The Language Book

A Perma-Bound Teach-and-Use Handbook for the Middle Level

by Florence W. Harris

Developed by National Curriculum Publishing, Inc.
Framingham, Massachusetts

Published by Perma-Bound Books
A Division of Hertzberg-New Method, Inc.

CONSULTANT: Faith Delaney
Supervisor of Reading and Language Arts
West Milford Township Public Schools
West Milford, New Jersey

EDITOR: Lucille Waugh
Salem, Massachusetts

The developers of this project have made every effort to locate the owner of each copyrighted selection reprinted here and make full acknowledgment for its use. In the case of an omission or error, the publisher will be pleased to make suitable acknowledgment in future printings.

Pages 5,6: Information from *Be an Inventor* by Barbara Taylor. Harcourt Brace Jovanovich, Publishers. Copyright © 1987 by Field Publications. *Page 7: All Creatures*

Acknowledgments continue on page 353.

Published by PERMA-BOUND
Vandalia Road
Jacksonville, Illinois
62650

ISBN: 0-8000-9338-0

Printed in the United States of America

The Language Book

A Perma-Bound Teach-and-Use Handbook for the Middle Level

Table of Contents

Part 1 –
Figuring It Out

Opening Your Mind

Ways to Find Ideas

☐ **Idea** A thought, a plan, a belief, or a picture in the mind

Driving past a company parking lot one day, Walter Fred Morrison noticed some workers relaxing by tossing a pie pan back and forth. The scene reminded him of similar scenes in his own youth, when he and his friends had played the same makeshift game with pie pans. The year was 1948, and the company was the Frisbie Pie Company. Morrison's observation that day started his thoughts going, and he went home to invent the plastic "Flyin' Saucer" that was to become the Frisbee.

Where do you find good ideas? Usually the best place to look is in your own mind. You have been collecting memories, facts, and ideas all your life. All you need to do is open your mind and set those thoughts free. Then you will find that one idea leads to another and another and another.

Any word or event can start you thinking, just as the pie pan game started Walter Fred Morrison thinking. You do not have to wait for a lucky chance, however. You can use some of the following ways to unlock your mind and release your thoughts.

How to Open Your Mind

1. **Brainstorming** You can brainstorm by yourself or with a group. Concentrate on something, such as an object, a word, or an idea. Write down every thought that occurs to you, no matter how silly or unrelated it may seem. Let one thought lead to another. Do not ignore any ideas. On the next page are the thoughts of one student who brainstormed about the word *cup*.

Some Ideas That Lasted

Poor Chester Greenwood could not enjoy winter weather because his ears got so cold. Desperate, he thought and thought. Then he had an idea. He bent wire into two loops, covered them with fur, and attached them to a metal strip that fit over his head. In 1873, still in his teens, Chester had invented earmuffs.

After a walk in the woods of Switzerland, George de Mestral struggled to pull burrs off his dog's coat. If only he could invent something that held as tightly as those burrs! Mestral set about to discover the burrs' secret. Eventually he succeeded and created one of the world's great fasteners — Velcro.

cup
Round, smooth
Could there be a square cup?
Had yellow cup with kittens on it when I was 2
Still love yellow -- because of that cup?
Handle -- lets you hold cup when hot
Who first thought of putting on a handle?
Makes it easy to drink hot chocolate
Love hot chocolate!
Needs to be prepared, even when instant
IDEA! Readymade hot chocolate in cup
to be heated in microwave!

2. **Freewriting**   Write freely for a set period of time, such as five minutes. You can just start writing and see what comes out, or you can use an object, a word, or a subject to get your thoughts moving. Do not stop to think. Do not lift your pen from the page. Do not worry about spelling, punctuation, or usage. Just keep writing, putting down whatever comes to mind.

cup
Rhymes with pup, yup, not much else --
bup, lup, dup, rup, sup -- is sup a word?
Think it's an old-fashioned way to say
"have supper" -- "Let's sup." This isn't
getting me anywhere. Try something else.
How do I use a cup? Love to drink hot
chocolate, especially after ice skating.
Tastes wonderful. Wonder why sweet
tastes good. How can our mouths tell
sweet from sour? And what makes
spicy hot food burn our mouths? Now
that's something I'd really like to
find out about. I could even go to
Mexican and Chinese restaurants to
do research!

Some Ideas That Lasted

How do you pack potato chips tightly without crushing them? One worker at a potato chip company got an idea from watching leaves fall. He noticed that dry leaves crumbled but wet leaves did not. Using this observation, he stacked some potato chips in a container while they were still wet. Then he dried them and found that the chips stayed tightly stacked. He had packed the first container of Pringle's potato chips.

3. **Clustering** A cluster diagram helps to lead you from one idea to another. To make a diagram, write a subject in the middle of a blank sheet of paper and circle it. Around it write words that the subject makes you think of. Circle each new word and connect it to the subject. Then let each of those words lead your thoughts to still other words, as you draw lines to connect them. Soon you will have a map of your thoughts in which related words are clustered together.

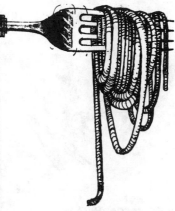

Some Ideas That Didn't Last

Automatically rotating spaghetti fork   1971

Turn on the motor and the fork will spin, wrapping strands of spaghetti neatly around it.

A way to escape from a burning building   1879

Attach the parachute and land safely on the padded soles.

More Ideas That Didn't Last

Hunting decoy 1897

This cow hides the hunter from ducks and other flying game.

Wrong-way boots 1974

— Information from
Be An Inventor, Barbara Taylor

4. **Listing**   Concentrate hard and make a list of everything you know about a subject. Try to include all different kinds of items related to your subject, such as songs and quotations.

> Cup
> Round container used for drinking
> Has a handle
> Glass, pottery, china, plastic, metal, paper, Styrofoam
> Usually used for hot liquids
> The denser the material, the longer the liquid stays hot
> "My cup runneth over" – where from?
> Measurement in cooking – 8 ounces or 16 tablespoons
> Prize or trophy
> Verb – to cup your hands

5. **Questioning**   Use *Who? What? Where? When? Why? How?* to list all the questions you can think of about a subject.

> Who uses cups? Who doesn't? Why?
> What else might they be used for?
> When in history did they first appear?
> Where were the earliest cups discovered?
> Why are they round? Why couldn't they be square?
> How are the handles attached to cups?

> ### TIPS for Opening Your Mind
> - Brainstorm about something.
> - Do some freewriting.
> - Draw a cluster.
> - Make a list.
> - Ask yourself questions.

Recalling

☐ **Recalling** Bringing back to mind, remembering

> It was easy to flick back over the years — right back to the time I had decided to become a veterinary surgeon. I could remember the very moment. I was thirteen and I was reading an article about careers for boys in the Meccano Magazine and as I read, I felt a surging conviction that this was for me.
>
> — *All Creatures Great and Small*, James Herriot

Memories are the richest source of ideas, as James Herriot knows. In the paragraph above, Herriot recalls the moment he decided to become a veterinarian. He remembers how old he was, what he was reading, and how he felt. To bring a past experience back to life, you too must dig deeply into your mind to recall the details.

How to Recall

1. **Open your mind.** You have so many memories stored away that it is difficult to recall everything that you have seen, done, and felt. When you are looking for an experience to write about or trying to remember something for any other reason, use the following strategies to unblock your memories.

   a. **Look around.** What person or thing reminds you of an experience?
   b. **Write a list of words that pop into your head.** What experiences do they remind you of?
   c. **In your mind, go back to different times and places in your life.** What memories do they stir up?
   d. **Use brainstorming, freewriting, clusters, lists, and questions.** They will help you to recall things that have happened to you. (See pages 3 – 6.)

2. **Put yourself in the time and place.** To recall the details of an experience, relive it in your mind. Close your eyes, picture the scene, and imagine that you are there. Concentrate on what things looked like, how you felt, and what you did.

A Memory Moment

SCENE	*Drugstore*
CHARACTERS	*Pharmacist*
	Customer (a chemist with a headache)
Pharmacist	Yes, ma'am, what can I do for you?
Customer	I'd like some prepared mona-ceticacidester of salicylic acid, please.
Pharmacist	Do you mean aspirin?
Customer	Right! I can never remember that name.

On Recalling . . .

Memory is the diary that we all carry about with us.
— *Oscar Wilde 1895*

Life is all memory, except for the one present moment that goes by you so quick you hardly catch it going.
— *Tennessee Williams 1963*

We do not remember days, we remember moments.
— *Cesare Pavese 1961*

To be able to enjoy one's past life is to live twice.
— *Martial* A.D. 86

3. **Imagine you are watching a movie of the experience.** Sit through the entire event. Run the film forward and backward. Speed it up and slow it down. Zoom in for close-ups, and back off for distance shots.

4. **Use all your senses.** Recall how things looked, sounded, smelled, felt, and tasted.

5. **Focus on your feelings.** As you relive the events, try to relive your feelings too. Were you happy? sad? relieved? cold? nervous? comfortable?

6. **Open your mind to details.** Details make an experience come to life. Recall little things, such as colors, textures, clothing, words, objects. Use brainstorming, freewriting, clusters, lists, and questions to help you track down details. (See pages 3 – 6.)

7. **Talk to others who were there.** Make a list of people who observed the experience or shared it with you in some other way. Speak to them and find out what they remember. Write down what they say. (See pages 130 – 131 on interviewing.)

8. **Take notes.** No matter which of the above strategies you use, always have a pad and pencil ready to take notes. Otherwise the details will disappear behind the doors of your memory.

TIPS for Recalling

- Open your memory with techniques such as brainstorming.
- Imagine you are back in the time and place.
- Relive the experience like a movie.
- Alert all your senses.
- Focus on your feelings.
- Open your mind to the details.
- Talk to people who were there.
- Take notes.

Observing

☐ Observing — Noticing things closely and carefully

We all expected to hear a roar followed by a charging lion, but nothing happened. Instead, we heard the excited barking of baboons, a sure sign that they had seen something alarming, either a lion or a leopard; after pausing, with ears and eyes strained, we moved on. Then, as George stooped to pass under a bush, something light-colored caught his eye; in a real fortress of thornbush crouched a lion, apparently ready to charge. George was about to fire when the loud buzzing of flies told him that the animal was dead.

— *Born Free*, Joy Adamson

Joy and George Adamson had to be good observers. Their lives depended on it as they moved through the wild-animal reserves of Africa. Although you may never face a lion or a leopard, you need to be a good observer too — when you explore a story idea, perform a science experiment, play basketball, or just cross a street. The strategies that follow will help you notice things closely and carefully. Use them whenever you are observing.

How to Observe

1. **Know why you are observing.** When you watch for lions, you concentrate on details such as barking baboons and buzzing flies. When you observe a scene to write about, you may want to concentrate on different details, such as the feel of the air and the shapes of the leaves. First ask yourself *why* you are observing. Then you can better decide *what* to observe.

2. **Use all your senses.** Observing means more than just seeing. Use all your senses, one at a time. Look, listen, touch, smell, and taste, whenever possible.

3. **Concentrate.** Direct all your attention to what you are observing. Block out other thoughts.

Special!

How many shapes do you see below? There's only one! What is it?

— *The World's Best Optical Illusion*, Charles H. Paraquin

Answer

4. **Think about what things mean**.   In the previous passage, it would not have done George any good to observe barking baboons if he had not thought about why the baboons were barking. George's life depended on not only observing the right things but also deciding what those things meant. When you observe, use your mind as well as your senses. Ask yourself, "What does that mean?"

5. **Move around**.   Observe the same thing from different places and angles. Move far away and very close. Observe from above and from below, inside out and upside down. You will notice features you never noticed before.

6. **Observe as someone or something else**.   "Borrow" another set of senses. Imagine you are a different person or a plant, an animal, or an object — a blade of grass, an elephant, an ant, a bird, a sneaker, for example. How would things appear to you?

7. **Use your pencil to help you see**.   Look hard at something and sketch it. Try not to look at your paper. Just let your pencil follow your eyes.

8. **Look through a "telescope."**   Shape your hand into a circle or roll a sheet of paper into a tube. Peer through your "telescope" with one eye, keeping the other eye closed. Slowly scan the scene. Then focus on details.

9. **Take notes**.   Notes help you remember. Carry a pad or journal. Jot down the things you observe.

TIPS for Observing

- Know your purpose.
- Use all your senses.
- Concentrate.
- Think. What does it mean?
- Move around.
- Observe as someone or something else.
- Draw.
- Use a "telescope."
- Take notes.

Creative Thinking and Imagining

☐ **Imagining** Forming pictures or words in the mind
Creating new ideas from old

In 1816, a small group of friends sat and discussed ways to amuse themselves. The group included nineteen-year-old Mary Shelley and her husband, the poet Percy Bysshe Shelley. They decided that each would compose a horror story. Mary Shelley wanted to write a tale that "would awaken thrilling horror—one to make the reader dread to look round, to curdle the blood, and quicken the beatings of the heart." For days she struggled to find an idea. Then, one evening, she heard her companions discussing whether it might ever be possible to manufacture life. When Mary Shelley went to bed that night, here is what happened.

When I placed my head on my pillow I did not sleep, nor could I be said to think. My imagination, unbidden, possessed and guided me, gifting the successive images that arose in my mind with a vividness far beyond the usual bound of reverie. I saw—with shut eyes, but acute mental vision—I saw the pale student . . . kneeling beside the thing he had put together. I saw the hideous phantasm of a man stretched out, and then, on the working of some powerful engine, show signs of life and stir with an uneasy, half-vital motion. . . .

The next morning Mary Shelley put pen to paper and began to write the story of *Frankenstein*.

The pictures that Mary Shelley saw existed only in her mind. Like her, you can use your mind to see anything, go anywhere, or do anything. As your mind travels, you may find that you produce fresh new ideas for a horror story or a breakfast cereal, a painting or a space probe.

Shelley's imagination was awakened by a conversation she happened to overhear. You need not wait for some event to start your imagination moving, however. You can use methods like those on the next page.

Imagination is more important than knowledge.

— Albert Einstein

Anagrams

Anagrams *are words or phrases formed from the letters of other words or phrases. Anagrams give you practice in looking at familiar things in new ways.*

Below, the words on the left are rearranged to form the words on the right. Can you find new words to replace the question marks?

team	—	meat
enters	—	resent
unclear	—	nuclear
Californian	—	African lion
rats	—	???
grin	—	???
night	—	???
thread	—	???
astronomer	—	moon starer
punishment	—	nine thumps
waitress	—	a stew, sir?
measurements	—	???

What if . . . ?

What if . . . horses walked on their hind legs?
What if . . . my sneakers could talk?
What if . . . the wheel had never been invented?
What if . . . color disappeared from the world?
What if . . . my cat and I changed places?
What if . . . we slept during the day and stayed awake at night?
What if . . . airplanes had feathers?
What if . . . time went backwards?

Creating Punchlines

Jokes are funny because they look at usual things in unusual ways. Create punchlines for these jokes. Then compare your creations with the answers given.

(1) Why can't a bike stand on one wheel?
(2) What do you call a frightened skin diver?
(3) Why do elephants have trunks?
(4) Why does a mother kangaroo dislike rainy weather?

Punchlines (1) because it's too tired (2) chicken of the sea (3) because they don't have glove compartments (4) because the children have to play inside

Answers

How to Imagine

1. **Relax and set your mind free.** Make yourself very comfortable. Close your eyes and try to relax every part of your body. Then let your thoughts travel wherever they want to go. Watch with your mind's eye.

2. **Create crazy pictures.** Picture a familiar item or scene. Then add something unusual. For example, picture a skyscraper and then put wings on it. What ideas does it give you? Where do your thoughts lead you?

3. **Try random combinations.** In two columns, list some words that pop into your mind. Then connect words in the two columns in any order. What combinations do you create? What do they make you think of?

pink	cloud	— pink secret?
hop	handlebar	— cloud that hops?
toenail	secret	— toenail contest?
fold	contest	— folding handlebars?
icy	rumble	— icy rumble?
		rumbling ice?

4. **Ask *What if?* questions.** Ask yourself, "What might happen if . . . ?" There are no limits to the questions you can ask. Here are a few you can use over and over. Just add your own words.

What if ____ disappeared from the world?
What if ____ could talk?
What if ____ had never been invented?
What if ____ had wings? feathers? wheels? eyes? roots?
What if someone invented a ____ ?
What if everything turned ____ ?
What if ____ and ____ changed places?

TIPS for Imagining

- Relax and set your mind free.
- Create crazy pictures.
- Combine words at random.
- Ask *What if?* questions.

Comparing and Contrasting

☐ **Comparing** Finding similarities — ways in which things are alike

☐ **Contrasting** Finding differences — ways in which things are not alike

Although all lizards are reptiles and are covered with dry and scaly skin, they can still show striking differences. In fact, almost three thousand kinds of lizards have been identified.

The dragon of Komodo stands out because of its size. The largest and oldest of all lizards, it can be ten feet long. Its long, forked tongue can actually smell out decaying animals, and its long, powerful tail is a weapon for killing its prey. This fearsome lizard eats monkeys, wild boars, and even deer, which it swallows whole. It hunts during the day and digs out a cave in which to hide at night.

In contrast, the chameleon is small enough to be held in the hand. Its special feature is its ability to change color, depending on temperature, surroundings, and mood. While this lizard moves slowly, its long tongue — as long as its body — darts out like a whip and pulls insects and small birds into its mouth. The chameleon is one of the few lizards that can curl its long tail, which it uses for grasping. This ability comes in handy, for the chameleon usually lives in trees.

While you probably do not spend much of your day comparing lizards, you do think about similarities and differences all the time — when you choose one TV show over another, for example, or when you describe a friend's house by comparing it with yours. Learning to make careful comparisons and contrasts can help you understand the world around you and explain it to others.

How to Compare and Contrast

1. **Compare and contrast things that have something in common.** You can learn a lot from comparing a Komodo dragon and a chameleon, a book and a movie, or the city and the country. You can learn very little from comparing a lizard and the city or a pencil and a cat. Compare things that have something in common. (Exception: Unusual comparisons can be used in figurative language to create special effects. See pages 193–194.)

MORE REPTILE RELATIVES

Toad vs Frog

TOAD

1. broader and bigger
2. usually darker in color
3. dry, rough skin, often covered with warts
4. slower and clumsier

FROG

1. more streamlined
2. lighter in color
3. smoother skin
4. faster moving

You've just seen a strange animal. Quickly you run to friends to describe it. You say "um," you stumble a lot, then you begin.

COMPARE	CONTRAST
"Well, it looked like a lion . . .	but it had the head of a lizard.
It had spots like a leopard . . .	but the spots were purple.
It had hooves like a horse . . .	but they were bigger!"

Comic Comparisons and Contrasts

— Why is a baseball game like a pancake?

They both depend on the batter.

— Why is an island like a *t*?

Both are in the middle of water.

— What's the difference between a jeweler and a jailer?

One sells watches; the other watches cells.

2. **List the features by which the things can be compared.** What kinds of features determine how the things look, how they are used, what they do, who they are, how they are built? List those general features. Here are some features by which animals might be compared and contrasted.

type of animal
skin
tongue
tail
food
size
color
habitat

3. **List the ways in which the things are alike.** Here are the features that two kinds of lizards have in common.

Komodo dragons and Chameleons

1. reptiles
2. scaly skin
3. long tongues
4. long tails
5. meat-eaters

4. **List the ways in which the things are different.** List related differences side by side.

	Komodo dragons	*Chameleons*
1. size	ten feet long	can be held in hand
2. tongue	used to smell	used to catch prey
3. tail	used to catch prey	used for grasping
4. color	does not change	changes
5. habitat	on ground	in trees

TIPS for Comparing and Contrasting

- Compare and contrast things that have something in common.
- List the features by which they can be compared.
- List the ways in which they are alike.
- List the ways in which they are different.

Understanding Cause and Effect

☐ **Cause** The reason something happens
☐ **Effect** Something that happens as a result of something else

People who entertain you with "magic" tricks may seem to defy nature, but they have simply learned how to use the laws of nature to achieve their special effects. Here, for example, is a simple trick that you can use to impress an audience and illustrate a physical law at the same time.

You will need a flat balloon and a glass jug or bottle. Put the jug in the refrigerator for about an hour. Then take it out and quickly place the mouth of the balloon tightly over the mouth of the jug. Mysteriously, the balloon will blow itself up.

What seems like magic is just a basic physical law in action. As air becomes warmer, it expands. As the cold air in the jug warms up, it expands, moving through the mouth of the jug into the balloon and causing the balloon to inflate.

The balloon trick, like a rainbow, a toothache, or just about any other event, can be explained in terms of cause and effect.

CAUSE The air inside the jug expands as it warms up.
EFFECT The balloon inflates.

How to Determine Cause and Effect

1. **Ask "Why did it happen?"** Find the cause of something by asking questions: Why did it happen? What made it happen? What caused it to happen?

		CAUSE
The cat ran up a tree.	(Why?)	A dog chased it.
The pond dried up.	(Why?)	There has been no rain for weeks.

2. **Ask "What effect did it have?"** Find the effect of something by asking questions like these: What effect did it have? What was the result? What happened because of it?

		EFFECT
A mosquito bites you.	(Result?)	You itch.
Garbage is dumped at sea.	(Result?)	The sea becomes polluted.

What Causes . . . ?

☐ *What causes a rainbow?*

Sunlight contains a mixture of colors. When a ray of sunlight passes through a raindrop, the ray is bent. Like a string unraveling, the ray separates into threads of violet, indigo, blue, green, yellow, orange, and red. The particular colors are determined by the angles at which the ray reaches the eye, for each color has its own angle.

☐ *What causes lightning to strike trees?*

When lightning flashes from a cloud, it seeks out the easiest path to the ground. Most objects conduct electricity more easily than air does. Therefore, a flash of lightning is attracted to the nearest high object, usually a tall tree or building, through which it can travel to the ground.

☐ *What causes the air to be colder in higher places?*

You might think that high places are warmer than low ones because they are closer to the sun. However, as you move up, the air grows thinner. Air absorbs heat from the sun. Since there is less air higher up, less heat is absorbed. Therefore, the higher you go, the colder you will be.

Your Turn

☐ What causes the earth to look bluish from space?
☐ What causes ice to be slippery?
☐ What causes the sea to be salty?

Cause and Effect Confusions

Do you think that if you go outdoors with wet hair you will catch a cold? Actually, germs cause colds, not drafts. Here are some other events that are NOT *examples of cause and effect.*

Making a funny face will *not* cause your face to freeze that way.

Eating fish will *not* make you smarter (although it may be smart to eat fish).

Touching a toad will *not* give you warts.

Dropping a knife will *not* make company come.

Eating bread crusts will *not* make your hair curl.

Watching a pot will *not* keep the water from boiling (but it will make it seem to take longer.)

Sneezing with your eyes open will *not* make your eyes pop out. (It's impossible to sneeze with your eyes open!)

3. **Do not confuse before and after with cause and effect.** Just because one event happened before another does not mean that the first event caused the second.

BEFORE You got a new kitten. AFTER Your dog became ill.

CAUSE Your dog ate candy. EFFECT Your dog became ill.

4. **Look for more than one cause or effect.**

CAUSE / CAUSES   EFFECT / EFFECTS
Winter arrived.
You wanted new boots. → You bought new boots.
You earned some money.

Spring arrived. ← Trees began to bud.
The dog began to shed.
Baseball season opened.

5. **Look for a chain of causes and effects.**   One event can cause another, which in turn can cause another, and so on.

A cold jug is exposed to warm air.
↓
The air inside the jug becomes warmer.
↓
The warmed air expands.
↓
The expanding air moves into a balloon.
↓
The balloon inflates.

6. **An event can have underlying causes as well as direct causes.** Find the direct cause. Then ask what else had to be true.

EFFECT   Your bike fell out of the bike rack.
DIRECT CAUSE   Someone accidentally knocked the bike over.
UNDERLYING CAUSE You did not place it in the rack properly.

TIPS for Determining Cause and Effect

- To find the cause of something, ask "Why did it happen?"
- To find the effect, ask "What happened as a result?"
- Do not confuse cause and effect with before and after.
- Look for more than one cause or effect.
- Look for a cause-and-effect chain.
- Look for underlying causes as well as direct causes.

Understanding General and Specific

☐ **General** Common to many things
☐ **Specific** Special to a few things or a single thing

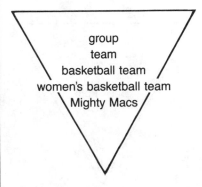

group
team
basketball team
women's basketball team
Mighty Macs

Although basketball was invented for a group of boys in a Massachusetts school, females adopted the sport quickly. Just a few weeks after the game was created in 1891, a junior high school girls' team had been formed, and within a year the first women's college game was played at Smith College. By the early 1900s, large numbers of women were playing basketball.

Some people began to object, however, claiming that females were too delicate and modest for such athletic activities. As a result, support for women's sports fell seriously behind support for men's sports.

Not until the 1970s did women's athletics leap forward. In 1972 the United States Congress stated that all school programs, including athletics, were to be available to males and females equally. As a result of this renewed support, girls and women poured out onto gyms and playing fields all over the country.

person
athlete
basketball player
guard
Carol Blazejowski

The experience of one team illustrates the rapid progress in women's sports in the seventies. In 1970 few people knew or cared about the women's basketball team from Immaculata College in Pennsylvania. Nevertheless, this team won the tournament run by the Association for Intercollegiate Athletics for Women in 1972, 1973, and 1974. By 1974 the national news services were covering the team's games. The following year their games appeared on national television. Then the Mighty Macs, as they were known, became the first women to play in New York City's famed Madison Square Garden. In just four years, the team had gone from an unknown group to one that received national attention.

clothing
footwear
sneakers
hightops

Sport is a general term. It can include many types of sports, such as basketball, archery, gymnastics, and running. *Basketball* is a specific term. It names a particular type of sport.

Basketball can be made more and more specific.

SPECIFIC	basketball
MORE SPECIFIC	girls' basketball
MORE SPECIFIC	girls' high school basketball
MORE SPECIFIC	state championship girls' high school basketball

How would you complete these general-to-specific triangles?

(1)

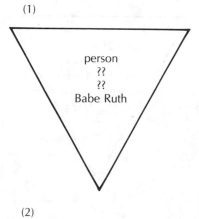

```
        person
          ??
          ??
       Babe Ruth
```

(2)

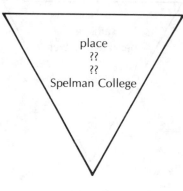

```
        place
          ??
          ??
     Spelman College
```

(3)

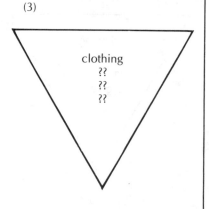

```
       clothing
          ??
          ??
          ??
```

How to Distinguish Between General and Specific

1. **A general term applies to many things.**   The word *team* is general. It expresses a general idea that covers many groups — basketball teams, teams of workers, even teams of horses.

2. **A general term groups related things.**   The general word *team* groups individuals who work together toward the same goal. That is what they have in common. Aside from that they can be as different as swimmers and horses.

3. **A specific term applies to just a few things or to a single thing.**   *Women's basketball team* applies to far fewer things than *team* does. *University of Georgia Women's Basketball Team* is even more specific, for it applies to one thing only.

4. **A specific term separates one thing from others like it.** *Montréal Canadiens* is a specific term standing for a single thing. It separates that team from every other team.

5. **A term can be more general than some things and less general than others.**

GENERAL	team	SPECIFIC	basketball player
MORE GENERAL	group	MORE SPECIFIC	guard
		MORE SPECIFIC	center guard
		MORE SPECIFIC	Carol Blazejowski

6. **Proper nouns are always specific.**   Proper nouns, such as the Celtics or Immaculata College, name specific persons, places, or things. They are always capitalized. (See page 261.)

TIPS for Understanding General and Specific

- A general term covers many things. It groups related things together.
- A specific term applies to just a few things or one thing. It separates that thing from others like it.
- A term can be more general than some terms and less general than others.
- Proper nouns are always specific.

Classifying

☐ Classifying   Grouping similar things together

Let's look back at the Emmy Award-winning TV shows of 1988.

Primetime
DRAMA SERIES *Thirtysomething*
COMEDY SERIES *The Wonder Years*
MINI-SERIES *The Murder of Mary Phagan*
VARIETY, MUSIC, OR COMEDY PROGRAM "Irving Berlin's Hundredth Birthday Celebration"

Daytime
DRAMA SERIES *Santa Barbara*
TALK/SERVICE SERIES *The Oprah Winfrey Show*
GAME/AUDIENCE PARTICIPATION SHOW *The Price Is Right*
ANIMATED PROGRAM "Jim Henson's Muppet Babies"
CHILDREN'S SERIES *Sesame Street*

It would make little sense to watch hundreds of different kinds of TV shows and then try to choose the best ones. How would you judge a talk show against a musical special, for example? Instead, before they are judged, TV programs are *classified*. That is, they are sorted into "classes" according to the kinds of programs they are. Then the judges can compare similar programs.

All sorts of things are classified. As a result, you can find, understand, and explain them more easily. For example, items in a department store are classified. As a result, you know where to find a sweatshirt or a tape player. Animals are classified too. As a result, if someone tells you that the rufous-sided towhee is a bird, then you know that it has feathers and wings, even if you have never seen a rufous-sided towhee.

CLASSIFYING SQUIRRELS

Notice that the groups grow smaller as the shared features grow larger.

KINGDOM: *Animalia*
Animals
    squirrels, humans, elephants, chipmunks, beavers, snakes, birds, fish, starfish, worms, snails, insects . . .

PHYLUM: *Chordata*
Animals that have backbones
    squirrels, humans, elephants, chipmunks, beavers, snakes, birds, fish . . .

CLASS: *Mammalia*
Animals that have backbones and that nurse their young
    squirrels, humans, elephants, chipmunks, beavers . . .

ORDER: *Rodentia*
Animals that have backbones, that nurse their young, and that have long and sharp front teeth
    squirrels, chipmunks, beavers . . .

FAMILY: *Sciuridae*
Animals that have backbones, that nurse their young, that have long and sharp front teeth, and that have bushy tails
    squirrels, chipmunks . . .

GENUS: *Sciurus*
Animals that have backbones, that nurse their young, that have long and sharp front teeth, that have bushy tails, and that climb trees
    squirrels (gray squirrel, fox squirrel . . .)

SPECIES: *Sciurus niger*
Animals that have backbones, that nurse their young, that have long and sharp front teeth, that have bushy tails, that climb trees, and that have rusty or grayish fur
    fox squirrel

Item! Want to remember the categories used in animal classification?

Kingdom, **P**hylum, **C**lass, **O**rder, **F**amily, **G**enus, **S**pecies

Then just remember this sentence:

King Philip Chews On Fat Green Snakes.

How to Classify

1. **Classifying means sorting things out.** When you classify, you put things of the same kind into one group, or class. Different kinds of things, then, will be in different classes.

   CLASSES (TYPES) OF TV SHOWS: drama series, game shows . . .
   GAME-SHOW CLASS: *Jeopardy, Wheel of Fortune* . . .

2. **Draw a tree diagram to sort things out.** A tree diagram can help you see how the parts of something are related. Below is part of a tree diagram of TV shows.

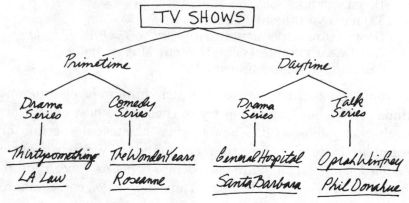

3. **Find features that are alike.** To classify, you put like things together. Things can be similar in various ways — shape, color, loudness, personality, first letter of their names, number of toes, and so on. When classifying, look for similar features. What do *General Hospital* and *Oprah Winfrey* have in common? They are both on in the afternoon.

4. **Use the like features as categories.** A *category* is the feature or features by which you classify. Suppose some of the TV programs you are classifying are about animals. Then you might create a class using the category *animal shows*.

5. **Make a category chart.** Charts like the one below can help you group things.

DAYTIME

DRAMA SERIES	CHILDREN'S SERIES	GAME SHOWS
General Hospital	*Mr. Rogers*	*The Price Is Right*
Guiding Light	*Sesame Street*	*Wheel of Fortune*
One Life to Live	*Kids, Inc.*	*Jeopardy*

6. **Be aware that things can be classified in different ways.** TV shows are classified a certain way for the Emmy Awards, but they can be classified in other ways too. How many different categories can you think of for TV programs? Here are a few.

Westerns	family sitcoms	shows appealing
mysteries	detective stories	to teens
dance specials	hour-long programs	shows starring
		teens

7. **Choose a classification that fits your purpose.** Your purpose helps you decide what classification to use. If you are scheduling a commercial for jeans, you might classify TV shows by the age of the audience. If you are a casting agent, you might classify shows by the types of performers involved.

8. **Be sure your categories make sense.** All your categories should fit your way of classifying. Suppose you are grouping TV shows by their content, such as Westerns, mysteries, and so on. Then it would make no sense to add a category such as shows starring redheads, which has nothing to do with content. A tree diagram like the one in item 2 will help you be sure that your categories are related in a way that makes sense.

9. **Be aware that classes sometimes overlap.** Items may sometimes belong to more than one class. *The Cosby Show*, for example, would fit into the class of shows starring teenagers as well as the class of shows appealing to whole families.

```
                    TIPS for Classifying

  • Classifying means sorting things out.
    To classify, first find common features.
    Use those features as categories.
  • Choose categories that fit your purpose.
  • Be sure your categories make sense.
  • Make a tree diagram and a category chart.
  • Be aware that items can be classified in
    different ways.
  • Be aware that classes can overlap.
```

Understanding Time Order

□ **Time Order** The order in which things happen

The modern bicycle has come a long way since 1790, when the first two wheeler was created. That toylike vehicle was made of wood, and the rider moved it by pushing both feet along the ground. People began to take two wheelers more seriously in 1816, when a German baron connected a steering bar to the front wheel. Then, in 1839, a Scottish blacksmith lifted riders' feet off the ground by adding foot pedals to the front wheel. By 1866, a French firm had sold about 400 pedal bicycles. Soon a U.S. patent was taken out, and the North American bicycle industry was born.

In the 1870s the high-wheeler appeared, with a front wheel that towered over the rear wheel by as much as five feet. This odd cycle was replaced in about 1885 by the safety bicycle. A popular bike, its wheels were of equal size, and its pedals were centered and linked to a chain that moved the rear wheel. Air-filled rubber tires, coaster brakes, and adjustable handlebars all followed in the 1890s. By 1897 these improvements had attracted about four million people in America to the bicycle.

The modern bicycle was not created all at once. Instead, it was developed step by step, one step after another. To understand the history of the bicycle, you need to understand the order of those steps. In fact, to understand just about anything — a story, a baseball game, a recipe — you need to understand the order in which things happen.

How to Understand Time Order

1. **Think about the order.**   When you read or listen, be aware of the order in which things happen. You will understand and remember more.

2. **Look for key words and dates.**   In the passage about bicycles, the dates helped you figure out the time order. You knew that an event in 1866 came before an event in 1897. Certain words, too, can give you clues about order. Here are examples.

first   second   next   then   before   after   last   finally

3. **Ask yourself questions.** What happened next? What came before that? What did they do then? What happened first?

4. **Does the order make sense?** Some things must occur before other things. For example, there had to be some way to steer a bicycle before pedals could be added. When you think about time order, ask yourself whether the order makes sense.

5. **Draw a diagram.** A time line or a sequence chain can help you see the order of events.

History of the Bicycle
TIME LINE

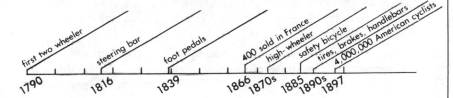

SEQUENCE CHAIN

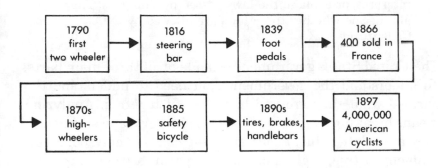

```
┌──────────┐   ┌──────────┐   ┌──────────┐   ┌──────────┐
│ 1790     │ → │ 1816     │ → │ 1839     │ → │ 1866     │
│ first    │   │ steering │   │ foot     │   │ 400 sold │
│ two wheeler│  │ bar      │   │ pedals   │   │ in France│
└──────────┘   └──────────┘   └──────────┘   └──────────┘

┌──────────┐   ┌──────────┐   ┌──────────┐   ┌──────────┐
│ 1870s    │ → │ 1885     │ → │ 1890s    │ → │ 1897     │
│ high-    │   │ safety   │   │ tires,   │   │ 4,000,000│
│ wheelers │   │ bicycle  │   │ brakes,  │   │ American │
│          │   │          │   │ handlebars│  │ cyclists │
└──────────┘   └──────────┘   └──────────┘   └──────────┘
```

> ## TIPS on Understanding Time Order
> - Think about the order.
> - Look for key words and dates.
> - Ask "What happened next?"
> - Ask "Does the order make sense?"
> - Draw a time line or sequence chain.

PHASES OF THE MOON

Time order becomes very obvious in the phases of the moon.

One half of our moon is always lit by the sun. As the moon moves around, or orbits, the earth, different parts of the moon's lighted section become visible.

Here are some of the phases the moon goes through every $29\frac{1}{2}$ days.

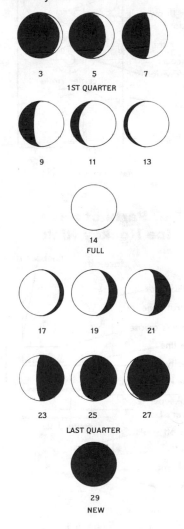

Understanding Time Order **23**

Parts of a Basketball Court

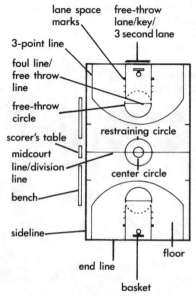

lane space marks
free-throw lane/key/ 3 second lane
3-point line
foul line/ free throw line
free-throw circle
restraining circle
scorer's table
midcourt line/division line
center circle
bench
sideline
floor
end line
basket

Parts of an Ice Hockey Rink

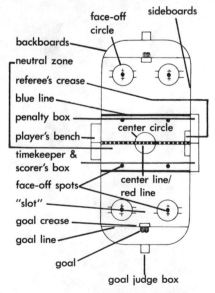

face-off circle
sideboards
backboards
neutral zone
referee's crease
blue line
penalty box
center circle
player's bench
timekeeper & scorer's box
face-off spots
center line/ red line
"slot"
goal crease
goal line
goal
goal judge box

— *What's What*, R. Bragonier, Jr., D. Fisher, Eds.

☐ Analyzing   Breaking something down into its parts or steps

The 200-year-old system of government of the United States of America is spelled out in its Constitution. In fact, the United States was the first nation in history to be based on a written constitution.

The framers of the Constitution wanted to prevent a single person or group from becoming too powerful. Their solution was to divide the government into three branches — executive, legislative, and judicial. Each branch acts as a check on the other two branches.

The *executive branch* is centered around the President. It includes departments such as defense and commerce, as well as agencies that regulate areas such as banking and atomic energy. The task of the President is to enforce the laws of the land.

The *legislative branch* is made up of the two parts of Congress — the House of Representatives and the Senate. Congress makes and revises the laws by which the people live.

The *judicial branch* is made up of the Supreme Court of the United States and other federal courts. The courts interpret, or explain, the laws passed by Congress. They also decide whether these laws are allowed by the Constitution.

The United States government is made up of three main parts. To understand the government, you need to understand the parts — what they are and how they fit together. Analyzing means breaking something down into its parts and seeing how they are related. Just about anything can be analyzed: a government, a tree, a glass of water, a poem, a friendship, or a problem.

How to Analyze

1. **Ask "What are its parts?"**   Ask yourself questions about what you are analyzing. What are its parts? What is it made of? How is it divided? What does each part do?

2. **Make a list.**   When you analyze, write down the parts you find. Sometimes just a list will do, like the one on the next page.

BRANCHES OF U.S. GOVERNMENT
Executive
Legislative
Judicial

3. **Make a chart.**   A chart can be even more useful than a list. It can help you see what the different parts are and how they relate to one another.

BRANCHES OF U.S. GOVERNMENT

	Task	*Make-up*
Executive	enforces laws	President, departments, agencies
Legislative	makes laws	Congress — Senate, House of Representatives
Judicial	interprets laws	Supreme Court, federal courts

4. **Draw a spider map.**   A spider map is another kind of diagram that can help you see how the main parts fit together.

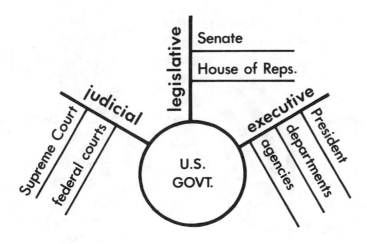

Patterns can be analyzed too — patterns of words, numbers, designs, poems. The following poems are limericks. Read them aloud and listen for a pattern.

A mouse in her room woke Miss Dowd;
She was frightened and
   screamed very loud,
   Then a happy thought hit her
   To scare off the critter,
She sat up in bed and meowed.
   — Edward Lear

There was a young lady from
   Niger,
Who smiled as she rode on a
   tiger.
   They came back from the ride
   With the lady inside,
And the smile on the face of the
   tiger.
   — Attributed to
   Cosmo Monkhouse

A puppy whose hair was so
    flowing
There really was no means of
    knowing
  Which end was his head,
  Once stopped me and said,
"Please, sir, am I coming or
    going?"

— Oliver Herford

A cheerful old bear at the zoo
Could always find something
    to do.
  When it bored him to go
  On a walk to and fro,
He reversed it and walked fro
    and to.

— *Laughable Limericks*,
    Sara and John E.
    Brewton, eds.

5. **Draw a tree.**   You often need to break down the main parts into still smaller parts. Drawing a "tree" can help you see how all these parts fit together.

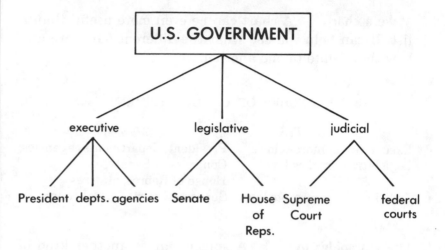

6. **Draw a labeled sketch.**   Sometimes the best way to understand something is to draw it and then label its parts. The drawing can be realistic, or it can be a sketch like the one below.

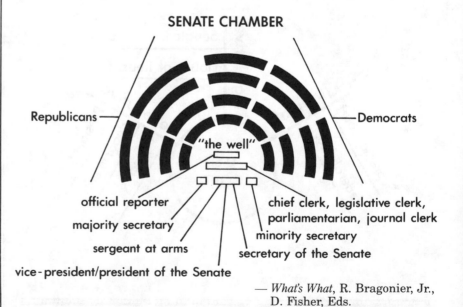

— *What's What*, R. Bragonier, Jr.,
    D. Fisher, Eds.

7. **For a process, ask "What are its steps?"** A *process* is a series of steps by which something is done or made. Knitting and doing homework are processes, and so is the growth of a chick inside an egg. Breaking a process into its steps is a form of analyzing. You must be sure to give the steps in the order in which they occur (see pages 22–23). You can make either a numbered list or a sequence chain like the one below.

HOW A BILL BECOMES A LAW

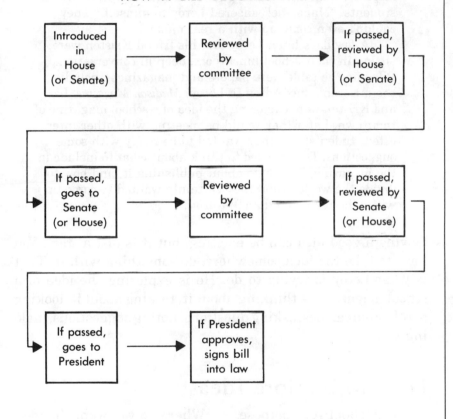

Writing Limericks

Here is the basic limerick pattern. (Some ta ta's can be added or left out.)

1. ta TUM ta ta TUM ta ta TUM
2. ta TUM ta ta TUM ta ta TUM.
3. ta ta TUM ta ta TUM,
4. ta ta TUM ta ta TUM,
5. ta ta TUM ta ta TUM ta ta TUM.

Lines 1, 2, and 5 rhyme.
Lines 3 and 4 rhyme.

Now try writing limericks of your own, following the above pattern. Here are opening lines you might use:

There once was a young man from Po, . . .

A lady who lost a blue shoe, . . .

There once was a nice boy named Zamp, . . .

TIPS for Analyzing

- Ask "What are its parts?"
- For a process, ask "What are the steps?"
- List the parts or steps.
- Make a diagram, such as a spider map, tree, labeled sketch, or sequence chain.

Exploring Ideas

Exploring an idea
Looking at an idea from all directions

"We sure could do better than this!" Leroy thought as he thumbed through the sheets of paper his cousin Amanda had given him. In clumsy hand-drawn letters on the front page were written the words *Madison Magazine*. Madison Middle School was Amanda's school, and the *Madison Magazine* was written and published each month by its students. "Magazine!" sneered Leroy to himself. "They couldn't even come up with a real name."

A few days later, Leroy and his friend Kristen were sitting in their school lunchroom, deep in conversation. Piled on the table were papers and magazines, including the miserable (according to Leroy) *Madison Magazine*. Leroy and Kristen were exploring the idea of a school magazine of their own. Later they would be meeting with other interested students, and they wanted to be ready with some suggestions. They needed to think about what to include in the magazine, how to go about publishing it, and how to divide the work — and they certainly wanted to come up with a better name than *Magazine!*

Having a good idea can be exciting, but it is just a start. You have to take the idea somewhere, do something with it. That is what Leroy is trying to do. He is exploring the idea of a school magazine — thinking about it, talking about it, looking at other magazines, asking questions, noting suggestions, making plans.

How to Explore Ideas

1. **Think about your purpose.** Where do you want the idea to go? Your purpose may not be as clear as Leroy's at first. In fact, you may need to explore to find a purpose. Still, having a general direction can help to move your thoughts along.

2. **Ask yourself questions.** What do you want to accomplish? Where might your idea lead? What do you need to do? What do you need to find out? On the next page is a list of questions that Leroy jotted down.

Exploring by Seeing Better

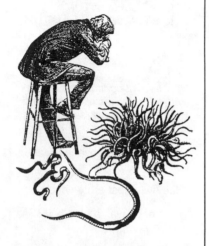

Antoni van Leeuwenhoek, a fabric merchant in Holland in the 1600s, often used magnifying glasses to inspect pieces of cloth. He wanted to develop more powerful magnifying glasses. After grinding hundreds and hundreds of lenses by hand, he succeeded. Then he clamped a lens between two metal plates, attached something to hold it with, and created a microscope.

In 1674, exploring new uses for his microscope, he aimed it at a drop of water. There, to his astonishment, he saw what he described as "little eels, or worms, lying all huddled up together and wriggling . . . and the whole water seemed to be alive with these multifarious animalcules."

Leeuwenhoek's lens had revealed a whole new world —the world of microscopic life.

Whom should we ask for permission to publish?
Whom should we ask to be our advisor?
What kinds of articles should be in the magazine?
Should we assign articles? ask students to submit them? both?
How should the magazine be printed?
How often should it be published — every month? every two
   months? every term?
What jobs need to be done? Who should do them?

3. **Talk to people.**   Discuss your idea with others. Just talking to a friend can be helpful. Talking to people who are experienced or knowledgeable can be even more helpful. Here, for example, is Leroy's list of people with whom he planned to discuss the idea of a school magazine.

classmates
teachers
editors of other student magazines

4. **Observe.**   Observe places, events, and objects that have something to do with your idea. Look, listen, touch, taste, smell. Measure things. Think about what your observations mean. (See pages 9 – 10.) Leroy looked through other student magazines, paying special attention to the following features:

contents	type of paper	title
size of page	illustrations	color
number of pages	number of workers	headings

5. **Describe.**   Describe what you observe. Write down the details and draw sketches. Describing will not only help you remember things but may also give you new ideas. Leroy, for example, made sketches of some page designs that he liked and that he might adapt for his own magazine.

6. **Do research.**   Go to the library. Interview people. Go wherever your idea leads you in order to find information. Leroy looked at all kinds of magazines for suggestions, and he read books and articles giving advice about school publications. He also interviewed editors and students at schools that had magazines.

Santorio Santorio was a doctor who lived from 1561 to 1636. In those years people believed that good health depended on a balance between the body and the outside world. Disease came from a lack of balance between what the body took in and what it put out.

Santorio set out to study this balance. He attached a chair to a specially made scale, and he sat there to weigh himself before and after every activity. He also weighed everything that went into and came out of his body, even calculating the amount of perspiration. To his surprise, there was no balance at all. The food he took in weighed much more than his body could possibly account for.

On the one hand, Santorio's desire to explore an idea destroyed the medical beliefs of his time. On the other hand, it introduced a useful approach to science — measurement.

Exploring Ideas | **29**

Go to the Person Who Knows

Want to explore an idea with an expert? These books can help you find one. Look for them in your library's reference section.

ENCYCLOPEDIA OF ASSOCIATIONS

People with shared interests often join organizations. This encyclopedia lists them all. Just look for your subject. You are bound to find some experts. Here, for example, are some groups interested in humor.

Comedy Writers Association
Humor Stamp Club
International Organization of Nerds
Marx Brothers Study Unit
Mister Ed Fan Club
Nurses for Laughter
Puns Corps

STANDARD PERIODICAL DICTIONARY

Listed in this dictionary are more than 68,000 periodicals on 230 subjects. One of them might contain just what you need. Here are just a few of the periodicals listed under the *A*'s in the music section.

ASCAP Jazz Notes
ASUC Journal of Music Scores
Accordion and Guitar World Magazine
Amateur Chamber Music Players
American Fiddler News
American Folk Music Occasional
American Guild of Authors and Composers Bulletin
American Guild of English Handbell Ringers Roster
American Record Guide

7. **Think about relationships.** When you explore an idea, think about how its parts connect with one another and with other ideas. (See pages 13–27.) Ask yourself questions like these.

- How do things compare and contrast with other things?
- What caused them?
- What effects do they have?
- What parts do they have?
- What things might be grouped together?
- What order should they be in?

Leroy looked at other student magazines and thought about how they were alike and how they were different. He also analyzed their contents. Then, to explore a plan for his own magazine, he made a list of different kinds of articles, such as fiction and nonfiction.

8. **Draw diagrams.** Charts, clusters, spider maps, trees, sketches, and other kinds of diagrams can help you organize and develop any idea. (See pages 5, 25, 26, 88 – 91.) Here is a map that Leroy drew to help him explore the kinds of articles the school magazine might include.

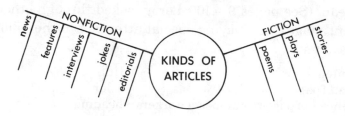

9. **Take notes.** When you are exploring an idea, always write down your thoughts and your discoveries. You might want to keep your notes together in a small notebook so that they do not get lost.

TIPS on Exploring Ideas

- Think about your purpose.
- Ask yourself questions.
- Talk to people.
- Observe.
- Describe.
- Do research.
- Think about relationships.
- Draw diagrams.
- Take notes.

Making Generalizations

☐ Making a generalization   Applying what you know about a few things to a whole group of things

Contrary to one more tenet[1] of the wolf myth, I never saw a wolf attempt to hamstring[2] a deer. Drawing upon all his strength, the wolf would forge up alongside the caribou and leap for its shoulder. The impact was usually enough to send the deer off balance and, before it could recover, the wolf would seize it by the back of the neck and bring it down, taking care to avoid the wildly thrashing hoofs, a blow from any one of which could cave in the wolf's ribcage like so much brittle candy.

The kill was quickly, and usually cleanly, made and I doubt very much if the deer suffered any more than a hog suffers when it is being butchered for human consumption.

The wolf never kills for fun, which is probably one of the main differences distinguishing him from man.

— *Never Cry Wolf,* Farley Mowat

Farley Mowat spent more than a year in the Arctic, studying wolves. After observing a number of wolves, he felt that he could make statements about most or all wolves: for example, *The wolf never kills for fun*. Such statements are called *generalizations*.

Mowat could not observe every wolf in the world to make his generalization. A young boy who touches a hot stove does not have to touch every stove in the world to make the generalization that stoves are hot — and that he had better keep his hands off. Without generalizations, we would all have burned hands, for we would not be able to generalize from one experience to another.

How to Make Generalizations

1. **Observe closely.**   You want to be sure that your observations are accurate and complete. Note as many facts and details as you can.

   Mowat watched wolves hunting many times and took careful notes on what he observed.

[1] belief
[2] cripple by damaging the knees

Grand Generalizations

Did you know that proverbs are kinds of generalizations? They state general truths about life. Perhaps a bird in the hand is not always better than two birds in the bush . . . but most of the time it is.

   Think about what these generalizations mean. Do you agree with them?

Fine words butter no parsnips.

What can you expect from a pig but a grunt?

Blessed is he who expects nothing, for he shall never be disappointed.

Whispered words are heard afar.

He was a bold man who first ate an oyster.

Every shoe fits not every foot.

Wishes can never fill a sack.

You cannot prevent the birds of sadness from flying over your head, but you can prevent them from nesting in your hair.

To make your dreams come true, you have to stay awake.

If you plant your feet firmly on the ground, you'll end up with dirty socks.

2. **Think about what you observe.** What do the things you observe have in common? What do they share with other things? What does this suggest to you? Observations become meaningful only when you relate them to other facts.

Mowat noticed that a wolf killed a deer cleanly and quickly. When he put this observation together with other observations, he decided that wolves seem to kill only for hunger, not fun.

3. **Make a generalization.** If your observation is true for some, might it be true for many? For what group?

If you know several poodles who are very smart, you might generalize and say that most poodles are smart. Your generalization applies only to poodles, not to other dogs.

4. **Do not be hasty.** Do you have enough examples? Do you have different kinds of examples? Are the examples typical? Avoid *hasty generalizations* — generalizations made from too few examples or from examples that are not typical.

You cannot assume that most people eat tuna fish for lunch just because you and your sister do. Furthermore, you cannot tell what most people eat for lunch just by observing a school cafeteria, for students represent only one group of people.

5. **Never say *never*.** Few generalizations are always true or true for everyone. Avoid words like *never, always, all*. Instead use *sometimes, often, some, many, most*.

Unfortunately, Mowat used the word *never*. Thus, if one wolf somewhere kills for fun, Mowat's generalization is false.

6. **Remember that a generalization is not a fact.** You may have to change your statement if new facts come along.

TIPS for Making Generalizations
- Observe closely.
- Think about what you observe.
- Apply your observation to a group.
- Avoid hasty generalizations.
- Use *sometimes, often, some, many, most*.
- Remember that a generalization is not a fact.

Drawing Conclusions and Making Inferences

☐ **Drawing a conclusion** Making an educated guess
☐ **Making an inference** Drawing a conclusion by
combining new information with what you already know

When a plane goes down, the tale of the accident is written somewhere in the wreckage. The clues may be obvious: a stalled engine, broken control cables, sabotage. Or they may pop out only when experts using microscopes find a telltale crack, or magnify a light bulb's filament to show that a warning signal had failed. . . .

Jack Young, whose specialty is aircraft engines, recalls poking through the wreckage of a plane that had crash-landed and skidded through a brick wall. He noticed a piece of brick lodged in the compressor blades of one of the engines. Not until a day or two later did its significance strike him: "The fan blades weren't torn up — so the engine must not have been running." That pointed to engine failure as a cause of the crash.

—*The Boston Globe,* November 24, 1989

After a plane crash, a "Go Team" of investigators rushes to the scene. These experts go over the crash site inch by inch, looking for clues. They are painstaking in their work, for the tiniest detail can help them to *make an inference* about the cause of the accident. Here is how they do it.

1. **They observe something.** A piece of brick is lodged in the blades of an engine. The blades are not torn up.
2. **They use their experience and knowledge to decide what it might mean.** The engine must not have been running.
3. **They draw a conclusion.** Engine failure caused the crash.

A detective follows the same steps to discover who committed a crime. A scientist follows the same steps to find a cure for a disease. And you follow the same steps to help you make decisions, figure things out, and discover things. For example, if you hear the doorbell ring, you conclude that someone wants to come in. If you notice that people wearing seatbelts survive accidents better, you conclude that seatbelts save lives.

1.

2.

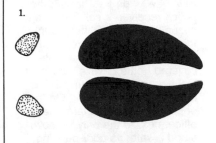

3.

4. 5.

Answers
1. moose
2. dog
3. wolf
4. skunk
5. cat

At 7:14 A.M. on February 7, the police received a call from the security guard at Glittery Gems, Inc. During a routine check of the ninth floor, the guard had discovered Lottie Lavelle, assistant to the president of Glittery Gems, handcuffed to her desk. On the opposite side of the large, fancy office, next to the only window, stood a safe, its door hanging open.

When Detective Ruiz and Officer Brian arrived on the scene, Lottie told them her story. She had arrived at the office early to discover a man and a woman robbing the safe. Both wore plain white T-shirts and jeans, and only their eyes showed above red bandanas tied around their faces. Taking the cuffs out of a backpack full of tools, they secured Lottie to her desk. Then they stuffed the contents of the safe into another backpack and ran out the door, tossing the red bandanas onto the floor. Clearheaded Lottie looked out the window and saw the two thieves rush into a new green pickup truck.

Detective Ruiz listened to every word, looked around carefully, and figured out just what had happened. Can you?

How to Draw Conclusions and Make Inferences

1. **Observe carefully.** Think of yourself as a detective looking for clues. To the crash team, a brick in an engine was a major piece of evidence. To you, a voice on the phone, the handwriting on a note, or a sentence in the newspaper may turn out to be important. Examine evidence with care, for a small detail can lead to a big discovery.

2. **What do you already know that could help you?** Look into your mind. Ask yourself what you have done or learned that could shed some light on what you are observing.

3. **Ask "What does it mean?"** How do the facts fit together? Where might they lead? Go beyond what you see and know to make guesses. That is how real discoveries are made.

4. **Draw a conclusion.** Make an educated guess about where the information leads. The crash expert guessed that the accident was due to engine failure. He used what he observed plus what he already knew to draw a conclusion. Here is the way the process works.

WHAT YOU OBSERVE +	WHAT YOU KNOW ⟶	CONCLUSION
The house is quiet.	The dog always barks when someone enters.	The dog is not here.
The flashlight does not work.	Flashlights run on batteries. Batteries wear out.	The flashlight needs new batteries.
Your friend is smiling.	She just took a French test.	She did well on the test.

5. **Make sure your conclusion is sound.** Ask yourself these questions to be sure your conclusion makes sense.

   a. **Are there enough examples?** Do not draw a conclusion from one or two examples. One growling German shepherd does not mean that all German shepherds are unfriendly.

   b. **Are there enough facts?** Get all the facts you need to draw your conclusion. If a light goes out, you cannot conclude that there has been a power failure. First find out whether other lights are working.

   c. **Does the evidence fit the conclusion?** A toothpaste may taste good, but that does not mean it cleans well.

   d. **Is the conclusion the most obvious one?** If you did poorly on a test, that does not mean that the test was too hard. There are more obvious possibilities. Did you study enough? Did you understand the material?

   e. **Does the conclusion follow from the evidence?** If one thing happened before another, that does not mean the first event caused the second. If you start out for the beach and then it rains, you cannot conclude that the rain started because you were going to the beach.

6. **Remember that a conclusion is not a fact.** A conclusion is based on facts, but it is not a fact itself. It is an educated guess, and it may or may not turn out to be correct. Only if it is proven can it be taken as a fact.

TIPS for Drawing Conclusions and Making Inferences

- Observe carefully. Look for clues.
- What do you already know that could help you?
- What might it all mean?
- Make an educated guess. Draw a conclusion.
- Be sure your conclusion is sound.
  Do you have enough evidence?
  Do you have enough facts?
  Does your evidence fit the conclusion?
  Is your conclusion the most obvious one?
  Does the conclusion follow from the evidence?
- Remember that a conclusion is not a fact.

Playing Sherlock Holmes

Sherlock Holmes, the detective created by Sir Arthur Conan Doyle, was a master of inference. He could look at a footprint or a hat and tell that the owner was a six-foot-tall blond man in his twenties who ran marathons, was very neat, collected stamps as a hobby, and preferred dogs to cats.

How much can you tell about a person by looking at something that belongs to him or her? Have some classmates or friends each borrow something from a relative or friend — a stuffed animal, a jacket, a notebook, for example. If the item contains clues such as notes or tickets, so much the better. Then examine each item carefully and see what the group can figure out about its owner.

Telling Fact from Opinion

Some More Facts

Dogs have their own pawprints, just as people have their own fingerprints.

The greyhound is not only the fastest dog but also the dog with the sharpest eyesight.

There is only one mammal with a poisonous bite — the short-tailed shrew.

Cats were worshiped by the ancient Egyptians.

The elephant is the only mammal that cannot jump.

Hair goes on growing for a while after a person dies.

People stop growing when their bones do, which is usually between the ages of 15 and 20.

The Dead Sea is the world's lowest and saltiest body of water. It contains about 11,600,000,000 tons of salt.

The first postage stamp was used in England in May 1840.

A football is from 10 $^7/_8$" to 11 $^7/_{16}$" long.

In 1987, attendance at major league football games topped 52,008,9l8.

The maximum weight of a bowling ball is 16 pounds.

☐ **Fact** Something that can be proven to be true
☐ **Opinion** A belief or judgment about something

Here are some facts you might not know.

- In Texas it's against the law to milk somebody else's cow.
- Noise can dull the sense of smell. Therefore, professional perfume sniffers, called "noses," work in soundproof rooms.
- The pigeon is the only bird that can drink water without lifting its head to swallow.
- The lower jawbone is the hardest bone in the body.
- There are about 2,200 feathers on every canary.
- There are about 13,000 different parts in the average car.

The statements above are *facts* because they can be proven. People have read the Texas laws and studied the sense of smell and counted the feathers on a canary. The statements below, on the other hand, are *opinions*. They cannot be proven.

Greyhounds are beautiful dogs.
That perfume has a perfectly horrible smell.
I think that canaries should not be kept in cages.

How to Tell Fact from Opinion

1. **A fact can be proven.** Someone, including you, can observe or test or measure or count to prove that the statement is true. The testimony of an expert is also a kind of proof.

2. **An opinion is a belief.** An opinion states what someone thinks. Someone else may think differently. Opinions cannot be proven. Phrases like *I think, I believe,* or *in my opinion* sometimes accompany an opinion.

> **TIPS** for Telling Fact from Opinion
> - If it can be proven, it is a fact.
> - If it is just what someone thinks or believes, it is an opinion.

Using Logic

Kinds of Reasoning

☐ **Logic**   Clear, sound thinking or reasoning

LISA: Did you know that "Cinderella" isn't logical?
DEREK: What are you talking about?
LISA: I was reading "Cinderella" to my little sister last night. The story doesn't make sense.
DEREK: Of course it doesn't. It's got a pumpkin that turns into a coach, and mice who turn into horses or something, and lots of other silly stuff. It's just a fairy tale. Fairy tales don't make sense.
LISA: I don't mean that. That's imaginary stuff. I mean the details of the story aren't logical.
DEREK: I don't get it.
LISA: At midnight things changed back the way they were, right?
DEREK: Right. Cinderella's gown changed back into rags, the coach changed back into a pumpkin, and the horses changed back into mice. So what?
LISA: Well, if everything else changed back, then why didn't Cinderella's glass slipper change back too?
DEREK: . . . Oops!

When you figure out why something does or does not make sense, you are thinking logically. That is, you are finding reasons that lead you to a certain conclusion. If the reasons take you there in a clear, step-by-step way, then your conclusion is likely to be reliable. In other words, if your reasoning is sound, then your conclusion will be sound. Sound reasoning is important. It helps you solve problems, understand the world around you, and make intelligent judgments.

How to Understand Reasoning

1. **Know the two kinds of reasoning.**   There are two main kinds of reasoning — inductive and deductive. (See also pages 31, 32, 33, 35).

    INDUCTIVE   Drawing a conclusion about many things on the basis of a few things

      Example   "Cinderella" has mice, *Stuart Little* stars a mouse, and *The Rescuers* features mice too. Therefore, some children's literature features mice.

About *logic*

logic study of principles of reason; system of reasoning (from Greek *logos*, "speech, reason, word")

SOME NEAR SYNONYMS

judgment	reasoning
wisdom	deduction
reason	induction
sense	argumentation

-ology WORDS

Many other words with *log* have the same origin as *logic* — for example, words ending with *-logy*, "science or study of."

anthropology	study of human beings
biology	study of life
cosmetology	study of cosmetics
criminology	study of crime
cryptology	study of codes
entomology	study of insects
geology	study of the earth
herpetology	study of reptiles
meteorology	study of weather
ornithology	study of birds
paleontology	study of fossils
psychology	study of the mind
seismology	study of earthquakes
sociology	study of society
zoology	study of animals

DEDUCTIVE Drawing a conclusion that must follow from the statements given

> *Example* All fairy tales are imaginary. "Cinderella" is a fairy tale. Therefore, it is imaginary.

2. **Don't stay away from arguments.** When you offer reasons and then draw a conclusion from them, you are presenting an *argument*. Both examples in item 1 above are arguments.

3. **Recognize the signals.** Words like *because, since, for* are often used to mark reasons. Words and phrases like *therefore, so, it follows that* mark a conclusion.

Because Cinderella's clothes, coach, and horses all changed back to what they were before, *it follows that* her glass slipper should have changed back too.

4. **Try to follow the argument.**

   a. When you listen and read, be alert for arguments. Pay attention to signals like *because* and *therefore*. Look for the parts of the argument and decide whether they make sense — whether the conclusion follows from the reasons.

   b. When you speak and write, use words like *because* and *therefore* to mark the parts of your arguments. Go over the arguments you give to be sure that they make sense.

   c. Use the guidelines that follow to help you judge your own arguments as well as those of others.

How to Use Inductive Reasoning

1. **Get the facts.** Gather as many facts as you can. Be sure your information is correct and complete. Check it yourself when possible. Otherwise, use reference books and other reliable sources.

2. **Ask yourself what you know about the facts.** Use your own knowledge and experience. What do the facts mean? How do they fit together? What else do they apply to? What do they have in common? What predictions might you make?

3. **Draw a general conclusion.** A general conclusion is one that is true for examples in addition to the specific ones you give.

Facts and observations
My two little brothers like stories about animals.
My little cousin likes stories about animals.
All the children I babysit for like stories about animals.
Conclusion
Many children like stories about animals.

4. **Is your conclusion sound?** Ask these questions:

a. **Have you looked at enough examples?** If you know two children who like scary stories, that does not mean that all children like scary stories.

b. **Are your observations correct?** Have you checked them either yourself or with expert sources?

c. **Do your examples fit your conclusion?** For instance, if your conclusion relates to what children read, do not use anything but children's literature in your examples.

NOT RELEVANT	Many children like Mickey Mouse cartoons.
NOT RELEVANT	Many children like the movie *Bambi*.
RELEVANT	Many children like stories about Peter Rabbit.
RELEVANT	Many children like the book *Make Way for Ducklings*.
CONCLUSION	Many children like to read about animals.

d. **Do you have all the facts you need?** The fact that most children like animal stories does not mean that only children like them. Have you asked teen-agers and adults?

e. **Does your conclusion follow from the facts?** The fact that many fairy tale heroines married princes does not mean that at one time many women really married princes.

f. **Have you limited your conclusion?** Few statements are true in all cases. Use words like *sometimes, most, many, often, some* to limit your conclusion. (See also page 32.)

TOO GENERAL	Children's stories are about animals.
IMPROVED	Many children's stories are about animals.

Hearts or Clubs?

There are three playing cards, two red (hearts) and one black (clubs). One card is placed in front of you and one in front of a partner. The third is placed in the middle. All are face down. You pick up your card and, in a few seconds, you can guess what card your partner has. How?

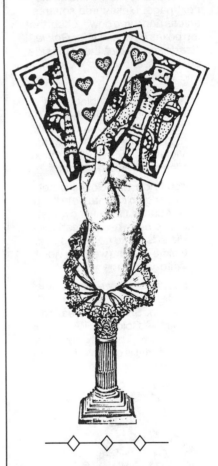

Answer

If you have a black card, then you know your partner must have a red card, because both of the other cards are red. If you have a red card, all you have to do is wait a few seconds. If your partner has the black card, he or she will probably figure out that you have a red card and say something. If your partner says nothing, then he or she is likely to have a red card too.

Table Logic

The three friends Scarlet, Violet, and Goldie always wear the colors scarlet, violet, and gold. However, no one wears the color that matches her name. Today, furthermore, Violet is not wearing gold. How can you figure out what color each girl is wearing?

Use a table like the one on the next page. Make three squares across and three down. Label the top boxes *G, S,* and *V* for *Goldie, Scarlet,* and *Violet.* Label the side boxes *g, s,* and *v* for *gold, scarlet,* and *violet.*

1. You know that Violet is not wearing gold or violet. Write *no* in the *g* and *v* boxes in Violet's column. The only box left for Violet is *s.* Put *yes* in the *s* box. Violet is wearing scarlet.

2. You know that Goldie is not wearing gold. Write *no* in the *g* box under *G.* You know that she is not wearing scarlet — Violet is. Write *no* in the *s* box. Goldie must be wearing violet. Write *yes* in the *v* box.

3. Scarlet is not wearing scarlet. Write *no* in the *s* box in her column. She is not wearing violet — Goldie is. Write *no* in the *v* box. The only color left for Scarlet is gold. Write *yes* in the *g* box.

5. **Be prepared to change your conclusion.** A conclusion, even a sound one, is not a fact. See if the conclusion still holds when other examples come up. If not, you may have to modify it or even give it up entirely.

How to Use Deductive Reasoning

1. **Go from all to some.** Go from a general statement to a specific one. (See pages 17–18.) Then combine the two in your conclusion. In other words, show that what is true for a group is true for a member of that group.

> GENERAL All my friends like stories about horses.
> SPECIFIC Rowena is my friend.
> CONCLUSION Rowena likes stories about horses.

2. **Try a syllogism.** The argument in item 1 is in the form of a *syllogism.* It contains two *premises,* or reasons, that lead to a conclusion.

> PREMISE 1 All my friends like stories about horses.
> PREMISE 2 Rowena is my friend.
> CONCLUSION Rowena likes stories about horses.

a. You can express a syllogism as an *if-then* sentence.

If all my friends like stories about horses *and* Rowena is my friend, *then* Rowena likes stories about horses.

b. The first premise makes a general statement with the word *all, every,* or *no.* The second premise makes a specific statement.

3. **Is the syllogism sound?** If both premises are true, or sound, the conclusion is sound. If a premise is false, or not sound, the conclusion is not sound.

> UNSOUND All dogs have three legs.
> Gremlin is a dog.
> Gremlin has three legs.

Poor Gremlin may have been hurt by a car and have three legs. Nevertheless, the syllogism is false because the first premise is false: all dogs do *not* have three legs.

4. Is the syllogism valid? If the conclusion does not follow from the premises, the syllogism is not logical. It is then said to be *invalid*. A syllogism can be invalid even if the premises are true.

INVALID   All horses have four legs.
           My dog has four legs.
           My dog is a horse.

The fact that all horses have four legs does not mean that all animals with four legs are horses. In a *valid*, or logical, syllogism, the specific item in premise 2 is likely to be a member of the general group in premise 1.

TIPS on Using Logic

UNDERSTANDING REASONING
- Know the two kinds of reasoning — inductive and deductive.
- Don't stay away from arguments — the logical kind.
- Recognize the words that signal an argument.
- Try to follow the argument.

USING INDUCTIVE REASONING
- Get the facts.
- Consider what you know about the facts.
- Draw a general conclusion — one that will apply to other examples.
- Be sure your reasoning is sound.
      Have you looked at enough examples?
      Are your observations accurate?
      Do all your examples fit your conclusion?
      Do you have all the facts you need?
      Does your conclusion follow from the facts?
      Have you limited your conclusion?

USING DEDUCTIVE REASONING
- Go from all to some.
- Try a syllogism.
- Be sure your reasoning is sound.
      Are the premises true?
- Be sure your reasoning is valid.
      Does the conclusion follow from the premises?

Table Logic

(See problem on previous page)

	G	S	V
g	no	yes	no
s	no	no	yes
v	yes	no	no

Syllogism Circles

VALID
All poodles are dogs.
Romeo is a poodle.
Romeo is a dog.

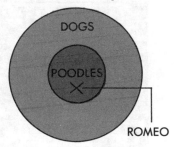

INVALID
All poodles are dogs.
Romeo is a dog.
Romeo is a poodle.

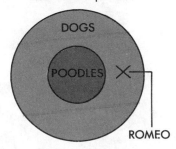

Faulty Reasoning and Propaganda

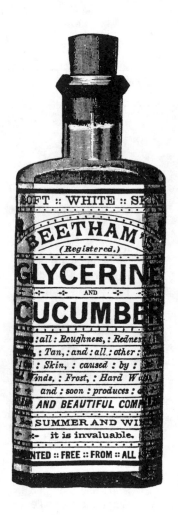

☐ **Propaganda** An attempt to spread an opinion or belief, sometimes using unfair or untrue information

Supermarket shelves are being flooded with "natural" products, some of them containing a long list of chemical additives. And some products that never did contain additives have suddenly sprouted "natural" or "no preservative" labels. . . .

"Natural" foods are not necessarily preferable nor necessarily natural.

Consider "natural" potato chips. They are often cut thick from unpeeled potatoes, packaged without preservatives in heavy foil bags with fancy lettering, and sold at a premium price. . . . The packaging is intended to give the impression that "natural" potato chips are less of a junk food than regular chips. But nutritionally there is no difference. Both are made from the same food, the potato, and both have been processed so that they are high in salt and in calories.

— "It's Natural! It's Organic! Or Is It?"
Consumer Reports, July 1980

"Buy my product!" "Vote for me!" "That is bad for you!" "That is good for you!" Almost everywhere you turn, people are trying to convince you to do something or believe something.

An organized attempt to convince many people of something is called *propaganda*. The aim of the propaganda may be worthwhile — to get people to work for a good cause or eat healthful foods, for example. The methods used, however, may be questionable.

How do you avoid being misled? You look at the facts and arguments carefully. Then you ask yourself, "Are the facts true?" "Does the argument make sense?" Below are the most common kinds of faulty reasoning. Watch out for them. (See also pages 37 – 41.)

Kinds of Faulty Reasoning

1. **Hasty generalization, overgeneralization**   A conclusion that is too broad or that is based on too little evidence (see page 32).

All natural foods are good for you.

As you saw above, "natural" oil is still fattening. Watch out for absolute words like *all* and *always*.

2. **Bandwagon**   An argument that says to jump on the bandwagon — to do something because "everybody else is doing it"

Natural foods are in. Don't be left behind — go natural with Goodie's Good 'n' Natural Graham Bars!

The fact that other people are buying something does not necessarily mean the item is worthwhile or right for you.

3. **Testimonial**   An argument based on what a famous person says

Popular movie star Lana Lala says, "Goodie's Good 'n' Natural Graham Bars help get me through the long days on a movie set. They keep me going — and they're good and natural too."

If somebody is famous for making movies, that does not mean the person knows about food or what's good for people. Also, what is good for that person may or may not be good for you.

4. **Name-calling**   Attacking a person rather than an issue

Careful Customers president Dodie Wheaton criticizes the sugar in Goodie's Bars. How can you take seriously the comment of someone who always wears jeans and a T-shirt!

How Dodie Wheaton dresses has nothing to do with the issue, namely, how much sugar the graham bars have. Name-calling is a way of avoiding the real issue.

5. **Transfer**   An attempt to transfer people's favorable feelings about one thing to something else

The wrapper on a Goodie's Good 'n' Natural Graham Bar shows a waterfall in a beautiful forest setting.

Waterfalls and forests are thought of as clean, beautiful parts of nature. The makers of Goodie's bars want you to think of the bars as clean, beautiful, and part of nature too. The facts, however, are to be found not in the picture but in the list of ingredients on the wrapper.

bias: a strong feeling for or against something, preventing a person from being open-minded on an issue; prejudice; a slanted line across the weave of a fabric (from Old French *biais*, "slanting")

A *bias* is a personal slant toward one side of an issue. Which way the slant goes depends on a person's (1) *point of view*, or feeling about the matter, and (2) *motive*, or reason. To understand a person's motive, ask these questions: Why does the person feel that way? Will he or she benefit personally?
Compare these statements:

Without preservatives in food, dangerous molds would form on food, and we would not be able to feed so many people so cheaply and safely.

Preservatives put chemicals in our bodies that may be unhealthful, even dangerous.

Both statements may be true, but the writers have chosen different facts. People's biases affect the facts they choose.
Ask: What are the points of view? The first person is in favor of preservatives, and the second is against them.
Ask: What might their motives be? Are they in the food industry, for example?
Be alert for bias. Try to find out *all* the facts.

Purrs and Snarls

A word is more than a word. It is often tied to a whole set of feelings. Some words are like purrs. They stir up positive, pleasant feelings. Others are like snarls, negative and nasty. Here are some examples. (See also page 163.)

PURRS	SNARLS
wealthy	filthy rich
determined	pigheaded
slender	scrawny
devoted	clingy
traditional	out-of-date
cosy	cramped
confident	swell-headed
colorful	flashy
expensive	overpriced
mischievous	bratty
advise	nag
extravagant	showy

6. **"Loaded" words**   Use of emotional words instead of arguments

Avoid dangerous chemicals. Stick to pure, natural products of the earth. Eat Goodie's Good 'n' Natural Graham Bars.

Words may be chosen to appeal to your emotions rather than your common sense. *Dangerous* frightens you. *Pure, natural, products of the earth* make you feel good and healthy. The feelings, however, are not enough. What are they based on? How are chemicals dangerous? *Which* are dangerous? Why should you think of the bars as pure and natural?

7. **Either-or**   An argument based only on the two extremes of an issue

Either eat foods labeled *natural* or fill your body with chemicals.

If you want to avoid artificial ingredients, then eat Goodie's Good 'n' Natural Graham Bars.

An *either-or* argument wants you to think there are no other choices, when actually there are many. For example, the first statement above wants you to think that only foods labeled *natural* have no chemicals. That is obviously not true. The second statement wants you to forget that you can avoid artificial ingredients without ever going near a Goodie's Graham Bar.

8. **It doesn't follow.**   An argument in which the conclusion does not follow from the reasons given

The label says *natural*, so Goodie's Graham Bars must be good for you.

This argument is illogical: it does not follow from the reason given. (See the discussion of deductive reasoning on pages 40 – 41.) There are many questions it leaves unanswered. What exactly is a "natural" food? What kinds of foods are labeled *natural*? Do you have to believe what the label says? Are all natural foods good for you?

9. **Faulty cause and effect**   A claim that one event caused another just because it happened first

I've been eating foods labeled *natural* for two weeks now, and today I have lots more energy.

This argument confuses *before and after* with *cause and effect*. The fact that one thing happened before another does not mean the first thing caused the second.

10. **Reasoning in a circle**   An argument that something is so just because it is so

Natural foods are good for you because they are natural.

Natural foods may really be good for you, but this argument does not tell you why. Because the reason and the conclusion are the same, the reasoning just goes round and round.

11. **Red herring**   The use of a side issue to distract from the real issue

No artificial preservatives in Nature's Best Strawberry Jam!

Jams have never needed or contained preservatives. The statement is made for two reasons: (1) to attract health-conscious people, and (2) to distract from the fact that jams contain large amounts of sugar.

TIPS on Recognizing Faulty Reasoning and Propaganda

Look for these kinds of faulty reasoning:

- Hasty generalization or overgeneralization
- Bandwagon
- Testimonial
- Name-calling
- Transfer

- "Loaded" words
- Either-or
- It doesn't follow
- Faulty cause and effect
- Reasoning in a circle
- Red herring

"No one can give you a better deal."
[*Everyone gives the same deal and we're no worse.*]

"You can save as much as . . ."
[*But you'll probably save much less.*]

"IT gives you more cleaning power."
[*More than what?*]

"IT saves you more."
[*More than what?*]

Weasel Words

Weasel words weasel out of things. They're the opposite of direct words. Here are some of advertising's pet weasel words.

like
It's like getting a box free.
It's like a trip to the beach.

help
Helps prevent cavities
Helps you look . . .
Helps you feel . . .
Helps stop . . .
Helps fight . . .

acts
Acts like a brush to . . .
Acts against decay

works
Works to prevent upset stomach
Works against stomach acid

Critical Thinking and Evaluating

☐ **Critical thinking** Evaluating in a sound way

☐ **Evaluating** Figuring out the value, worth, or importance of something

FILM REVIEW: *Young Guns II*

"Kid" is the operative[1] word in describing the "Young Guns" approach to the Billy the Kid legend, since these films regard Billy as more of a gun-toting cut-up than a true desperado.[2] As played again by Emilio Estevez in "Young Guns II," Billy tends to giggle at tense moments and, during important ones, to mumble.

The other members of the Lincoln County Regulators, Billy's gang, share a similar boyishness that's geared far more carefully to the tastes of today's teen-age audiences than to the folklore of the Old West. . . .

Mr. Estevez, who first appears in old-coot[3] makeup during a prologue that suggests Billy actually got away, is a sturdy if unspectacular presence, best when he's not asked to take center stage. . . .

A larger problem with the screen play is that it's never quite sure where its sympathies lie. Billy and his gang are presented affectionately enough for a while, but their eventual sad fate is depicted without emotion. The fact that these outlaws became famous, and are being impersonated by attractive young stars, seems to be deemed[4] reason enough for the film's existence.

— Janet Maslin, *New York Times*, August 1, 1990

If you saw *Young Guns II* (and perhaps you did), you might write a very different review. How something is evaluated can depend on what it is and who is doing the evaluating. If you do your judging in a sound and sensible way, then your judgment will be as worthy as the reviewer's. You will be able to say not just "That is good" or "That is bad," but "That is good (or bad) *because* . . ." If you follow *because* with sound reasons, then you have learned the important skill of critical thinking. That is, you have learned how to look at something, judge it, and draw a reasonable conclusion about it. (See pages 33 – 35 .)

[1]in operation, effective
[2]desperate, dangerous criminal, especially in the Old West
[3]foolish old man
[4]judged, considered

How to Evaluate

1. **What is evaluating?**   Evaluating means judging how good something is — whether it does what it is supposed to do. You answer questions such as "Does it work?" "Is it accurate?" "Is it worthwhile?" and you back up your answer with reasons.

2. **Analyze the item.**   How do you judge something as complicated as a movie? Break it into parts. Then you can judge each part separately. (See page 24). Here are some movie parts.

   acting, screenplay, setting, direction, camera work, . . .

   If you were evaluating a book, a new pair of shoes, or a plot idea, the parts would of course be different.

3. **Set standards.**   Ask a question about the quality of each part. For a movie, you might ask quesions like these:

   Was each actor convincing? moving?
   Was the screen play believable? suspenseful? entertaining?
   Was the setting interesting? Did it create a mood?

   These questions set standards, or *criteria*. Different items will have different criteria. If you were evaluating an idea for a research report, for instance, you would ask a different set of questions. Also, different people may set different criteria. You might use standards different from those used by the movie reviewer on page 46.

4. **Decide how well the item meets the standards.**   *Young Guns II* did not meet Maslin's standards for acting or screenplays.

5. **Draw a conclusion.**   Base your conclusion on the results of Step 4. Here is Janet Maslin's conclusion.

   This approach has its appeal in limited doses, but it makes for a western that's smaller than life.

TIPS for Evaluating

- Analyze the item.
- Set standards for it.
- See whether it meets the standards.
- Draw a conclusion.

A Difference of Opinion

There's nothing that everyone agrees on. Here are some real rotten reviews received by the world's most admired writer, Shakespeare.

ON WILLIAM SHAKESPEARE'S PLAY *Romeo and Juliet*, 1662

— To the Opera and there saw Romeo and Juliet, the first time it was ever acted; but it is a play of itself the worst that ever I heard in my life . . .
— Samuel Pepys, *Diary*

ON WILLIAM SHAKESPEARE

— Shakespeare's name, you may depend on it, stands absurdly too high and will go down. He had no invention as to stories, none whatever. He took all his plots from old novels . . .
— Lord Byron, 1814

— from *Rotten Reviews*, Bill Henderson, ed.

Problem Solving

Problem solving
Answering a question or working out a situation that presents difficulty

Here is a situation that researchers set up to investigate how people solve problems. Someone is placed in a room and given a candle, a book of matches, and a box of tacks. The person is asked to figure out how to hang up the candle so that it will burn properly and provide light in the room. How does the person go about looking for a solution?

First of all, almost no one picks up the items and starts working immediately. People start out by looking at the items and thinking, "What do I know about these things? How do they work?"

Next, the subjects consider possible solutions and explore each one to see whether it will work. Then they choose the one they think will work best and try it out. Most people think of putting a tack through the candle and attaching it to the wall. Or they try making a row of nails and placing the candle on it. Or they melt some wax and try using it to glue the candle to the wall. Usually they try more than one approach.

These solutions are clumsy: the tack barely goes through the candle or bends it, the wax does not stick, the candle falls as it melts the wax holding it up, and so on. Still, they can be made to work for a while. A few people, however, are not satisfied. They go on thinking and trying, and they sometimes come up with the best solution of all. They empty the box of tacks, tack it to the wall, and use it as a candle holder!

The way people handle this problem is not very different from the way you handle — or should handle — the problems you face every day. The basic approach is the same whether you are looking for a way to earn money, finish a puzzle, write a well-organized paragraph, or build a robot.

Here are the important points to notice. In the experiment, no one came up with the best solution right away. People stopped to think before getting to work, and they all started just about the same way, no matter what solution they found.

Problem solving, then, is not a matter of just sitting around and waiting for an idea to strike. When an idea does appear, it usually comes as the result of a step-by-step process of figuring things out. The people who get the best ideas are likely to be those who keep figuring . . . and figuring . . . and figuring.

Solve This One

There are at least two solutions to the problem below. To find them, you need to break out of the usual way of looking at things. One of the solutions is a particular challenge. Few people think of it.

Try to find one or both solutions yourself before you look at the answers. Keep track of the way you go about attacking the problem. Do you follow the steps in the TIPS?

PROBLEM: Without lifting your pencil from the paper, draw no more than four straight lines that will cross through all nine dots. (Try it on your own paper, of course, not in this book.)

How to Solve a Problem

1. **Define the problem.** State it to yourself. Be specific.

> TOO GENERAL I need to light this room somehow.
> SPECIFIC I need to keep this candle lit, using this book of matches and box of tacks.

2. **Explore the problem.** Describe it to yourself. Take it apart in your mind. Ask yourself questions about it.

I can light the candle with one of these matches. But how do I make the candle stand up? Candles tend to drip wax, too, so I have to watch out for that. I can hang something up with the tacks. Can I get them into these walls? Is there anything else in the room? The matches . . .

3. **Consider solutions.** Don't stop at the most obvious ones.

I could tack the candle to the wall. Maybe I could rest the candle on some tacks in the wall. How else do you hang things up? With glue — but I don't have any. Is there anything I could use instead? Well, candles drip wax. Maybe . . .

4. **Examine each solution.** What will it do? What will happen?

The nail might bend the candle so it doesn't burn straight. Also, the candle might singe the wall. If I use wax as glue, the candle will melt the wax and fall. . . .

5. **Decide on a solution.** Choose the one that works best.

6. **Consider the results.** Can you improve on them? Then try something else, starting again from the beginning.

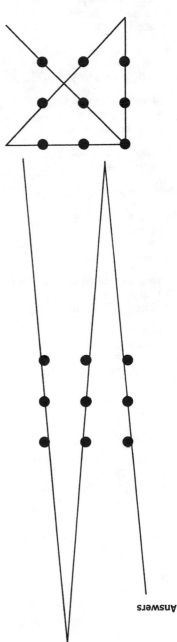

TIPS on Solving a Problem

- Define the problem.
- Explore the problem.
- List possible solutions.
- Examine each solution.
- Decide on a solution.
- Consider the results.

Answers

Synthesizing

☐ **Synthesizing** Combining different parts or activities to create a new whole

Some Inventors Groups

American Society of Inventors
23 Palisades Avenue
Absecon, NJ 08207

Appalachian Inventors Group
P.O. Box 388
Oak Ridge, TN 37830

California Inventors Council
P.O. Box 2096
Sunnyvale, CA 94087

Inventors' Association of
New England
P.O. Box 3110
Cambridge, MA 02139

Inventors Workshop
International
121 North Fir Street
Ventura, CA 91003

Midwestern Inventors Society
P.O. Box 335
St. Cloud, MN 56301

National Congress of Inventor
Organizations
P.O. Box 158
Rheem Valley, CA 94570

Northwest Inventors
Association
723 East Highland Drive
Arlington, WA 98223

Society of American Inventors
P.O. Box 7284
Charlotte, NC 28217

** Seventh-grader Matthew Peters won a prize for inventing the S.I.T. Skoot after he watched his dad skate fast and then sit on his hockey stick and glide over the ice. Matthew's invention consists of a pole and wheels. The pole is held between the legs and the wheels roll over ice or other smooth surfaces.

** Katie Harding, a kindergartner, invented the Mudpuddle-Spotter — an umbrella with a flashlight attached to the handle. It helps her avoid puddles while walking after dark.

** Suzanna Goodin, a first-grader, won a prize for her Edible Pet Food Server. Tired of washing spoons after feeding her cats, she designed a spoon-shaped cracker. After it has been used to serve the food, the pet just eats it.

Often a "new" invention is simply two existing products or things combined in a new way. An answering machine, for example, is a combination of a tape recorder and a telephone.

Let's invent something by combining two inventions that already exist — a broom and a radio. How about a musical broom? Then you can dance your way around the room as you sweep!

— Adapted from *Be an Inventor*, Barbara Taylor

You're an inventor too. When you prepare a salad, put together an outfit, predict the outcome of a game, write a story, or solve any kind of problem, you are inventing something. That is, you are *synthesizing* — bringing together ideas and combining them in a new way. You are doing what professional inventors, architects, artists, detectives, and writers do.

How to Synthesize

1. **Observe.**   Don't just look at things. Train yourself to look around them, under them, above them, inside them. Listen to them, touch them, smell them, even taste them. Take them apart. Look at them as if you were someone else. You will see things you never saw before. (See also pages 9 – 10.)

2. **Associate.**   What does the object or idea remind you of? What is it like? What is it different from?

3. **Ask questions.**   Questioning is one of the most important parts of the creative process.

   a. **Information questions**   Ask *Who? What? Where? When? Why? How?*

   b. **Comprehension questions**   Certain questions will help you understand the item you are considering — what it is, what it is like, what you and others know and think about it.

   • How do I define it? How does the dictionary define it?
   • What kind of thing is it? What group is it a member of?
   • What are some examples of it?
   • What parts does it have? How would I break it down?
   • What is its purpose? How is it used? How else might it be used? How is it not used? Why?
   • What are its causes? its effects?
   • Is it possible? Why or why not?
   • Is it practical? Why or why not?
   • Has it been done before? When? How? By whom?
   • What facts do I know about it? Where can I learn more?
   • What songs, programs, paintings, movies, sayings, articles do I know about it?
   • What do people say about it?

   c. **Creative questions**   Ask "What if" questions. Don't be afraid to be original, even silly. (See page 12.)

   • What if I changed just one part?
   • What if something had never happened?
   • What if I moved it somewhere else?
   • What if it disappeared?

4. **Try random combinations.**   Make lists of items. Draw lines from one list to the other at random. See what you can do with the combinations you come up with. (See page 12.)

Some Wild Combinations

Put some of these items together. What can you think of?

TV game show	fingernail
poem	bell
sewing machine	odor
writing tool	Mars

EXAMPLES

— Writing with your fingernail?
— Game show in which people try to guess odors?
— Sewing machine with a bell?
— Poem about Mars?

┌─────────────────────────────────────┐
Tips on Synthesizing

• Observe.   • Ask yourself questions.
• Associate.   • Try random combinations.
└─────────────────────────────────────┘

Part II –
Finding and Using Information

Using the Library

Where to Start

☐ **Library**   A collection of books, magazines, and other forms of information for reference, reading, or borrowing

The Main Floor of One Library

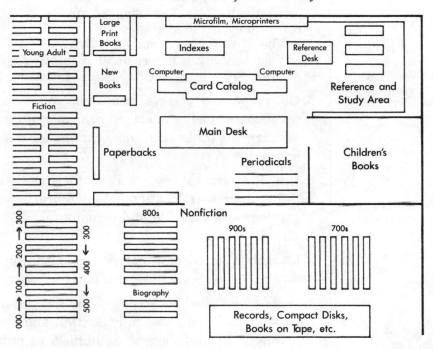

How to Use the Library

1. **Know the layout.**   Your library may be arranged differently than the one above, but it will have most of the same sections. Learn where the sections are, especially these:

Nonfiction	Children or Juvenile	Reference
Fiction	Young Adults or Young People	

2. **Know what's happening.**   Libraries are lively places. They offer movies, CDs, pictures, and other material and sponsor special events such as film showings and contests. Look around. Pick up handouts. Find out what is going on at *your* library.

!!!
About Libraries

- The first libraries were libraries of clay! Early "books" were written on clay tablets.

- The Egyptians wrote on *papyrus*, a plant they cut into strips, pressed into sheets, and rolled into scrolls.

- The greatest library of ancient times was the Greek library in Alexandria, Egypt. It had a copy of every known scroll of the time and probably held more than 700,000 scrolls!

More About Libraries

- The public library goes back to ancient Greece and Rome. However, since few people could read in those days, public libraries were not really very public.

- In 1638 John Harvard gave his school about 400 books to start a library. His gift was so highly prized that the school was renamed in his honor. That is how Harvard University got its name — and the future nation got its first library.

- Canada's first college library was established earlier — in 1635 at the Jesuit College of Quebec.

- The spread of the free library in the United States dates back to the 1830s.

- The Library of Congress in Washington D.C. has over 530 miles of book shelves!

3. **Get a library card.**   You will need a library card to check out items. Apply at the main desk. There may be a small fee.

4. **Learn the rules.**   Some libraries hand out a printed sheet of rules. If yours does not, ask the librarian these questions:

- How do you check out books, tapes, and records?
- How long may material be kept out?
- What is the fine for overdue material?
- What hours is the library open?
- Where in the library may you study?
- What behavior is expected? Plan on being quiet and polite. Never leave your belongings unattended.

5. **Go prepared.**   Have whatever you need, such as a notebook or pad, a pencil or pen, your library card, a bag for carrying books, and some change for the copy machine or printer.

6. **Find the card catalog.**   Look for the listing of library items and their location. Many libraries now have two catalogs — a card file and a computerized catalog (pages 55 – 59).

7. **Learn how to request material.**   Usually you find your own material. Sometimes you must fill out a request form.

8. **Learn how to find material.**   Use the call number (pages 57 – 58) to locate the right section and shelf. Books are arranged in alphabetical or numerical order, depending on what kinds of books they are (page 57).

9. **Learn how to use special equipment.**   More and more libraries are installing microprinters, computers, copiers, and other equipment. Check with a librarian before using any equipment.

10. **Ask for help.**   The librarian is there to help you.

TIPS on Using the Library

- Know the layout.
- Know what goes on.
- Get a library card.
- Learn the rules.
- Go prepared.

- Find the card catalog.
- Learn how to request material.
- Learn how to find material.
- Learn how to use the equipment.
- Ask the librarian for help.

Card and Computerized Catalogs

☐ **Catalog** A list of items

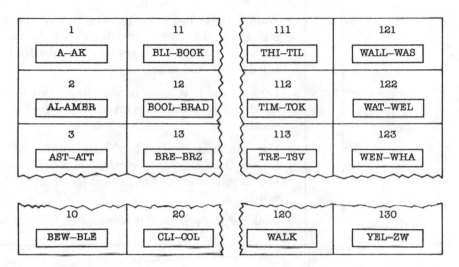

1 A–AK	**11** BLI–BOOK	**111** THI–TIL	**121** WALL–WAS
2 AL–AMER	**12** BOOL–BRAD	**112** TIM–TOK	**122** WAT–WEL
3 AST–ATT	**13** BRE–BRZ	**113** TRE–TSV	**123** WEN–WHA
10 BEW–BLE	**20** CLI–COL	**120** WALK	**130** YEL–ZW

Every library has a *card catalog* — a set of cards listing every work in the library and where it is located. In addition, libraries are now installing computers that give the same information. Here are guidelines for both kinds of catalogs.

How to Use the Card Catalog

1. **Find the card catalog.** The card catalog is usually located in stacks of labeled drawers, like those shown above.

2. **Find the right drawer.** Each drawer is labeled for a part of the alphabet. The drawers are arranged in alphabetical order. Inside the drawer are cards for subjects, titles, and authors of works in the library. Find the drawer whose letters match the first few letters of the term you are looking for.

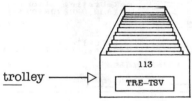

trolley ⟶ ▷ 113
TRE–TSV

The Fine Art of Browsing

Some books are to be tasted, others to be swallowed, and some few to be chewed and digested.
— *Sir Francis Bacon*

Browsing can help you "taste" more books. *Browse* means "look over or read in a casual way." When you are in the library, take time to walk by the shelves and browse. (You can browse using the computer too.)

Look for tempting topics and titles. Then "taste" a few of the books. New tastes help you discover, learn, and grow — and they can give you some interesting ideas to chew on.

3. Find the card.   The cards are alphabetized.

Finding Items in Alphabetical Order

- Words that begin with the same letter are alphabetized by the second letter. Words that begin with the same two letters are alphabetized by the third letter, and so on.

- Look for the first letter of your first word. Then look for the second letter. Go on until you find what you want.

- Use the *guide cards*. They have labels that stand higher than the other cards. They can help guide you to your word. Do not count *the* or *an* as the first word.

- Look for *Mc* or *St.* as if it were spelled *Mac* or *Saint*.

---

4. Know the 3 kinds of cards.   Works are listed in three ways: (a) by title, (b) by author, and (c) by subject. The cards give the same information but arrange it differently.

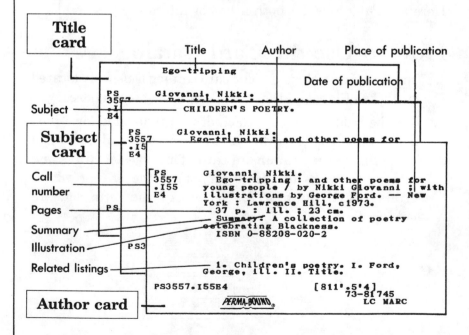

5. **Read the card.**   The card contains helpful information. For example, the summary tells you what the book is about. The copyright date tells you how recent its facts are.

6. **Follow the call number.**   Every book has its own call number, listed in the catalog and on the book spine. The number tells what section of the library the book is in. Think of the number as the book's address, and follow it to the book's home on the library shelf. The call number depends on the kind of book and the library's classification system.

   a. **Kind of book**

   FICTION   *F* or *Fic* identifies a book as fiction. Fiction is alphabetized by the author's last name.

   NONFICTION   Nonfiction books are arranged by subject. Each subject has its own number or letter.

   Other classifications point you to a particular section of the library, such as Young Adult, Biography, or Reference.

   b. **Library system**   Libraries arrange their books using one of the two groups of categories shown below. (See the margins for some breakdowns of these categories.) On the next page are sample call numbers.

Library Classification Systems

DEWEY DECIMAL

000–099	General (Reference)	500–599	Science
100–199	Philosophy	600–699	Technology
200–299	Religion	700–799	Fine Arts
300–399	Social Science	800–899	Literature
400–499	Language	900–999	History

LIBRARY OF CONGRESS

A	General Works	M	Music
B	Philosophy, Religion	N	Fine Arts
C	History-Related Sciences	P	Language and Literature
D	History: General, Old World	Q	Science
E-F	History: America	R	Medicine
G	Geography, Anthropology	S	Agriculture
H	Social Sciences	T	Technology
J	Political Science	U-V	Military Science
K	Law	Z	Bibliography, Library Science
L	Education		

A System Breakdown

Here is a breakdown of the Dewey *History* category.

DEWEY DECIMAL SYSTEM

900–999   History
910–919	Geography, travel, description
920–929	Biography
930–939	Ancient history
940–949	Europe
950–959	Asia
960–969	Africa
970–979	North America
980–989	South America
990–999	Other areas

The subtopics under *History* are broken down into still smaller topics. Here, for example, is the breakdown of the subtopic *North America*.

970–979   North America
971	Canada
972	Middle America
973	United States
974	Northwestern states
975	Southeastern states
976	South central states
977	North central states
978	Western states
979	States of the Great Basin and Pacific Slope

More System Breakdowns

Here are breakdowns of some Library of Congress categories.

LIBRARY OF CONGRESS SYSTEM

P **Language and Literature**
PN Literature

80–99	Criticism
101–245	Authorship
441–1009.5	Literary history
1010–1551	Poetry
1560–1590	The performing arts, show business
1600–3307	Drama
1660–1693	Dramatic composition
1865–1999	Special types (tragedy, comedy, puppet plays, ballet, radio and TV, movies, . . .)
2000–3307	The theater (stage, management, . . .)
3311–3503	Prose, prose fiction
4400	Letters
4500	Essays
4699–5650	Journalism

Q **Science**
QH Natural history, biology

1–278.5	Natural history
75–77	Conservation
301–705	Biology
426–470	Genetics
471–489	Reproduction
501–531	Life
540–549	Ecology

Sample Call Numbers

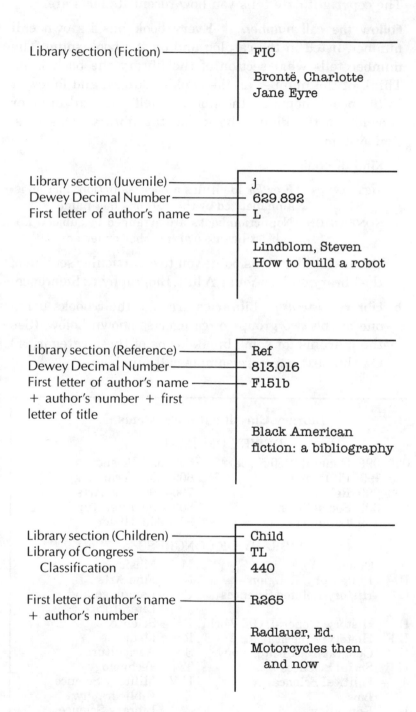

Library section (Fiction) — FIC

Brontë, Charlotte
Jane Eyre

Library section (Juvenile) — j
Dewey Decimal Number — 629.892
First letter of author's name — L

Lindblom, Steven
How to build a robot

Library section (Reference) — Ref
Dewey Decimal Number — 813.016
First letter of author's name + author's number + first letter of title — F151b

Black American fiction: a bibliography

Library section (Children) — Child
Library of Congress Classification — TL 440

First letter of author's name + author's number — R265

Radlauer, Ed.
Motorcycles then and now

How to Use a Computerized Catalog

1. **Find out what it can do.**   Computerized catalogs give the same information as card catalogs, but they also do other things. If your library has a computerized catalog, find out what it can do for you. Here are some possibilities:

   - Allows you to scan the resources quickly and easily
   - Tells you whether or not a book is checked out
   - Tells you what is available at other libraries
   - Gives you a printed list of works on your subject

2. **Learn how to use it.**   First find out whether you are permitted to use the computerized catalog yourself. If you are, ask the librarian for step-by-step instructions or read the posted instructions carefully. (See pages 132–133 for tips on following instructions.)

3. **Follow the call number.**   Computers have not changed the way books are arranged. To find a book on the shelves, you must still know its call number. In a computerized catalog, the call number will appear on the screen rather than on a card. Copy the number and then follow it to the library shelves.

Most book people are famous for what they wrote. The American librarian Melvil Dewey (1851–1931) is famous for what he numbered.

Dewey thought of a system for numbering everything in the library. As a result, the library could keep track of its books and the reader could find them. The system, which is based on 10s and 100s, is called the Dewey Decimal System.

TIPS for Using Card Catalogs and Computerized Catalogs

CARD CATALOG
- Find the card catalog.
- Find the right drawer.
- Find the card.
- Know the three kinds of cards.
- Follow the call letters to the right section and shelf.

COMPUTERIZED CATALOG
- Find out what it can do.
- Find out whether you may use it yourself.
- If so, learn how to use it. Follow the instructions step by step.
- Follow the call letters to the right section and shelf.

Readers' Guide to Periodical Literature

POST, ELIZABETH L.
How to get out of 19 sticky situations
Redbook 170:92-93

POSTAGE STAMPS
    See also
    Covers (Philately)
Cycling takes a licking. il *Bicycling*
    29:88–9 Je '88
Post Office honors astronomer on
    stamp. il *Sky and Telescope* 76:233 S '88
Some words from Fairplay for Frogs
    addressing stamp oversight. il
    Country Journal 15:23 Ap '88
        History
Other uses for stamps. H. Herst, Jr.
    il *Antiques & Collecting Hobbies*
    3:74–5 Ap '88
        Rates
    See Postal rates

What it Means . . .

POST, ELIZABETH L.
    [Author entry]
How to get out of 19 sticky situations
    [Article title]
Redbook 170:92-93
    [Magazine]
POSTAGE STAMPS
    [Subject entry]
    See also
    Covers (Philately)
    [Cross-reference]
Cycling takes a licking. il *Bicycling*
    29:88–9 Je '88   [Illustrated]
Post Office honors astronomer on
    stamp il *Sky and Telescope* 76:233 S '88
        [Volume, page(s)]
Some words from Fairplay for Frogs
    addressing stamp oversight. il
    Country Journal 15:23 Ap '88
        [Month, year]
        History
       [Subtopic]
Other uses for stamps. H. Herst, Jr.
        [Author]
    il *Antiques & Collecting Hobbies*
    3:74–5 Ap '88
        Rates
    See Postal rates
    ["See" reference]

Reference Material

☐ **Reference material**   Books, pamphlets, tapes, disks, and other material used for information

How to Use Reference Material

1. **Know what is available.**   Information at the library comes packaged in different ways.

   a. **Books**   There are books on just about any subject you can think of. Use the card or computer catalog to find books on whatever interests you. Look at special reference books to find specific information. (See item 4 on the next page.)

   b. **Periodicals**   Recent issues of newspapers and magazines are usually kept in a special periodicals section. Older issues may be stored elsewhere.

   c. **Pamphlets, booklets, clippings**   Material such as pamphlets, booklets, and clippings that cannot stand on shelves is kept in a special place called a *vertical file*.

   d. **Microfilm and microfiche**   Newspapers, magazines, and telephone directories are often stored as rolls or sheets of film. They are viewed on special machines.

   e. **Computerized aids**   Some computerized aids are for use by librarians. Others are for your use. Ask.

2. **Learn how to use equipment.**   Ask for and follow step-by-step instructions for computers, microfilm and microfiche machines, copy machines, and all other equipment.

3. **Pick a place to start.**   Start with one of the following:

   a. **The card or computerized catalog**   See pages 55 – 59.

   b. **A reference work**   See item 4.

   c. **A lead from a book**   Look on the copyright page of a book that interests you, for it may tell you what subjects to look up in the card catalog for more information. Also follow cross-references in encyclopedias and subtopic heads in the *Readers' Guide* and in computerized indexes. (See page 61.)

4. **Use reference works.** Look for information in these sources (and the dictionary, pages 62 – 64, and thesaurus, page 65):

Main Types of Reference Works

Almanacs, yearbooks　Facts on many topics, such as sports, world events, awards; updated every year
EXAMPLES　*Facts on File, The Information Please Almanac*

Atlases　Maps and related information, such as population, weather, resources, industry, history
EXAMPLES　*Hammond's New World Atlas*
Atlas of World History

Biographies　Facts about people's lives
EXAMPLES　*Current Biography, Men and Women of Science*

Encyclopedias　Alphabetized articles on many topics; a good place to begin research on a topic
EXAMPLES:　GENERAL　*The World Book Encyclopedia*
SPECIFIC　*Encyclopedia of Space*
World Encyclopedia of Comics

Guidebooks, handbooks, manuals　Specialized information
EXAMPLES　*Simon and Schuster's Guide to Mammals*
Chilton's 1990 Auto Repair Manual: 1983–1990

Readers' Guide to Periodical Literature　Indexed list of magazine articles by subject; books once a year plus current indexes during the year (see margin, page 60)

Magazine Index　Computerized index of magazine articles by subject; supplements or replaces *Readers' Guide* in many libraries (see margin)

Other indexes　Alphabetical listings of items
EXAMPLES　*New York Times Index, Short Story Index*

---

5. **Use the reference librarian as a source.**　The reference librarian is there to help you find information. Just ask.

TIPS on Using Reference Material
- Know what is available.
- Learn how to use equipment.
- Pick a place to start.
- Use specialized references.
- Ask the reference librarian.

Magazine Index

Using a Dictionary

!!!
About *dictionary*

Like most people, you have probably used the dictionary to answer a question or settle a disagreement, for the dictionary is the "last word" on words. The word *dictionary* comes from Latin *dicēre*, "to say."

Speaking of Dictionaries

Here are a few of the special dictionaries you can probably find in your library.

Audio Dictionary
Compton's Illustrated Science Dictionary
Dictionary of Astronomy
Crossword Puzzle Dictionary
Dictionary of Days
Dictionary of Microcomputer Terms
Dictionary of Music
New Dinosaur Dictionary
Perigree Visual Dictionary of Signing
Rhyming Dictionary
Sports Dictionary

☐ **Dictionary**   List of words and their meanings, arranged in alphabetical order

How to Use the Dictionary

1. **Choose the right one.**   There are many kinds of dictionaries. Use one that will tell you exactly what you want to know.

TYPES OF DICTIONARIES

General (abridged) dictionary   Lists most words in a language, plus meanings and pronunciations
  EXAMPLES   *The American Heritage Student's Dictionary*
        Webster's New World Dictionary of the American Language

Unabridged dictionary   Similar to a general dictionary but longer, more complete, and more detailed
  EXAMPLES   *Oxford English Dictionary*
        Webster's Third New International Dictionary

Special dictionaries   List words related to a subject
  EXAMPLES   *Dictionary of American Slang*
        Webster's New Dictionary of Proper Names
        Dictionary of Mythology, Folklore, and Symbols

---

2. Know what is in it. Besides words and their meanings, a dictionary often gives other facts. Here are examples.

Biographies	Holidays	Braille alphabet
Weights and measures	Abbreviations	Manual alphabet
Proofreading symbols	Morse Code	Maps

3. Follow alphabetical order. These hints will help you find a particular word.

a. Look for the first different letter. Words that begin with the same letter are alphabetized by the second letter. Words that begin with the same two letters are alphabetized by the third letter, and so on.

fancy	fancy	fancy
feat	farm	fang
fidget	fashion	fantastic

b. Follow letter-by-letter alphabetical order. A compound word is alphabetized as if there were no space or hyphen. A prefix or suffix is listed as if it were a full word. An abbreviation is alphabetized by its own spelling, not by the spelling of the word it stands for. The following words are in their dictionary order:

SINGLE WORD	laboratory
2-WORD COMPOUND	Labor Day
SUFFIX	-like
HYPHENATED COMPOUND	like-minded
ABBREVIATION	Lt. (lieutenant)

c. Let the guide words guide you. *Guide words* are pairs of words that appear at the top of each page, usually printed in heavy type. They show the first and last words on the page. The other words on that page will fall between the two guide words alphabetically.

Guide words	**geyser / gigantic**	**giggle / giraffe**
Words on the page	geyser, ghastly, ghetto, . . . gift, gifted, gigantic	giggle, Gila monster, gild, . . . gingerly, gingham, giraffe

dan·de·li·on [dan′di li′en] *n.* A common weedy plant with many-rayed yellow flowers and with toothed leaves that are sometimes eaten in salads. After the flowers have bloomed, the ripe seeds form a fluffy, rounded mass.

part of speech label
syllables   pronunciation
definition

dandelion

The name **dandelion** comes from Old French *dent de lion*, "lion's tooth"; its leaves are sharply indented and resemble rows or teeth. See note at **indent.**

word history

date¹ [dat] *n.* **1.a.** Time stated in terms of the month, day, and year or any of these: *The date was May 13, 1851.* **b.** A statement of calendar time: *Put a comma between the day of the month and the year in dates.* **2.** The day of the month: *The date changes at midnight. On what date was*

homograph
definitions
example

7. *Informal.* **a.** An appointment [usage label] to go out socially with a member of the opposite sex: *Tom asked Ann for a date.* **b.** One's partner on a date or dates: *He danced with his* [related forms] *date.* —*v.* **dat·ed, dat·ing.** **1.** To [new part of speech] mark with a date: *a letter dated May 1; a deed dated 1865.* **2.** To determine the age, time, or origin of: *They dated the rock by studying the fossils in it.* **3.** *Informal.* To go on a date or dates with: *Ann dates several boys.*

idiom. out of date. No longer [usage label] current, valid or useful: *That information is out of date.*

date² [dāt] *n.* The sweet, one- [homograph] seeded, oval or oblong fruit of a tropical palm tree, the **date palm.**

— Adapted from *The American Heritage Student's Dictionary*

64

---

4. Study the entry. An *entry* lists a single term plus all the information about it. (See the margin for sample entries.)

a. Entry The entry word is written in dark type and broken up into syllables. The syllables show how to divide a word at the end of a line. The entry word also shows spelling and capitalization. If two spellings are given, the first is usually preferred.

b. Pronunciation The entry uses symbols to show how to pronounce the word. A key to the symbols appears at the bottom of the page and at the front of the dictionary.

ACCENT MARKS ′ marks a syllable that is said strongly
′ marks the syllable said most strongly

c. Part of speech label Each word is labeled with its part of speech. If a word is used as more than one part of speech, look carefully for the use you want.

n. noun   *adv.* adverb   *conj.* conjunction
v. verb   *pron.* pronoun   *interj.* interjection
adj. adjective   *prep.* preposition

d. Definition The *definition* is the meaning. Different meanings are numbered. Find the meaning that you need.

e. Homographs *Homographs* — words that look alike but have different meanings and origins — have separate entries.

f. Usage aids Some entries include notes, illustrations, examples, and usage labels such as *idiom* or *informal.*

g. Forms Entries may show forms such as principal parts or plurals, or they may show related words (*dig* – *digger*).

h. Word history Some entries show *etymology*, or word origin.

TIPS on Using a Dictionary
- Choose the right dictionary.
- Know what is in it.
- Follow alphabetical order.
- Study the entry.

Using a Thesaurus

☐ **Thesaurus**   Dictionary of synonyms and antonyms
☐ **Synonyms**   Words that have similar meanings
☐ **Antonyms**   Words that have opposite meanings

entry word — **silly** ⎰ foolish, ridiculous, inane, senseless, asinine ⎱ *(Slang* — *synonyms*   *usage label*   **sensible** *antonym*
screwy, nutty, goofy, daffy, loony, batty, dizzy, wacky)

skip 1. spring, jump, leap. 2. pass over, omit, bypass **include**
different meanings

— *The Clear and Simple Thesaurus Dictionary*

How to Use a Thesaurus

1. **Know how to find what you need.**   Do you need a lively synonym for a word? Find a thesaurus. Read the introduction to find out whether words are arranged alphabetically or by idea. If they are arranged by idea, they will also be listed in an index of words. Look up your word alphabetically in the main section or in the index.

2. **Study the entry.**   See the example above. Each entry gives synonyms and other information for a word. When an entry word has more than one meaning, the synonyms for each meaning are usually numbered or punctuated differently.

3. **Pick an exact fit.**   Synonyms rarely mean exactly the same thing. Most lipsticks are *red*, but they go from *pink* to *crimson*. All heat is *warm*, but it goes from *lukewarm* to *fiery*. How do you choose just the right word? Try these tips.

   a. **Picture it.**   What are you trying to describe or tell? What does it look like? sound like? How does it move?

   b. **Ask *who? what? where? when? why? how?***   How fast? handsome? bright? clumsy? What kind? motion? result?

   c. **Experiment.**   Try different synonyms in your sentence. Pick the one that has the effect you want.

> ### TIPS on Using a Thesaurus
> - Know how to find what you need.
> - Study the entry.
> - Pick an exact fit.

!!!
About *thesaurus*

Thesaurus is from a Greek word meaning "storehouse." Peter Mark Roget (pronounced roe-jay′) published the first one in 1852. Here is an early title page — though not the original one.

> ROGET's
>
> **THESAURUS**
>
> OF THE
>
> **ENGLISH LANGUAGE**
>
> IN DICTIONARY FORM
>
> *Being a Presentation of Roget's Thesaurus of English Words and Phrases in a Modernized, More Complete, and More Convenient Dictionary Form, Together with Briefer Synonymies for the Busy Writer, the Whole Comprised in One Alphabetical Arrangement*

How Many Words for It?

Snow is not just snow in Eskimo. There is one word for snow on the ground, one for falling snow, one for slushy snow, one for hard-packed snow, and so on.

English has many words for things that fly, such as *bird, insect, plane, pilot,* but Hopi has only two — one for birds and one for everything else.

In native Australian languages, there are different words for a hole formed by a rock, a hole in an object, a hole in a spear, a hole in the ground, and so on.

Using a Book

□ **Book** Pages bound together and placed between covers

MAIN PARTS OF A NONFICTION BOOK

PART AND LOCATION	INFORMATION
Jacket Removable paper cover	Title, author's name, information about the book such as book summary or author biography
Spine Joins back and front	Title, author, publisher, call number if a library book
Title page First printed page	Title and subtitle, if any, author or editor, publisher
Copyright page Reverse of title page	Date of publication, owner of printing rights, Library of Congress data, sometimes a book summary and list of related topics
Foreword, Preface, Introduction Near the beginning	Author's purpose, background, organization of book, instructions on use, names of people who helped
Table of Contents Near the beginning	Listing of what is in the book, in order, plus page numbers
Text Main section	Actual contents of the book; may have titles, headings, illustrations
Index At or near the end	Alphabetized list of terms mentioned, plus page numbers
Appendix At or near the end	Maps, charts, tables, documents, notes, or other special material
Glossary At or near the end	Dictionary of terms used
Bibliography	List of sources used; sometimes a list of additional readings

NOTE: Not every book has every part listed.

Check This Out

Do you know the meaning of each of these "bookish" terms? Check the dictionary if you do not.

1. bookworm
2. to book
3. to throw the book at
4. by the book

More Numbers

Every new book is given an ISBN number, which appears on the copyright page. *ISBN* stands for International Standard Book Number.

Answers

(1) someone who spends a lot of time reading; (2) to arrange for ahead of time, as in *to book plane tickets*, or to write charges against in a police record; (3) *slang* — to punish or scold severely; (4) *idiom* — strictly according to rule

Wolf Pack
Tracking Wolves in the Wild

Sylvia A. Johnson
&
Alice Aamodt

· LERNER PUBLICATIONS COMPANY ·
MINNEAPOLIS

Introduction

THE TRACKS IN THE CRUSTY SNOW ARE DEEP AND WIDE. They look like the footprints of a large, heavy dog—a husky, perhaps, or a Great Dane. The marks made by the round pads and the sharp claws of the animal's feet can be seen clearly in the slanting light of the late afternoon sun. Placed neatly one behind the other, the tracks cross the clearing in a straight line and disappear into the deep shadows of the pine forest.

Behind the first set of tracks are the footprints of several other four-footed travelers. They are similar in form to the marks made by the lead animal, but most are smaller. These tracks too move in neat, straight lines over the snow-covered ground. They seem to be made by animals traveling swiftly over familiar territory, creatures confident and at home in the cold northern forest.

Index

Contents

Glossary

active submission—approaching a dominant wolf and licking or nipping its muzzle. Pack members often greet the alpha male in this manner.

alpha female—the female wolf at the top of a wolf pack's social structure

alpha male—the male wolf at the top of a wolf pack's social structure

beta male—the male wolf second in rank to the alpha male of a pack

cache (KASH)—a spot near a den where meat is buried for the use of a female wolf with pups

...als that eat meat

TIPS on Using a Book

- If the book has a jacket, read the information it contains.
- Check the different parts. What are the introductory sections? How is the text divided? Are there illustrations? charts? Is there an index? an appendix? a glossary?
- Find the date on the copyright page. Depending on the subject, the date of the information may be important.
- Look through the book. To see what is in it, skim. To find specific information, scan. (See pages 205 – 206.)
- Start with the introductory material.
- Look at the table of contents to see what the book covers.
- Look through the text. Look for titles, heads, illustrations. Read the beginnings and endings of the sections.
- Look at the index. See what facts and terms are listed.
- Look at any special sections at the end.

Using a Newspaper

Newspaper Language

Newspaper people, like people in other fields, have a special work language, or *jargon*. Here are some examples:

banner Headline spread across the top of a page

crop To cut a photo to fit a space or blank out a part

filler Material used just to fill space

hard news Actual events

kill To throw away all or part of a story

makeup Layout of each page

morgue The newspaper library

proof Printed draft for revising

scoop Important news learned by one reporter or newspaper before anyone else

• **Newspaper** Sheets of news printed daily or weekly

MAIN SECTIONS OF A NEWSPAPER	
News	Events of the day; may have sections for local, national, and international news
Topical Sections	
Arts and Films	News and reviews of music, dance, theater, art, and so on
Business	Business news, stock market and other financial listings
Living	Homemaking, human interest, and so on
Sports	Sports news, scores, and statistics
Announcements	Engagements, marriages, births
Classifieds	Advertisements for things to buy and sell, job opportunities, legal notices
Columns	Personal comments and opinions of individual writers, some appearing regularly
Comics	Comic strip section
Editorial page	Opinions expressed in editors' unsigned articles, readers' letters, and cartoons
Obituaries (Deaths)	Announcements of recent deaths
Op-ed page	Page opposite editorial page, with opinions expressed in signed columns
Weather	Weather map, national and international temperature listings, local forecasts

"Flag"

Lead headline

Lead story

Byline

Caption

Jumpline

Index of features

How to Use a Newspaper

1. **Study the front page.**   The front page has the most important stories of the day. Here are its other main parts. (Some, such as headlines, bylines, and jumplines, appear throughout the paper.)

    a. **Flag**   The *flag* is a term for the name of the paper.

    b. **Ears**   These are two small sections on either side of the flag with weather reports, sayings, or other information.

    c. **Headline**   Lines in large dark print announce what each story is about. The biggest headline, the *lead headline*, tops the most important story, the *lead story*.

    d. **Byline**   The *byline* gives the writer's name.

    e. **Jumpline**   The *jumpline* tells where an article continues.

    f. **Caption**   The *caption* explains an illustration.

    g. **Index**   The index of features tells where to find the various sections. It usually appears on page 1, 2, or 3.

2. **Follow the jumplines.**   Finish the articles you start.

3. **Use the index.**   It will help you find what you want.

4. **Look for the "5 W's."**   To get the important information from a story, look for the answers to *Who? What? Where? When? Why?*

5. **Separate fact from opinion.**   As you read, be aware of what is fact and what is opinion. (See page 36.)

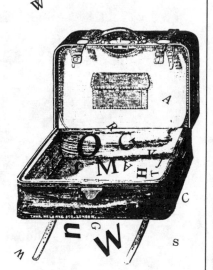

A Case History

Did you know that capital letters are called *upper case* and small letters are called *lower case*? Here's why.

Newspapers used to be printed with inked pieces of metal type. Originally each piece of type was put in place by hand, one letter at a time.

The pieces of type were kept in a tray, or *case*. Since the small letters were used more often, they were kept in the lower part of the case, which was easier to reach. The capital letters were stored in the upper case.

TIPS on Using a Newspaper

- Know the main sections.
- Study the front page.
- Use the index.

- Follow the jumplines.
- Look for the "5 W's."
- Separate fact from opinion.

Studying

Getting Organized

How to Get Organized

1. **Get your act together.** Have these basic tools on hand:
   - Notebook divided by subjects, with pockets for handouts
   - Assignment pad or date book
   - Pencils, erasers, and pen
   - Dictionary
   - Library card
   - Two copies of your school schedule, one in your notebook and one in an obvious place at home
   - Large calendar with space for writing
   - Phone numbers of classmates to call about assignments
   - Book bag

2. **Keep a calendar.** On a large calendar, keep track of appointments, dates of tests, dates when projects are due. Keep the calendar in an obvious place.

3. **Make a weekly plan.** Plan each week. Reserve time for regular assignments and special projects. Even better, chart your whole day. A chart like the one below can be a big help.

Weekly Time Chart								
Time	**MON.**	**TUES.**	**WED.**	**THURS.**	**FRI.**	**SAT.**	**SUN.**
7:00 A.M.							
8:00							
9:00							
10:00							
11:00							
12:00 Noon							
1:00 P.M.							

4. **Avoid morning madness.** Pack your book bag at night. Put in everything you need for the next day, including your homework, wallet, transportation pass or money, and keys. Put your packed bag in the same place every night.

One Student's Schedule

Monday

7:00 Meet Oscar at bus stop to get geo. book – 7:15

8:00 School – 8:15

9:00

10:00

11:00 Math Test – Chs. 4, 5

12:00 Lunch – Get Burbank biog. from libr.

1:00 Study Hall – Take notes on Burbank

2:00 Band – 2:15

3:00 Home – 3:45
Into soccer uniform

4:00 Mr. Murphy – car pool to soccer

5:00

6:00 Dinner – make salad

7:00 Call Trina about Luther's gift – clean desk!

8:00 First draft – Burbank report

9:00 Math assgnmt – Look at French notes for Thursday's test

Studying

Geography
February 24, 1991

North Africa
A. Countries
Morocco
Algeria
Libya
(Egypt, too, but
more part of Mid-East)

Atlantic
Ocean
Mediterranean
Morocco
Tunisia   Sea
Algeria   Libya   Egypt   Red
Sea

B. Location
– NE tip of Africa
– On Med. Sea
– Morocco also on
Atlantic O.

C. Region
– Mostly desert !!
Few live there
– Some oases (places
with water) = settlements
– Rainfall on Med. Coast =
most people live there
(?? What Languages ??
Find out.)

Class Time

How to Get the Most out of Class

1. **Be prepared.**   At night, check what you need for each class the next day. Put it in your school bag or put a note on the bag to get it in the morning. In class, get out your assignment, open your notebook, and have your pen or pencil in hand. Be ready to start when your teacher is. If you miss a class, find out what you missed.

2. **Listen.**   See the lessons on "Listening" (page 122) and "Following and Giving Instructions" (pages 132 – 133).

3. **Take notes.**   Notes help you focus on and remember the main points you hear. Here are some note-taking tips.

Taking Notes in Class

- Write the date.
- To write quickly, use abbreviations and other symbols.
- Write anything the teacher says to write.
- Copy words and diagrams the teacher puts on the board.
- Write only the main points of what the teacher says.
  Pay special attention to opening and closing comments.
  Write down words or ideas that keep being repeated.
  Listen for key words and for word clues such as *first, next, furthermore, finally,* and *remember, notice.*
  Notice gestures and voice changes that cue main points.
- Summarize the main points in a few words. (See page 217.)
- Mark important words. Use an underline, circle, star, box, arrow, or your own symbol.
- Go over your notes later to be sure you understand them.

---

4. **Speak up.**   Ask questions when you do not understand. Make comments when you have thoughts to share.

5. **Save handouts and assignments.**   Keep everything from one class in the same section of your notebook.

6. **Write down the assignment.**   Keep an assignment book. Write all your assignments for each day. Cross them out when done.

Assignments

How to Do Your Assignments

1. **Keep track.** Keep a daily record of your assignments. Include the following:

> #### Assignment Information
> – Date given
> – Subject
> – Assignment
> – Date due

Check your assignment pad every day. Cross out an assignment when you have finished it.

2. **Get it straight.** Be sure you understand the assignment — its purpose and what you are expected to do. Ask about anything that is not clear. Listen for direction words such as *Read! Write! Answer! Explain! Describe!* Write them down and know exactly what your teacher means by them.

3. **Get what you need.** Does your assignment require a particular book or pen or some other material? Note it when you write the assignment. Be sure to get it in time.

4. **Set goals.** Do you put things off until the last minute? Do you just plunge in to get assignments over with? Don't do either. Instead, plan. Set goals and build them into a weekly schedule (page 71). Here are two kinds of goals:

   a. **Short-term** Reserve time for the next day's assignments. Include daily study time in your plan for the week.

   b. **Long-term** Break big projects into small steps. (See "Analyzing," pages 24 – 27.) Build each step into your weekly plan. Note big projects and tests on your calendar (page 71), and don't forget to look at the calendar!

5. **Begin where you please.** Some students attack the hard parts first, when they have energy. Others get discouraged and like to build up to the hard parts. Do whatever works.

6. **Take a break.** Stretch. Take a walk. Eat an apple.

An Assignment Book . . .

March 12, 1991

MATH
- Problems 3-16, p. 146
Use graph paper!
Due tomorrow.

- QUIZ FRIDAY!! Ch. 5
(Especially pp. 140-6)

SPANISH
- Memorize pres. tense
estar - for tomorrow

ENGLISH
- Think about book
report topic - Decide
by Thurs.

Practice SQ3R

DETECTIVE STORIES
A HISTORY

The First Detective. In one form or another, detectives have been around forever, but the detective story as we know it is fairly new. The American writer Edgar Allan Poe started the form in 1841 with *The Murders in the Rue Morgue*. His detective, C. Auguste Dupin, was the first in a long line of nosy, brilliant amateur detectives. Logic was the detective's best weapon then, and so it remains in the detective stories of today.

The Great Sherlock. Poe created the detective story, but a British doctor named Sir Arthur Conan Doyle gave it its best-known character — the great Sherlock Holmes.

After the publication of *A Study in Scarlet* in 1887, Holmes quickly became a popular hero. In England, whenever a new Sherlock Holmes story appeared in *The Strand Magazine*, lines of eager customers stretched for several blocks!

Brilliant Holmes, with his magnifying glass, his attention to detail, and his whiz-bang logic became so real that visitors to London still look for his house. Over a century later, Holmes remains the most famous and popular detective ever — and the one most imitated by other writers.

7. Follow SQ3R! Use the following method when you study.

Study with SQ3R

SURVEY! First look over what you need to read. Get a general idea (pages 205 – 206).

QUESTION! List questions to ask yourself later. Turn each heading into a question. Also use any study questions provided.

READ! Concentrate. Look for answers to your questions. (See pages 115 – 116.)

RECORD! Take notes.
- Write main points and important details only.
- Write key words and phrases only. Abbreviate.
- Use your own words whenever possible.
- Use a simple outline (page 211).
Write answers to your list of questions.

REVIEW! Look over headings, highlighted words, and the beginning and ending. Go over your notes.

---

8. Stuck? Here are some suggestions.

   a. Don't give up. Reread. Look ahead. You may find a clue you overlooked, or things may just click.

   b. Keep going. Skip over the confusing part and finish everything you can. Then come back and try again.

   c. Ask for help. Still stuck? You might want to ask a classmate or relative to help clear up the confusion.

   d. Write a note. If all else fails, include a note with the assignment. Speak to the teacher before class.

9. Check it. Reread it. Check spelling and punctuation. Check your assignment pad. Have you done everything?

10. Get it ready. Put your work in your school bag.

11. Go over comments. See what was right, what was wrong, and why. Clear up questions.

Memorizing

How to Memorize

1. **Don't put it off.** Do your memorizing near the beginning of your study time. Memorizing gets harder as you get tired.

2. **First, understand.** Before you try to memorize anything, understand it. You will remember it better and longer.

3. **Read, read, read and write, write, write.** Read the material over and over. Write it over and over. "See" it in your mind.

4. **Talk to yourself.** Say the words out loud. Use a tape recorder and listen to yourself.

5. **Make a connection.** Connect new material to facts you already know. Find examples for general statements.

6. **Put things in order.** Order your items. For example, put words in alphabetical order or events in time order.

7. **Make groups.** Put similar things together (pages 19 – 21).

8. **Concentrate on key words.** Let key words unlock your mind.

9. **Memorize the number.** Know how many items there are to learn. Then you can be sure that you know them all.

10. **Repeat.** Keep repeating. Have someone quiz you.

11. **Use memory tricks.** See the margin for examples.

MNEMONICS

Make up a word.	Create an *acrostic* — a word made up of the first letters of the items.
Make up a sentence.	Make up a sentence whose words begin with the same letters as the items.
Make up a saying.	Catchy sayings stick in the mind.
Make up a rhyme.	Rhyming statements are easy to learn.
Repeat a letter.	Make up a sentence with alliteration — words that begin with the same letter.

Using Memory Tricks

MAKE UP A WORD.
Roy G. Biv helps you remember the colors of the spectrum: *R*ed, *O*range, *Y*ellow, *G*reen, *B*lue, *I*ndigo, *V*iolet.

MAKE UP A SENTENCE.
Silly Milly hates eating onions cues you on the Great Lakes, from west to east: *S*uperior, *M*ichigan, *H*uron, *E*rie, *O*ntario.

Every good boy does fine gives you the names of the musical notes on the lines of the treble staff: *E, G, B, D, F.*

MAKE UP A SAYING.
Spring forward, fall back tells you when to set the clock ahead an hour and when to set it back.

MAKE UP A RHYME.
Thirty days has September, April, June, and November. . . .

In fourteen hundred ninety-two Columbus sailed the ocean blue.

REPEAT A LETTER.
Red to right returning reminds sailors to keep the red harbor light on their right when entering a harbor.

Your Turn

Make up a sentence that cues
— Snow White's seven dwarfs
— the last five presidents

A Summary of TIPS

TIPS on Getting Organized

- Get your act together. Keep your basic tools on hand.
- Keep a calendar in an obvious place. Use it.
- Make a weekly plan. Reserve study time.
- Avoid morning madness. Get things ready at night.

TIPS on Doing Well in Class

- Be ready to start when the teacher is.
- Listen carefully.
- Take notes on the main points.
- Speak up. Ask questions.
- Save handouts and assignments with your class notes.
- Write assignments in an assignment book or pad.

TIPS on Doing Assignments

- Keep track. Write assignments in your assignment book.
- Understand what you have to do.
- Prepare everything you will need.
- Set long-term and short-term goals. Make a plan.
- Decide whether to start with the hardest or easiest part.
- Take a break once in a while. Reward yourself.
- Use the SQ3R plan: Survey. Question. Read. Record. Review.
- If you get stuck, keep trying. Then ask for help.
- Check your assignment when done.
- Put your completed work in your school bag.
- Go over your teacher's comments.

TIPS on Memorizing

- Don't put it off. Memorize when you feel alert.
- Be sure you understand the material first.
- Read, read, read. Write, write, write.
- Say, say, say the material aloud. Use a tape recorder.
- Connect new material to what you already know.
- Arrange items in a suitable order. Group similar items together.
- Concentrate on key words. Use them as cues.
- Know the number of items you are learning.
- Use memory tricks. Make up words, sentences, sayings, rhymes.

A Grammar Book of 1880

English Grammar.

PART I.

AN OUTLINE FOR BEGINNERS.

"I am convinced that the method of teaching which approaches most nearly to the method of investigation, is incomparably the best; since, not content with serving up a few barren and lifeless truths, it leads to the stalk on which they grow."
BURKE.

THOUGHT AND ITS EXPRESSION.

1. We *think*, or have *thoughts*.
2. We express our thoughts by means of *words*.
3. Words are either spoken or written.
4. The expressing of our thoughts by means of words, is called *language*, or *speech*.
5. Language is made to suit the world, and consists of many thousands of words; but, like trees or persons, they can all be divided into a small number of classes.
6. To express our thoughts, we use nine classes of words, which are therefore called the *Parts of Speech*.
7. The PARTS OF SPEECH are Nouns, Pronouns, Articles, Adjectives, Verbs, Adverbs, Prepositions, Conjunctions, and Interjections.
8. To these nine classes of words belong eight chief

Taking a Test

General TIPS

TIPS on Getting Ready

- Find out what will be on the test so you know what to study.
- Find out what kind of test it will be so you know how to study. (See pages 71 – 76.)
- Keep a calendar. Mark the date of the test on your calendar.
- Catch up on any missing assignments and notes.
- Don't cram — make a plan! (See page 71.) Do some studying every day. Do more right before the test.
- Go over class notes, handouts, assignments, and textbook. Skim. (See pages 205 – 206.)
- Mark or take brief notes on important points.
- Memorize. (See page 75.)
- Drill yourself. Hand-made flash cards can help.
- Make up questions and answer them. Answer the questions in your textbook.
- Ask for help if you do not understand something.
- If you must cram, do it right. Skim, take notes, memorize.
- Quiz yourself the night before or have someone quiz you.
- Get what you need — pen, pencil, eraser. Put it by the door.
- Try to get a good night's sleep.

TIPS on Taking a Test

- Get there on time!
- Have everything you need — pens, pencils, eraser.
- Listen carefully to the teacher's directions.
- Write your name and the date first so you don't forget.
- Read written directions carefully. Underline important words:

choose	circle	underline	fill in	cross out
write	explain	match	answer	compare

- Decide how much time to spend on each question. Give more time to questions that are worth more. Leave time for review.
- Do the easiest questions first.
- Read every word before you answer. Look for key words:

all	always	every	sometimes	alike	opposite	most
none	never	some	only	different	same as	not

- If you will be marked wrong for not answering, guess!
- Reread! Look for mistakes. Look for unanswered questions. Don't make last-minute changes without a very good reason.

!!!
It's About Time!

Time . . . It can be your friend or your enemy during a test. Furthermore, time may not be what it seems. A day isn't always a day, 1 o'clock isn't always 1 o'clock, an hour isn't always an hour. Get to know time better.

From Day to Day! Our standard day runs from midnight to midnight, but that has not always been true. Some ancient people measured the day from dawn to dawn. Others counted the day from sunset to sunset . . . and still do.

13 O'Clock! We use a 12-hour system to keep track of time, but the armed forces and most Europeans use a 24-hour system. For example, the first hour after noon is not 1:00 P.M. but 13:00, and the hour before midnight is not 11:00 P.M. but 23:00.

A 56-Minute Hour! You think you have trouble keeping track of time? Before mechanical clocks appeared in Europe in the thirteenth century, the length of an hour could vary by several minutes.

Taking a Test

Could You Pass These Tests?

Here are some test questions given to different kinds of specialists. How would *you* do?

AIR TRAFFIC CONTROLLER

1. How are nonradar environment aircraft in a holding pattern separated?
   (a) Vertically
   (b) Longitudinally
   (c) By 2 miles
   (d) By 5 miles

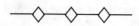

UMPIRE

2. With a zero-two count on him, the batter steps back out of the batter's box while the pitcher is in his windup. The pitcher continues to pitch anyway, and throws a pitch that does not enter the strike zone. What should the umpire call?

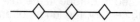

U.S. CITIZENSHIP

3. What are some of the rights the Bill of Rights guarantees?

— *Can You Pass These Tests?*
Allen D. Bragdon, ed.

Kinds of Tests and Questions

```
KINDS OF TESTS

Classroom Tests

WHAT THEY TEST    Knowledge of specific information
HOW TO PREPARE    Study the information (pages 73 – 74,
                  75).

Standardized Tests

WHAT THEY TEST    Overall knowledge, abilities in different
                  areas
HOW TO PREPARE    Keep up with your work. You can't cram.
                  Get to know the different test forms.
                  Practice.
```

```
KINDS OF TEST QUESTIONS

True-False        Decide whether a statement is true or false.
Multiple-Choice   Choose the best of several answers.
Matching          Match pairs of items from two lists.
Fill-in           Supply a missing word or phrase.
Analogy           Find a word related to another in a
                  given way.
Essay             Write an answer of a paragraph or more.
```

How to Answer Test Questions

TRUE-FALSE   Decide whether a statement is true or false.

EXAMPLES (1) Deserts never have rainfall.   T   Ⓕ

          (2) Many deserts have very little rainfall.   Ⓣ   F

          (3) The Sahara, in Alaska, is a hot desert.   T   Ⓕ

TIPS on True-False Questions

- Read carefully. Just one word can make a difference.

- Pay attention to words like those below. They mean that if there are any exceptions, the statement is false (example 1).

  all   none   no   every   always   never

- Pay attention to words like those below. They mean that if there are any exceptions, the statement can still be true (example 2).

  may   many   most   some   often   sometimes   usually

- If a part is false, the whole statement is false (example 3).

MULTIPLE-CHOICE   Choose the best of several answers.

EXAMPLE   (4) An *oasis* is a

          (a) sand dune.

          (b) section of some deserts.

          Ⓒ desert area that has water.

          (d) animal of the desert.

TIPS on Multiple-Choice Questions

- Read the directions carefully.
  Check to see whether each item is used only once.
  Check to see whether every item must be used.

- Pay special attention to words like these:
  most   best   right   correct   least   not   wrong   incorrect

- Read all the choices before you decide on an answer.

- Eliminate answers that are obviously wrong.

- Then choose the best of the remaining answers.

- Beware of answers that are only partly right (4b above).

- Check grammar and usage. (Because the part to be completed in 4 ends with *a*, not *an*, the answer is likely to begin with a consonant, which rules out 4d.)

Could You Pass These Tests?

COAST GUARD CAPTAIN

4. If you are standing a wheel watch and you hear that someone has fallen overboard on the starboard side, you should prepare to
   (a) Turn hard to starboard
   (b) Turn hard to port
   (c) Proceed to throw a life ring to mark the spot
   (d) Hold the rudder amidships

PILOT: GLIDER

5. What minimum upward current must a glider encounter to maintain altitude?
   (a) 2 feet per second
   (b) The same as the glider's sink rate
   (c) The same as the adjacent down currents
   (d) Greater than the adjacent down currents

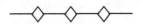

TRUCKER

6. The road is MOST slippery
   (a) Just after it starts to rain
   (b) After it rains long enough to "wash" the road
   (c) Just as the rain stops

— *Can You Pass These Tests?*
  Allen D. Bragdon, ed.

MATCHING   Match pairs of items from two separate lists.

EXAMPLE   (5) Atacama Desert — Africa
Kalahari Desert — Asia
Gobi Desert — South America

TIPS on Matching Questions

- Look at all the items before you start.

- Work your way down one list. Avoid switching back and forth.

- If the lists are unequal, work on the shorter one.

- Do the easy items first to narrow your choices.

- If you are unsure, try different pairings. See which set of matches works best.

FILL-IN   Complete a statement with a word or phrase.

EXAMPLE   (6) A sand hill is called a *dune* .

TIPS on Fill-in Questions

- Read every word carefully.

- Answer easy questions first. Then go back to the hard ones.

- Find an answer that fits the sentence grammatically.

- Look for language clues. (In example 6, the article *a* tells you the answer must be a noun that begins with a consonant.)

- Take a guess. (A blank space may be marked as wrong.)

ANALOGY   Find a word that is related to another word in a certain way.

EXAMPLES   (7) *Big* is to *large* as *little* is to _small_ .

(8) *Big* is to *little* as *fast* is to _slow_ .

(9) *Toe* is to *foot* as *finger* is to _hand_ .

(10) music : composer :: book : _author_ .

(11) painter : brush :: dentist : _drill_ .

TIPS on Analogy Questions

- In analogy formulas, : means "is to" and :: means "as."
- Decide how the first two words are related. For example

Word / synonym	(*big / large*, example 7)
Word / antonym	(*big / little*, example 8)
Part / whole	(*toe / foot*, example 9)
Product / producer	(*music / composer*, example 10)
User / tool	(*painter / brush*, example 11)
Item / group	(*poodle / dog*)
Object / purpose	(*pen / write*)

- In your mind, form a sentence that tells the relationship.

  Big means the same as *large*. (example 7)

  A *toe* is part of a *foot*. (example 9)

- Now replace the pair of words with the incomplete pair.

  Little means the same as _____ . (example 7)

  A *finger* is part of a _____ . (example 9)

- Find a word that completes the sentence.

ESSAY   Write an answer of a paragraph or more.

EXAMPLE   (12) Explain how desert animals have adapted to life in the desert.

The animals who live in the desert have had to adapt to both the lack of water and the heat. For example, camels do not sweat much and can go without water for a long time. Smaller animals hardly drink water at all. Some of them get moisture from the juice of plants and seeds they eat, while others get it from the animals they eat. To escape the blazing sun, smaller animals usually live underground during the day. Then at night they come out to eat. Without adapting in such ways, the animals could not survive in the harsh conditions of the desert.

TIPS for Essay Questions

- Read the question carefully. Know what these words mean:

Compare	Show how two things are alike and different.
Contrast	Show how two things are different.
Describe	Give details showing the features of something.
Define	Tell what the term or subject means.
Discuss	Tell about something in detail.
Explain	Tell how, what, or why.
Summarize	Give the main points briefly.

- Jot down all the details you can think of for your answer.

- Avoid what you're not sure of. Concentrate on what you know.

- Make a simple outline of the main points and details.

- State your main idea in a short introduction.

- Then follow your outline.

- Use facts, examples, and other supporting details.

- Write a conclusion. Summarize or restate the main idea.

- Avoid empty expressions such as *I think, I feel, it seems.*

- Go over your answer carefully. Correct any errors.

Taking a Test

Standardized Tests

TIPS on Standardized Tests

- Listen to the general directions. Follow them exactly.
- Read the directions for each part. Notice every word.
- Go over the sample question. Be sure you understand it.
- Read each question carefully. Read all the choices before you answer.
- Skip questions you cannot answer easily. Go back if you can.
- Keep your eye on the clock or on your watch.
- Use the test booklet to make notes if you need them.
- Mark all answers on the answer sheet. Use No. 2 pencil only.
- Find the number on the answer sheet that matches the number of the question.
- Find the circle that has the same letter as your answer.

ANSWER SHEET (completed)

1. Ⓐ Ⓑ Ⓒ ●D Ⓔ
2. Ⓐ ●B Ⓒ Ⓓ Ⓔ
3. Ⓐ ●B Ⓒ Ⓓ Ⓔ
4. Ⓐ Ⓑ Ⓒ Ⓓ ●E
5. ●A Ⓑ Ⓒ Ⓓ Ⓔ
6. Ⓐ Ⓑ Ⓒ ●D Ⓔ

- Fill in the circle completely. Make your mark dark.
- Mark only one answer for each question.
- To change an answer, erase your first mark completely.
- Check your answers if you have time.
- The common kinds of standardized tests are

Reading Comprehension
Writing
Vocabulary
  Synonyms
  Antonyms
  Sentence completions
  Analogies
Grammar, Usage, Mechanics

Questions You Won't Find on Standardized Tests!

1. Why did twenty-two people get up and leave their tables at Pizza Paradise in Butte, Montana, on March 7, 1990, at 5:52 P.M.?

2. What kind of ant lives in a house?

3. What is left with just a nose after it loses an eye?

4. Where is the center of gravity located?

5. What is the most efficient way to make a fire with two sticks?

Answers

(1) They were finished eating; (2) Occu-pant; (3) The word noise; (4) At the bottom of the v in gravity; (5) Be sure that one of them is a match.

83

More Questions You Won't Find on Standardized Tests!

6. What did the mother sardine say to the baby sardine when it saw its first submarine?

7. I occur once in every minute but not once in a hundred thousand years. What am I?

8. If a pen with an eraser costs $2.10 and the pen costs $2.00 more than the eraser, what does the eraser cost?

9. A duck, a frog, and a skunk wanted to go to the movies, which cost a dollar. Who could afford to go and who couldn't?

10. Although life can be tough, what is something you can always count on?

Answers

(6) Don't worry — it's only a can of people; (7) The letter m; (8) The eraser costs 5 cents, and the pen costs $2.05; (9) The duck could afford to go because it had a bill; the frog could afford to go because it had a green back; the skunk could not afford to go because it had only a (s)cent — and even that was bad! (10) Your fingers

How to Take Standardized Tests

READING COMPREHENSION   Read a passage. Answer questions on it.

EXAMPLE

The Inca people began as a family that ruled a small area in Peru. By the 15th century, the Incas had established a large, well-ordered empire, with splendid cities, roads, arts, and crafts. Every person in Inca society had a place in the order and a specific job. At the top was the emperor and his queen, who ruled with absolute power. Immediately below them were the high priest, the commander of the army, and four chief officials. One level lower were the privileged classes — the head civil servants, judges, and generals who performed the daily tasks of governing. Next came lesser officials and craftspeople and, at the bottom, the great masses of people who grew food and raised livestock.

(1) What is the main idea of the passage?

  A The Incas built a large, splendid empire.
  B In the well-ordered Inca society, everyone had a place and a job.
  C The emperor and queen ruled with absolute power.

(2) What did most of the Inca people do?

  A Grow food and raise livestock
  B Participate in the government
  C Work on crafts

(3) The word *privileged* in this passage means

  A Military
  B Unimportant
  C Having special rights or advantages

TIPS on Reading Comprehension Questions

• Read the questions first so you know what to look for.

• Read the passage. Look for the main idea and supporting details. (See pages 147 – 149.)

• Look at the questions again. Then read the passage again.

• Read all the answer choices before you pick one.

• Beware of answers that are only partly correct (example 3a).

WRITING

EXAMPLES Choose the best supporting detail for the
sentence.

(4) The Incas treasured beautiful handmade
objects.

    A Their empire grew rapidly.
    B Most people grew crops or tended
      livestock.
    Ⓒ They produced lovely cloth and fine
      pottery.

Choose the word that best completes the
sentence.

(5) _____ the Spanish conquered the
Incas, many of the Inca traditions were lost.

    Ⓐ After
    B Although
    C If
    D Usually

TIPS for Questions on Writing

- Read the instructions carefully.

- Read the entire question before choosing an answer. For fill-ins,
  try out each answer in the sentence.

- Use your knowledge of grammar and usage. (Choice 5d produces
  a run-on sentence and does not make sense. It can therefore be
  ruled out.)

Riddle History

*Here are two riddles that go back
to ancient times.*

What flies forever and rests
never?
    — The wind

What has one voice and yet
becomes four-footed and two-
footed and three-footed?
    — A person, who crawls
      on all fours as a baby, then
      stands erect, and when
      older may walk with a cane

*In ancient times, riddles were
serious puzzles. In fact, people
thought that the gods spoke in
riddles. Over time, riddles became lighter and more fun.
Shakespeare, writing in sixteenth-
century England, referred to the*
Booke of Merry Riddles *in one of
his plays. Jonathan Swift, who
wrote* Gulliver's Travels *in the
1700s, wrote riddles too. Test
yourself on this riddle by Swift.*

We are little airy creatures,
All of different voice and features;
One of us in glass is set,
One of us you'll find in jet,
T'other you may see in tin,
And the fourth a box within.
If the fifth you should
    pursue,
It can never fly from you.

*The answer is the five vowels —
a,e,i,o,u. Can you figure out why?*

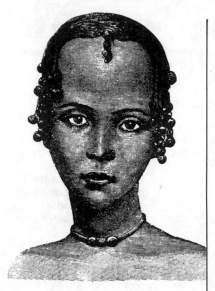

VOCABULARY

Synonym Questions Find the word closest in meaning to the given word. (See page 249.)

EXAMPLE (6) beautiful

A pleasant Ⓑ attractive C cheerful
D homely E slim

Antonym Questions Find the word that is most nearly the opposite of the given word. (See page 249.)

EXAMPLE (7) cheerful

A happy B cautious C empty
D tired Ⓔ unhappy

Sentence Completions Choose the word or words that best fit the meaning of the sentence.

EXAMPLE (8) Because the Incas treasured beautiful
objects, they _____ the craftspeople
who made them.

Ⓐ respected B hated C amazed
D knew

Analogy Questions (See page 81.)

TIPS on Vocabulary Questions

- Synonyms rarely have exactly the same meaning. (*Beautiful* is stronger than *attractive*.) Choose the word that comes closest in meaning (page 249).

- Antonyms are rarely exact opposites. Choose the word that is most nearly the opposite (page 249).

- Think about all the different meanings of a word.

- For sentence completions, be sure the finished sentence is grammatical and makes sense.

GRAMMAR, USAGE, MECHANICS

EXAMPLES   Find the error if there is one.

(9) <u>She</u> and <u>I</u> <u>was</u> <u>there</u> yesterday. <u>No error</u>
       A   B C   D   E

Choose the best way to write the underlined part.

(10) Can <u>Maria and me</u> go to the movies?

   A Maria and me   D I and Maria
   B Me and Maria   E Myself and Maria
   C Maria and I

Choose the best way to complete the new sentence. Keep the meaning of the original sentence.

(11) As soon as the bell rings, we will begin.
     Rewrite, beginning with the following:
     <u>We will begin</u>

   A the ringing of the bell.
   B when the bell rings.
   C but the bell rings.

TIPS on Grammar, Usage, Mechanics Questions

- Look for subjects and verbs that agree.
- Look for pronouns and verbs that agree.
- Look for pronouns and antecedents that agree.
- Look for correct forms of verbs, pronouns, and modifiers.
- Look for correct capital letters.
- Look for correct punctuation.
- Look for words used correctly.

Using Graphic Aids

Your Turn

Greek *dia-*, as in *diagram*, can mean "through, across, between, apart." Use that fact to guess at the origins of the *dia-* words below. Check your guesses in a dictionary.

1. diagonal
2. dialogue
3. diameter

☐ **Graphic aid**   Visual aid used to organize and present information

COMMON GRAPHIC AIDS	
TYPE	**PURPOSE**
Picture	To illustrate a text
Chart, Table, Schedule	To present a set of facts in an organized way, often in labeled columns
Diagram	To show the parts or workings of something, usually by a labeled sketch
Graph	To show how certain facts are related
Map	To show where things are located, usually by a sketch representing a section of the earth's surface

If you had read the above facts in a paragraph instead of in a chart, you might have found them harder to follow. The chart makes the facts clearer and easier to read. That is the purpose of all visual aids — to help you understand and use information.

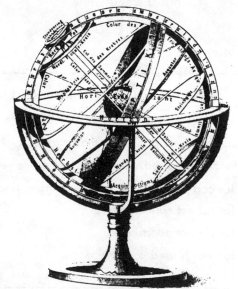

Answers
1. *dia-*, "across," + *gonia*, "angle" 2. *dia-*, "between, one with another," + *legein*, "tell" 3. *dia-*, "through," + *metron*, "measure"

Charts and Tables

STANDINGS — American League East (April 21, 1990)

TEAM	HOME WINS	HOME LOSSES	AWAY WINS	AWAY LOSSES	TOTAL WINS	TOTAL LOSSES
Toronto	4	2	2	2	6	4
Yankees	3	1	1	2	4	3
Boston	4	2	1	2	5	4
Milwaukee . .	0	1	4	3	4	4
Baltimore . . .	1	0	3	5	4	5
Detroit	4	2	0	4	4	6
Cleveland . . .	1	0	2	5	3	5

TIPS on Charts and Tables

- Read the title to find out what the subject is.

  EXAMPLE   The chart above shows the standings within the American League East on April 21, 1990.

- Read across (horizontally) and up and down (vertically).
  The horizontal lines of facts are called *rows*.
  The vertical lines of facts are called *columns*.

- Check the heading of each column to see what is listed.

  EXAMPLE   (Column 1) For each *Team*, the chart lists
  (Column 2) Number of *Wins* at *Home*
  (Column 3) Number of *Losses* at *Home*
  (Column 4) Number of *Wins Away*
  (Column 5) Number of *Losses Away*
  (Column 6) Number of *Total Wins*
  (Column 7) Number of *Total Losses*

- Use the column headings to find specific facts.

  EXAMPLE   How many games did Milwaukee lose?
  Step 1: Find the column labeled *Team*.
  Step 2: Move down the column to find *Milwaukee*.
  Step 3: Find the column labeled *Losses* under *Total*.
  Step 4: Read across the row from *Milwaukee* to the number in the *Losses* column, which is 4.

- Use the information to draw one or more conclusions.

  EXAMPLE   Most teams have more losses than wins when away.

Schedules

Train No.	Frequency	Dp. Wash.	Dp. Balt.	Dp. Phila. (30th St.)	New York (Penn. Station) Ar.	New York (Penn. Station) Dp.	Ar. New Haven	Ar. Provi- dence	Ar. Boston (South Sta.)
■ 66	Daily	⊛●10 20 p	⊘11 15 p	□12 54 a	2 52 a	3 25 a	5 00 a	7 39 a	8 34 a
■866	Daily	●10 20 p	⊘11 15 p	□12 54 a	⊛2 52 a	⊛8 00 a	—	—	—
★290	②SaSuonly	—	—	5 41 a	7 50 a	—	9 26 a	□11 22 a	12 12 p
200	①ExSaSu	—	—	5 41 a	7 21 a	—	—	—	—
150	Mo only	—	—	—	—	8 05 a	9 51 a	12 07 p	12 58 p
12	Ex Mo	3 45 a	4 22 a	5 53 a	7 40 a	8 05 a	9 51 a	12 07 p	1 12 p
202	①ExSaSu	—	—	6 20 a	8 08 a	—	—	—	—
180	④Mo only	● 4 50 a	5 26 a	□6 48 a	8 15 a	—	—	—	—
204	①ExSuMo	—	—	□6 48 a	8 15 a	—	—	—	—
206	②ExSaSu	—	—	7 05 a	8 50 a	—	—	—	—
★198	Daily	—	—	7 20 a	8 52 a	9 07 a	10 44 a	12 59 p	1 48 p
★100	①ExSaSu	—	—	7 35 a	8 57 a	9 07 a	10 44 a	12 59 p	1 46 p
★190	①ExSaSu	—	—	8 00 a	9 27 a	—	—	—	—
42	①ExSaSu	—	● 6 20 a	⊘ 6 58 a	□8 14 a	9 52 a	10 16 a	12 01 p	2 05 p	2 55 p
★168	Daily	—	—	—	9 30 a	—	—	—	—
★280	⑥ExSaSu	▲6 50 a	—	—	9 30 a	—	—	—	—
★102	①ExSaSu	▲7 00 a	⊘ 7 38 a	□8 44 a	9 59 a	—	—	—	—
182	Daily	● 7 20 a	7 54 a	□9 08 a	10 38 a	—	—	—	—
★104	①ExSu	●8 00 a	8 35 a	□9 40 a	10 55 a	—	—	—	—
44	SaSu only	—	—	10 10 a	11 38 a	—	—	—	—
★170	Daily	● 8 30 a	⊘ 9 13 a	□10 24 a	11 59 a	12 19 p	2 06 p	4 20 p	5 05 p
★106	Daily	▲9 00 a	9 35 a	□10 40 a	11 55 a	—	—	—	—
86	Daily	● 9 20 a	⊘10 00 a	□11 14 a	12 53 p	—	—	—	—
★108	④ExSaSu	10 00 a	10 31 a	□11 35 a	12 49 p	—	—	—	—
★174	Daily	●10 20 a	10 55 a	□12 10 p	1 37 p	1 52 p	3 29 p	5 41 p	6 31 p
★110	①ExSaSu	11 00 a	11 31 a	□12 36 p	1 55 p	—	—	—	—
★114	②Suonly	—	—	1 00 p	2 25 p	—	—	—	—
Daily	●11 20 a	□12 00 n	□1 12	2 52 p	3 25 p	5 00 p			

— Amtrak

TIPS for Schedules

• Schedules are special kinds of tables. They show when certain things happen.

EXAMPLE A train schedule shows when trains arrive and depart.

• Read the title and column headings to see what is listed.

EXAMPLE Northbound trains in the Northeast corridor

• Read the column headings. Look at the explanations of symbols.

• Use the column headings to help you find a particular item.

EXAMPLE Step 1: For a train from Baltimore to New Haven, find the column headed *Dp. Balt.* (*Dp.* = "depart") and look at departure times.

Step 2: Find a convenient time to leave. Read across that line to the *Ar. New Haven* column (*Ar.* = "arrive") to find the arrival time.

Step 3: Look left on that line to see the number of the train and the days on which it operates.

Step 4: Check the meanings of all symbols. The circled 1 after Train No. 202 means it will not run on three days: 5/29, 7/4, 9/4.

Diagrams

Space Suit

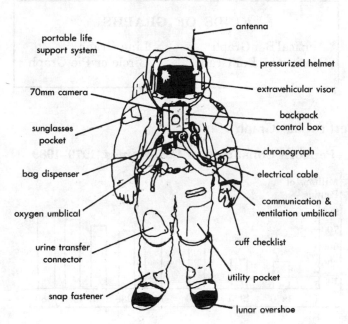

- portable life support system
- antenna
- pressurized helmet
- extravehicular visor
- 70mm camera
- backpack control box
- sunglasses pocket
- chronograph
- bag dispenser
- electrical cable
- oxygen umbilical
- communication & ventilation umbilical
- urine transfer connector
- cuff checklist
- snap fastener
- utility pocket
- lunar overshoe

— *What's What*, R. Bragonier, Jr., and D. Fisher, eds.

TIPS on Diagrams

- A diagram is a sketch showing the parts of something or how something works. Diagrams are useful in analyzing. (See pages 24 – 27.)

- Read the title of the diagram, if there is one, to find out what the diagram shows.

  EXAMPLE   The above title tells you the diagram shows a space suit.

- Read the *caption*, if there is one. The caption is a label below the diagram. It tells what the diagram shows and sometimes gives an explanation.

- Read the labels. They tell the names of the parts.

- Follow the lines from the labels to the diagram. They show where the parts are located.

Pop the Question

Is popcorn really corn?

— Yes. It is a specific type of corn with small, hard kernels. The plant is smaller than most other corn plants.

Why does popcorn pop?

— Popcorn kernels contain a great deal of moisture. When the kernel is heated, the moisture turns into steam, and pressure builds up. Finally the pressure bursts the hard covering around the kernel, and the corn pops out.

How much does popcorn pop?

— Good popcorn kernels can pop to 35 times their size!

Where did popcorn come from?

— Popcorn originated in America. In fact, the native Indians probably introduced it to the Pilgrims.

Graphs

+---+
| **KINDS OF GRAPHS** |
| |
| Vertical Bar Graph   Line Graph |
| Horizontal Bar Graph   Circle or Pie Graph |
+---+

A. Vertical Bar Graph

Popcorn Consumed in U.S. Homes, 1970–1989

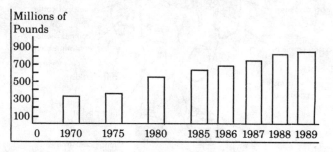

— *Source: The Popcorn Institute*

+--+
| **TIPS** on Vertical Bar Graphs |
| |
| • A graph is a chart that shows how sets of facts are related. |
| EXAMPLE   The graph above shows the relationship between |
| (1) the amount of popcorn eaten in U.S. homes, and|
| (2) the year the popcorn was eaten. |
| |
| • Read the title to find out what the graph shows. |
| |
| • Look at the *horizontal axis* — the facts that go across. |
| Look at the *vertical axis* — the facts that go up and down.|
| |
| • Read labels and all other information. |
| EXAMPLE   The vertical axis shows millions of pounds. |
| |
| • Look at the highest point of a bar. Follow that point across the |
| graph. You will see a connection between the facts. |
| EXAMPLE   The bar for 1988 hits the vertical axis at about 800. That means |
| in the year 1988 about 800 million pounds of popcorn |
| was eaten in U.S. homes. |
| |
| • Draw one or more conclusions from the information. |
| EXAMPLE   More and more popcorn is being eaten in U.S. homes. |
+--+

B. Horizontal Bar Graph

Goals and Winners, World Cup Soccer Tournaments, 1930–1986

Average goals per game and winner of each World Cup

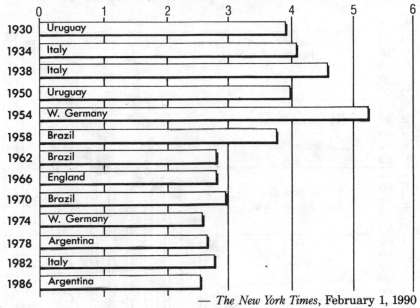

— *The New York Times*, February 1, 1990

TIPS on Horizontal Bar Graphs

- A graph is a chart that shows how sets of facts are related.

  EXAMPLE   The graph above shows the relationship among
  - (1) the average goals per World Cup soccer game,
  - (2) the nation winning the World Cup tournament,
  - (3) the year the tournament was played.

- Read the title to find out what the graph shows.

- Read labels and all other information.

  EXAMPLE   The label near the top tells you that (1) the numbers on the horizontal axis (across the top) stand for average goals per game, and (2) the countries written on the bars are the winners.

- Look at the tip of a bar. Follow that point to the top. You will see a connection in the sets of facts.

  EXAMPLE   In the year 1934, an average of 4 goals was scored in each game of the World Cup.

- Draw one or more conclusions from the information.

  EXAMPLE   On the whole, the number of goals scored in the World Cup has been decreasing.

C. Double Bar Graph

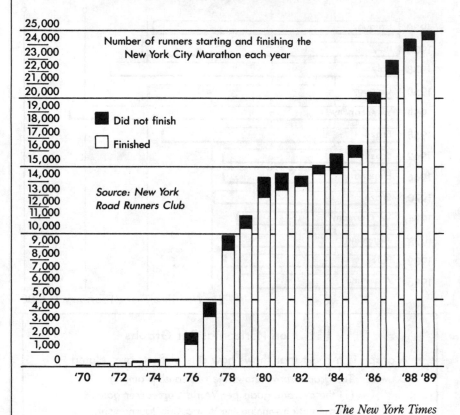

Starting and Finishing Runners, New York Marathon, 1970–1989

Number of runners starting and finishing the New York City Marathon each year

■ Did not finish

□ Finished

Source: New York Road Runners Club

— *The New York Times*

TIPS on Double Graphs

- A double graph compares and contrasts sets of facts. (See pages 13 – 14.)

  EXAMPLE   In the graph on page 94, you can compare and contrast
  (1) starting runners with finishing runners
  (2) in different years.

- Read the title to find out what the graph shows.

- Read labels and all other information.

  EXAMPLE   Look at the labels next to the small light and dark squares on the left. They tell you that the light bars show the number of runners who finished the race and the dark bars show the number of runners who did not finish.

- Get information from the graph.

  EXAMPLE   Step 1: Choose a year listed along the bottom.
  Step 2: Follow the bar above that year to the tip of the light portion.
  Step 3: Follow an imaginary line across to the numbers listed at the left.
  Step 4: The point where your lines meet shows the number of runners who finished that year.
  Step 5: Go back to the same bar. Follow the top of the dark portion across to the numbers.
  Step 6: The point where your lines meet shows the total number of people who ran that year.
  Step 7: Subtract the finishers from the total to find out how many did not finish that year.

- Draw one or more conclusions from the information.

  EXAMPLE   The total number of New York Marathon runners has increased, and so has the number of runners who finish the race.

The Earliest U.S. Stamps

The first U.S. postage stamps were issued in 1847. One pictured George Washington, the first U.S. president. The other showed Benjamin Franklin, the first U.S. postmaster general.

D. Line Graph

Price of U. S. First-Class Stamp, 1958–1991

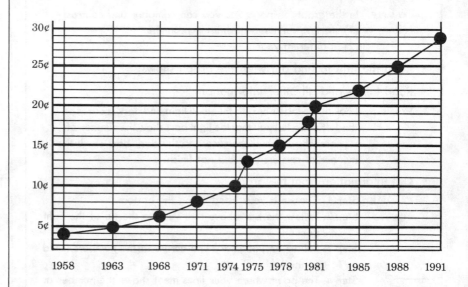

TIPS on Line Graphs

- A graph is a chart that shows how sets of facts are related.

  EXAMPLE   The graph above shows the relationship between
  (1) the price of a first-class stamp, and
  (2) the year the stamp was bought.

- Read the title to find out what the graph shows.

- Read labels and all other information.

  EXAMPLE   The label above the numbers tells you that they show prices.

- Follow points on the line across (the *horizontal axis*) and down (the *vertical axis*). See where the two sets of facts meet. Each point will show a connection.

  EXAMPLE   Find 1978 on the horizontal axis. Follow it up to the line. At that point, look across to the vertical axis. You will see that in 1978 a first-class stamp cost 15¢.

- Draw one or more conclusions from the information.

  EXAMPLE   The cost of a first-class stamp has risen steadily.

E. Circle (Pie) Graph

Breakdown of U.S. Population by Age, in Percentages, 1980
Total population 1980: 228 million

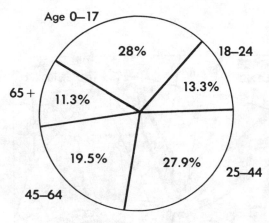

— Figures from *Statistical Abstract of the United States*

TIPS for Circle or Pie Graphs

- A graph is a chart that shows how sets of facts are related. A circle graph shows how one part is related to the whole and to the other parts.

  EXAMPLE (1) The circle above stands for the total U.S. population in 1980.
  (2) Each part stands for a certain age group.
  (3) The graph shows what part of the population belonged to each age group in 1980.

- Read the title to find out what the graph shows.

- Read the labels on the parts of the circle.

  EXAMPLE The labels show the age group and the percentage of the population represented by each part.

- Get information by looking at the size of the parts.

  EXAMPLE In 1980, to which age group did the largest number of people belong? The answer is from 0 to 17.

- Compare and contrast. (See pages 13 – 14.)

  EXAMPLE In 1980, there were fewer people over 65 than there were people between 18 and 24.

Watch for Map Traps!

A map shows you where to make
　　your car go,
To drive through Dakota to Fargo.
　　But follow those lines,
　　And watch all the signs,
Or you may head instead for
　　Chicago.

A map is a wonderful way,
To avoid getting lost in L.A.
　　But watch what you're doing
　　Or you may end up chewing
Some hot curried rice in Bombay.

— Florence Harris

Maps

A. Road and Street Maps

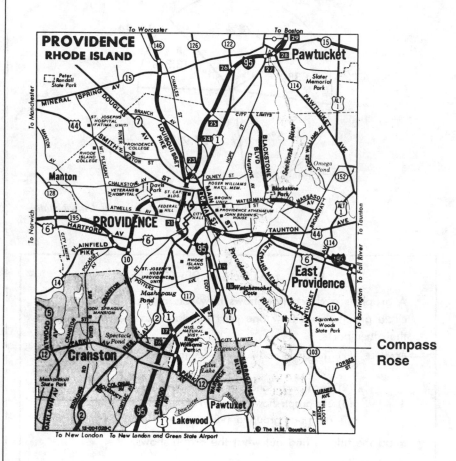

Compass
Rose

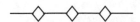

Legend —————

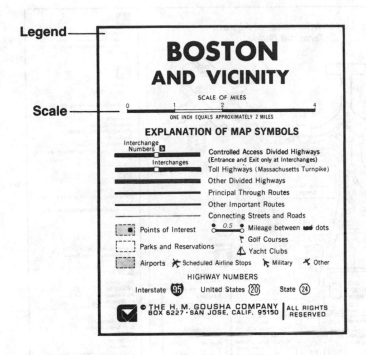

BOSTON
AND VICINITY

SCALE OF MILES

Scale —————

0   1   2   4

ONE INCH EQUALS APPROXIMATELY 2 MILES

EXPLANATION OF MAP SYMBOLS

Interchange Numbers ⑤

Interchanges

Controlled Access Divided Highways
(Entrance and Exit only at Interchanges)

Toll Highways (Massachusetts Turnpike)

Other Divided Highways

Principal Through Routes

Other Important Routes

Connecting Streets and Roads

Points of Interest   •—0.5—• Mileage between ⬛ dots

Parks and Reservations   ⛳ Golf Courses

   ⚓ Yacht Clubs

Airports   ✈ Scheduled Airline Stops   ✈ Military   ✈ Other

HIGHWAY NUMBERS

Interstate 95   United States 20   State 24

© THE H. M. GOUSHA COMPANY
BOX 6227 · SAN JOSE, CALIF. 95150 | ALL RIGHTS RESERVED

TIPS on Road and Street Maps

- Look at the *legend* or *key* to see what the symbols mean.

- Look at the *scale*. The scale shows the distance on the map that equals a mile or a kilometer.

- Look at the *compass rose*. Use the arrows to find the directions north, south, east, and west.

- Use the map to see where places are.

  EXAMPLE   Rhode Island College is in the northwest corner of Providence, on Mt. Pleasant Avenue.

- Use the map to see how to get from one place to another.

  EXAMPLE   To get to Rhode Island College from East Providence, take Route 195 to Main Street, turn left on Smith Street, and turn left again on Mt. Pleasant Avenue.

Using Graphic Aids | **99**

B. Diagram Maps

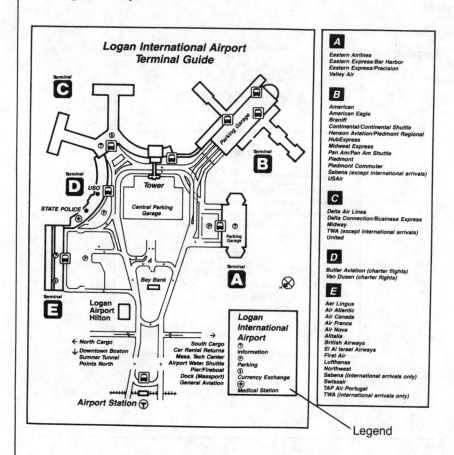

Logan International Airport Terminal Guide

Terminal **C**

Parking Garage

Terminal **B**

Terminal **D**   USO

STATE POLICE

Tower

Central Parking Garage

Parking Garage

Terminal **A**

Bay Bank

Logan Airport Hilton

Terminal **E**

← North Cargo
↓ Downtown Boston
 Sumner Tunnel
 Points North

South Cargo
Car Rental Returns
Mass. Tech Center
Airport Water Shuttle
Pier/Fireboat
Dock (Massport)
General Aviation

Logan International Airport
ⓘ Information
ⓟ Parking
Ⓢ Currency Exchange
⊕ Medical Station

Airport Station Ⓣ

A
Eastern Airlines
Eastern Express/Bar Harbor
Eastern Express/Precision
Valley Air

B
American
American Eagle
Braniff
Continental/Continental Shuttle
Henson Aviation/Piedmont Regional
HubExpress
Midwest Express
Pan Am/Pan Am Shuttle
Piedmont
Piedmont Commuter
Sabena (except international arrivals)
USAir

C
Delta Air Lines
Delta Connection/Business Express
Midway
TWA (except international arrivals)
United

D
Butler Aviation (charter flights)
Van Dusen (charter flights)

E
Aer Lingus
Air Atlantic
Air Canada
Air France
Air Nova
Alitalia
British Airways
El Al Israel Airways
First Air
Lufthansa
Northwest
Sabena (international arrivals only)
Swissair
TAP Air Portugal
TWA (international arrivals only)

Legend

— Massport

TIPS on Diagram Maps

- Read the title to see what the map shows.
- Look at the *legend* or *key* to see what the symbols mean.
- Look at the labels to see what the parts of the diagram are.
- Use the map to find out where places are.

  EXAMPLE   Delta Air Lines is located in Terminal C.

- Use the map to see how to get from one place to another.

  EXAMPLE   To go from Delta to American, drive down the main road past the Hilton, take two left turns, and look for Terminal B on the right.

C. Weather Maps

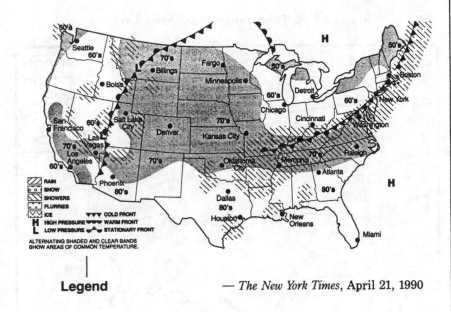

— *The New York Times*, April 21, 1990

Legend

TIPS on Weather Maps

- Look at the *legend* or *key* to see the meanings of the symbols.

- Use the map to find out the temperature and other weather conditions in a particular area on a given day.

  EXAMPLE   On the day represented above, the weather was in the 50's with showers in the extreme Northwest.

- Use the map to compare and contrast weather conditions in different areas on a particular day.

  EXAMPLE   Much of the South was 30 degrees warmer than New England.

D. Time Zone Maps

Map of U.S. Time Zones and Area Codes

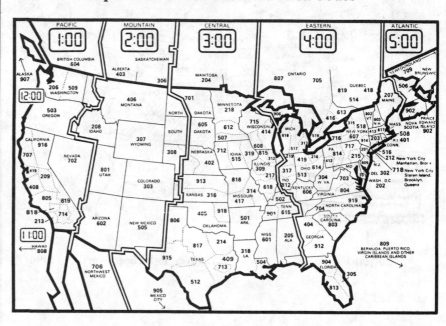

TIPS on Time Zone Maps

- Find the dividing lines between time zones. They do not necessarily match other boundaries.

  EXAMPLE   The state of Kentucky is split into two time zones.

- Look at the numbers that show the time in each zone. Figure out the difference in hours.

  EXAMPLE   When it is 5:00 in the Atlantic zone, it is 3:00 in the Central zone, which is two hours earlier.

- Figure out the time in specific places.

  EXAMPLE   When it is 8:00 in New Brunswick (Atlantic), it is two hours earlier, or 6:00, in Texas (Central).

- Notice that the above map shows telephone area codes too. When calling someone in another state or region, dial this number before you dial the person's telephone number.

  EXAMPLE   To reach northern Kansas, first dial 913. (In most areas, you must also dial 1 before the area code.)

Glossary

Computer Terms

address Number indicating a particular location in the **memory** of a computer

algorithm Step-by-step plan for solving a problem or carrying out a procedure

alphanumeric Set of symbols made up of letters and numbers

ASCII (pronounced "askey") Stands for American Standard Code for Information Interchange — an accepted code for representing letters and numbers

assembly language Computer language using specific names for instructions to the computer

backup Copy of **data** in case of loss or damage of the original

BASIC Stands for Beginner's All-purpose Symbolic Instruction Code, a widely used computer language for **programming**

baud Measurement (in **bits** per second) of speed at which information is transferred

binary Code using 0's and 1's to represent information

bit **Binary** number (0 or 1), smallest unit of information

boot To load the **operating system** into a computer after it has been turned on

bug Error in a **program** or system

byte Group of **bits** that the computer processes as a unit; a **character**

CAI Stands for Computer-Aided (or Assisted) Instruction — a question-and-answer system by which the computer teaches or practices lessons

central processing unit (See **CPU.**)

character Letter, number, or other symbol; generally, a **byte**

chip Tiny part, usually made of silicon, containing thousands of **circuits**

circuit Electrical path flowing out of and returning to a power source, performing work along the way

CMI Stands for Computer-Managed Instruction — system of teaching in which the computer becomes the teacher

COBOL Stands for COmmon Business-Oriented Language, a computer language used mainly for business **programs**

command Single instruction to the computer system, carried out immediately

CPU Stands for Central Processing Unit, the unit that contains the "brain" of the computer

CRT Stands for Cathode Ray Tube, a tube that acts as a video screen; a **video display terminal** or **monitor**

cursor Flashing symbol on a **CRT** screen to show where next **character** will appear

daisy wheel printer Printer with characters on a wheel, producing solid, typewriter-like characters (See also **dot matrix printer**.)

data Information presented to a computer

database **File** with information on a particular subject or subjects

debug To correct errors in a system or **program**

disk, diskette Flat, circular plate, usually magnetic, on which information is stored; usually wrapped in a protective envelope

disk drive Device that transfers information to and from a **disk**

documentation Written material explaining a computer **program** or system

DOS Stands for Disk Operating System; set of **programs** for communicating with the **disk drive**

dot matrix printer Printer producing characters made up of small dots (See also **daisy wheel printer**.)

file Organized collection of information that is given a name and that can be handled as a unit, like a file folder in a filing cabinet

floppy disk (See **disk**)

FORTRAN Stands for FORmula TRANslation, a computer language used mainly for science **programs**

GIGO Stands for Garbage In, Garbage Out, meaning what comes out of a computer can be no better than what is put in

hard copy Computer **output** printed on paper

hardware Physical objects that make up a computer system, such as the **monitor**, keyboard, and printer

input Information entered into a computer

I/O (Pronounced "eye-oh") General term for **input-output** activities of a computer

joystick A hand control, usually used for computer games

K Kilobyte; 2^{10} (1024) **bytes**; used to show the size of a computer's **memory** — for example, a computer with 64K can store 65,536 bytes (64×1024)

laser printer An extremely fast printer that forms characters as dots of static electricity that attract then melt metallic dust

LOGO Computer language used for **programming**, especially as a first computer language for young people

memory The part of a computer that stores information

menu List of choices, usually shown on a **monitor**, from which the user selects an action for the computer to perform

modem Stands for MOdulator/ DEModulator, a device by which computers can send information over regular telephone lines

monitor Viewing screen, like a TV screen, allowing a video display of the computer **input** and **output**

mouse Hand-held device that can control a pointer on the display screen

operating system The large, complicated master control **program** that runs a computer system

output The result of computer processing; for example, the printed report produced by a computer **program**

Pascal A popular **programming** language originally developed to teach structured programming; now used for business and scientific programs.

peripheral Device, usually attached to a computer, that handles **input/output** and information storage, such as a **disk drive** or a printer

program (1) Set of instructions that a computer can follow; (2) to create and run a set of instructions for a computer to follow

RAM Stands for Random Access Memory — temporary **memory** for information that can be changed or erased by the user

read To acquire information from **memory** or from a storage device such as a **disk**

ROM Stands for Read-Only Memory — fixed, permanent **memory** built into the computer that cannot be changed by the user; usually holds the **operating system**

software **Programs**, along with their **documentation**, created for use with **hardware**

syntax Rules for writing instructions in a **programming** language; similar to the grammar of a human language

terminal Device, usually consisting of a keyboard and **monitor**, by which the user communicates with a computer

tutorial Teaching **program** providing basic instruction

video display terminal (**VDT**) (See **CRT; monitor**.)

write-protect Method of preventing new information from being written on a **disk** or in a **file**; on disks, usually involves covering or uncovering a notch

Bits and Pieces

When You Don't Have a Ruler . . .

— Use a dollar bill, which measures 6¹⁄₈ by 2⁵⁄₈ inches.

— Use a quarter, which is about an inch in diameter.

— Use a penny, which is about ³⁄₄ of an inch in diameter.

— Use a credit card, which is usually 3³⁄₈ by 2¹⁄₈ inches.

— Use a standard sheet of paper, which is 8¹⁄₂ by 11 inches.

Some Measurements . . .

— A marathon race route is 26 miles, 385 yards long. That's 42.2 kilometers.

— The diameter of the earth at the equator is 7,930 miles or 12,756 kilometers.

— A football field is 120 yards (109.7 meters) from end line to end line.

— At its deepest part, the ocean is 6.9 miles or 11 kilometers deep.

— The highest point above sea level, Mt. Everest, rises 5.5 miles or 8.8 kilometers.

— The moon is 233,812 miles (376,274 kilometers) from the earth.

Weights and Measures

The Metric System

The metric system is used together with the U.S. customary system in the United States (the only country that has not yet fully adopted the metric system). Here are the basic metric units:

meter	unit of length
gram	unit of mass (weight)
liter	unit of fluid volume

Multiples of these units are all based on ten.

deka-	=	10 times	*deci-*	=	1/10 of
hecto-	=	100 times	*centi-*	=	1/100 of
kilo-	=	1,000 times	*milli-*	=	1/1000 of
mega-	=	1,000,000 times	*micro-*	=	1/1,000,000 of

Metric Weights and Measures

Linear measure

10 millimeters	= 1 centimeter
10 centimeters	= 1 decimeter
10 decimeters	= 1 meter
10 meters	= 1 dekameter
10 hectometers	= 1 kilometer
10 kilometers	= 1 myriameter

Square measure

100 sq. millimeters	= 1 sq. centimeter
10,000 sq. centimeters	= 1 sq. meter
100 sq. meters	= 1 are
100 ares	= 1 hectare
100 hectares	= 1 sq. kilometer

Fluid volume measure

10 milliliters	= 1 centiliter
10 centiliters	= 1 deciliter
10 deciliters	= 1 liter
10 dekaliters	= 1 hectoliter
10 hectoliters	= 1 kiloliter

Weight

10 milligrams	= 1 centigram
10 centigrams	= 1 decigram
10 decigrams	= 1 gram
10 grams	= 1 dekagram
10 hectograms	= 1 kilogram
1,000 kilograms	= 1 metric ton

Cubic measure

1,000 cu. millimeters	= 1 cu. centimeter
1,000 cu. centimeters	= 1 cu. decimeter
1,000 cu. decimeters	= 1 cu. meter

U.S. Customary System

U.S. CUSTOMARY		METRIC
Linear measure		
1 inch	= 1,000 mils	= 2.54 centimeters
12 inches	= 1 foot	= 0.3048 meter
3 feet	= 1 yard	= 0.9144 meter
5 ½ yards	= 1 rod	= 5.029 meters
40 rods	= 1 furlong	= 201.168 meters
8 furlongs (5,280 feet)	= 1 (statute) mile	= 1.6093 kilometers
3 miles	= 1 (land) league	= 4.83 kilometers
Area measure		
1 square inch		= 6.452 square centimeters
144 square inches	= 1 square foot	= 929.03 square centimeters
9 square feet	= 1 square yard	= 0.8361 square meter
30 ¼ square yards	= 1 square rod	= 25.292 square meters
160 square rods	= 1 acre	= 0.4047 hectare
640 acres	= 1 square mile	
Weight (Avoirdupois)		
1 dram		= 1.772 grams
16 drams	= 1 ounce	= 28.3495 grams
16 ounces	= 1 pound	= 453.59 grams
100 pounds	= 1 hundredweight	= 45.36 kilograms
2,000 pounds	= 1 ton	= 907.18 kilograms
Liquid measure		
1 teaspoon	= ⅓ tablespoon *or* ⅛ fluid ounce	
1 tablespoon	= 3 teaspoons *or* ½ fluid ounce	
1 fluid ounce	= 2 tablespoons	
1 cup	= 16 tablespoons *or* 8 fluid ounces	
1 pint	= 2 cups *or* 16 fluid ounces	= 0.4732 liter
1 quart	= 2 pints *or* 4 cups *or* 32 fluid ounces	= 0.9464 liter
1 gallon	= 4 quarts *or* 8 pints *or* 16 cups	= 3.7854 liters
1 barrel	= 31.5 U.S. gallons	= 119.24 liters

Temperature

Temperature too is commonly measured by two systems, Fahrenheit (F) and Celsius (C).

	F	C
(*Freezing*)	32°	0°
	50°	10°
	68°	20°
	86°	30°
(*Normal body temp*)	98.6°	37°
	104°	40°
(*Boiling*)	212°	100°

From One System to Another

TO GO FROM	TO	MULTIPLY BY
inches	millimeters	25
feet	centimeters	30
yards	meters	0.9
miles	kilometers	1.6
millimeters	inches	0.04
centimeters	inches	0.4
meters	yards	1.1
kilometers	miles	0.6
ounces	grams	28
pounds	kilograms	0.45
grams	ounces	0.035
kilograms	pounds	2.2
ounces	milliliters	30
pints	liters	0.47
quarts	liters	0.95
gallons	liters	3.8
milliliters	ounces	0.034
liters	pints	2.1
liters	quarts	1.06
liters	gallons	0.26

Alphabets and Numerals

Roman Numerals

(For some background on Roman numerals, see page 211.)

I	=	1
II	=	2
III	=	3
IV	=	4
V	=	5
VI	=	6
VII	=	7
VIII	=	8
IX	=	9
X	=	10
XI	=	11
XII	=	12
XIII	=	13
XIV	=	14
XV	=	15
XVI	=	16
XVII	=	17
XVIII	=	18
XIX	=	19
XX	=	20
XXI	=	21
XXII	=	22
XXIII	=	23
XXIV	=	24
XXV	=	25
XXVI	=	26
XXVII	=	27
XXVIII	=	28
XXIX	=	29
XXX	=	30
XL	=	40
L	=	50
LX	=	60
LXX	=	70
LXXX	=	80
XC	=	90
C	=	100
D	=	500
M	=	1000

HEBREW

Forms	Name	Sound
א	'aleph	'
ב	bēth	b (bh)
ג	gimel	g (gh)
ד	dāleth	d (dh)
ה	hē	h
ו	waw	w
ז	zayin	z
ח	ḥeth	ḥ
ט	ṭeth	ṭ
י	yodh	y
כ ד	kāph	k (kh)
ל	lāmedh	l
מ ם	mēm	m
נ ן	nūn	n
ס	samekh	s
ע	'ayin	'
פ ף	pē	p (ph)
צ ץ	ṣadhe	ṣ
ק	qōph	q
ר	rēsh	r
שׂ	sin	s
שׁ	shin	sh
ת	tāw	t (th)

GREEK

Forms	Name	Sound
A α	alpha	a.
B β	beta	b
Γ γ	gamma	g (n)
Δ δ	delta	d
E ε	epsilon	e
Z ζ	zēta	z
H η	ēta	ē
Θ θ	thēta	th
I ι	iota	i
K κ	kappa	k
Λ λ	lambda	l
M μ	mu	m
N ν	nu	n
Ξ ξ	xi	x
O o	omicron	o
Π π	pi	p
P ρ	rhō	r (rh)
Σ σ ς	sigma	s
T τ	tau	t
Υ υ	upsilon	u
Φ φ	phi	ph
X χ	khi	kh
Ψ ψ	psi	ps
Ω ω	ōmega	ō

RUSSIAN

Forms	Sound
А а	a
Б б	b
В в	v
Г г	g
Д д	d
Е е	e
Ж ж	zh
З з	z
И и Й й	i, ĭ
К к	k
Л л	l
М м	m
Н н	n
О о	o
П п	p
Р р	r
С с	s
Т т	t
У у	u
Ф ф	f
Х х	kh
Ц ц	ts
Ч ч	ch
Ш ш	sh
Щ щ	shch
Ы ы	y
Э э	e
Ю ю	yu
Я я	ya

Bits and Pieces

Holidays

Major U.S. Holidays

New Year's Day	January 1
Martin Luther King, Jr.'s Birthday	January 15*
Lincoln's Birthday	February 12
President's Day	Third Monday in February
Washington's Birthday	February 22
St. Patrick's Day	March 17
Easter Sunday	March or April (date varies)
Mother's Day	Second Sunday in May
Armed Forces Day	Third Saturday in May
Memorial Day	May 30*
Flag Day	June 14
Father's Day	Third Sunday in June
Independence Day	July 4
Labor Day	First Monday in September
Columbus Day	October 12*
Election Day	First Tuesday after the first Monday in November
Veterans' Day	November 11
Thanksgiving Day	Fourth Thursday in November
Christmas Day	December 25

Major Canadian Holidays

Easter Monday	March or April (date varies)
Victoria Day	First Monday before May 25
Canada Day	July 1
Labor Day	First Monday in September
Thanksgiving Day	Second Monday in October
Remembrance Day	November 11
Christmas Day	December 25
Boxing Day	December 26
Veteran's Day	November 11

*This is the official date. The holiday is actually celebrated on the Monday closest to the date.

More U.S. Holidays . . .

American Family Day
First Sunday in August, Arizona

Child Health Day
First Monday in October

Citizenship Day
September 17

Elizabeth Cady Stanton Day
(Birthday of leader in struggle for rights for women)
November 12

General Pulaski Memorial Day
(Death of Polish hero of American Revolution)
October 11

Grandparents' Day
First Sunday after Labor Day

Groundhog Day
(Legend has it that if the groundhog sees its shadow on this day, winter continues for another six weeks) February 2

Loyalty Day
May 1

Susan B. Anthony Day
(Birthday of crusader for equal rights for women) February 15

United Nations Day
October 24

Wright Brothers Day
December 17

Your Turn

When are these celebrated?

(1) Kwanzaa
(2) Chinese New Year
(3) Discovery Day (Puerto Rico)

Answers
(1) Dec. 26; (2) First new moon after sun enters Aquarius — between Jan. 21 and Feb. 19; (3) Nov. 19

Solar System

Our solar system is made up of the sun and all the objects that orbit, or move around, it. The sun, the only star in our system, is the source of light and heat. The nine known planets in the system move in two ways: (1) each planet *rotates*, or spins, on its own axis, and (2) each planet *revolves*, or moves in a circle, around the sun.

All the planets except Mercury and Venus have moons. Jupiter, Saturn, Uranus, and probably Neptune are circled by rings. There are other objects in the solar system too, including *asteroids* (minor planets), *comets* (frozen balls of gases), *meteoroids* (solid particles).

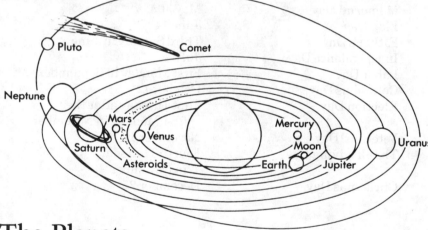

The Planets

	DIAMETER	DISTANCE FROM THE SUN	ORBITS SUN IN	ROTATES ON AXIS IN
Mercury	3,100 miles	36 million miles	88 days	59 days
Venus	7,700 miles	67 million miles	225 days	244 days
Earth	7,920 miles	93 million miles	365 days	24 hours
Mars	4,200 miles	141 million miles	687 days	24 hours, 24 minutes
Jupiter	88,640 miles	483 million miles	11.9 years	9 hours, 50 minutes
Saturn	74,500 miles	886 million miles	29.5 years	10 hours, 39 minutes
Uranus	32,000 miles	1,782 million miles	84 years	23 hours
Neptune	31,000 miles	2,793 million miles	165 days	15 hours, 48 minutes
Pluto	15,000 miles	3,670 million miles	248 years	6 days, 7 hours

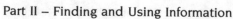

Bits and Pieces

Signs of the Zodiac

Do you see shapes in the stars? Ancient people did — a lion, a ram, a set of scales, for example. In fact, they named different groups of stars, or *constellations*, for these shapes.

The ancients imagined a belt above the earth within which the moon and planets seemed to travel. They divided this belt, or *zodiac*, into twelve equal parts, or *signs*, and named each sign for the constellation in that part of the sky. (The names are expressed in Latin.) In the thousands of years since then, the position of the earth's axis has changed, and the signs have shifted. As a result, the stars and the signs no longer match.

The Water Carrier	The Fishes	The Ram
The Bull	The Twins	The Crab
The Lion	The Virgin	The Scales
The Scorpion	The Archer	The Goat

Part III –
Communicating

Reading

Before You Read

You might think zookeepers spend all their time mucking out yards and dishing up meals. But they can also bathe chinchillas in volcanic dust, brush sea lions' teeth with meat-flavored tooth powder, and tend a special patch of sunflowers for gorilla snacks. The responsibilities of keepers at the National Zoo in Washington, D. C., are as diverse as the personalities of the creatures they care for.

> — Jacket copy, *Keepers and Creatures at the National Zoo,* Peggy Thomson

You may have heard the saying, "You can't judge a book by its cover." Actually, if you know where to look, clues on the cover and elsewhere can tell you a lot about a book before you read it.

What to Do Before You Read

1. **Look.** Read the title and the author's name. If the book has a jacket, read what it says. Flip through the book. Look for a table of contents, index, and illustrations. Read the introduction, preface, foreward, or dedication. Ask yourself questions like these:

   - What does the title tell me?
   - Who is the author? Have I read other books by the author?
   - What does the jacket tell me about the book? the author?
   - Is there a table of contents? an index? What do they tell me about what the book contains?
   - Are there illustrations? What do they show?
   - What kind of work is it? (See the margin for examples.)
   - What is it about?
   - If it is a story, where and when does it take place?
   - How long is it?

2. **Think about what you know.** Draw on what you know. Ask yourself questions like these:

   - What do I know about the subject? about the setting?
   - What have I read, seen on TV, or heard about that relates to the subject or the story?
   - Where have I been and what have I done that relates to the subject or story?
   - What does the subject or story remind me of?

Types of Reading

Here are the major kinds of works you will find in your reading. (See pages 224 – 229 for definitions of some of the terms.)

FICTION

Folklore
Myth, legend
Realistic fiction
Historical fiction
Science fiction
Fantasy
Mystery

Story
Novel
Narrative poem

NONFICTION

History
How-to
Reference
Factual information
Textbook
Biography
Personal narrative
Autobiography

Report
Article
Essay
Informational book

3. **Diagram what you know.** To see how much you know about the subject, story, or setting, use it as the center of a cluster diagram. (See pages 5 and 134.) Around the center, write the ideas that the topic makes you think of. Keep expanding the cluster until you run out of ideas.

4. **Think about what you don't know.** Ask yourself whether you have enough background to enjoy or understand what you read.

   • What might you need to know?
   • Is the story set in another time or place? Perhaps you want to find out more about the setting.
   • Is the information technical or specialized? Is there a special vocabulary? You may want to do some background reading first or keep a reference book handy.

5. **Make predictions.** A prediction is an educated guess about what will happen.

   • Predict what the work might be about and how it might begin.
   • If it is nonfiction (true to life), like *Keepers and Creatures at the National Zoo,* predict what information you will get.
   • If it is fiction (imaginary), predict what it might be about and what might happen.

6. **Decide what to look for.** To get the most out of what you read, don't just look at the words. Think about them.

   • If you are reading a narrative, look for details that tell you about the plot, setting, and characters.
   • If you are reading for information, look for details that tell you what you want to learn. Jot down some questions.

TIPS on What to Do Before You Read

• Look closely — at the title, cover, illustrations, contents.
• Think about what you know. Try a cluster diagram.
• Think about what you don't know. What should you find out?
• Make predictions. What will happen? What will you learn?
• Think about what to look for as you read.

Reading

While You Read

With no experience in the care and coddling of cuttlefish, the zoo lost its first batch. Now it knows: The water must be a good, close-to-perfect match for the sea water which the cuttlefish come from. The food must be just right and the way the food is offered just right, too, or the cuttlefish will droop and starve themselves rather than eat it.

— *Keepers and Creatures at the National Zoo*,
Peggy Thomson

Suppose you are reading along and you come to the paragraph above. Did you expect to learn about caring for cuttlefish? What are cuttlefish? The paragraph tells you only that they come from the sea. What do you do when you come across a challenge like cuttlefish? Here are some strategies to use when you read.

What to Do While You Read

1. **Think.**   Use your brain as well as your eyes.

   - If you are reading for information, think about what you want to learn. Make a list of questions before you begin. Keep asking, "Is that fact or opinion?" (page 36).
   - If you are reading a story, think about the setting, plot, and characters. (See pages 185 – 189.) Try to picture them as you read. Look for clues to the characters' personalities. Get to know them.
   - No matter what you are reading, think about its meaning — for the writer, for you, for the world.

2. **Predict.**   Keep making educated guesses about what is to come.

   - Before you begin, predict what the book will be about. What sorts of things will you learn? What will happen?
   - After you have read a few pages, a section, or a chapter, check your predictions.
   - If your predictions were right, go on to predict what will come next. (See *foreshadowing*, page 226.)
   - If your predictions turn out to be wrong, just go ahead and make new ones, based on what you have read.
   - Keep making and checking predictions. You don't have to be right. In fact, it is often more fun to be surprised.

3. **Paraphrase.** Retell in your own words what you have read. Paraphrasing (page 210) helps you to understand — and to discover what you *don't* understand.

4. **Pace yourself.** Adjust your speed to what you read. A selection full of facts and long words may need to be read slowly, for example. If you need to slow down, do it.

5. **Figure out puzzles.** Puzzled? Don't give up.

   a. **Reread.** Read the words again. Concentration may make things click, or you may find something you overlooked.

   b. **Read on.** The explanation may lie just ahead. If not, you can always come back to try to figure out the puzzle.

   c. **Look it up.** Still puzzled? Decide if a dictionary or other reference work will help. (See pages 60 – 65.)

6. **Ask questions.** At the end of a scene or a section, stop and ask yourself questions about what you just read. Then try to answer them. Here are some general questions. Add more specific ones based on whatever you are reading.

   • What was the author trying to tell me?
   • What did I actually find out?
   • What was the main idea? What details supported it?
   • Do I agree or disagree? Why?
   • What does it remind me of? What does it make me think of?
   • How does it make me feel? Why?
   • What are the characters like? What do I think of them?
   • What would I have done in the same situation?

7. **Take notes.** Write down facts you want to remember and ideas and questions you want to think about. Your notes can provide ideas for your own reports, compositions, or stories.

TIPS on What to Do While You Read

• Think.
• Keep on predicting.
• Paraphrase.
• Pace yourself.
• If you are puzzled, reread, read on, look it up.
• Ask questions.
• Take notes.

Reading

After You Read

> Wilbur never forgot Charlotte. Although he loved her children and grandchildren dearly, none of the new spiders ever quite took her place in his heart. She was in a class by herself. It is not often that someone comes along who is a true friend and a good writer. Charlotte was both.
>
> The End
>
> — *Charlotte's Web*, E. B. White

What do you do after you finish reading something? Do you put it down and forget about it? Do you sometimes read it again? Do you tell a friend about it? Do you look for something else by the same author? Do you look for something else on the same subject?

The effect of a good book can last for a long time after you read the last page. Sometimes it can last forever.

What to Do After Reading

1. **Think about it.**   Here are some of the questions you might ask yourself when you finish reading something:

   - Did I like it? Why or why not?
   - What did I like best? What did I like least?
   - Did I learn anything? If so, what?
   - What would I like to know more about?
   - Who do I know that might like this work?
   - Should I recommend it to a friend? Why or why not?
   - Would I like to know more about the author?
   - Would I like to read other works by the author?
   - Would I like to read more on the subject or theme?
   - What do I think of the main character?
   - What would I have done if I were the main character?
   - What else might have happened?
   - What places, situations, problems, or people in my own life are like those in the book?
   - How was this book like others I have read? How was it different?
   - What did the author want me to think about?
   - What did I think about?

Still More Prize Winners

Here are some more Newbery winners for different ages. (See pages 116 and 117 for more Newbery winners and pages 123, 124, 215 for still more books to read.)

Dear Mr. Henshaw, B. Cleary
Dicey's Song, C. Voigt
Door in the Wall, M. De Angeli
Gathering of Days, J. Blos
Ginger Pye, E. Estes
Grey King, S. Cooper
Hero and the Crown, R. McKinley
High King, L. Alexander
Invincible Louisa, C. Meigs
Jacob Have I Loved, K. Paterson
Julie of the Wolves, J. George
King of the Wind, M. Henry
M. C. Higgins, the Great,
    V. Hamilton
Miss Hickory, C. Bailey
Mrs. Frisby and the Rats of NIMH,
    R. O'Brien
Rabbit Hill, R. Lawson
Roll of Thunder, Hear My Cry,
    M. Taylor
Sarah, Plain and Tall,
    P. MacLachlan
Slave Dancer, P. Fox
Sounder, W. Armstrong
Strawberry Girl, L. Lenski
Summer of the Swans, B. Byars
21 Balloons, W. DuBois
*Visit to William Blake's Inn: Poems
    for Innocent and Experienced
    Travelers*, N. Willard
Westing Game, E. Raskin

2. **Try some follow-up activities.** Think about following up on what you read. Here are some suggestions:

- Write a summary (page 217). Share it with classmates, friends, or family. Keep a book of summaries for reference.
- Write a book report (pages 215 – 216).
- Keep a list or card file of everything you read.
- Write a letter telling a friend about the work. Can you persuade your friend to read it?
- Illustrate the work with a drawing, collage, or model.
- Keep journal entries as one of the characters.
- Try to "sell" the work to others. You can even develop an ad campaign, complete with a printed ad and a commercial.
- Do some research into the time or place.
- Write a play about one or more of the events.
- Write a play starring one of the characters.
- Appear on a "talk show" as one of the characters.
- Be part of a "readers' theater" and read sections aloud.
- Imagine you are a close friend of one of the characters. Write him or her a letter.
- Brainstorm related writing topics. Explore a few.
- Write a story about one of the characters or events or places.
- Write a story with the same conflict or theme.
- Find out more about the author.
- Read other works by the author.
- Read other works on the subject or theme. Compare them.
- Write a letter to the author, making a comment about the work or asking a question.
- Write a report on one of the topics.

TIPS on What to Do After You Read
- Think about what you read.
- Try some follow-up activities.
- Read more!

Thinking About Audience and Purpose

☐ **Audience** Person or people to whom you are speaking or writing

☐ **Purpose** Reason for speaking or writing

If the Queen is your audience

He took up his brush and went to work. Ben Rogers hove in sight presently — the very boy, of all boys, whose ridicule he had been dreading. . . . Ben said:

"Hello, old chap, you got to work, hey?" . . .

Tom contemplated the boy a bit, and said:

"What do you call work?"

"Why, ain't *that* work?"

Tom resumed his whitewashing, and answered carelessly:

"Well, maybe it is, and maybe it ain't. All I know is, it suits Tom Sawyer."

"Oh, come now, you don't mean to let on that you *like* it?"

The brush continued to move.

"Like it? Well, I don't see why I oughtn't to like it. Does a boy get a chance to whitewash a fence every day?"

That put the thing in a new light. Ben stopped nibbling his apple. Tom swept his brush daintily back and forth — stepped back to note the effect — added a touch here and there — criticized the effect again — Ben watching every move and getting more and more interested, more and more absorbed. Presently he said:

"Say, Tom, let *me* whitewash a little."

Tom Sawyer, Mark Twain

Tom Sawyer had an audience, his friend Ben. He also had a purpose. He wanted to persuade Ben that whitewashing the fence was fun. Then maybe Ben would take over the job and Tom could go off and enjoy a free day!

Whenever you speak or write, you have an audience and purpose too. Decide who and what they are. Then you will be better able to decide what to say and how to say it.

How to Think About Audience

1. **Decide who your audience is.** Your audience may be an individual or a group, a friend or a stranger. Tom Sawyer's audience was Ben, a boy Tom's age and a friend. If Ben had been older or younger or a stranger, Tom might have spoken quite differently. Know exactly who your audience is so that you know exactly how to address them.

How do you address different people when you speak to them? Most audiences are easy. You would probably use Ladies and gentlemen *for a group of adults and* Mr. So-and-so *or* Ms. What's-her-name *for an individual adult. But what would you call the Queen of England? the Prince of Wales? Be prepared!*

- **Queen**
  "Your Majesty," then "Ma'am"
- **King**
  "Your Majesty," then "Sir"
- **Prince**
  "Your Royal Highness" (if of royal blood)
  "Your Highness" (otherwise)
  Then "Sir"
- **Princess**
  "Your Royal Highness" (if of royal blood)
  "Your Highness" (otherwise)
  Then "Ma'am"
- **Earl**
  "My Lord" or "Lord Jones"
- **Countess**
  "Madam" or "Lady Jones"
- **Duke**
  "Your Grace" or "Sir"
- **Duchess**
  "Your Royal Highness" (if of royal blood) or "Ma'am"
  "Your Grace" (otherwise) or "Ma'am"

Audience and Advertising

Advertisers have to know their audiences too. Who buys jeans? Who buys pick-up trucks? Who buys chocolate-flavored cereal?

Here are questions that help advertisers target an audience.

1. How old are they?
2. Are they male or female?
3. What do they look like? Height? Size? Coloring?
4. Where do they live? Cold climate or warm? Country, city, or suburb? North, South, East, or West?
5. How much money do they make?
6. What work do they do?
7. How educated are they?
8. Do they own a car? What kind?
9. Are they married?
10. Do they have children? How many? How old?
11. Do they have a pet? What kind?
12. What language do they speak at home?
13. What foods do they eat most? least? not at all?
14. How often do they eat out? Where do they eat?
15. Where do they shop?
16. What do they do in their spare time?
17. How often do they watch TV? What do they watch?
18. What do they read?
19. What sports do they enjoy?
20. What music do they like?
21. What do they care about?
22. What do they worry about?

2. **Picture your audience.**   Tom spoke face-to-face with Ben. When you write, however, you cannot see your audience. You may not even know the people who will read what you write. In that case, make them up. Picture real people — what they look like and how they are dressed. Then "talk" to your imaginary audience. Your writing will be livelier and more focused.

3. **Think about what your audience knows.**   Would Tom try the same approach on the town judge? If so, he would probably fail, because the judge knows a lot more about people than Ben does. What does your audience know? What information do they have? What experience do they have? Answer questions like these as you plan what to say.

4. **Think about what your audience does *not* know.**   Ben did not know that Tom really hated his job. To achieve his purpose, Tom wisely kept the information to himself. Usually, however, you will want to share information with your audience. What don't they know about your topic? What do they need to know to understand? Explain words, background, and other details.

| TO A GROUP OF BUILDERS | Then we whitewashed the walls. |
| TO AN AVERAGE AUDIENCE | Then we whitewashed the walls. That is, we whitened them by applying a mixture of lime and water. |

5. **Think about what your audience wants to know.**   Ben might have been interested in some tips on whitewashing. What will your audience be interested in? The more interested they are, the closer attention they will pay.

6. **Match your language to your audience.**   Tom was speaking to a friend his own age, so he used everyday, informal language. If he had been speaking to the town judge, his style would probably have been more formal. Choose the language style that is right for your audience. (See pages 162 – 163.)

| TO A FRIEND | "What a pain! I've gotta paint the fence." |
| TO AN ADULT | "I'm afraid I have to paint the fence." |

How to Think About Purpose

Some Synonyms for *purpose*

aim
goal
objective
target
intention
mission
ambition
intention
plan

1. **Know your purpose.** Tom's purpose was to *persuade* Ben to help him. The most common purposes for speaking or writing are listed below. You may have a combination of these purposes.

PURPOSES FOR SPEAKING AND WRITING

To inform
To tell about something — to explain it, define it, describe it, or give some other kind of information about it

EXAMPLE "How to Whitewash a Fence"

To persuade
To try to convince someone to do something or believe something

EXAMPLE "Why You Should White-wash a Fence"

To entertain
To try to move your audience by making them feel amused, fascinated, frightened, or even sad

EXAMPLE "The Day I Whitewashed My Little Brother"

To express yourself
To share things that are important to you or that move you

EXAMPLE Poem about "A Freshly Whitewashed Fence"

---

2. **Choose details that support your purpose.** To persuade someone, find good reasons. To inform someone, find the right facts. (See page 148.)

TIPS on Audience and Purpose

- Ask yourself who your audience is. Picture them.
- Think about what your audience knows and does not know.
- Think about what your audience wants or needs to know.
- Match your language to your audience.
- Decide what your purpose is.
  To inform? To persuade? To entertain? To express yourself?
- Choose details that support your purpose.

Listening

"Telephone"

Test how carefully people listen by playing a game of "telephone" with a group of friends. Make up a sentence full of colorful details. Whisper it to one person, who will whisper it to another, who will whisper it to another, and so on until everyone has heard it. Then have the last person say it aloud. Is it still the same sentence?

᭰᭟᭰

It takes two to speak the truth — one to speak, and another to listen.

— Henry David Thoreau

Why listen carefully?

Picture a man wearing overalls and carrying a shovel over his shoulder. He is talking to some people dressed in fancy clothes. "Garden party?" he says. "I thought you said *gardening* party!"

• **Listening**   Paying careful attention to words or sounds

> As I was going to St. Ives,
> I met a man with seven wives.
> Each wife had seven sacks.
> Each sack had seven cats.
> Each cat had seven kits.
> Kits, cats, sacks, wives —
> How many were going to St. Ives?

Have you ever tried this brain teaser on anyone? If so, you know that the right answer depends not on careful arithmetic but on careful listening. While some people are counting wives, sacks, cats, and kits and multiplying by seven, the good listener already has the answer: one. *Met* is the key word. Only *I* was going to St. Ives. The others were probably headed in the opposite direction.

How to Listen

1. **Concentrate.**   Do not let your mind wander. Block out other thoughts or sounds by concentrating on what is important.

2. **Listen for main ideas and key words.**   Pick out the important points as you listen. Repeat them to yourself.

3. **Watch the speaker.**   Speakers "talk" with their bodies as well as their voices. Gestures and facial expressions add meaning.

4. **Think while you listen.**   Ask: What does that mean? How do I feel about that? What do I want to say to the speaker?

5. **Picture what you hear.**   The St. Ives brain teaser fools people who do not picture what is said.

TIPS for Listening

- Concentrate.
- Listen for main ideas and key words.
- Watch the speaker's body language.
- Think.
- Picture what you hear.

Telling a Story

☐ **Storytelling**   Orally telling a set of events in a creative, interesting way

> There was once a Princess, famous for her beauty, who had been so spoiled by her doting father that she had grown vain and proud, thinking only of herself and demanding that her every wish be immediately fulfilled. . . .
>
> — *The Singing Ringing Tree*, Selina Hastings

What will the princess demand? Will a prince arrive? Will the spoiled princess learn her lesson? If you began to wonder what might happen, you were already caught in the storyteller's net.

There have always been stories and people to tell them. Before people could read or write, they told stories to explain things, to teach things, and to entertain one another. In fact, Hastings is retelling a story that is hundreds of years old.

A good story is exciting for both listener and teller. Have you ever told a story and felt your audience hanging on to your words?

How to Tell a Story

1. **Plan the main events.**   Every story has a beginning, a middle, and an end (pages 185 – 189). Plan the order of events with the help of a story map — a list of events in the order in which they happen (pages 22 – 23). Then check that the order makes sense. Below is an example.

Story Map

BEGINNING: Spoiled princess introduced

1. Spoiled princess demands pet elephant
2. Elephant brought
3. Princess demands palace for elephant
4. Luxurious palace built
5. Child finds wounded bat and asks if it can live in palace until healed
6. Princess tosses out bat
7. Bat turns into prince

END: Princess stamps foot and demands prince come back, but he walks away

---

Where Do You Find Good Stories?

Selina Hastings was retelling a very old story when she wrote *The Singing Ringing Tree*. Here are some books in which you can find stories to retell.

TALES FROM
AROUND THE WORLD

American Tall Tales, A. Stoutenburg
Arrow to the Sun: A Pueblo Indian Tale, G. McDermott
Best-Loved Folktales of the World, J. Cole, ed.
Bringing the Rain to Kapiti Plain: A Nandi Tale, V. Aardema
Cow-Tail Switch and Other West African Stories, H. Courlander and G. Herzog
Dancing Kettle and Other Japanese Folk Tales, Y. Uchida
Fables of Aesop, J. Jacobs, ed.
Girl Who Cried Flowers and Other Tales, J. Yolen
Grandmother Stories of the Northwest, Nashone
Italian Folktales, I. Calvino
Magic Orange Tree and Other Haitian Folktales, D. Wolkstein
Mexican Folk Tales, A. Campos
People Could Fly: American Black Folktales, V. Hamilton
Sea of Gold and Other Tales from Japan, Y. Uchida
Tall Tale America, W. Blair

More Sources for Stories

FAIRY TALES

Black Fairy Tales, T. Berger
Hans Christian Andersen's Fairy Tales, H. C. Andersen
Tales from Grimm, W. Gag

ANCIENT MYTHS

Adventures of the Greek Heroes, McLean and Wiseman
Book of Greek Myths, I. and E. D'Aulaire
Children of Odin: Book of Northern Myths, P. Colum
D'Aulaire's Norse Gods and Giants, I. and E. D'Aulaire
Greek Gods and Heroes, R. Graves
Mythology, E. Hamilton

SCARY STORIES

Ghost Stories, F. Dixon
Great Ghost Stories, B. Schwartz, ed.
Scary Stories to Tell in the Dark, A. Schwartz
Science Fiction's Greatest Monsters, D. Cohen
Tales for the Midnight Hour, J. Stamper

Spin a Yarn

Fill a box with a collection of odd items, such as a toothpaste tube, a jar of peanut butter, an alarm clock, a book, a stuffed toy. Close your eyes and pick three items out of the box. Then spin them into a story.

2. **Tie up loose ends.** Plan your ending. Tell what happened to the main characters. Did they change or stay the same? get what they deserved? live happily ever after? Don't leave events dangling or you will leave your listeners unhappy.

3. **Watch a "movie" of your story.** The more vivid a picture you have, the more vivid your story will be. Close your eyes and picture the scene. Imagine how things look, feel, sound. Get to know your characters — what they wear, what color hair they have, what their faces look like, how they move and sound. Watch a "movie" of your story in your mind.

4. **Choose vivid words and details.** Help your listeners see and hear the events. Use words that tell color, shape, size, smell, feelings, and action (pages 167–168). Use words that sound like what they mean: *slam, pow, ouch, creak* (page 167). Compare things with other things. For example, later in the Hastings story, a prince brings "pearls as big as nectarines."

5. **Use your voice.** Telling a story is like being all the characters in a play at once. Give each character a voice. Speak softly in scary parts and loudly in exciting ones. Slow down and speed up to keep your listeners listening.

6. **Use your face and body.** Move around to show what is happening. Show how your characters look, move, and gesture. Lean forward in exciting parts.

7. **Practice.** Practice in front of a mirror to get your movements and gestures just right. Practice telling the story to whoever will listen. Ask for suggestions.

TIPS for Telling a Story

- Plan the main events. Make a story map.
- Tie up loose ends.
- Watch a "movie" of the story in your mind.
- Choose vivid words and details.
- Use your voice.
- Use your face and body.
- Practice.

Giving a Speech

☐ **Speech**   Oral composition presented to an audience

> Good evening. I want to acquaint you with a habit that fosters creativity. You might use it when you start to write your next speech. The good thing about it is that it's simple and requires no effort . . . except, of course, doing it! . . . What is involved? Literally, nothing! I call it the "nothing habit." Let me give you some examples of how great thinkers have used it.
>
> — Robert P. Paashaus

Would you like to know more about a way to get ideas that is simple and requires no effort? Robert Paashaus wanted to convince the audience to try the "nothing habit" — a method that worked for him. By making it sound so easy and giving it a catchy name, he caught his audience's attention.

How to Prepare a Speech

1. **Choose a topic that interests you.**   Can you hear Robert Paashaus's enthusiasm? He is excited about the "nothing habit," and his excitement comes through. If your topic is interesting to you, you can make it interesting to others.

2. **Know your subject.**   The more you know about a subject, the easier it is to talk about it. Read about your subject in an encyclopedia. Ask other people what they know or think about it.

3. **Think about your purpose and audience.**   Do you want to persuade? inform? entertain? express yourself? What do your listeners know? What don't they know? How do they feel about the topic? Should you use formal or informal language? (See pages 119–121, 162–163.)

4. **Plan.**   Think about what you want to say. Making an outline will help you plan (page 211).

5. **Think of a good beginning.**   You can begin with a striking example or incident. You can also begin, as Robert Paashaus did, by showing listeners how your subject will help them.

It usually takes more than three weeks to plan a good impromptu speech!
— Mark Twain

Follow the "Tell Them" Plan

Good speakers introduce what they are going to say, say it, and then review it. They follow the "Tell them" plan:

- Tell them what you are going to tell them.
- Tell it to them.
- Tell them what you have told them.

Teaser Topics

Challenge yourself or someone else to speak for one minute on one of these topics!

Growing Caterpillars in Siberia
Playing Basketball on the Moon
The Difference Between Alarm Clocks and Peanut Butter
My Life as a Bottle Cap Tester
Why Lamps Need Erasers
Teaching a Shark to Knit
Fridays in the Swamp
Tarantulas I Have Known and Loved

6. **Think of a good ending.**   Here are some ways to end a speech.
   a. Give a summary of important points.
   b. Suggest something listeners can do.
   c. Give an interesting example, incident, or quotation.
   d. Give listeners something to think about.

7. **Prepare note cards.**   Write your main ideas and key words on note cards. Use the cards as prompts. Do not write out your speech. If you do, you will sound like a robot.

8. **Practice, practice, practice.**   Give your speech to your dog, the mirror, your parents, a friend. Do not memorize it.

How to Deliver a Speech

1. **Stand straight.**   Put your weight on both feet. Do not sway. Think about your opening, take a deep breath, and begin.

2. **Speak slowly and clearly.**   Speak loudly enough to be heard, but do not shout. HINT: Ask a friend in the back to signal if you are not speaking clearly or loudly enough.

3. **Look at your audience.**   Search out people who look interested and speak to them. Make eye contact.

4. **Show enthusiasm.**   Look and sound interested. Smile.

TIPS for Giving a Speech

PREPARING A SPEECH
- Choose a subject that interests you.
- Know your subject.
- Identify your purpose and audience.
- Make a plan. Plan a specific beginning and ending.
- Prepare note cards to prompt you.
- Practice, practice, practice.

DELIVERING A SPEECH
- Stand straight.
- Speak slowly and clearly.
- Look at your audience.
- Show enthusiasm.

Having a Discussion

☐ Discussing — Talking about a subject within a group

"We're supposed to think of a class project. I think it should have something to do with the environment."

"Like what? Cleaning up the air?"

"How about water? I read about a class someplace that adopted a brook. They cleaned it up and took water samples and kept a record of what lived there. They noticed something funny, and it turned out that a factory was dumping stuff in their brook. That was illegal, so they got it stopped."

"It doesn't have to be a brook, does it? There's the pond over by the park."

"It doesn't even have to be water. What about the vacant lot on Fourth Street? . . ."

You may have heard the saying *Two heads are better than one*. Discussions are based on that idea. In a discussion, several people share ideas on a particular subject and decide which ones are best. Ideally, everybody contributes and everybody gains.

Group Games

A good discussion follows certain rules, and so does a good game. Try one of these with a group of friends.

WHAT'S YOUR FAVORITE FOOD?

Choose a leader. The leader makes a list of famous names. Then he or she calls each person by a name and asks, "What's your favorite food?" The person must answer with a food that has the same initials as the name. Anyone who does not think of an answer in four seconds is out.

Here are some examples:

— What's your favorite food, Charlie Brown? Crisp bananas.
— What's your favorite food, George Bush? Gooey brownies.
— What's your favorite food, Princess Diana? Pickled doughnuts.
—What's your favorite food, Bill Cosby? Baked cantaloupe.

WHO WANTS TO BE PRESIDENT?

One player thinks of a real person he or she would like to be. The other players ask questions that must be answered yes or no. If they do not guess who the person is in twenty questions, the same player gets to choose a person again.

How to Have a Discussion

1. **Know the subject.**   Before the discussion, you might want to read or speak to people about the subject. Explaining the subject is a good way to start a discussion. Ask questions about anything you do not understand. (You are probably not the only one who does not understand it.)

2. **Know the purpose.**   Here are the three most common purposes of a discussion and the steps involved in carrying them out.

CARRYING OUT YOUR PURPOSE

To make a decision
Gather suggestions.
Discuss the reasons for and against each suggestion.
Agree on the best decision.

To explain or analyze
Gather facts.
Consider the importance of each fact.
Agree on which facts are the most important.

To solve a problem
State the problem.
Brainstorm possible solutions.
Discuss the good and bad points of each solution.
Agree on an action.

---

3. **Stick to the point.**   Comments and examples are helpful only if you can connect them directly to the topic.

4. **Listen to others.**   Pay attention to what others say. Do not interrupt. Respond to the last comment before you make a new one. Say something like, "I see your point, but I think . . ."

5. **Ask questions.**   You can contribute to a discussion simply by asking someone to explain something you do not understand.

6. **Be polite.**   If you have something to say, say it to the group. If you disagree with something, do so politely.

How to Lead a Discussion

1. **Keep the discussion moving.** Invite different people to speak.

   "Anthony, do you think we could clean up the vacant lot?"

2. **Keep track of the main points.** Jot them down or ask someone near you to do it.

3. **Keep the discussion on the subject.** Do not get off the track.

   "That's a great story, Melissa, but we need to finish talking about the vacant lot now."

4. **Do not take sides.** Treat everyone with respect.

   "Both Jerome and Wanda have interesting ideas, but we can't accept them both. Let's look at Jerome's first, and then we'll talk about Wanda's."

5. **Help people come to an agreement.** That is why you are there.

   "Well, we've looked at both ideas pretty closely. Why don't we list the advantages and disadvantages of each one on the board and then take a vote."

6. **Watch the time.** Leave time to summarize and tie up things. Then people will feel they have accomplished something.

TIPS on Having a Discussion

AS A MEMBER
- Know your subject.
- Know your purpose. Is it to make a decision? to explain something? to solve a problem?
- Stick to the point.
- Listen to others.
- Ask questions.
- Be polite.

AS A LEADER
- Keep the talk moving.
- Keep track of ideas.
- Keep to the subject.
- Do not take sides.
- Help people come to an agreement.
- Watch the time.

Interviewing

On Interviewing Celebrities

Barbara Walters has probably interviewed more famous people on TV than any other interviewer in the world. Here is her advice on interviewing a celebrity.

You can safely begin a conversation with any famous person — or with anyone at all, for that matter — by indulging your natural impulse to express admiration. People tend to say flattering things to celebrities they don't even like, just to get a good look at them, and celebrities are well aware of this, but you're going to be different. Don't gush, don't take so long to say it that the smile begins to hurt [the celebrity's] face, and try to avoid empty superlatives, such as *just loved, marvelous, fabulous, fantastic,* and *divine.*

— Barbara Walters, *How to Talk with Practically Anybody About Practically Anything*

☐ **Interview**   A question-and-answer conversation for a purpose

Q. Are Soviet students different from American students?

A. They seem to work harder than Americans my age — or at least they have more planned time than play time. They go to school five and a half days a week, including Saturdays. Ugh! They study another language, usually English or German. They probably are not smarter than we are, but they might be learning and studying more.

— Gail Greco interviewing Samantha Smith, 1985, *Cobblestone* magazine

In 1983, eleven-year-old Samantha Smith of Manchester, Maine, wrote to Yuri Andropov, then general chairman of the Soviet Union, about world peace. To her surprise, Andropov invited her and her parents to visit Russia as his guests.

Reporter Gail Greco interviewed Samantha. In an interview, the person doing the interviewing asks questions of another person. An interview is a good way to find out about a person or a topic. To get the right information, however, the interviewer has to ask the right questions.

How to Conduct an Interview

1. **Plan. Know your purpose.**   An interview is *about* something. There is a reason for interviewing the person. Gail Greco wanted to know what Samantha Smith observed in the Soviet Union. She asked questions that would bring out Samantha's observations. When you interview, decide exactly what you want to find out. Then you will know what questions to ask.

2. **Plan. Inform yourself.**   Get as much information as you can beforehand. The more you know about the person and the topic, the sharper your questions will be and the more comfortable you will feel. Gail Greco got information about Samantha's trip from newspaper stories. Background information can also come from encyclopedias and other reference books (pages 60 – 65) and from talking to people.

3. **Plan. Write out key questions.** Brainstorm questions to ask and choose the best ones. Use your list of questions in the interview. You may want to leave space after each question for the answers. Here are some question guidelines.

What Kinds of Questions to Ask

- Questions that are specific, brief, and clear

  TOO GENERAL   What were the Soviet people like?

  MORE SPECIFIC   How were the Soviets like Americans?

- Questions that cannot be answered simply yes or no

  POOR   Did you like the Soviet people?

  BETTER   What did you like best about the Soviets?

- Questions that will bring out the information you want

---

4. **Be polite.** Make an appointment for the interview and be on time. Introduce yourself and state the purpose of the interview. Thank the person afterward.

5. **Listen!** Don't be in such a hurry to ask your next question that you miss the answer to the one you just asked. If you do miss an answer, apologize and ask the person to repeat it. Look at the person as much as possible.

6. **Ask follow-up questions.** Ask "Why?" or "How?" or other questions to get more information and to show you are interested. Ask for examples or explanations. Stick to the topics you decided on, but follow interesting leads.

7. **Keep a record.** Tape-record the interview if you can. Otherwise, take notes on main ideas and comments you want to quote. Be sure to quote accurately.

TIPS on Interviewing

BEFORE THE INTERVIEW
- Know your purpose.
- Do your homework.
- Write out key questions.

DURING THE INTERVIEW
- Be polite.
- Listen!
- Ask follow-up questions.
- Keep a record.

Zany Interviews

THE "THE-LESS" INTERVIEW

A common word such as *the, a, this, that* is not allowed to be used by the person being interviewed. See how long the person can last without saying the forbidden word!

Suppose *the* is forbidden. The interview might go like this.

Q. *When did you decide to become a clown?*
A. *Decision was really made first time I saw circus, at age of six. Make-up on the — oops!*

THE "I'M NOT MYSELF" INTERVIEW

One person answers interview questions as if he or she were another person in the room or a famous person. Others try to guess who is being interviewed.

Or . . . Everyone sits in a circle and answers interview questions as if he or she were the person on the left.

Answers NOT to Use

Q. How did you find the weather on your trip?
A. I just went outside and there it was!

Q. Did it take you long to become a hairdresser?
A. No, I took all the shortcuts.

Q. Where were you born?
A. Wyoming.
Q. What part?
A. All of me!

Q. How do you carve wood?
A. Whittle by whittle.

Q. Why did you become a printer?
A. I was the right type.

Following and Giving Instructions

More Riddle Tips

1. Start with a list of words on some subject.
   EXAMPLE "pig" words

2. Find words that rhyme with words in your list. (Use a rhyming dictionary.)
   EXAMPLE *fig* and *pig*

3. Replace the rhyming word with your word and use that as your riddle answer.
   EXAMPLE Use *pig* for *fig*.

4. Make up a riddle with that word in the answer.
   EXAMPLE What is a pig's favorite snack? A *Pig* Newton!

* * *

1. Pick a famous person, place, or thing and divide the name into syllables.
   EXAMPLE *Al-bert Ein-stein*

2. Find a word on your list that rhymes with one of the syllables and substitute your word for that syllable.
   EXAMPLE *Al-bert SWINE-stein*

3. Use your made-up word as the answer to your riddle.
   EXAMPLE What pig was a famous scientist? Albert *Swine*stein!

— Adapted from *Funny Side Up!* Mike Thaler

☐ Instructions Directions telling how to do something

    It's easy to make up your own riddles. First, pick a subject. Then list all the words you can think of on that subject. (A thesaurus, an encyclopedia, or a book on the subject can help you.) For example, suppose your subject is pigs. Then you might come up with a list like this one.

hog   boar swine sow swill slop   snort snout
grunt oink pen   mud ham sausage hock pork

    Next, take any word on the list and drop the first letter or first two letters. For example, if you drop the *h* on *ham*, you get *am*. Now use the dictionary to find words beginning with *am*.

America amnesia ambush ambulance

Put the *h* from *ham* back on each word and you have your riddle answers. As your last step, all you have to do is think of some riddle questions to go with the answers.

In what country are pigs free? *Ham*erica!
What do you call it when a pig loses his memory? *Ham*nesia!
What do you call it when some pigs attack you? A *ham*bush!
How do you take a pig to the hospital? In a *ham*bulance!

— Adapted from *Funny Side Up!* Mike Thaler

After reading these instructions, could you create your own riddles? If you read carefully, you probably could, for Mike Thaler gives you clear, easy steps to follow.

How to Follow Instructions

1. **Concentrate.** If you miss a step or sometimes even a word, you may not be able to carry out the instructions.

2. **Pay attention to the order.** One step depends on another, so pay attention to the number and order of steps. Words like *first, then, next, now, last* will help you.

3. **Picture each step.** Go over each step in your mind. Do you understand it? How does it follow from the step before? How does it lead to the next step? Can you do it?

4. **Review all the steps.** Imagine yourself following the instructions. Can you carry them out?

5. **Clear up what you don't understand.** Ask questions if you can. Do some research if needed. Try to work out problems.

6. **Take notes.** Notes will help you remember and follow long or complicated instructions.

How to Give Instructions

1. **Put yourself in your audience's place.** Who is your audience? What do they need to know to follow your instructions? What words do you need to explain?

2. **Plan.** Divide the task into separate steps. List the steps. Then imagine you are carrying out the instructions. Have you given all the necessary steps? Have you put them in order? Have you listed any materials that are needed?

3. **State your purpose.** Tell what the instructions are for.

4. **Give the steps in order.** Use words such as *first, then, next, finally* to make the order clear. (See pages 154, 157).

5. **Don't skip any steps.** Each step should lead to the next.

6. **Include all needed information.** Tell your audience everything they need to know to carry out the steps.

7. **Give examples.** If your instructions are complicated, examples will help your audience understand them.

Give These Instructions

How to make tacos
How to ride a unicycle
How to read a totem pole
How to take good photographs
How to talk to animals
How to milk a cow
How to memorize
How to pitch a tent
How to make a friend
How to lose a friend
How to catch a rainbow trout
How to steal bases
How to fly a kite
How to make a kite
How to juggle
How to put out a grease fire
How to treat a cut
How to stop hiccups
How to audition

Now Try Telling . . .

How to walk on the ceiling
How to spin a web
How to weigh a building
How to teach a snake to bark
How to walk to Mars
How to trap a cloud
How to brush a shark's teeth
How to melt a mountain
How to spy on a dinosaur

TIPS on Instructions

FOLLOWING INSTRUCTIONS
- Concentrate.
- Pay attention to the order.
- Picture each step.
- Review all the steps.
- Clear up problems.
- Take notes.

GIVING INSTRUCTIONS
- Know your audience.
- Plan. Picture each step.
- State your purpose.
- Give the steps in order.
- Give all the steps.
- Give all needed information.
- Give examples.

Following and Giving Instructions | **133**

The Writing Process

Where does our alphabet come from?

A
Egyptians, 3000 B.C.
  Stood for "ox"
Semites, 1500 B.C.
  Called *aleph*, "ox"
Phoenicians, 1000 B.C.
  Simplified the symbol
Greeks, 600 B.C.
  Called symbol *alpha*
Romans, A.D. 114

B
Egyptians, 3000 B.C.
  Stood for "house"
Semites, 1500 B.C.
  Called *beth*, "house"
Phoenicians, 1000 B.C.
  Drew doorway on house
Greeks, 600 B.C.
  Called symbol *beta*
Romans, A.D. 114

- *Alphabet* comes from the Greek names for the first two letters: *alpha* + *beth*

!!!

- If you used the original meanings of the letters, *alphabet* would mean "ox house"!

Prewriting

☐ **Prewriting**   Gathering and organizing ideas for a composition

You know by now that when you write, you do not just pick up your pencil and begin. Writing is a process, a series of steps that actually starts in your head, not on a piece of paper.

As a first step, any writer has to think of ideas and then choose one to write about. The writer above was asked to write about something important to her. She decided to try clustering. She wrote down *Something important to me* and followed the flow of her thoughts. Eventually they did lead her to a good writing idea — the problem of abandoned pets.

How to Prewrite

1. **Look for a topic.** The first place to look for a topic is inside your own mind. (See pages 3 – 6.) Clustering is one way to start your search, as you saw on the previous page. Try the mind-opening techniques below. Whichever you use, let the ideas flow out freely and collect as many ideas as you can.

Ways to Collect Ideas

Brainstorm (page 3)	Recall (pages 7 – 8)
Freewrite (page 4)	Talk to people
Cluster (page 5)	Read, use radio and TV
List (page 6)	Observe (pages 9 – 10)
Question (page 51)	Keep a journal

Keeping a journal is more than just a way of getting writing topics. By jotting down observations each day, you can keep in touch with your thoughts and hold on to special memories.

2. **Choose a topic.** Look over all the ideas you have collected. Choose a writing topic that fits the following guidelines:

How to Choose a Topic

Choose a topic that fits the assignment.
Choose a topic that interests you.
Choose a topic that you know about or can find out about.
Choose a topic that you can cover in your composition.

---

3. **Explore your topic.** Exploring your topic means discovering what there is to say about it. Use the library. Also use the techniques listed in item 1 to come up with thoughts and facts on the topic. Furthermore, try cubing and drawing, explained on the next page.

Taking a Personal Inventory

Look inside yourself for ideas. Take a *personal inventory.* Jot down as many answers as you can to questions like these:

Things you know and do

What do I know a lot about?
What do I like to do?
What do I like to read about?
What do I do outside school?
What do I do on vacation?
What can I fix or put together?
What could I teach somebody?
What would I like to learn how to do?
What are my favorite books? TV programs? movies? Why?

People

Who are the people closest to me — friends? relatives?
Who are other people I know?
Who are people I would like to know?
Who are people I want to be like? Why?
Who are people I do not want to be like? Why?
What fictional characters would I like as friends? Why?
If I were producing a movie of _____ (a book or story you like), whom would I choose to play the roles? Why?
Who is the funniest person I know? the nicest? the oldest? the youngest? the strangest?

People who keep journals live twice.
— *Jessamyn West*

More Personal Inventory Questions

Places

What places have I visited?

What places would I like to visit? Why?

What kinds of places do I find interesting? Why?

What would my dream room look like?

What would my dream country or city be like?

If I could live anywhere in the universe, where would I live? Why?

Firsts

What is the earliest thing I can remember?

What was my first day at school like?

What was my first trip to the dentist like?

What was my first taste of _____ (your favorite food) like?

What was my first big achievement?

What was my first big disappointment?

When was the first time I broke something?

Who was my first friend?

a. Cubing. Make a cube or draw six squares. On each side or square, write one of these instructions: *Describe it, Compare it, Associate it, Analyze it, Apply it, Argue for or against it.* Then take one instruction at a time and write about your topic, answering questions like those below. Use your imagination as well as your knowledge, and write both silly and serious answers.

Cubing Questions

- **Describe it.** What does it look like? feel like? smell like? sound like? taste like?
- **Compare it.** What is it like? What is it different from?
- **Associate it.** What does it remind you of? What does it make you think of? What is it related to?
- **Analyze it.** What are its parts? What is it made of?
- **Apply it.** What does it do? How might you use it?
- **Argue for or against it.** Is it good or is it bad? Why? Are you in favor of it? Why? Are you against it? Why?

---

b. Drawing Draw pictures or sketches to help you fill in the details about objects, places, and people you want to write about. Draw cartoons of events.

4. **Choose the best ideas.** Go over your exploring notes. Cross out unrelated ideas. Add any new ideas that occur to you.

5. **Organize your ideas.** Mark main ideas and details to identify them (pages 147 – 150). Then make a plan, using a spider map (page 25), chart (page 25), or outline (page 211).

   a. Charts Charts are helpful for organizing stories, narratives, and descriptions (pages 123, 165, 168).

b. Outlines For a one-paragraph composition, list the main idea and then the details in the best order (pages 151–154). For a longer composition, arrange the ideas into main topics, subtopics, and details, as shown below. List the main topics with Roman numerals, the subtopics with capital letters, and the details with numbers.

Outline

I. Problem of abandoned pets
   A. Many thousands each year
   B. Fate of abandoned pets
      1. Animal shelters — often put to sleep
      2. Struggle along or die
II. What to do
   A. Neutering
   B. Adoption of older pets
   C. Support of animal groups and shelters

---

6. **Know your audience and purpose.** Be clear about why you are writing and for whom. (See pages 119–121.)

TIPS on Prewriting

- **Look for a topic.**
  Brainstorm. Freewrite. Cluster. Make lists. Ask questions. Recall. Talk to people. Read. Use radio and TV. Observe. Keep a journal.
- **Choose a topic**
  That fits the assignment.
  That interests you.
  That you know about or can find out about.
  That is narrow enough to cover in your composition.
- **Explore your topic.**
  Get information from the library.
  Use the techniques under "Look for a topic," plus drawing and cubing.
- **Make a plan.**
  Choose the best ideas.
  Put ideas In an order that makes sense.
  Make a map, chart, or outline.
  Identify your audience and purpose.

. . . And Still More Personal Inventory Questions

Things to Think About

What would I change if I could?

What do I want to stay the same?

What kind of person do I want to be?

What do I want to be doing in 10 years? 30 years? 50 years?

What do I admire? approve of?

What do I dislike? disapprove of?

If I met the President of the United States, what would I say?

If I were President of the United States, what would I do?

What recent events made me happy? unhappy?

Why do bad things happen?

What do I like about TV? What do I dislike about TV?

If I were a TV producer, what would I do a show about?

Things to Find Out

How far away is the moon?

How did writing begin?

How many different kinds of spiders are there?

Did houses always have windows?

What is the history of pizza?

How did cameras develop?

How do trees grow?

How do you keep an iguana as a pet?

What and where is Timbuktu?

How many active volcanoes are there? Where are they?

Was there a real Count Dracula?

The Writing Process

Drafting

☐ **Draft**   An early version of a composition

> There are millions of stray animals in this country every year. Only a ~~tiny frac~~ few wandered away from home. Most have been dumped or delibritely abandoned.
>
> Why do people abandon cats? Every year, many thousands of pets are dumped by awful people who don't want them anymore. The lucky ones end up in animal shelters. People don't think when they get a cute kitten that it will be a cat and live for fifteen years and need it's litter box emptied. So they figure cats can get by on there own. So they just abandon it. A lot of the dead animals on highways are because they were left along the road by heartless, cruel, thoughtless people.
>
> I got my cat Puff that way. Everybody thinks he's beautiful. He has long hair white with pale gold spots, and playful and affecsionate. But you wouldn't think so when I found him. He was hungry and cold and dirty. And full of grease from sleeping under cars. He had been dumped by his previous owners. (Add ending)

After you have a topic and a plan, it is time to write. Put pen to paper and go. Don't try to write a perfect draft. Don't even stop to correct mistakes. Just get your ideas on paper. Once you have a draft, then you can fiddle with words, sentences, and ideas.

How to Write a First Draft

1. **Work from your prewriting notes.** Use your outline or chart as a guide. You may add or change ideas if new thoughts occur to you as you write. Always keep your audience and purpose in mind. (See pages 119 – 121.)

2. **Let the words flow out.** Write quickly. Don't worry about being messy. Cross out words, use abbreviations, leave blank spaces, move things around, if necessary, but keep writing. Do not stop to fix mistakes.

3. **Start anywhere.** If you can't think of a good beginning, start in the middle, or write the ending first. Write separate sections, if you like, and then put them together later.

4. **Jump around if necessary.** If your ideas are coming too fast for your pencil (or word processor), make a few notes and go on to the next idea. You can always come back.

5. **Do more prewriting.** If you get stuck, go back and use some prewriting techniques. A new idea or detail may be enough to get you going again. Sometimes you will need to adjust your plan or come up with a new one. Once in a while, you may even have to start over and choose another topic.

6. **Write on every other line.** Give yourself room to think. Skip a line as you write. Then you can make changes more easily.

7. **Put your draft aside.** Put away the draft for a day or even a few hours. Then you can look at it with fresher eyes.

TIPS for Writing a First Draft

- Work from your prewriting notes.
- Let the words flow out.
- Start anywhere. Jump around if necessary.
- Do more prewriting if you need more ideas.
- Write on every other line.
- Put your draft aside for a time.

The Writing Process

Your Turn

Go through the How to's and the Tips. Then come back and figure out why the student made the changes she did in her composition.

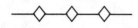

Every writer should own a wastebasket.
— *E. M. Forster*

I have never thought of myself as a good writer. . . . But I'm one of the world's great rewriters.
— *James Michener*

Revising Goals

- Clearly expressed ideas
- Well-organized ideas
- Ideas that support the topic
- Varied, interesting sentences

Revising

☐ **Revising**   Making changes to improve

> There are millions of stray animals in this country every year. Only a ~~tiny frac~~ few wandered away from home. Most have been ~~dumped or~~ deliberitely abandoned.
>
> Why do people abandon cats? ~~Every year, many thousands of pets are dumped by awful people who don't want them any more.~~ The lucky ones end up in animal shelters. People ~~don't~~ do not always think when they get a cute kitten that it will ~~be a cat and live~~ become a demanding cat who lives for fifteen years and need it's litter box emptied. So they figure cats can get by on there own, so they just abandon it. ~~A lot of the dead animals on highways are because they were left along the road by heartless, cruel, thoughtless people.~~ Most of the others suffer and starve. ~~I got my cat Puff that way.~~ Everybody thinks he's beautiful. ~~He has~~ long hair white with pale gold spots, and My cat Puff ^ playful and ~~he is~~ affecksionate. ~~But you wouldn't think so~~ when I found him, though, he ~~He~~ was hungry and cold ~~and dirty.~~ And full of grease from sleeping under cars. He had been ~~dumped by his previous owners~~ abandoned.

When you revise, you shape your early drafts into a finished product. You cross out, add, and shift material around until the composition says what you want it to say.

How to Revise

1. **Reread with a fresh eye.** Revise means "see again." When you see your draft again, try to see it as if it were someone else's. What is good? What could be better? What should go?

2. **Consider audience and purpose.** How can you make your composition appeal to your audience more? How can you make it achieve its purpose better? (See pages 119 – 121.)

3. **Outline what you wrote.** If the outline does not hold together, the draft will not either. Make needed changes.

4. **Find another eye.** If possible, exchange drafts with a classmate. Otherwise, ask a friend or relative for comments. Ask questions, and listen to the answers and suggestions. Make changes that will improve your composition.

5. **Expand your best ideas.** Develop interesting parts and descriptions with more details, examples, and incidents.

6. **Cut out unnecessary parts.** Take out repeated ideas. Take out points that do not relate to the main idea (page 155).

7. **Check your writing style.** Ask yourself questions like these:

   Which short, choppy sentences could be combined?
   Which long, complicated sentences should be broken up?
   Where can I use vivid words instead of dull ones?
   How can I vary my sentence beginnings? sentence structure?

8. **Use a checklist.** See the checklist on page 142.

TIPS for Revising

- Reread with a fresh eye.
- Consider audience and purpose.
- Outline what you have written.
- Ask someone else to look it over.
- Expand your best ideas.
- Cut out unnecessary parts.
- Check your writing style.
- Use a checklist.

Talking About Writing

What do you say when a classmate asks you for comments on a composition? Here are some suggestions.

1. Always start by saying something positive, such as, "Pete seemed so real," "The last argument really convinced me," "That was an interesting fact."

2. Never say something is "bad." Instead, say it might be "better" or "clearer" or "more exciting if . . ."

3. Go on to offer a positive suggestion.

4. Make your suggestions clear and direct. Do not say, "You need to be clearer." Instead say, "You might tell what Josie looks like since she's such an important character."

5. Try to answer questions like these:

   Could the beginning be more exciting?

   Are there any parts you had trouble following?

   Are the details arranged in a clear way?

   Can you picture people, places, and things?

   Are there places where more details should be used?

   Does the ending tie things up in an interesting way?

Checklist for Revising

AUDIENCE AND PURPOSE

See pages

[ ] Who is my audience? Have I written
    for them? . . . . (119–121)
[ ] What is my purpose? Have I achieved it? . . (119–121)

ORGANIZATION AND CONTENT

[ ] Does my topic sentence (or thesis statement)
    state the main idea clearly? . . . . (147–150)
[ ] Do I have enough details to support the
    main idea? . . . . (147–148)
[ ] Are details organized in a way that makes
    sense? . . . . (151–154)
[ ] Have I used transitions to make the
    order clear? . . . . (154, 157)
[ ] Have I used repeated words, synonyms, and
    pronouns to tie sentences together? . . . . . (156–157)
[ ] Does every main idea have its own
    paragraph? . . . . (147)
[ ] Do I begin in an interesting way? . . . . . . (150, 166)
[ ] Do I end in a way that ties ideas together? . . . (150)

WORDS AND SENTENCES

[ ] Have I taken out all unnecessary words? . . (158–159)
[ ] Have I used the most vivid words I can? . . . . . (163)
[ ] Does my language suit my audience? . . . . . . (162)
[ ] Have I combined short, choppy sentences
    to make longer, more interesting ones? . . (280–283)
[ ] Have I broken up rambling sentences? . . . . (158–159)
[ ] Have I used sentences of different form
    and length? . . . . (160–161)
[ ] Have I varied the beginnings of my
    sentences? . . . . (160–161)

The Writing Process

Proofreading

☐ **Proofreading**   Rereading to find and correct errors in grammar, spelling, punctuation, and capitalization

Remember these marks

dele~e~te

ins^e^rt

cl͜ose up

space#needed

transp⌒ose

capital letters

$mall /etters

Add period⊙

Add comma‸please.

Leave ⫶it⫶ as it was.

My cat Puff has long ~hair~ ⟨white⟩ with pale gold spots, and he is playful and ~affeckrionate~ *affectionate*. ~Everybody~ thinks he's beautiful. When I found him, though, he was hungry and cold♀. And full of grease from sleeping under cars. He had been abandoned.

~There are~ millions of stray animals‸ *appear* in this country every year. Only a few have wandered ~away~ from home. Most have been ~delibritely~ *deliberately* abandoned. Why do people abandon cats? People do not always think when they get a cute kitten that it will become a demanding ~cat~ who lives for fifteen years and need‸s it's̶e̲ litter box emptied. ~they~ figure cats can get by on ~there~ *their* own, so they just abandon ~it~ *the cats*⊙ The lucky ones end up in animal#shelters. Most of the others suffer and starve.

What can you and I do about this problem‸ *?* Before you get a pet, be sure you want it for its life͡time. Go to a shelter for a pet that needs a home. Most important‸ make sure your pet is neutered. If everyone did these things‸ the problem of abandoned ~A~nimals would just about disappear.

The point of writing is to communicate. The mistakes you look for in proofreading may seem minor, but they become major when they slow readers down and prevent them from understanding your ideas.

Ooops!

Proofread carefully, or you may end up with bloopers like these.

If you have a dictionary, there is no excuse for spelling mstakes.

This family restaurant takes pride in the way it serves fried chicken and children.

The heavy use of salt can help you get rid of your aunts.

Mr. Everest is every mountain climber's dream.

Dina's chicken won the cooking contest!

They hung the pitcher in the hallway.

Bear feet are not allowed.

He bought a sofa complete with cushions, boots, and an umbrella.

The new mall was panned by a famous architect.

How to Proofread

1. **Check for errors.** Look for the following kinds of details.

When You Proofread

☑ Check that paragraphs are indented.
☑ Check spelling. Use the dictionary.
☑ Check all punctuation.
☑ Check all capitalization.
☑ Check for grammar and usage errors.

---

2. **Look at one line at a time.** Look at each word and sentence to see that it is written correctly. Do not read for content.

3. **Go through your draft several times.** First look for spelling errors, then for punctuation errors, and so on.

4. **Use proofreading marks.** Use these marks to make changes:

    ℐ delete (take out)   ≡ make a capital letter
    ∧ insert here   / make a small letter
    ◡ close up space   ⊙ add a period
    # add space   ⌃ add a comma
    ∼ transpose words or letters   ... leave it as it was

5. **Swap papers with a friend.** If possible, ask a classmate to check your paper while you check his or hers.

6. **Use a checklist.** See the proofreading checklist on page 145.

TIPS for Proofreading

- Check for errors.
- Check one line at a time.
- Go through your draft several times.
- Use proofreader's marks.
- Swap papers with a classmate.
- Use a checklist.

The Writing Process

Checklist for Proofreading

See page

PARAGRAPHS
[　]　Have I indented each paragraph?

SPELLING
[　]　Have I checked every word I am not sure of
　　　in the dictionary? . . . . (62)
[　]　Have I spelled plurals correctly? . . . . . . (255 – 256)

PUNCTUATION
[　]　Have I ended each sentence with the
　　　right punctuation mark? . . . . (288)
[　]　Have I used commas between independent
　　　clauses? . . . . (333)
[　]　Have I used commas with introductory words,
　　　phrases, and clauses? . . . . (333)
[　]　Have I used commas correctly in series? . . . . . (332)
[　]　Have I used commas with interrupters? . . . . . (333)
[　]　Have I used periods with abbreviations? . . . . . (331)
[　]　Have I used apostrophes correctly with
　　　contractions? . . . . (337)
[　]　Have I used apostrophes correctly with
　　　possessives? . . . . (337)
[　]　Have I used quotation marks correctly? . . (338 – 339)
[　]　Have I used semicolons and colons correctly? . . (335)
[　]　Have I used hyphens correctly? . . . . (336)

CAPITALIZATION
[　]　Does every sentence begin with a capital letter? . (327)
[　]　Have I capitalized proper nouns and adjectives? . (328)
[　]　Have I written titles correctly? . . . . (330)

GRAMMAR AND USAGE
[　]　Have I corrected fragments and run-ons? . (320 – 321)
[　]　Does every verb agree with its subject? . . (305 – 308)
[　]　Have I used the correct forms of irregular verbs? . (300)
[　]　Have I used pronouns correctly? . . . . . . (309 – 315)
[　]　Have I used adjectives and adverbs
　　　correctly? . . . . (316 – 319)
[　]　Have I used words correctly? . . . . (322 – 326)

The Writing Process

Some Magazines That Publish Student Writing

Cobblestone
20 Grove Street
Peterborough, NH 03458

Cricket
P.O. Box 300
Peru, IL 61354

Merlyn's Pen,
P.O. Box 1058
East Greenwich, RI 02818-9946

Reflections (poetry)
P.O. Box 368
Duncan Falls, OH 43734

Scholastic Voice
Scholastic, Inc.
2931 East McCarty St.
P.O. Box 3710
Jefferson City, MO 65102-9957

Shoe Tree
National Association for
Young Writers
215 Valle del Sol Drive
Santa Fe, NM 87501

Stone Soup
P.O. Box 83
Santa Cruz, CA 95063

Some Other Ways to Publish

- Write and perform a song
- Write and send a greeting card
- Write a "How-to" book
- Make a tape
- Create a cartoon strip
- Publish a neighborhood newspaper
- Write a commercial
- Circulate an announcement
- Write a bumper sticker
- Produce a radio program
- Create a family album

Publishing

☐ **Publish**   Make your writing public

To the Editor:
    In your January 12 article about the Lowe Animal Shelter, you did not mention that the shelter needs volunteers. The shelter can use people of any age who can give an hour or two a week. I am in the seventh grade, and I work there on Tuesdays after school. I walk dogs, clean cages, and play with the animals. The only pay I get is a good feeling from doing something helpful, but I think that is enough. The shelter could use more help.

You do not have to be a professional writer to be published. In fact, anything you compose and make public can be thought of as published — a letter printed in a newspaper (like the letter above), a story shared with classmates, a poem hung on a bulletin board, or even an announcement read over the intercom.

How to Publish

1. **Add a title or heading to your final draft.**

2. **Make a neat copy.**

3. **Check your writing for errors a final time.**

4. **Find a way to make the writing public.**

TIPS on Publishing

- Post your paper on the bulletin board. Add illustrations.
- Read your writing to the class or another group. Add slides, music, or other aids.
- Share your writing with your family by mail or in person.
- Start a school or a class magazine.
- Submit a piece of writing to a newspaper or magazine.
- Write and put on a play.
- Produce an illustrated book, alone or with others.
- Exchange writing with a class in another school, perhaps in another country.
- Make a poster that includes your writing.
- Help produce a class book and present it to the library.

Writing a Paragraph

☐ **Paragraph**   Group of sentences about one main idea

The gerbil is a popular pet for several reasons. While most other rodents are primarily nocturnal, the gerbil is active during the day. It has a gentle disposition, a natural curiosity, and no fear of people. It seldom makes more noise than an occasional *cheep*, and if it gets loose, it doesn't try to hide.

— *Care of Uncommon Pets*, William J. Weber, DVM

What is the paragraph about? The first sentence tells you. It is about the reasons gerbils are such popular pets.

The sentence in a paragraph that tells you the main idea, or topic, is called the *topic sentence*. All the other sentences support the main idea, as shown in the diagram below.

TOPIC SENTENCE:	The gerbil is a popular pet for several reasons.

Supporting detail: active during the day
Supporting detail: gentle
Supporting detail: natural curiosity
Supporting detail: no fear of people
Supporting detail: seldom makes noise
Supporting detail: doesn't hide

Notice that the paragraph is indented. The indented line serves as a signal that an idea is going to be developed. If the paragraph is part of a longer composition, the indented line signals that a *new* idea is going to be developed.

Pets to Avoid

Certain animals produce venom, or poison, that can be passed to humans through a bite or a sting. Not all bites are fatal, but they can certainly be very uncomfortable. Here is a list of some venomous animals.

SNAKES

Coral snake
Rattlesnake
Cottonmouth water moccasin
Copperhead snake
Asian pit viper
Boomslang
King cobra

LIZARDS

Gila monster
Mexican beaded lizard

INSECTS

Bee
Wasp
Hornet

SPIDERS, SCORPIONS

Black widow spider
Brown recluse spider
Fiddleback spider
Tarantula
Scorpion

SEA CREATURES

Portuguese man-of-war
Octopus
Stingray

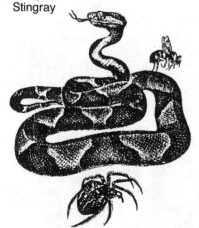

How to Write a Paragraph

1. **What is your main idea?**   A paragraph has one main idea. If it is to be clear to your reader, it must first be clear to you. Write down the idea. Does it capture exactly what you want your paragraph to say? Rework it until it does.

2. **What should your topic sentence say?**   State the main idea clearly. Tell exactly what the paragraph is about — no more, no less. Notice why neither of the sentences below would make a good topic sentence for the gerbil paragraph.

   TOO GENERAL   Some animals make better pets than others.
   TOO SPECIFIC   Gerbils are gentle pets.

3. **How will you develop your main idea?**   Find and use details that help tell about your main idea. Here are some examples.

Kinds of Supporting Details	
facts	The gerbil is not a nocturnal animal.
examples	My friend Eva's gerbil is gentle and friendly.
reasons	Think carefully before getting a pet, because any pet needs attention.
description	Gerbils make only an occasional *cheep*.
events	Then Eva put the gerbil back in its cage.
steps	Next, find a suitable cage for the gerbil.

4. **Do your details stick to the topic?**   Ask yourself whether each detail supports your main idea. In the opening paragraph, every sentence develops one specific topic — why gerbils are popular pets. The sentences below tell about pets and gerbils, but they do not support that topic. Why not? They do not help to tell why gerbils are popular pets.

   UNRELATED   Rats and mice, on the other hand, will try to hide.
   UNRELATED   Gerbils love to eat sunflower seeds.

5. **Who is your audience? What is your purpose?**   Always consider your audience and purpose when you write. (See pages 119 – 121.)

6. **How will you organize your details?** Different kinds of paragraphs call for different kinds of organization. Before you write, decide what order makes sense for your paragraph. (See pages 151 – 154.) Then list your details in that order. Here are some examples:

PURPOSE OF PARAGRAPH	ORDER OF DETAILS
To describe a gerbil	From head to toe From toe to head
To tell an incident about a pet gerbil	From first event to last
To tell how to build a gerbil playground	From first step to last
To explain how to take care of a gerbil	From most to least important From least to most important

7. **Where should you put your topic sentence?** In the gerbil paragraph, the topic sentence begins the paragraph. However, the topic sentence does not always have to be first.

TOPIC SENTENCE LAST

Gerbils are cleaner and less smelly than other rodent pets. For caged pets, they require relatively little equipment and care. They are quiet and gentle, as well as affectionate and curious. *No wonder gerbils are popular pets.*

TOPIC SENTENCE WITHIN THE PARAGRAPH

Gerbils were first imported into this country in 1954. *They quickly became popular as pets.* They were not smelly, required little care, and were inexpensive to keep. They had affectionate dispositions and were easy to handle. Their gentleness and curiosity won the hearts of many owners.

Placing Your Topic Sentence

A paragraph has a shape. Think about the shape of your paragraph when you write.

START WITH THE BIG IDEA AND SUPPORT IT.

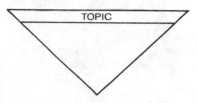

BUILD UP TO THE BIG IDEA

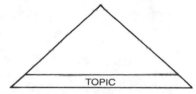

DO BOTH! BUILD UP TO THE BIG IDEA AND THEN SUPPORT IT.

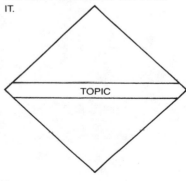

Sometimes writers only suggest, or imply, the main idea.

IMPLIED TOPIC SENTENCE
The ideal pet is one that does not need constant care. A good pet should also be interesting and fun, but it does not have to be affectionate. Fish, for example, do not show affection but are beautiful and fascinating to watch.

Even without a topic sentence, the main idea is clear — the features of an ideal pet. In your own writing, however, to be sure your ideas come across, use topic sentences.

8. **How will you begin?** You might want to begin with your topic sentence. Make it interesting and appropriate.

NOT INTERESTING   This paragraph is about gerbils.
MORE INTERESTING   Would you like to own a member
of the *Gerbillinae* family?

9. **How will you end?** Write a concluding sentence that ties up the paragraph neatly. Here are some suggestions.

WAYS TO CONCLUDE A PARAGRAPH

- **Restate the main idea in different words.**
  It is easy to see why the gerbil appeals to many pet owners.
- **Pick up key words or details and summarize.**
  Gentle, curious, affectionate, and quiet, the gerbil appeals to many pet owners.
- **Add a new detail or understanding.**
  Gerbils have been popular pets ever since they were imported to this country in 1954.

TIPS on Writing a Paragraph

- State your main idea clearly in a topic sentence.
- Develop your main idea with facts, examples, reasons, descriptive details, events, steps.
- Stick to the topic.
- Organize your sentences in a way that makes sense.
- Write an interesting beginning and ending.

Organizing Details

□ **Organizing** Arranging things in an orderly way

Putting things in an order that makes sense

Before you get yourself moving on roller skates, think about how you're going to get yourself to stop. The easiest way to stop, of course, is to drop to the floor or head for the railing. To save wear and tear on your body, however, try learning the T-stop. First, glide on your left skate, with your right skate trailing behind you. Lift the right foot slightly and turn it to form a 90° angle with the left. Think of the right foot as the top of a *T* and the left foot as the base. Then, as you bend your left knee, slowly lower your right skate to the floor, keeping it in the T position. Finally, press the wheels of the right skate firmly into the floor. By the time your skates touch, your right skate will have braked you to a stop.

If you touch one skate to the other before getting into the T position, you may end up doing the fall-stop instead of the T-stop. The order in which you do things is important when you are trying to stop. Accordingly, the order in which you say things is important when you are *explaining* how to stop. In fact, order is important whenever you are trying to communicate. If your details are arranged in an order that makes sense, your reader will be better able to understand them.

How to Organize Details

1. **Think about your purpose.** Are you telling a story? giving directions? describing? explaining? trying to persuade? sharing your feelings? (See pages 119–121.) Are you using facts? events? reasons? descriptive details?

2. **Arrange your details in an order that makes sense.** When you explain how to do a T-stop, you arrange your details in the order in which they happen, as in the opening paragraph. Other kinds of details will call for other kinds of arrangements, as you will see on the next page.

3. **Be aware of different arrangements.** On the next page are listed the most common ways to arrange supporting details.

A History of Roller Skates

While people have ice-skated for centuries, roller-skating is fairly new. Here are the main events in the development of the roller skate.

1760 Joseph Merlin fit two metal spools onto a strip of wood and strapped the wood to his foot. To show off his invention, Merlin strapped on a pair of these skates and wore them to a London ball. Unfortunately, he had been so busy thinking about how to move that he forgot to think about how to stop. He rolled right into a large mirror, destroying the mirror and almost destroying himself.

Early 1800s J. Garcin created simple skates for the summer training of ice skaters.

1863 American James L. Plimpton patented the first roller skates with four wheels.

1870s Many rinks opened, and roller-skating became very popular.

Organizing Details | **151**

The Modern
Roller Skate

How might you arrange your details if you were describing this skate?

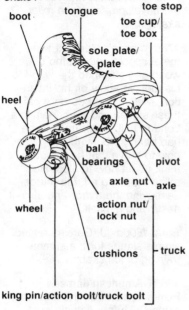

boot · tongue · toe stop · toe cup/toe box · sole plate/plate · heel · ball bearings · pivot · axle nut · axle · wheel · action nut/lock nut · cushions · truck · king pin/action bolt/truck bolt

— *What's What*, R Bragonier, Jr., and D. Fisher, eds.

WAYS TO ARRANGE DETAILS

Time order   Arrange details in the order in which they happen.

USE   narratives, histories, directions, instructions
DETAILS   events, steps in a process

EXAMPLE
The first wheels on roller skates were made of wood. Then came metal and, later, polyurethane.

Spatial order   Arrange details by location. For example, go from near to far, up to down, side to side.

USE   descriptions
DETAILS   descriptive details

EXAMPLE
Just inside the locker room door, cubbyholes holding skates covered both walls. Long benches stood in the middle of the room, and lockers filled the back wall.

Order of importance
a. Arrange details from most important to least important, or
b. Arrange details from least important to most important.

USE   explanations, persuasion
DETAILS   facts, reasons

EXAMPLES
How do you choose a pair of skates? First of all, be sure they fit well. Also think about how and where you will use them. Finally, consider how they look on you.

How do you choose a pair of skates? Consider how they look on you. Also think about how and where you will use them. Most important of all, be sure they fit well.

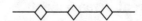

WAYS TO ARRANGE DETAILS (continued)

Cause and effect (See pages 15 – 16.)
  a. Begin with a cause and give its effects, or
  b. Begin with an effect and give its causes.

  USE   explanations, persuasion
  DETAILS   facts, reasons, events

  EXAMPLES
  In 1863, a practical roller skate was invented at last. As a result, interest in skating grew.

  Interest in roller-skating grew after 1863. In that year, a practical skate was invented at last.

Comparison and contrast (See pages 13 – 14.)
  a. Tell how two things are alike, or
  b. Tell how two things are different, or
  c. Compare and contrast two things point by point.

  USE   descriptions, explanation, persuasion
  DETAILS   description, facts

  EXAMPLES
  Both roller-skating and ice-skating can take place indoors and out. Also, both are split into figure skating and racing activities.

  Roller skaters skate on a hard surface such as pavement or wood. The skates have four wheels, so balancing is fairly easy. Ice skaters, of course, skate on ice. The skates have blades, so balancing is harder.

  Roller skaters skate on a hard surface such as pavement or wood, but ice skaters glide on ice. While roller skates have four wheels, ice skates have blades. Therefore, balancing is easier on roller skates than on ice skates.

The ??????

Here's the main character in your science fiction story. How would you arrange your details to describe it?

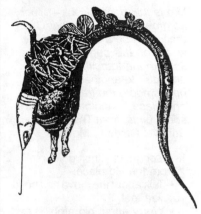

Two-Way Writing

The way letters are arranged is important. Take n, w, and o.

  Word 1:   now
  Word 2:   own
  Word 3:   won
  No word: wno

In English, letters are arranged from left to right (although in some other languages, such as Hebrew, the letters go the other way). Sometimes, as a challenge, people like to find ways to arrange letters so that they go both ways! A word, phrase, or sentence that reads the same in both directions is called a palindrome. (See also page 258.) Here are examples.

did   Mom
noon   Pop
level Hannah

Madam, I'm Adam.
Never odd or even.
No lemons, no melon.
Step on no pets.
Name no one man.
A man, a plan, a canal, Panama!
Marge lets Norah see Sharon's
  telegram.

Another Kind of Transition

Transition: "The process of moving from one thing to another"

Life is full of transitions — such as growing up or moving. Often these can be a bit bumpy. The words on this page can help smooth the transition from one idea to another. What can help smooth the transition from one place to another? Here are some hints, from The Teenager's Survival Guide to Moving.

1. *Disconnect.* Unplug yourself from the old place.
   - Talk about the move and how you feel.
   - Worry about big problems, not little ones.
   - Say your good-bys to friends and to places.
   - Keep souvenirs.
   - Find out about the new place and school.
   - Make sure your records get to your new school.

2. *Change.* Make the move.
   - Pack for the trip — maps, games, food, books.
   - Keep a diary and take pictures. Get souvenirs.

3. *Reconnect.* Plug yourself into your new place.
   - Fill your new space with your favorite things.
   - Get a map and walk around.
   - Ask for help — from classmates, teachers, neighbors.
   - Remember that fitting in takes time.
   - Get involved.

4. **Use transition words.**   Transition words and phrases make the order clearer, such as *First, Then,* and *Finally* in the paragraph about the T-stop. Here are other transition words.

SOME TRANSITION WORDS

Time order

first	then	earlier	meanwhile	next week
second	before	later	suddenly	finally
next	after	at noon	as soon as	last

Spatial order

Near to far or far to near

near	farther	at the end	around	beyond
close by	across	in front of	north	behind

Top to bottom or bottom to top

above	higher	in the middle	at the top
below	lower	between	at the bottom

Side to side

right	between	in the middle	at the other end
left	next to	at one end	to the east

Inside to outside or outside to inside

inside   outside   within   in the middle

Order of importance

also	finally	furthermore	more important
besides	first	in addition	most important

Cause and effect

because   therefore   as a result   for this reason

Comparison and contrast

like	same as	different from	on the contrary
unlike	similarly	in contrast	on the other hand

TIPS on Organizing Details

- Think about your purpose.
- Arrange your details in an order that makes sense.
- Use transition words.

Making Your Writing Unified

☐ **Unified**   Joined to form a single whole
☐ **Unified writing**   Writing in which every sentence belongs to the topic

> Animals in the oceans follow one of three life styles. Members of one group, which includes jellyfish and the tiny young of some large fish, drift with the currents. They are unable to swim or too weak to swim against the currents. Those in another group, which includes most adult fish as well as squid, octopus, and whales, are the strong swimmers. Members of the third group, which includes corals and barnacles, stay put. They settle to the bottom or attach themselves to a stone or to a plant or to another creature and stay there for the rest of their lives.
>
> — *Amazing Creatures of the Sea*, National Wildlife Federation

The writer of the paragraph above knows that a paragraph sticks to one topic, or main idea. In this case, the topic is stated in the first sentence: *Animals in the oceans follow one of three life styles*. The sentences that follow discuss the three life styles and give examples. Because all the sentences stick to the topic, the paragraph has *unity*.

How to Make Your Writing Unified

1. **State your main idea in a topic sentence.**   The topic sentence in the opening paragraph is clear and specific: *Animals in the oceans follow one of three life styles*. It tells which animals are discussed and what is said about them.

2. **Make every sentence relate to the main idea.**   As you write, ask yourself: Is this sentence really about my main idea?

3. **Weed out unrelated ideas.**   As you revise, cross out ideas that do not belong to your topic sentence. If you start discussing a new idea, then start a new paragraph.

TIPS for Making Your Writing Unified

- State your main idea in a topic sentence.
- Be sure every sentence relates to the main idea.
- Weed out unrelated ideas.

!!!
About *unity*

The word *unity* comes from Latin *unus*, "one."

SOME SYNONYMS

oneness
wholeness
solidarity

accord
harmony
cooperation

RELATED WORDS

unified
unite
union
unit
unison

Your Turn

How does *uni-*, related to *unus*, "one," help form the meaning of these words?

unicorn
uniform
unicycle
universe
unilateral

155

Making Your Writing Coherent

The Bones of the Body

The human skeleton has about 206 separate bones, with 64 in the hands and arms alone. Here are the names of the major bones of the body:

Head and face bones	*Skull*: *frontal, temporal, nasal, malar, maxilla, mandible, hyoid*
Collar bone	*Clavicle*
Shoulder bone	*Scapula*
Breast bone	*Sternum*
Chest bones	*Ribs*
Spinal column	*Vertebrae*
End of spinal column	*Sacrum*
Tail bone	*Coccyx*
Hip bones	*Pelvis*: *ilium, pubis, ischium*
Upper arm bone	*Humerus*
Forearm bones	*Radius Ulna*
Wrist bones	*Carpals*
Hand bones	*Metacarpals*
Finger bones	*Phalanges*
Thigh bone	*Femur*
Knee cap	*Patella*
Calf bone	*Fibula*
Shin bone	*Tibia*
Heel bones	*Tarsals*
Front foot bones	*Metatarsals*
Toe bones	*Phalanges*

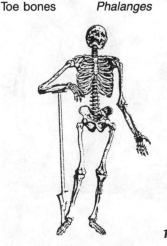

☐ **Coherent**   Clearly and logically connected

☐ **Coherent writing**   Writing that shows how ideas are connected

> The healing process begins the instant a bone snaps. Torn vessels inside the bone release blood into the fracture. The blood clots, or thickens, forming a substance that helps produce new cells. Gradually, strong tissue called callus replaces the clot. It binds the fracture ends together and eventually holds it like a splint. Meanwhile, the torn blood vessels and nerves are healing. When the callus turns into bone, mending is complete. The process takes a few weeks to several months — the younger the patient, the faster the recovery.
>
> — *National Geographic World*, November 1989

The healing of a broken bone is a complicated process. To explain the process clearly, the writer of the passage above has done two important things: (1) connect facts in a way that makes sense, and (2) use connectors to help show how the facts go together. The result is a *coherent* paragraph. When you write, you too need to tie ideas and facts together into a coherent paragraph.

How to Make Your Writing Coherent

1. **Arrange ideas logically.**   Always put your ideas in an order that makes sense. Time order — the order in which things happen — makes sense when you are discussing a process, such as healing. With other kinds of topics, other arrangements make sense. (See pages 151 – 154.)

2. **Repeat key words.**   Notice how key words such as *blood, bone, callus* are repeated in the opening passage. Such repetition helps to link ideas.

3. **Use synonyms.**   A lot of repeated words can make a paragraph boring. Besides repeating words, use synonyms or near synonyms to link ideas. (See page 249.) For example, the words *healing, mending, recovery*, which have similar meanings, are all used in the opening passage.

4. **Use pronouns.** Another way to link ideas is to replace some nouns with pronouns, that is, with words such as *it, they, she.* (See pages 263 – 265.) Notice how the opening passage uses the pronoun *It* instead of repeating the word *callus.*

5. **Use transitions.** Transitions are words and phrases that connect ideas and show how they are related, like the words *Gradually, eventually,* and *Meanwhile* in the opening passage. Below are transitions that show different kinds of relationships. (See page 154 for more transitions.)

Some Transitions

To show time	since	during	afterward
	meanwhile	later	as time passed
	eventually	until	soon
	at last	finally	next
	first, second	soon after	gradually
To show place	here	there	elsewhere
	beyond	opposite	in front of
	nearby	to the left	next to
	east	far away	on top of
To show result or effect	therefore	as a result	accordingly
	due to	because of	consequently
	for this reason	thus	hence
To give an example	for example	that is	such as
	for instance	specifically	to illustrate
To add a point	in addition	furthermore	also
	moreover	besides	second
To compare	similarly	likewise	also
To contrast	however	yet	nevertheless
	on the other hand	in contrast	but
To emphasize	in particular	most important	note that
To conclude	in conclusion	to conclude	finally
To summarize	in other words	in short	to sum up

TIPS for Making Your Writing Coherent

- Arrange ideas in a logical order.
- Use repeated words, synonyms, and pronouns.
- Use transitions.

Making Your Writing Concise

Can You Recognize These?

Below are examples of wordiness gone wild! What familiar lines are hiding there? Make the passages concise to find out.

A. Here before you is a set of triplets all belonging to a well-known and familiar group of rodents. It is important to point out that all three of these particular representatives of the mouse family have totally and completely lost the ability to see with their eyes and are, as a result of this fact, unable to view anything at all. As a point of interest, you are instructed to watch carefully with your own eyes and observe the manner in which these rodents move around on their legs with great swiftness.

B. The fact of the matter is that a threesome of rather youngish members of the cat family who are, in point of fact, somewhat small little kittens have, we are forced to admit, lost or misplaced in a location that is unknown to them and others the warmish coverings for their hands that formerly belonged to them and, to make a sad tale even worse, have not the least idea in what place in the world these possessions of theirs can possibly be found.

☐ **Concise**   Clear and direct, with no unnecessary words

A. Of all of the living creatures who now live on the earth, whales are the very largest animals of all in size. As an example of this, take the blue whale, for instance, which is just about the size of two semi-trailer trucks that have been put together end to end. The point is that the size of them makes blue whales somewhat like six elephants in size! The fact is that whales are mammals for the reason that they give birth to young whales that are live and also because they produce milk as other mammals do, and, also like other mammals, they breathe air with their lungs.

B. Of all living creatures, whales are the largest. The blue whale, for example, is about the size of two semi-trailers end to end or six elephants! Whales are mammals. They give birth to live young, produce milk, and breathe air.

Passage B gives the same facts as A does, but B is shorter and clearer. *Concise* writing is direct and to the point. Make your writing concise by using only the words that you need.

How to Write Concisely

1. **Avoid empty words and phrases.**   Words like *very* and *somewhat* are often unnecessary. Do not use them unless you are certain they add needed emphasis.

WORDY	the very largest animals	somewhat like six elephants
CONCISE	the largest animals	like six elephants

Phrases like those below are empty of meaning. Avoid them.

<table>
<tr><td colspan="2" align="center">Empty Expressions</td></tr>
<tr><td>the point is that</td><td>due to the fact that</td></tr>
<tr><td>the fact is that</td><td>it seems as if</td></tr>
<tr><td>the thing is that</td><td>because of the fact that</td></tr>
<tr><td>it is my opinion that</td><td>for the reason that</td></tr>
<tr><td>if you ask me</td><td>what I mean is</td></tr>
<tr><td>on account of</td><td>what I want is</td></tr>
</table>

2. **Avoid redundant words and phrases.** When you repeat words or meanings without a good reason, you are being *redundant*. Here are examples from the opening paragraph:

REDUNDANT
As an example of this, take the blue whale, *for instance*
Of all of the *living* creatures *who now live*
Of all of the living *creatures* who now live on the earth, whales are the very largest *animals* of all
whales are the very *largest* animals of all *in size*

3. **Combine related sentences.** To cut words and sharpen meaning, join related sentences. (See pages 280 – 283).

WORDY	As an example of this, take the blue whale, for instance, which is just about the size of two semi-trailer trucks that have been put together end to end. The point is that the size of them makes blue whales somewhat like six elephants in size!
CONCISE	The blue whale, for example, is about the size of two semi-trailers end to end or six elephants!

4. **Break up rambling sentences.** Sentences that go on and on are like overloaded trucks. They break down. Unload them by separating them into shorter sentences. The final sentence in Passage A was separated into two sentences in Passage B.

5. **Reduce phrases and clauses.** Shorten wordy phrases and clauses when you can. (See pages 278 – 283, 284 – 287.)

WORDY	the size *of them*
CONCISE	their size
WORDY	semi-trailers *that have been put together* end to end
CONCISE	semi-trailers end to end
WORDY	They give birth to young *whales that are live*.
CONCISE	They give birth to live young.

TIPS on Writing Concisely

• Avoid empty expressions and redundant expressions.
• Combine related sentences.
• Break up rambling sentences.
• Reduce words and clauses.

Take It Away!

A letter is taken away from each word on the right. The letters are then rearranged to form a new word, with the meaning shown on the left.

rock	S T O N E
short letter	N O T E
2,000 pounds	T O N
negative word	N O
exclamation	O

discovered	L E A R N E D
thinner	L E A N E R
find out	L E A R N
close by	N E A R
is, plural	A R E

Your Turn

Using the above as models, complete these Take-aways.

tool used to cut	K N I F E
good	_ _ _ _
part of a fish	_ _ _
not out	_ _
me	_

beginning	S T A R T I N G
looking	_ _ _ _ _ _ _
cord	_ _ _ _ _ _
bee bite	_ _ _ _ _
make vocal music	_ _ _ _
bad deed	_ _ _
inside	_ _
1st person singular pronoun	_

Can you create some Take-aways of your own?

Writing Varied Sentences

Vary Your Food, Too!

Sam found that liver made him feel better because it contained vitamins his body needed. Eat a variety of foods so that you get the different vitamins you need to stay healthy.

Vitamin A: Butter, cheese, egg yolk, milk, liver, leafy green vegetables, carrots

Vitamin B_1 (Thiamine): Whole-grain cereals, peas, beans, peanuts, oranges, liver, nuts, many vegetables and fruits

Vitamin B_2 (Riboflavin): Eggs, green vegetables, liver, lean meat, milk, wheat germ

Niacin: Lean meat, fish, beans, whole-grain cereals, peanuts

Vitamin B_6: Molasses, meat, cereal

Vitamin B_{12}: Liver, milk, cheese

Vitamin C: Oranges, grapefruit, tangerines, tomatoes, other fruits and vegetables

Vitamin D: Butter, egg yolks, salmon, tuna, sardines, liver

Vitamin E: Lettuce and other leafy green vegetables, rice

Folacin: Liver, leafy green vegetables

☐ **Varied sentences** Sentences of different structure and length

A. On that same day, Frightful caught a rabbit in the meadow. As I cleaned it, the liver suddenly looked so tempting that I could hardly wait to prepare it. For the next week, I craved liver and ate all I could get. The tiredness ended, the bones stopped aching, and I had no more nosebleeds. Hunger is a funny thing. It has a kind of intelligence all its own. I ate liver almost every day until the first plants emerged, and I never had any more trouble. I have looked up vitamins since. I am not surprised to find that liver is rich in vitamin C. So are citrus fruits and green vegetables, the foods I lacked. Wild plants like sorrel and dock are rich in this vitamin. Even if I had known this at that time, it would have done me no good, for they were but roots in the earth. As it turned out, liver was the only available source of vitamin C — and on liver I stuffed, without knowing why.

— *My Side of the Mountain*, Jean George

Sam, a teen-ager from New York City, is trying to live on his own in the woods. Jean George knows that no matter how interesting Sam's adventures are, they can seem boring if they are told in a boring way.

B. Frightful caught a rabbit. I cleaned the rabbit. Its liver looked tempting. I craved liver a lot. I got more. I ate it all.

Why do these sentences sound choppy and babyish? They are all short simple sentences, and they all start with the subject. Interesting sentences are varied, like George's sentences.

How to Write Varied Sentences

1. **Vary beginnings.** Do not avoid sentences that begin with the subject. Just be sure that some begin in other ways as well. Here are some beginnings George used:

PHRASE *On that same day,* Frightful caught a rabbit . . .
ADVERB *So* are citrus fruits and green vegetables . . .
CLAUSE *As I cleaned it,* the liver suddenly looked . . .

2. **Vary length.** In Passage B, the sentences ar[...]
same length, and the rhythm becomes monoto[...]
varying the length, you also vary the rhythm —[...]
your reader to stay awake. In Passage A, for exa[...]
short sentence *Hunger is a funny thing* follows sev[...]
sentences. The change creates an interesting rhy[...]
makes the reader notice the sentence.

3. **Vary structure.** Sentences come in different fo[...]
page 293.)

SIMPLE	Hunger is a funny thing.
	Wild plants like sorrel and dock are rich in this vitamin.
COMPOUND	The tiredness ended, the bones stopped aching, and I had no more nosebleeds.
COMPLEX	I am not surprised to find that liver is rich in vitamin C.
	As I cleaned it, the liver suddenly looked so tempting that I could hardly wait to prepare it.
COMPOUND COMPLEX	I ate liver almost every day until the first plants emerged, and I never had any more trouble.

Use different structures to keep the rhythm of your writing interesting. Use different structures also to show how ideas are related.

I cleaned the liver. It suddenly looked tempting.
As I cleaned it, the liver suddenly looked tempting.

When the ideas are combined with *as*, the reader understands just how the two events are related. When you write and revise, look for ideas that can be combined (pages 280 – 283.)

TIPS on Writing Varied Sentences

- Vary sentence beginnings.
- Vary sentence length.
- Vary sentence structure.

like this one on cereal boxes and other food packages — even on bags of chips. Do you know what they tell you?

The federal government has set Recommended Daily Allowances (RDA) of vitamins and other nutrients. These are the amounts you need to stay strong and healthy. The chart on each food package tells you what percentage of the recommended amounts you get in one serving of that food. Learn how to read your food so you know how much nutrition you are getting.

PERCENTAGE OF
U.S. RECOMMENDED
DAILY ALLOWANCES
(U.S. RDA)

- - - - - - - - - - - - - - -

	1 oz. cereal	1 oz. cereal plus 1/2 cup milk
Protein	8	20
Vitamin A	*	2
Vitamin C	*	*
Thiamine	2	6
Riboflavin	4	15
Niacin	4	4
Calcium	*	15
Iron	10	10

Diction

☐ Diction   Word choice

A.   Dear Mr. Walton:

I regret that I must cancel our meeting scheduled for Tuesday, June 8. An unforeseen conflict has arisen which cannot be resolved. Since I am extremely interested in hearing your latest proposal, I shall contact you as soon as I am able to reschedule.

B.   Dear Billy,

I'm awfully sorry, but next Tuesday's get-together is off. Something important came up for the same day, and there's no way I can get out of it. Being nosy, I'm dying to hear your news, and I'll call you as soon as I figure out when I'm free again.

The two letters may say the same thing, but they say it in very different ways. The difference lies mostly in the word choice, or *diction*. When you speak or write, you make choices not only about what to say but also about how to say it.

How to Choose the Right Words

1.   **Choose the appropriate level.**   Letters A and B show the two basic levels of diction, *formal* and *informal*, which are outlined below. Your school writing, like the writing in newspapers and magazines, usually falls somewhere between these extremes. Whatever you write, think carefully about the level that suits your audience and purpose.

Strange things can happen when you mix levels of language.

Consult the railroad timetable for the departure times of the Chicago choo-choos.

Scientists are conducting experiments to determine whether there is an ideal time for humans to hit the sack.

I'll grab a snack and meet you at five sharp at Jamie's abode.

Since the facilities will accommodate only a limited number of guests, each member may be accompanied by only one buddy.

Despite the inclement weather, the official reception was swell.

I can't bike over because my vehicle is in disrepair.

Formal and Informal Diction	
INFORMAL	Ordinary, everyday conversational words Contractions; relaxed usage Use with friends, family
Example	*There's no way I can get out of it.*
FORMAL	Learned, scholarly words No contractions; usage rules followed Use for business, serious occasions
Example	*The conflict cannot be resolved.*

2. **Stick to the same level.**   Once you choose a level, stay with it. Choose only words and expressions that fit.

3. **Think about connotation.**   Do *nosy* and *interested* mean the same? Both mean "eager to find something out," but a *nosy* person may be *too* eager. Words have two kinds of meaning:

Denotation   Dictionary definition of a word
Connotation   Meaning beyond the dictionary definition

A word's connotation depends on the way it is used and the feelings associated with it. For example, you might respect an *interested* person but not a *nosy* one. Connotations are often, but not always, positive or negative.

Some Connotations

POSITIVE	NEGATIVE
relaxed	lazy
thrifty	stingy
determined	stubborn
neat	fussy
carefree	irresponsible
calm	dull
cautious	cowardly
brave	reckless
famous	notorious
confident	conceited
synthetic	false, phony
filled	crammed
bright	glaring

4. **Choose specific words.**   If letter writer A had chosen the general word *thing* or *situation* instead of the specific word *conflict*, the message would have been less clear. Specific words help you say exactly what you want to say.

TIPS on Choosing the Right Words

- Use words that suit your audience and purpose. Then stick to the same level of diction throughout.
- Use words that have the appropriate connotation.
- Use specific words.

Changing the Connotation

When something has a negative connotation, people may try to give it a new name to make it sound more positive or impressive. The result is a *euphemism*, that is, a tasteful term that is substituted for one considered less tasteful. Sometimes euphemisms work, but sometimes they go too far. What do you think of these?

garbage collector: sanitation engineer
lie: embroider the truth
burglar alarm: security system
stomachache: abdominal discomfort
pen or pencil: writing implement
cowboy or cowgirl: mobile mountain range technician
newsboy or newsgirl: media courier
bank holdup: unauthorized withdrawal
desk: work station
pigpen: hog containment unit
bookmobile: traveling library center
laundry: fabric care center
secondhand: previously owned

Your Turn

What euphemisms would you create for these terms?

garbage
constantly barking dog
unfriendly cat
failing grade
used clothing
exam jitters

Types of Writing

Writing to Tell Events

☐ **Narrative writing**   Writing that tells what happens, writing that tells a story

☐ **Personal narrative**   A story about yourself

> I dreaded the long seven-block walk to school, but shortly after lunch I set out with a scarf wrapped around my head so it covered my nose and mouth as well. By the time I was half way to Block 41, the wind grew so intense, I felt as though I were caught in the eye of a dust hurricane. Feeling panicky, I thought of running home, but realized I was as far from my own barrack now as I was from school, and it was possible some children might be at the school.
>
> Soon barracks only a few feet away were completely obscured by walls of dust and I was terrified the wind would knock me off my feet. Every few yards, I stopped to lean against a barrack to catch my breath, then lowering my head against the wind, I plodded on. When I got to school, I discovered many children had braved the storm as well and were waiting for me in the dust-filled classroom.
>
> — *Desert Exile*, Yoshiko Uchida

Yoshiko Uchida was a schoolteacher in the Utah desert, where she and other Japanese Americans were forced to relocate during World War II. When she describes her experience, her details bring it to life for you.

When you write about what happened, real or made up, you are writing a narrative. When you write about what happened to *you*, you are writing a personal narrative.

Features of a Narrative

- Tells about something that happens or has happened
- Tells events in the order in which they happen
- Has a clear beginning, middle, and end
- Is set in a certain place and time
- Focuses on someone to whom things happen

For story writing, see pages 185 – 189. Here you will learn how to write a personal narrative — a narrative about yourself.

How to Write a Personal Narrative

1. **Recall.**   What has happened to you that is exciting? moving? interesting? funny? Jot down incidents you remember. (See pages 7 – 8 for tips on recalling.)

2. **Choose an incident.**   Use these guidelines to choose an incident to write about in a personal narrative.

Choosing a Subject for a Personal Narrative

Choose an experience . . .
- that you remember well.
- that your readers will enjoy reading about.
- that you will enjoy writing about.
- that you can tell about in a short narrative.

---

3. **Narrow it.**   Narrow the incident so you can tell about it in detail. Although Yoshiko's dust storm went on all day, she tells only a small part of it — her walk to school. Similarly, do not write about your whole vacation. Write about one incident, such as the few moments you were caught in a storm.

4. **Make a plan.**   A chart like the one below can help you plan your narrative. Add as many events as you need.

Narrative Plan

WHAT happened: _____

WHERE and WHEN it happened: _____

WHO was there: _____

HOW it started: _____

    Next: _____

    Next: _____

    Next: _____

HOW it ended: _____

HOW I felt: _____

Some True Personal Details

You can relive the experiences of some "Black Women Who Changed the World" through the personal details they reveal below. These women were interviewed by Brian Lanker for his book I Dream a World.

I never thought that I was a pretty girl because I thought you had to be light-skinned, have a pointed nose and thin lips in order to be pretty. The thought of being pretty was a foreign idea to me. So I decided to be smart instead.
— Oprah Winfrey,
    performer and producer

For the most part we were raised on welfare. I can remember the visits from the social worker, who, in my estimation, was a very important person. Not only was the social worker someone who was dressed nicely, with a briefcase, who came to your house, she appeared to have a lot of power. That's what I wanted to be, a very important social worker.
— Maxine Waters,
    California state
    representative

When I was a sophomore in high school, I had a microscope given to me in a laboratory to look through, and that was it. I said, "That's for me, biology."
— Jewel Plummer Cobb,
    scientist and college
    president

Some Time-Order Transitions

after
after a while
at last
as soon as
before
during
earlier
finally
first
immediately
just as
later
meanwhile
next
shortly
soon
suddenly
then
when
while

5. **Write a strong beginning.** Capture your reader.

> ### Beginning a Narrative
> - **Begin with an action.**
>   When I opened the door, the wind slapped me.
> - **Begin with details about the place, or setting.**
>   My lonely school sat in the middle of the desert.
> - **Begin with details about someone in the narrative.**
>   I dreaded the long seven-block walk to school.
> - **Begin with dialogue — somebody's words.**
>   "I hate dust storms!" I roared back to the wind.
> - **Begin with a general statement.**
>   In the desert, dust was my constant companion.

6. **Tell events in time order.** Time order (pages 22–23) helps readers follow events. In the opening passage, for example, you follow Yoshiko on her way from home to school.

7. **Use transitions.** Transitions, or connecting words like *before, suddenly*, tie events together (pages 154, 157). Note Yoshiko's phrases: *shortly after lunch, By the time I* . . .

8. **Use lots of personal details.** *I dreaded . . . I set out with a scarf wrapped around my head so it covered my nose and mouth.* Such details bring the desert experience to life. Use personal details in your narratives too. Tell what you did, what you saw, what you heard, how you felt, what you thought.

9. **Write a strong ending.** Write an ending that completes the action. Do not just tell what happens — show it.

> WEAK I was glad to get there.
> IMPROVED I leaned against the door and sighed with relief.

> ## TIPS for Writing a Personal Narrative
> - Choose an incident you want to write about. Narrow it.
> - Chart your narrative.
> - Write a beginning that grabs the reader.
> - Tell the events in time order. Use transitions.
> - Include lots of details.
> - Write an ending that ties up the action. *Show* what happens.

Writing to Describe

☐ **Descriptive writing**   Writing that appeals to the senses — sight, hearing, smell, taste, and touch

The first light on the roof outside; very early morning. The leaves on all the trees tremble with a soft awakening to any breeze the dawn may offer. And then, far off, around a curve of silver track, comes the trolley, balanced on four small steel-blue wheels, and it is painted the color of tangerines. Epaulets[1] of shimmery brass cover it, and pipings of gold; and its chrome bell bings if the ancient motorman taps it with a wrinkled shoe. The numerals on the trolley's front and sides are bright as lemons. Within, its seats prickle with cool green moss. Something like a buggy whip flings up from its roof to brush the spider thread high in the passing trees from which it takes its juice. From every window blows an incense,[2] the all-pervasive blue and secret smell of summer storms and lightning.

— *Dandelion Wine*, Ray Bradbury

Bradbury creates a living picture with words. His colors, shapes, smells, sounds, and feelings surround you.

How to Write a Description

1. **Observe.**   Use your senses first and then your pen. Jot down what you see, hear, smell, taste, or feel when you observe or imagine your subject. (See pages 9 – 10.)

2. **Describe how it looks.**   Bradbury does not tell you just that there is a track. He tells you that there is *a curve of silver track*. Tell what is in a scene and what it looks like.

3. **Describe how it sounds.**   Mention sounds, like the bing of the trolley bell. Take advantage of words that sound like what they mean, like Bradbury's *bing, clatter, tap, whisper.*

4. **Describe how it smells and tastes.**   Name things that have smells or tastes, such as incense and summer storms. Use words that describe smells or tastes, such as *smoky, lemony.*

[1]Trimming on the shoulder of an officer's uniform
[2]Substance giving off a sweet smell when burned

Featuring . . . Sight Words

COLOR!

Red	rose, crimson, scarlet	
Blue	azure, aqua, turquoise	
Green	emerald, kelly, lime	
Brown	russet, bronze, tan	
Yellow	canary, straw, lemon	
Black	ebony, raven, jet	
White	ivory, pearl, milky	

SHAPE!

angular	flat	pointed
broad	long	scalloped
crooked	narrow	square
curved	oval	twisted

SIZE!

deep	shallow	sturdy
high	slim	tiny

BRIGHTNESS!

bright	glazed	shadowy
cloudy	glistening	shimmery
dull	glowing	shiny
fuzzy	misty	sunny

MOVEMENT!

Fast	speed, zoom, careen, hurl, dart, fly, gallop
Slow	amble, creep, trail, plod, waddle, droop, slink

Featuring . . . Sound Words

bang	hiss	sigh
beep	hush	sizzle
boom	meow	slurp
buzz	moan	snarl
chatter	murmur	splash
clatter	pluck	squeak
cluck	purr	squeal
coo	quack	squish
crackle	ring	tap
creak	roar	thud
crunch	rumble	thump
drip	rustle	twang
giggle	scream	twitter
groan	screech	whine
growl	shout	whisper

---

bitter	lemony	smoky
burnt	musty	sour
clean	nutty	spicy
delicious	oily	stale
fishy	peppery	stuffy
floral	pungent	sweet
fragrant	ripe	tangy
fresh	rotten	tart
juicy	salty	tasteless

**Featuring . . .
Touch Words and
Feeling Words**

breezy	furry	silky
bumpy	fuzzy	slick
chilly	gooey	slimy
clammy	greasy	slippery
coarse	gritty	slushy
cold	grubby	smooth
cool	gusty	soft
creepy	hard	solid
crisp	hot	steamy
cuddly	icy	sticky
damp	oozy	stinging
downy	prickly	uneven
dry	rough	velvety
fluffy	sandy	wet
frosty	sharp	windy

Your Turn

How many words can you add to
these lists of "sense" words?

5. **Describe how it feels.** Use words that describe textures, temperatures, and sensations, like Bradbury's *prickle, cool, incense blows.* Tell not only how something feels but also how it makes *you* feel, such as *shivery* or *feverish.*

6. **Use figurative language.** Figurative language tells what things are like rather than what they really are. (See page 192.) The trolley car cable is not a buggy whip but is *like a buggy whip.* The *smell of summer storms* is not really secret, but *secret* gives a sense of what the smell is like. Two kinds of figurative language are *simile* and *metaphor.*

   a. **Simile** A simile says something is *like* something else. The word *like* or *as* is used.

   Something like a buggy whip . . .
   The numerals are as bright as lemons.

   b. **Metaphor** A metaphor says something *is* something else.

   The trolley wires were a spider thread.

7. **Collect details in a chart.** Fill out a chart like this one.

Detail Chart

Subject: _____

Item	Sight	Sound	Smell/Taste	Touch/Feeling
___	___	___	___	___
___	___	___	___	___
___	___	___	___	___
___	___	___	___	___

8. **Order your details.** Arrange your details in some sort of spatial order, such as high to low. (See pages 151 – 154.)

TIPS for Writing a Description

• First observe.
• Use details of sight, sound, smell, taste, and touch/feeling.
• Use figurative language.
• Collect your details in a chart.
• Order your details.

Types of Writing

Writing to Inform

☐ **Expository writing**   Writing that informs or explains

> Fossil teeth are clues to what dinosaurs ate. By studying teeth, paleontologists[1] have learned that most dinosaurs were plant eaters, but some ate animals. Duck-billed dinosaurs, for example, had hundreds of teeth in their jaws. The teeth in each jaw were suited to grinding up plants. *Tyrannosaurus rex* had teeth that were six inches long, with edges like saws. These teeth were suited to tearing through flesh.
>
> — *Dinosaurs Walked Here*, Patricia Lauber

How do we know what dinosaurs ate? Patricia Lauber explains. When you write to explain or inform, you write exposition.

How to Write Exposition

1. **Choose a topic.**   Follow these guidelines.

   ┌───┐

   ### Choosing a Topic for Expository Writing
   • Choose a topic that interests you.
   • Choose a topic that will interest your audience.
   • Choose a topic you know about or can learn about.

   └───┘

2. **Ask a question and answer it.**   Patricia Lauber might have gotten the idea for her paragraph by asking, "What did dinosaurs eat? How do we know?" Questioning can help you find a topic, narrow it, and develop it into a composition.

3. **Gather facts.**   A fact is a piece of information that can be proven. Your own observations, plus the observations of experts that you find in your library, are your best sources of facts.

4. **Remember your audience.**   How much do they already know? What do they need to know to understand you?

[1]Scientists who study fossils

Daffy Explanations

Why is tennis such a noisy game?
— Because every player raises a racket

Why did the woman stand next to the bank vault?
— Because she wanted to be on the safe side

Why doesn't it ever rain for two days continuously?
— Because there's a night in between

Why don't we pay our bills with a smile?
— Because we have to pay with money

Why do you always find things in the last place you look?
— Because then you stop looking

Why does the Statue of Liberty stand in New York harbor?
— Because it can't sit down

Why shouldn't we pollute the ocean?
— Because it makes the sea sick

Why are story writers strange creatures?
— Because their tales come out of their heads

*Looking for a topic? Try one of
these.*

How do you write a riddle?

How are dinosaurs related to
  birds?

Who was the original
  Engelbert Humperdinck?

How does the lead get inside
  a pencil?

What really happened when
  Benjamin Franklin flew a
  kite in a thunderstorm?

How do you write a computer
  program?

Are there any good effects
  from watching TV? If so,
  what are they?

What holds up a skyscraper?

What was it like to ride in
  a stagecoach?

What is Green Slime really
  made of?

How can we create less
  garbage?

What are the differences, if
  any, between a turtle and a
  tortoise?

How is sound recorded onto
  a compact disk?

How do deserts come to be?

What is trigonometry?

How does someone become a
  citizen of this country?

What causes glass to fog up?

Why do top musical groups
  earn so much money?

Why do people smile?

Why do people cry?

5. **List reasons.**   Reasons explain why something happened
or is or is not true. *Because* often signals a reason.

Because Tyrannosaurus rex had long teeth with sawlike
edges, experts believe it was a meat eater.

6. **Find examples.**   The first two statements in the dinosaur
paragraph are followed by two examples. Examples are
needed to support general statements and make them
clearer.

7. **Write a topic sentence and support it.**   Lauber opens with
the topic sentence. She then gives reasons and examples
to support that statement (pages 147 – 150). A composition
of more than one paragraph has a thesis statement instead
(page 204).

8. **Organize.**   How do you arrange your details in expository
writing? Here are your main choices. (See pages 151 – 154.)

Arranging Details		
Purpose	*Details*	*Order*
To explain	Facts, reasons, examples	Order of importance Cause-effect Comparison-contrast
To explain a process	Steps	Time order
To give instructions	Steps	Time order

9. **Use transitions.**   Words and phrases such as *for example*
tie statements together. (See pages 154 and 157.)

10. **Write a conclusion.**   Restate the main idea, sum up the
details, or add an observation or fact.

TIPS for Writing Exposition

- Ask a question and try to answer it.
- Gather facts, reasons, and examples.
- Remember your audience.
- Write a topic sentence (or thesis statement) and support it.
- Organize details logically. Use transitions.
- Write a concluding statement.

Types of Writing

Writing to Persuade

☐ **Persuasive writing**   Writing that tries to convince people to think a certain way or take an action

> One way to fight the greenhouse effect[1] is to soak up carbon dioxide (CO_2) in our atmosphere. If each of our one million readers planted a tree, we could neutralize the CO_2 produced from burning one million tons of coal. Planting trees is especially beneficial in urban areas, where they shade "heat islands" that are normally three to five degrees warmer than outlying areas. Why not "green" your neighborhood? For further information, write: National Arbor Day Foundation, Conservation Trees, 100 Arbor Ave., Nebraska City, NE 68410 and/or American Forestry Association, Global ReLeaf, P.O. Box 2000, Washington, DC 20013.
>
> — *Greenpeace* Magazine

Perhaps you don't worry about the greenhouse effect, or perhaps you don't think you can do anything about it. The editors of *Greenpeace* want you to worry about it — and do something about it. To try to make you agree with them, they offer arguments, or reasons.

How to Write Persuasion

1. **Choose an issue that can be argued.**   You may be against pollution in general, but who isn't? There is nothing to argue about. However, you can argue for or against a way to fight one kind of pollution, just as the *Greenpeace* article argues for a certain way to fight the greenhouse effect.

2. **Do not choose an issue that is a matter of personal taste.** You cannot persuade someone that *trees are beautiful*. That is a matter of personal taste. However, you can try to persuade someone that *more trees should be planted in cities*.

   a. Choose an issue that can be argued.
   b. Choose an issue that is important to you.
   c. Choose an issue that involves more than personal taste.
   d. Choose an issue for which you can gather sound evidence.

[1]The possible warming of the planet as a result of air pollution

---

!!!
About Trees . . .

Trees are the largest plants.

Some trees have lived for thousands of years. They are the oldest known living things.

Unlike people, trees keep growing as long as they live.

There are about 20,000 different kinds of trees.

How are trees different from other plants?
- Trees grow taller.
- A tree has one stem, the trunk.
- The trunk is woody and at least three inches thick.
- The trunk can stand by itself.

What good do trees do?
- They act as windbreakers.
- They keep soil from blowing or washing away.
- They help store water.
- They provide homes and shelter for wildlife.
- They provide shade.
- They provide beauty.

What do we get from trees?
- Wood for lumber, paper, and other products
- Food, such as oranges, mangoes, apples, cherries, peaches, coconuts, chocolate, maple syrup, and olives
- Other products, such as cork, rubber, and medicines.

Argue for or against

We must recycle paper in order to save trees.

We should use our feet instead of our cars.

Farmers must use pesticides.

Cars should be kept out of certain areas of cities.

We do not have to change our life styles to fight pollution.

Students should get more homework.

School sports should receive less attention.

Young people should not have curfews.

Schools should have dress codes.

Our schools must not cut back on physical education.

Students should wear uniforms.

Teachers should be able to censor student newspapers.

Foreign languages should not be taught in schools.

The school cafeteria should be run like a fast-food restaurant.

Children should be given their mother's last name instead of their father's.

Star athletes deserve their high salaries.

We need new heroes.

3. **Write a thesis statement.** Write a sentence that states your opinion. Tell exactly what you want others to think or do. Use a word like *must* or *should* to give your statement force. For special effect, you can use a question, as the *Greenpeace* article does.

The world must find safe new sources of energy.
We should all take steps to reduce air pollution.
Why not "green" your neighborhood?

4. **Gather evidence.** Why should we plant trees? The *Greenpeace* editors argue that trees soak up CO_2 and shade hot cities. What arguments support your opinion? What kinds of facts would support each point? Where can you find them? Collect supporting facts, reasons, and examples.

5. **Use facts, not opinions.** Your thesis statement gives your opinion. Go on to support it with facts, not more opinions. Remember that facts can be proved, but opinions tell only what someone believes or thinks.

OPINION   I don't think the greenhouse effect is serious.

FACT   Scientists do not agree on how serious a threat the greenhouse effect actually is.

6. **Collect opposing arguments.** Know the arguments on the other side. Argue against them when you can. Grant the points when you cannot.

OPPOSING POINT   Although scientists do not agree about the greenhouse effect,

ARGUMENT AGAINST IT   we cannot afford to wait until they do. That may be too late.

7. **Organize your arguments.** Arrange your arguments from least to most important or, if you prefer, from most to least important. Use transitions such as *next, furthermore, more important* to show how the points fit together. (See pages 151 – 154 and 157.)

8. **Know your audience.** If you are going to persuade your audience of anything, you must know who they are. What is important to them? How much do they already know? What might their opinion be now? What sorts of arguments might move them? (See pages 119 – 121.)

9. **Try the "you" approach.** Point out how your proposal will help the readers. Will it make them safer? healthier? wiser? more popular?

10. **Make sense.** Be sure your arguments are logical (pages 37 – 41). Also be sure your reader can follow your reasoning.

11. **Avoid overblown language.** By appealing to people's emotions, you can make your arguments more forceful. Do not overdo such appeals, however, and do not use language that is loaded or insulting.

LOADED	People who ignore air pollution are murderers.
INSULTING	The idiots who do nothing are endangering us all.
EFFECTIVE	Plant a tree. Your future children and your children's children will thank you.

12. **Recommend an action.** The *Greenpeace* editors suggest that everyone plant a tree. You can suggest that people volunteer time, write letters, join a group, or take some other action. Be specific. For example, the Greenpeace article lists addresses readers can write to for help.

Argue for . . .

Try to persuade people of the following.

All trees should be painted blue.

Bare trees should be dressed in the winter.

People should live in trees instead of houses.

Dogs must be taught to walk on their hind legs only.

Rulers should be curved, not straight.

All doors should open from the bottom.

Only people over thirty should be allowed to wear purple.

Clouds must be outlawed.

Our flag colors should be changed to pink, aqua, and orange.

Our national anthem should be changed to "Old MacDonald Had a Farm."

People should keep spiders as pets instead of dogs or cats.

TIPS for Writing Persuasion

PREWRITING

- Choose an issue that is arguable.
- Write a thesis statement that tells what you are arguing.
- Gather facts, reasons, examples on both sides.
- Arrange arguments in order of importance.
- Know your audience.

DRAFTING

- Tell readers how they will benefit.
- Make sense. Be logical.
- Use emotional appeals carefully.
- Use transitions.
- Recommend that readers take an action.

Types of Writing – Writing to Persuade | 173

Writing a Friendly Letter

Post Office Abbreviations for States

Alabama	AL
Alaska	AK
Arizona	AZ
Arkansas	AR
California	CA
Colorado	CO
Connecticut	CT
Delaware	DE
Florida	FL
Georgia	GA
Hawaii	HI
Idaho	ID
Illinois	IL
Indiana	IN
Iowa	IO
Kansas	KS
Kentucky	KY
Louisiana	LA
Maine	ME
Maryland	MD
Massachusetts	MA
Michigan	MI
Minnesota	MN
Mississippi	MS
Missouri	MO
Montana	MT
Nebraska	NB
Nevada	NV
New Hampshire	NH
New Jersey	NJ
New Mexico	NM

☐ Friendly letter Informal note or letter to friend or relative

HEADING
Street address
City, State, ZIP Code
Month, Day, Year

SALUTATION

BODY

CLOSING
SIGNATURE

> 44 First Avenue
> Alamosa, CO 81101
> December 22, 1990
>
> Dear Matt,
>   It was great to hear that you made the basketball team. I'm still not good at shooting baskets, but I'm working on it.
>   I have some news too. We started a chess club at school, and I was elected president! Last week we won our first tournament. It was pretty exciting. If I practice basketball, will you learn chess?
>   Your friend,
>   Michael

ENVELOPE

RETURN ADDRESS

> Michael Choi
> 44 First Avenue
> Alamosa, CO 81101

STAMP

> Matthew Levin
> 2 Winston Way
> Benton, AR 72015

A friendly letter shares personal news or feelings, usually with a friend or a relative. There are different kinds of friendly letters — informal notes like the one on page 174, thank-you notes, sympathy notes, and invitations.

How to Write a Friendly Letter

1. **Include all five parts.**   The five parts of a friendly letter are the heading, salutation (greeting), body, closing, and signature. Notice where they are placed in the model letter.

2. **Punctuate and capitalize correctly.**   Follow these rules.

Punctuation and Capitalization in Friendly Letters

USE COMMA	Between city and state	*Alamosa, CO*
	Between day and year	*December 22, 1990*
	After the salutation	*Dear Matt,*
	After the closing	*Your friend,*
CAPITALIZE	Street name	*First Avenue*
	City, state	*Alamosa, CO*
	Month	*December 22*
	Salutation: first word, name	*Dear Matt*
	Closing: first word	*Your friend,*

---

3. **Use an informal closing.**   Here are some appropriate closings.

Some Closings for Friendly Letters

Sincerely,	Love,
With love,	Affectionately,
Fondly,	Your friend, niece, cousin, ...

---

4. **Address the envelope properly.**   Follow the model.

5. **Be friendly.**   A friendly letter is just that — friendly. First show interest in the person you are writing to, and then tell about yourself. Some models follow.

New York	NY
North Carolina	NC
North Dakota	ND
Ohio	OH
Oklahoma	OK
Oregon	OR
Pennsylvania	PA
Rhode Island	RI
South Carolina	SC
South Dakota	SD
Tennessee	TN
Texas	TX
Utah	UT
Vermont	VT
Virginia	VA
Washington	WA
West Virginia	WV
Wisconsin	WI
Wyoming	WY

Some Other Post Office Abbreviations

American Samoa	AS
District of Columbia	DC
Federated States of Micronesia	FM
Guam	GU
Marshall Islands	MI
Northern Mariana Islands	MP
Puerto Rico	PR
Palau	PW
Virgin Islands	VI

When you address a letter, do you ever wonder where the name of the city or town came from?

Amwell, New Jersey Named for a town in England

Aroostook, Maine Algonquian for "beautiful river"

Arkansas Name of a tribe and a village

Battleship Island, Washington Named for its shape

Bear Poplar, North Carolina Place where an early settler chased a bear into a poplar

INFORMAL NOTE

23 West Mansfield Avenue
Fairfield, IO 62556
November 18, 1990

Dear Aunt Carmen,

It was wonderful to get your letter and hear the news about Eva! I'm so glad that she made the orchestra. She must be getting really good on the flute.

I'm involved in music too. I'm in a bell choir. Everyone gets a different note and has to play it at the right time. Last week I was the high E flat. You really have to concentrate. Otherwise you can play at the wrong time or miss your note completely. It gets easier with practice, though.

I hope you can come for a visit soon.

Love,
Gloria

THANK-YOU NOTE

189 South Grove Street
Rutland, VT 05701
April 1, 1991

Dear Uncle Ronald,

Thank you for the great sweater. It fits perfectly and goes with everything. I have already worn it twice and have gotten lots of compliments.

I'm glad I have an uncle with such great taste. Thank you!

Your nephew,
Leroy

Breedlove, West Virginia   Named for a family of settlers

California   From the name of a lush island in a romantic Spanish poem of about 1500

Charleston, South Carolina   Named for King Charles II of England (*-ton* = "town")

Cincinnati, Ohio   Named for a hero of ancient Rome

Cobleskill, New York   Named for Jacob Kobell, whose mill was powered by the stream (*kil* = "stream" in Dutch)

Erdahl, Minnesota   Named for a place in Norway from which early settlers came

Grenola, Kansas   From the combining of the settlements of Greenfield and Canola

SYMPATHY NOTE

Still More Place Name Origins

Leoncito, New Mexico From Spanish "little lion," probably meaning mountain lion

Louisiana Named for King Louis XIV of France

Minnesota Siouan for "cloudy water"

Memphis, Tennessee Named for the city in Egypt

Nome, Alaska From a misreading of *no name* or *? name* on an early map

St. Paul, Minnesota From the name of a church on the site

St. Petersburg, Florida Named for a city in Russia

Salem, Massachusetts From Hebrew for "peace"; also a shortening of *Jerusalem*

823 Lincoln Terrace
East Point, GA 30344
January 18, 1991

Dear Kirsten,

I was very sorry to hear about your grandfather's death. I know how much he meant to you and your parents.

Do you remember the time you took me to visit your grandparents on their farm? They were so friendly. I will never forget your grandfather showing me a baby calf!

Please let me know if there is anything I can do to help you and your family. I am thinking of you and will call soon.

Sincerely,
Margaret

INVITATION

> 1013 Thirteenth Avenue
> Eugene, OR 97401
> May 18, 1990
>
> Dear Dale,
>   I am having a birthday party on Saturday, June 16. It will start at noon. We will have a cookout and games in the back yard. Please come. Wear jeans!
>   Please let me know soon whether or not you can make it.
>
>   Your friend,
>
>   Winona

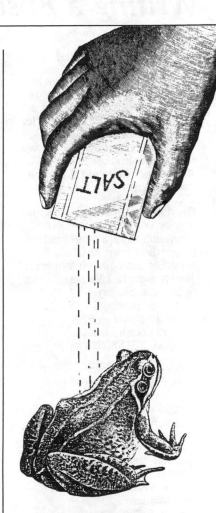

Still More Place Name Origins

Sallisaw, Oklahoma   From French *salaison*, "salting" — a place where hunters salted their meat to preserve it

Seattle, Washington   Named for local Indian chief

Sniktaw, California   Named for W. F. Watkins, a journalist who liked to spell his name backwards

Tarzana, California   Named for fictional character Tarzan

Utah   For the Ute, an Indian tribe

Vermont   From French *vert*, "green," and *mont*, "mountain"

TIPS for Writing Friendly Letters

- Include all five parts: heading, salutation (greeting), body, closing, signature.
- Use correct punctuation and capitalization.
- Be friendly and informal.
- Use an informal closing.
- Address the envelope correctly.

Writing a Business Letter

Order These!

Did you know that there are lots of interesting and FREE things you can order by mail? Here are some, selected from Free Stuff for Kids, *published by Meadbrook, Inc. (When you see SASE below, that means enclose a Self-Addressed, Stamped Envelope measuring 9 1/2 X 4 1/4 inches.)*

Send for a football fan package that includes a team sticker, information and photos about the players and team, an official NFL schedule, and other information. Twenty-eight NFL teams offer the package including

Denver Broncos
Fan Package — FSK
5700 Logan Street
Denver, CO 80216

Green Bay Packers
Fan Package — FSK
P.O. Box 10628
1265 Lombardi Avenue
Green Bay, WI 54307

Want bowling tips? Write to this address and ask for Bif's Fun-Damentals of Bowling. SASE
Young American Bowling
 Alliance
5301 S. 76th St.
Greendale, WI 53129

Yo-yo fans can send for the *Duncan Yo-Yo Trick Sheet* by writing to
Duncan Toys Company
Department FSFK
P.O. Box 5
Middlefield, OH 44062

Find out how to make paper by writing for:
How You Can Make Paper
American Paper Institute,
 Inc.
260 Madison Ave.
New York, NY 10016

☐ Business letter   Formal letter for business purposes

HEADING	Street address ——— 725 Main Street City, State, ZIP Code —— Pocahontas, AK 72455 Month, Day, Year ——— May 11, 1991
INSIDE ADDRESS	Fleetfoot Footwear, Inc. 2134 Highway 27 Greeley, CO 80631
SALUTATION	Dear Sir or Madam:
BODY	My local shoe store, Tap Toes, no longer carries Fleetfoot sneakers. Since I would like to buy another pair, would you please send me a list of stores in my area that sell them. Thank you for your help.
CLOSING SIGNATURE	Yours truly, *Jan Fischer* Jan Fischer

You write business letters to companies, government agencies, and people you do not know. The most common business letters are (1) requests for information or services, (2) orders, and (3) complaints.

How to Write a Business Letter

1. **Include all six parts.**   A business letter has these parts:

   a. **Heading**   Write your full address and the date.

   b. **Inside address**   Skip a line and write the name and address of the company. Write the name and title of the person who will receive the letter, if you know them.

   c. **Salutation (greeting)**   Skip a line after the inside address. Use the person's name if you know it. Otherwise, use *Dear Sir or Madam* or *Dear* and the company's name.

   d. **Body**   Write the letter. Indent paragraphs or skip a line between them or do both.

   e. **Closing**   Use a formal closing, such as *Sincerely, Sincerely yours, Yours truly, Very truly yours*.

   f. **Signature**   Sign your full name. Print or type it below.

2. **Place the parts correctly.**   Follow one of the models. The letters on pages 180 and 182 are arranged in *modified block style*. Those on pages 183 and 184 follow *block style*.

3. **Punctuate and capitalize correctly.**   Follow these rules.

Punctuation and Capitalization in Business Letters

USE COMMA	Between city and state	*Pocahontas,* AK
	Between day and year	*May 11,* 1991
	After closing	*Yours truly,*
USE COLON	After greeting	*Dear Sir or Madam:*
CAPITALIZE	Street name	*2134 **H**ighway 27*
	City, state	*Greeley, **CO***
	Month	***M**ay 11, 1991*
	Salutation: first word, name	*Dear Sir or Madam:*
	Closing: first word	*Yours truly,*

---

4. **Address the envelope correctly.**   See page 174.

5. **Give complete information.**   Provide all information needed to respond to your letter. Be specific, clear, and direct.

6. **Use formal language.**   Be polite and formal (page 162). Say please and thank you. Study the models on the next page.

Want to know more about the harmonica? Just ask for "A Brief History of the Harmonica" or "Easyreeding" from
Hohner, Inc.
Department FD
P.O. Box 9375
Richmond, VA 23227-5035

Chess players can improve their game with the booklet "Ten Tips to Winning Chess." Send your request and SASE to
Barbara DeMaro
U.S. Chess Federation
186 Rt. 9W
New Windsor, NY 12550

Want a pen pal anywhere in the world? Send your request and SASE to
Student Letter Exchange
215 5th Avenue S.E.
Waseca, MN 56093

Send for the "Bicycle Safety Pamphlet" by writing to
Aetna Life & Casualty
Corporate Communications
DA/23
151 Farmington Ave
Hartford, CT 06156

Find out about the weather and how it affects passenger jets. Send SASE and ask for the "What's the Weather Pamphlet."
Air France Distributing
Center
NYC DX
2039 9th Ave.
Ronkonkoma, NY 11779

Send for *So You Want to Know about Orienteering* a 10-page booklet that tells about orienteering — using a map and compass to find your way. SASE
Orienteering Services, USA
P.O. Box 1604
Dept. FS
Binghamton, NY 13902-1604

LETTER OF REQUEST

323 Mountain Terrace
Mobile, Alabama 36619
January 7, 1991

New York Knickerbockers
4 Pennsylvania Plaza
New York, New York 10001

Dear New York Knickerbockers:

I will be visiting New York next month with my family, and we would like to attend one of your games. Would you please send me a copy of this year's schedule.

I have also heard that you mail out free Knicks bumper stickers. Would you kindly send me a bumper sticker too. I have enclosed a self-addressed stamped envelope.

Thank you very much.

Sincerely yours,

Manuel Garcia
Manuel Garcia

Enc.*

*Add *Enc.* at the left, below your typed or printed name to signal the person who receives the letter to look for an enclosure.

ORDER LETTER

17 Buenavista Lane
Bend, OR 97701
March 12, 1991

Poster Palace
312 Grand Avenue
Austin, TX 78756

Dear Poster Palace:

Please send me the following items from your Spring
1991 catalog:

1 panda poster, #371, unframed	$4.50
1 Love the Earth poster, #771A,	
with metal frame	8.50
	$13.00
Postage and handling	3.40
TOTAL	$16.40

I have enclosed a money order for $16.40 to cover the
price of the posters plus postage and handling.

Thank you.

Sincerely yours,

Patricia Finnerty
Patricia Finnerty

Enc.

Want to know more about money
matters? Send a postcard asking
for "The Story of Money" and
"Once Upon a Dime"
   Federal Reserve Bank of
      New York
   Public Information Department
   33 Liberty Street
   New York, NY 10045

Love horses? Send for informa-
tion about the American Quarter
Horse and the American Junior
Quarter Horse Association, an
organization you can join. Ask for
the "American Junior Quarter
Horse Association Booklet"
and "For You, AQH Booklet".
   AQHA
   Department FS
   P.O. Box 200
   Amarillo, TX 79168

LETTER OF COMPLAINT

Want some wildlife wisdom? Send a SASE asking for any or all of these:
"Hit the Trail for Bluebirds"
"Animal Orphans? No!"
"Fishing FUNdamentals"

Write to
Publication Center
Ohio Department of Natural
Resources
4383 Fountain Square Drive
Columbus, OH 43224

People have always searched for ways to light up the darkness. Learn about the quest for light by sending a postcard asking for one or all of these booklets:

"History of Human Achievement"
"Radiant Energy"
"Saving Lighting Energy"

Write to
Barbara Sitzman
GTE Products Corporation
Marketing Services Center
70 Empire Drive
West Seneca, NY 14224

1803 Highland Avenue, Apt. 3
Broken Arrow, Oklahoma 74728
February 14, 1991

Dennis White Cloud, Manager
Customer Service Department
Woodward Computers
887 Jenks Boulevard
Oklahoma City, Oklahoma 73125

Dear Mr. White Cloud:

The Ace Computer Model #125-77 I ordered on February 1 arrived today. However, the instruction manual was missing. I would appreciate your sending me the manual as soon as possible, since I need the instructions in order to use the computer.

Thank you.

Very truly yours,
Cassandra MacDonald

TIPS for Writing Business Letters

- Include all six parts: heading, inside address, salutation, body, closing, and signature.
- Use modified block or block style.
- Punctuate and capitalize correctly.
- Complete the envelope correctly.
- Include all the needed information.
- Be formal and polite.

Writing a Story

☐ **Story**   Series of events with a plot, setting, and characters

An Assortment of Stories

Adventure   Myths
Detective   Legends
Mystery   Fables
Science   Folk tales
Fantasy   Tall tales
Western
Romance
Horror
History
Humor

> I looked at Mr. Rodriguez in disbelief.
> "D?" I asked. He fumbled with his marking book.
> "Yes, D." He closed the book and looked up at me.
> Advice time, I thought. I knew this ritual only too well. He flung the navy book on his mahogany desk and stood up. I'd never noticed how big he was before. . . .
>
> —"Theft," Elizabeth Webster, *Merlyn's Pen*, October 1989

Someone once suggested this formula for writing a story: "Find a character. Get him up a tree. Throw stones at him. Get him down." In other words, get your characters into trouble and then get them out of it. Elizabeth Webster, who wrote "Theft" when she was an eighth grader, seems to know the formula. When she introduces her main character, he is already "up a tree."

How do you develop this formula into a story? You include the basic parts, or elements, shown below.

Stories for Reading . . .

On pages 123 – 124 is a list of stories you might want to read. Reading may give you good ideas for your own stories.

PLOT	A series of events tied to a problem
CONFLICT	The problem that sets off the events
CLIMAX	Point at which the problem peaks
RESOLUTION	The way the problem is finally handled
CHARACTER(S)	Person, animal, or thing involved in the events
MAIN CHARACTER(S)	The character who faces the main problem
SETTING	Time and place in which the events happen

To plan a story, start with an idea for a setting, character, or plot. Then build the rest of the story around it.

How to Plan a Story

1. **Plan the setting.**   Set the right scene for your story. Pick a setting that fits the events, conflict, characters, and mood. Scary events can be scarier in a dark, lonely place.

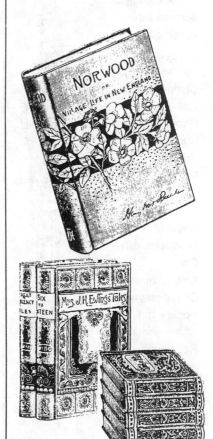

Story Ideas

START WITH A SETTING

A staircase
Saturn
The ocean floor
Pet show
Treetop
Video store
Inside a telephone
Blue jeans factory
Cloud
Closet
Tunnel
Bus
Anthill
Skating rink
Box of crayons
Shark's stomach
Science lab
Volcano

START WITH A
CHARACTER

Clarinet player
Bee
Robot
Snowflake
Toll taker
Perfume salesperson
Mail carrier
Soccer ball
Cactus plant
Limousine driver
Frog
King or queen
Chess player
Hockey fan
Young seal
Rainbow-colored cat

2. **Plan your characters.** Your story can be about anyone or anything you decide to bring to life — a person, a snake, a plane, a cloud. Sketch each character in a chart.

Character Profile
NAME AND AGE: _____
OCCUPATION, INTERESTS: _____
BACKGROUND, FAMILY: _____
APPEARANCE, CLOTHING: _____
WAY OF SPEAKING: _____
WAYS OF ACTING, MOVING: _____
LIKES AND DISLIKES: _____
BEHAVIOR TOWARD OTHERS: _____
STRENGTHS: _____
WEAKNESSES: _____

3. **Plan the conflict.** The conflict, or problem, can be as dramatic as a blizzard or as ordinary as a case of hiccups. Below are the main kinds of conflicts.

Conflict between the main character and another character

A student complains to a teacher about a test grade.

Conflict between the main character and a force of nature

A bear cub gets lost in a sudden storm.

Conflict between feelings inside the main character

A space explorer is torn between duty and curiosity.

---

4. **Plan the plot.** Tell the events in time order (page 22). Use the opening event to introduce the conflict. Then let the conflict build to a high point, event by event. Finally, resolve the conflict. A diagram of a plot looks like this:

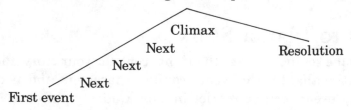

5. **Make a story chart.** A story chart is a plan. Even if you change your plan as you write, it will get your thoughts moving. Use as many events as you need in your chart.

Story Chart

SETTING: _____

MAIN CHARACTER(S): _____

OTHER CHARACTERS: _____

CONFLICT OR PROBLEM: _____

FIRST THING THAT HAPPENS: _____

NEXT: _____

NEXT: _____

CLIMAX: _____

RESOLUTION: _____

How to Write a Story

1. **Choose a point of view.** Who tells your story? Through whose eyes does the reader view the events? Stick to one narrator, or storyteller, and one point of view.

   a. First person

NARRATOR	One of the characters
PRONOUNS	First person pronouns, such as *I, me, our*
TELLS	Only what that character sees, hears, feels
EFFECT	Personal — lets reader get "inside" a character

   I smiled at Rona. Was she glad to see *me?*

   b. Third person limited

NARRATOR	One of the characters
PRONOUNS	Third person pronouns, such as *she, his, their*
TELLS	Only what that character sees, hears, feels
EFFECT	Focused, but less personal than first person

   He smiled at Rona. Was she glad to see *him?*

   c. Third person omniscient ("all-knowing")

NARRATOR	Observes the action but is not part of it
PRONOUNS	Third person pronouns, such as *she, his, their*
TELLS	Everything about all characters
EFFECT	Not personal but reader can be told everything

   He smiled at Rona. She was not glad to see *him*.

More Story Ideas . . .

START WITH A PROBLEM
Mixed message
Train that never comes
Telephone with a mind of its own
Uninvited guest
Empty fuel tank
Broken baseball bat
Unanswered letter
Tight shoe
Failed audition
Guilty conscience
Hurricane
Disobedient computer
Wild anteater
Sudden freeze
Invasion of wild fish
Poisonous potato chip
Missing earring

START WITH A DETAIL
Footsteps
Calm ocean
Empty cereal box
Blowing car horn
Silence
Moth hole
Deep brown eyes
Cold pizza
Worn-down eraser
Paw print
Eerie howl
Open door
Single shoe lace
Green traffic light
Stand-up ears
Whisper

And More Story Ideas . . .

2. **Fill in the setting.**   What mood do you want your story to have? What do you want the reader to "see"? Think of the setting as a stage set, and set the stage for your events. Sometimes you can just leave clues, as in the opening story. More often, you will want to fill in details that carry your reader away to the time and place of your story.

3. **Tell events in time order.**   If you skip around, your reader will have trouble following the story. As you write, ask yourself, "What happens next?" Be sure each event leads naturally to the next one. Use transitions, such as *a month later, as soon as, by the time I got there,* to connect events and show just when they happen (pages 154, 157).

4. **Bring your characters to life.**   Read this description of a character in Elizabeth Webster's story and picture him.

I had Bradley English, "the momma's boy," walking me home. He lived in one of those rich, three-story houses — you know, the kind with an attic so big you can fit a whole apartment into it. . . . He looked like a big, fat stuffed animal, wearing tons and tons of woolen articles and a down jacket that must have taken five hundred ducks to stuff. His combat boots clunked against the cement sidewalk . . .

Here are ways to bring the characters in *your* story to life.

a. **Give details about how they look, sound, dress, move.**

   She was small, but she walked with her head high.

b. **Give details about how they act.**

   As far as I know, no one had ever heard her laugh.

c. **Give details about how others react to them.**

   Even Ben, the class clown, did not try to tease her.

d. **Put words in their mouths.**

   "Gotta go now," she said quietly but firmly.

Dialogue — what characters say — is especially important. Webster's story would be flat without it.

I couldn't believe I'd gotten a D. I looked at Mr. Rodriguez. He said it really was a D.

5. **Show, show show!**   Don't just tell readers what happens or what the setting is like or how characters feel. Show them by using details. Compare the two sentences below, for example. The first just tells you someone was angry. The second, taken from the opening story, uses vivid details to show you just how angry he was.

TELLING   He was angry.
SHOWING His eyebrows were all scrunched together
           and he looked about ready to howl.

6. **Build to a climax.**   The conflict is what keeps the reader reading. You want the reader to ask, "What will happen next? What will the character do? How will it all turn out?" Try to add excitement, event by event, as you build to the climax of your story.

7. **Settle the problem.**   Your ending can be happy or it can be sad, but it should resolve the conflict in a way that fits the story. Do not leave your characters dangling. Tie up loose ends.

TIPS on How to Write a Story

PLAN!
- Plan the setting.
- Plan the characters.
- Plan the plot — conflict, events, and resolution.
- Make a story chart to help you.

WRITE!
- Choose a point of view.
- Fill in the setting.
- Tell events in time order. Use transitions.
- Bring your characters to life. Use description and dialogue.
- Show, don't just tell. Use details.
- Build to a climax.
- Resolve the problem in a fitting way.

Writing a Poem

How does it feel to...?

Reach the finish line
Dive into the ocean
Be lost
Wear new shoes
Catch a snowflake
Walk in the rain
Quarrel with a friend
Find a quarter
Pet a cat
Hit a home run
Get angry
Eat an ice cream cone
Meet someone special
Be alone
Walk into a subway
Ride an elevator
Watch a race
Wake up in the morning
Be afraid
Write a poem
Be two years old

The Topic

☐ **Poetry**   A form of writing in which feelings are expressed through word pictures and sounds

Heat Wave

On those days
when
prairie grass stands up so tall
reaching up to find
the breeze
that is not there
to sway it from side to side
I sneak
away
to find a cool place
to rest.

— Cheri Johnson, age 10,
Cricket, December 1987

Heat Wave

When the days get long,
And the grass turns brown,
The best thing to do
Is to go way down
To the cool, dark woods
And the tall shady trees,
To the chirping of the crickets
And the buzzing of the bees.
Find a nice soft spot
Where the moss grows deep
To lay yourself down
And drift off to sleep.
When you awaken,
And dusk begins to fall,
The shadows will be getting longer,
And it won't be hot at all.

— Jeremy Bell, age 13,
Cricket, December 1987

How do you feel on a hot day? Cheri Johnson and Jeremy Bell have told you how *they* feel, and you can share their feelings through their poems. The two poems are different, though. A poem about a heat wave is also about *how the poet feels* about a heat wave.

How to Find a Topic for a Poem

1. **Open your mind.**   Anything that can trigger a response in you can trigger a poem. Start with any subject, from a moth to a movie star, from a leaf to a broken window. Get your thoughts moving and see where they take you.

2. **Make an idea chart.**   Try putting some ideas on paper. Make a chart like the one begun below. List some general subjects and then brainstorm ideas for each subject.

<table>
<tr><td colspan="2" align="center">Idea Chart</td></tr>
<tr><td>PEOPLE</td><td>Grandmother, Geronimo, Rosa Parks</td></tr>
<tr><td>EVENTS</td><td>Heat wave, satellite launch, birthday</td></tr>
<tr><td>OBJECTS</td><td>Door to my house, rocket, watch, TV</td></tr>
<tr><td>SCENES</td><td>City street in heat wave, Mars</td></tr>
<tr><td>SENSATIONS</td><td>Touch: velvety, sandpapery, prickly</td></tr>
</table>

3. **Have fun with words.**   Collect words that you like, such as *silvery, hanky-panky, extraterrestrial*. Find other words that go with them: for example, *iridescent, glisteny* might go with *silvery*. Try writing some lines. See what happens.

4. **Just write!**   When you are feeling down or up or nervous or sentimental, pick up a pen and let your feelings flow onto a page. You may end up with the beginning of a poem.

TIPS on Finding a Poem Topic

- Open your mind.   • Play with words and lines.
- Make an idea chart.   • Write your feelings.

More Poem Ideas

- *Who Am I?* "Just call me . . ." Who are you? What are you like? What do you adore? What do you despise?

- *Make a wish.* "If I were . . ." In a wish poem, you can be anything, do anything, go anywhere.

- *Start with a color.* "When I see red, . . ." What does a certain color make you think of? How does it make you feel? Don't stick to obvious colors. Think about all the colors in a big crayon box!

- *Who? What? Where? When? Why? How?* Answer each question In a line of a poem.

Who?	A red-headed runner
What?	Paces impatiently
Where?	At the corner
When?	As the traffic light glows red—
Why?	Eager to cross the street and dash away,
How?	Her soft shoes bouncing on the stony sidewalk

- *Make a list.* "Snakes and snails and . . ." What slithers? What shines? What can't you buy? What is friendship made of? Answer a question with a list and use the list in a poem.

Writing a Poem

The Literal Way

SUNRISE The first appearance of the upper rim of the sun each day above the eastern horizon as a result of the daily rotation of the earth, with accompanying light reaching the earth, made up of all the colors of the rainbow blending to form white light, the brightness of which depends upon the particular conditions of the earth's atmosphere at that moment

DRUM A musical instrument played by percussion, or striking, made of either an open cylinder or a kettle with a drumhead, or skin, stretched tightly across the opening which, when struck, vibrates and produces a sound that is enlarged by the drum shell

Figurative Language

☐ **Figurative language**   Words and images that appeal to the imagination and tell what things are *like*

☐ **Literal language**   Words that tell what things are

I'll tell you how the Sun rose

I'll tell you how the Sun rose—
A ribbon at a time.
The steeples swam in amethyst,[1]
The news like squirrels ran.

The hills untied their bonnets,
The bobolinks begun.
Then I said softly to myself,
"That must have been the sun!"

But how he set I know not.
There seemed a purple stile[2]
Which little boys and girls
Were climbing all the while.

Till when they reached the other side,
A dominie[3] in gray
Put gently up the evening bars
And led the flock away.

— Emily Dickinson

the drum

daddy says the world
is a drum tight and hard
and I told him
i'm gonna beat
out my own rhythm

— Nikki Giovanni

To describe a sunrise in a science class, you use *literal language.* To describe what a sunrise is like to you or to express your feelings about yourself, you use *figurative language*, as in the two poems above.

[1] Violet color   [2] A step over a fence or wall   [3] Schoolteacher

How to Use Figurative Language

Collect Comparisons

Write some adjectives that have to do with the way things look, sound, smell, taste, or feel. Then list things that can be described by each adjective.

As *glaring* as a cat's eyes
a spotlight
the morning sun

.
.
.

1. **Create an image.**   Clear, sharp details help the mind "see." Create word pictures, or images, that will strike your reader's inner eye. (See pages 167 – 168.) Try to imagine both pictures below. Which can you "see" more clearly?

   WEAK   The buildings were a beautiful color.
   STRONG   The steeples swam in amethyst.

2. **Use your senses.**   Do you experience things only with your eyes? No, you use all your senses — sound, smell, taste, and feeling, as well as sight. When you describe things, then, give details that appeal to more than just the reader's eyes. For example, Emily Dickinson mentions the "bobolink," the sound made by a bird of the same name. Nikki Giovanni creates drumbeats with words. Below, Jeremy Bell tells how some things sound and feel in a heat wave (page 190).

   SOUND   To the chirping of the crickets
   And the buzzing of the bees
   TOUCH/FEEL   Find a nice soft spot
   Where the moss grows deep

Your Turn

As *slithery* as . . .
As *crinkly* as . . .
As *peppery* as . . .
As *thunderous* as . . .
As *mammoth* as . . .
As *stale* as . . .
As *gooey* as . . .
As *fuzzy* as . . .
As *hushed* as . . .
As *shrill* as . . .
As *bitter* as . . .
As *clammy* as . . .
As *stinging* as . . .
As *glossy* as . . .
As *murky* as . . .
As *sturdy* as . . .
As *whiny* as . . .
As *melodic* as . . .
As *venomous* as . . .

3. **Use figures of speech.**   Similes, metaphors, and personification can help you create images that appeal to your reader's imagination. (See also page 168.)

   a. **Simile**   A simile makes a comparison. It says something is like something else, and it uses *like* or *as*.

   FIGURATIVE   The news *like* squirrels ran.
   LITERAL   The news spread fast.

To *show*, not just tell you, how news of the sunrise traveled, Emily Dickinson compares it to fast-moving squirrels. The literal statement might be fine in a newscast, but it does not spark your imagination.

Writing a Poem – Figurative Language | **193**

Avoid clichés — similes, metaphors, and other figures of speech that have become tired and dull from overuse. Here are some examples:

As quiet as a mouse
As light as a feather
As rough as sandpaper
As deep as the ocean
As busy as a bee
As smooth as glass
As sweet as honey
As quick as a wink
As stubborn as a mule

Eyes like stars
Worked like a horse
Sparkled like diamonds

She is a walking encyclopedia.
His heart is an iceberg.
The car was a lemon.
He's a shining star.
She's a fountain of kindness.

b. Metaphor   A metaphor also makes a comparison, but without using *like* or *as*. Instead, it says or suggests that something *is* something else.

FIGURATIVE   daddy says the world is
a drum tight and hard
and I told him
i'm gonna beat
out my own rhythm

LITERAL   The world is a hard place, and I'm going to deal with it my way.

Nikki Giovanni's poem is a metaphor comparing the world to a drum. Notice how even the rhythm of the poem carries out the metaphor. Now look back at the last two stanzas of Dickinson's poem (page 192). What is she describing? The whole picture — the purple ladder, the boys and girls, the schoolteacher gently raising the evening bars — is a long metaphor for the setting sun.

c. Personification   Personification gives human qualities to something that is not human.

The steeples swam in amethyst

The hills untied their bonnets

Steeples cannot really swim, and hills cannot really untie anything. However, the "living" verbs make the steeples and the hills — and the images — come alive.

TIPS on Using Figurative Language

- Create images — word pictures that appeal to the reader's senses and imagination.
- Appeal to the senses — sight, sound, smell, taste, touch or feeling.
- Use figures of speech.
  Similes say one thing is like another, using *like* or *as*.
  Metaphors say one thing *is* another, without *like* or *as*.
  Personification uses human qualities for something not human.

Writing a Poem

Sound Effects

Whispers

Whispers
   tickle through your ear
   telling things you like to hear.

Whispers
   are as soft as skin
   letting little words curl in.

Whispers
   come so they can blow
   secrets others never know.

— Myra Cohn Livingston

A Lazy Thought

There go the grownups
To the office,
To the store.
Subway rush,
Traffic crush;
Hurry, scurry,
Worry, flurry.

No wonder
Grownups
Don't grow up
Any more.

It takes a lot
Of slow
To grow.

— Eve Merriam

Higgledy Piggledy

Sometimes rhyming words are put together to make good sound rather than good sense.

namby-pamby
ragtag
flip-flop
helter-skelter
fuddy-duddy
willy-nilly
hanky-panky
hoity-tolty
wingding
mumbo jumbo
hickory, dickory, dock

REALLY Using Rhyme!

Can you catch all the rhymes in the last line of this limerick?

The bottle of perfume that
   Willie sent
Was highly displeasing to
   Millicent;
  Her thanks were so cold
  They quarreled, I'm told,
Through that silly scent Willie
   sent Millicent.

!!!
Rhymeless Words

Try to end a line of a rhyming poem with any of these words and you may never finish your poem. There are no individual words that rhyme with them!

orange   silver   sugar
elephant   radio

Say the word *whisper* softly to yourself and really listen. What does it sound like? A whisper!

Poetry is meant to be read aloud. Therefore, more than any other kind of writing, poems make use of the sound of words as well as the meaning. Learn to use the natural sound effects of language when you write your own poems.

Stinkety-Pinkety

What's an overweight kitty? A fat cat, of course. A rhyming pair like fat cat *can be called a "stinkety-pinkety."*

Tight smile	*thin grin*
Seat for a grizzly	*bear chair*
Seafood platter	*fish dish*
Angry employer	*cross boss*
Stupid fruit	*dumb plum*

Your Turn

What "stinkety-pinkety" rhyming pairs fit these definitions?

Unhappy father
Mind ache
Reddish lemonade
Crooked penny

Now think of a definition for each "stinkety-pinkety" below.

mellow fellow
rare pair
dark ark
funny money

How to Use Sound Effects in a Poem

1. **Rhyme time?**   Words that *rhyme* end with the same vowel and consonant sounds, such as *sound* and *round*. Some poems use rhyme, and others do not. The two opening poems use rhyme, for example, but one of the poems on page 192 does not. Should you use rhyme in your poem? The decision is up to you. If you like rhyme, make lists of rhyming words: *there/scare/rare/dare/bear/care/hair* . . . See what ideas the words bring to mind. (For some rhyme schemes, see page 199.)

2. **Beat out a meter?**   Some poems, especially rhymed ones, have a *meter*. That is, the lines have a regular pattern of strong beats, or *accents*. Jeremy Bell's poem (page 190), for example, has two accents per line. (Below, **/** stands for a strong beat and **⌣** for a weak one.)

    When the days get long,
    And the grass turns brown,

    "Whispers" has a meter, too — a four-beat line.

    Whispers tickle through your ear
    telling things you like to hear.

3. **Get the rhythm.**   Not every poem has a meter, but every poem has a rhythm. The rhythm comes from the natural rhythm of the language. Read Cheri Johnson's lines aloud (page 190) and listen to the natural rhythm. Also read Eve Merriam's lines (page 195) and notice how the rhythm helps carry the meaning. *Hurry, scurry, worry, flurry* rushes you along, while the last lines slow you down.

    It takes a lot
    Of slow
    To grow.

    As you write your own poem, read your lines aloud. Play with them until the rhythm sounds right to you.

4. **Play with word sounds.** Take advantage of the way words sound when you put them together.

   a. **Onomatopoeia** Use words that sound like what they mean. *Whisper* is one example. *Chirping* and *buzzing* in the poem on page 190 are other examples. Here are a few more. (See page 167 for a longer list.)

   whiz hiss hum plop slurp thump twang
   clomp quack

   b. **Alliteration** Repeat a sound at the beginnings of words.

   *s*oft as *s*kin
   *s*way it from *s*ide to *s*ide

   c. **Consonance** Repeat a consonant sound or sounds within words that have different vowel sounds.

   *l*et*t*ing *l*it*t*le words cur*l* in

   d. **Assonance** Repeat a vowel sound within words.

   N*o* w*o*nder / Gr*o*wnups / D*o*n't gr*o*w up / Any m*o*re.

5. **Collect words.** Do you like the sounds of certain words, such as *rutabaga, clitter-clatter, quadrennium, Machu Picchu*? Collect words with interesting sounds. You may be able to use them in a poem or even build a poem around them.

TIPS on Using Sound Effects in a Poem

- Use rhyme if you like to work with rhyming words.
- Beat out a rhythm.
  Use a strong, regular beat, or meter, OR
  Use just the natural rhythm of the language.
- Play with the sounds of words.
  Onomatopoeia — words that sound like what they mean
  Alliteration — repeated sounds at the beginnings of words
  Consonance — repeated consonant sounds within words
  Assonance — repeated vowel sounds within words
- Collect words. Enjoy them!

S is the letter most often used in alliteration, and for a good reason. *S* begins more words than any other letter! Furthermore, it can be used before any letter except *b* or *x*.

Consonance Pairs

hippity-hoppity
shilly-shally
whippersnapper

Tongue Twisters

What happens when alliteration goes wild? A tongue twister! Try twisting your tongue around these (especially the last one, which some say is the hardest tongue twister of all).

Six slim slender saplings

Frisky Freddy feeds on fresh fried fish.

Around the rugged rocks the ragged rascal ran.

They threw three thick thistles at three thrilled thrushes.

Shiver and slither shoveling slushy, squishy snow.

The sixth sick sheik's sixth sheep's sick.

Writing a Poem

Form

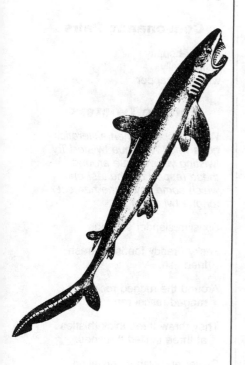

About the Teeth of Sharks

The thing about a shark is — teeth,
One row above, one row beneath.

Now take a close look. Do you find
It has another row behind?

Still closer — here, I'll hold your hat:
Has it a third row behind that?

Now look in and . . . Look out! Oh my,
I'll *never* know now! Well, goodbye.

— John Ciardi

Love Song for a Jellyfish

How amazed I was, when I was a child
To see your life on the sand.
To see you living in your jelly shape,
Round and slippery and dangerous.
You seemed to have fallen
Not from the rim of the sea,
But from the galaxies.
Stranger, you delighted me. Weird
    object of
The stinging world.

— Sandra Hochman

The poem about sharks has rhyme and meter and is divided into parts. The poem about jellyfish has no rhyme or meter and no separate parts. The shark poem is simple and funny and tells a kind of story. The jellyfish poem is serious and descriptive and tells a personal reaction.

Poems come in different forms and styles. Experiment. See what works best for you and for your poem.

How to Choose the Form of a Poem

1. **Rhyme scheme**   Rhymed poems often follow a rhyming pattern, or *rhyme scheme*. The rhyme scheme can be indicated by letters of the alphabet. The letter *a* stands for the first rhyming sound, *b* for the second, and so on.

Neither Out Far Nor In Deep

The people along the **sand**	*a*
All turn and look one **way.**	*b*
They turn their back on the **land.**	*a*
They look at the sea all **day.**	*b*
As long as it takes to **pass**	*c*
A ship keeps raising its **hull;**	*d*
The wetter ground like **glass**	*c*
Reflects a standing **gull.**	*d*
The land may vary **more;**	*e*
But wherever the truth may **be —**	*f*
The water comes **ashore,**	*e*
And the people look at the **sea.**	*f*
They cannot look out **far.**	*g*
They cannot look in **deep.**	*h*
But when was that ever a **bar**	*g*
To any watch they **keep?**	*h*

— Robert Frost

The Termite

Some primal termite knocked on **wood**	*a*
And tasted it, and found it **good,**	*a*
And that is why your Cousin **May**	*b*
Fell through the parlor floor **today.**	*b*

— Ogden Nash

The Sloth

In moving-slow he has no **Peer**	*a*
You ask him something in his **Ear,**	*a*
He thinks about it for a **Year;**	*a*
And, then, before he says a **Word**	*b*
There, upside down (unlike a **Bird**),	*b*
He will assume that you have **Heard —**	*b*
A most Ex-as-per-at-ing **Lug**	*c*
But should you call his manner **Smug,**	*c*
He'll sigh and give his branch a **Hug;**	*c*
Then off again to sleep he **goes,**	*d*
Still swaying gently by his **Toes,**	*d*
And you just know he knows he **knows.**	*d*

— Theodore Roethke

About the Sloth

A sloth is a slow-moving furry animal that likes to hang upside-down from the branches of trees.

Writing a Poem – Form | **199**

Write an Acrostic Poem

Spell out the subject of your poem in the first letter of each line. Here's an example.

L ong flowing mane
I dentifies the king of beasts.
O n guard and alert,
N oble even at rest.

Finish a Limerick

There once was a turtle named Nell
Who grew tired of wearing her shell
  She left it at home
  When she went out to roam,

2. **Stanzas**   Poems may be divided into parts, or *stanzas*, with similar rhyme schemes and rhythms. The poems by Ciardi (page 198), Frost (page 199), and Roethke (page 199) have stanzas.

3. **Free Verse**   *Free verse* is verse without meter (a regular beat). However, free verse is not without rhythm. It makes use of the natural rhythm of the language. Hochman's poem is an example (page 198). Free verse may or may not be rhymed.

4. **Couplet**   A *couplet* is a pair of rhymed lines.

A rude and noisy bird is the seagull —
Its behavior is anything but regal.

5. **Haiku**   *Haiku* is a verse form from Japan. It uses seventeen syllables arranged in three lines to create a single strong image. The lines do not rhyme and need not be sentences.

From the velvet darkness of night
The trill of a lone bird
Declares dawn.

6. **Cinquain**   The *cinquain* is an unrhymed poem of five lines with a set number of syllables in each line.

LINE	SYLLABLES	
1	*two*	Purple
2	*four*	A shade, a mood
3	*six*	A ribbon dangling loose
4	*eight*	A sunset blanketing the sky
5	*two*	Lilac

7. **Limerick**   The *limerick* is a five-line rhymed poem. Lines one, two, and five rhyme; lines three and four may or may not rhyme. Limericks are usually humorous. (See page 27.)

A diner while dining at Crewe
Found a rather large mouse in his stew.
  Said the waiter, "Don't shout
  And wave it about,
Or the rest will be wanting one too."

8. **Concrete poetry**   Some poems use the arrangement of the words on the page to help get their meaning across. Such "shape poems" are called *concrete poetry*. They are written to be seen as well as to be read and heard.

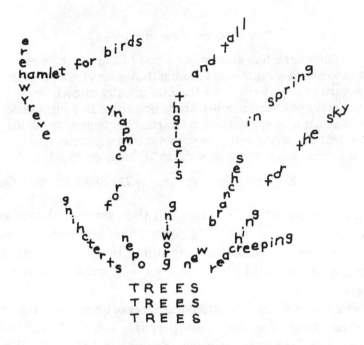

— "Trees," Denise F., *The English Journal*, April 1973

Some Poems to Read

Complete Poems of Emily Dickinson

Edna St. Vincent Millay's Poems Selected for Young People

Ego-Tripping and Other Poems for Young People; My House: Poems; Spin a Soft Black Song, Nikki Giovanni

Evangeline and Selected Tales and Poems, Henry Wadsworth Longfellow

I Am the Darker Brother: An Anthology of Modern Poems by Black Americans

100 Selected Poems, e. e. cummings

Pocket Book of Robert Frost's Poems

Oxford Book of Poetry for Children

Complete Nonsense of Edward Lear

All the Small Poems, V. Worth

Light in the Attic and *Where the Sidewalk Ends,* Shel Silverstein

Rainbows Are Made, Carl Sandburg

One at a Time: His Collected Poems for the Young, David McCord

---

TIPS on Forms of Poetry

Some questions:
- What will your rhyme scheme be?
- Will you divide your poem into stanzas?
- Will you write free verse or a poem with meter?

Some forms to consider:
- Couplet
- Haiku
- Cinquain
- Limerick
- Concrete Poetry

The Process

☐ **Report**   A composition presenting facts gathered by research

A Different View of the Shark

The Shark
How many Scientists have
  written
The shark is gentle as a kitten!
Yet I know about the shark:
His bite is worser than his bark.
— Ogden Nash

The Modern View of Sharks

    The shark has always been one of the most feared creatures on earth. Recent studies, however, give a different picture of the shark from the one usually shown in monster books and movies. According to Dr. Eugenie Clark, a scientist who specializes in sharks, "Neglecting to buckle the seat belt while riding in your car is many times more dangerous than meeting a shark" (Clark preface).

    — Eugenie Clark, Preface to *The Shark Watchers' Guide**

From the introduction, you can tell that you will learn something about sharks from this report. The student who wrote it learned even more. Before beginning to write, he found out as much as he could about sharks — a subject that really interested him.

    The main steps in composing a report are the same as in any other kind of writing. You prepare, you draft, you revise, you proofread, and you publish. (See pages 134–146.) Why do you do all this? You want to inform your reader about some subject. Therefore, as you go through the steps, you focus on gathering information and presenting it to the reader clearly and accurately.

    Here are the main parts of a report:

> Title
> Introduction
> Body
> Conclusion
> List of Sources

How to Write a Report

1. Choose a topic.   The world around you is full of possible report topics. How do you choose one?

* *The Shark Watchers' Guide* is written by Guido Dingerkus.

Choosing a Topic for a Report

- Choose a topic you would like to know more about.
- Choose a topic that will interest your audience.
- Choose a topic for which you can find information.
- Choose a topic you can cover in a brief report.

Need a Report Topic?

African Americans in the Revolution
Language of whales
Moons of Jupiter
Early Disney films
The useful firefly
Beginnings of television
Fashions of the sixties
Lasers in eye surgery
Flower paintings of O'Keeffe
How constellations are named
New uses for robots
Training of a jet pilot
League of Five Nations
Chinese calendar
How the bald eagle became endangered
Murals of Diego Rivera
Pros and cons of wind power
Geography of Vietnam
Sand painting
Poetry of Gwendolyn Brooks
Life inside a space capsule
Chicago fire of 1871
History of corn
Puerto Rico's relationship to the United States
How (your state) became a state
Apes learn sign language
Death of Sitting Bull
Measuring earthquakes
Origin of some slang expressions
Middle School in Japan

Suppose you are interested in ocean creatures. It is a topic that will interest your audience (namely, your classmates), and information is easily available in the library. However, can you cover ocean life in a brief report? No. You need to narrow, or limit, the topic. Here is one way to do it.

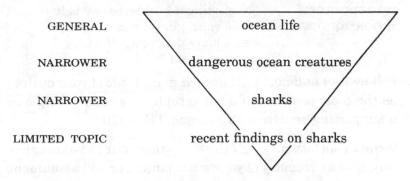

GENERAL	ocean life
NARROWER	dangerous ocean creatures
NARROWER	sharks
LIMITED TOPIC	recent findings on sharks

3. **Ask questions.** What do you need to find out to explain your topic? Make a list of questions your report should answer.

   What old beliefs about sharks have been changed?
   What have we learned about how sharks find food?
   How have we learned about how sharks move?

4. **Gather information.** Find information to answer the questions on your list. Use encyclopedias for general background information, the library catalog for books on your topic, and the *Readers' Guide to Periodical Literature* for magazine articles. (See pages 60 – 61.) You might also interview an expert on your topic. (See pages 130 – 131.)

5. **Take notes.** On separate note cards, write each fact you find and its source — the book, article, or interview it came from. You can then organize your notes simply by putting together cards with similar details. (See pages 207 – 209.)

!!! About Sharks . . .

There are between 250 and 350 different kinds of shark.

Sharks have no bones. Instead, they have cartilage, a gristly, rubberlike material.

Tiger sharks eat anything, including cans and other trash. They are very dangerous because they swim close to shore.

There are fewer than 100 shark attacks reported a year.

Female sharks are thought to be more dangerous than males.

The fearsome shark of books and movies is the *great white shark*. It can grow as long as 30 feet and weigh as much as three tons.

The great white shark often eats large animals such as seals and porpoises.

The *mako shark* is one of the fastest fish. Some move as fast as 60 miles an hour!

The *whale shark* is the world's largest fish, growing to more than 50 feet. (Remember, the whale is a mammal, not a fish.)

6. **Make an outline.** After putting together note cards on the same topic or subtopic, use the topics to make an outline for your first draft. (See page 211 for outlining tips.)

7. **Write a thesis statement.** Decide what your main point, or thesis, will be. Write a sentence that states it clearly and specifically. Tell the reader exactly what to expect.

> THESIS STATEMENT Recent studies give a different picture of the shark from the one shown in monster books and movies.

8. **Write an introduction.** Write an introduction around your thesis statement. Add a catchy detail or quotation to "hook" the reader.

> INTRODUCTORY "HOOK" (QUOTATION) "Neglecting to buckle the seat belt while riding in your car is many times more dangerous than meeting a shark."

9. **Follow your outline.** Use each main topic of your outline as the topic sentence of a paragraph. Use each subtopic as a supporting sentence. (See pages 147 – 150.)

10. **Write a conclusion.** At the end, state your thesis another way, give a summary of your main points, or add a comment on your information. Avoid empty expressions such as "I have just shown you" or "Now you have seen."

> CONCLUSION The shark is not a monster but an efficient and fascinating creature whom we are just beginning to know.

11. **Identify your sources.** Identify the source of every quotation. (See pages 212 – 213.) List all your sources in a list at the end. (See page 214.)

TIPS on Writing a Report

- Choose a limited topic.
- Ask questions about the topic.
- Find answers to the questions.
- Take notes on cards.
- Use the cards to make an outline.
- Write a thesis statement.
- Write an introduction.
- Follow your outline.
- Draft a conclusion.
- Identify your sources.

Writing a Report

Skimming and Scanning

☐ **Skim** Look over a page, picking out important parts

☐ **Scan** Look over a page, searching for specific information

The Body of a Shark

Teeth. A shark's mouth is on the underside of the head among all species except whale sharks. The mouth of a whale shark is at the front of the head. A shark has several rows of teeth. When an old tooth wears out or is lost, a new one grows in and replaces it. . . . Some persons believe that sharks must turn over on their backs to bite, but this is not true.

Senses. Sharks have keen senses, which they use in hunting. Their sense of smell is particularly well developed. As much as two thirds of a shark's brain may be used in connection with smelling. Sharks can sense some odors, such as that of blood, ¼ mile (.4 kilometers) away. Sharks also have excellent hearing. They can hear a struggling fish or a human swimmer at a considerable distance, perhaps as far as 1,000 yards (910 meters).

Sharks were once thought to have poor vision. They cannot see sharp details, but they use their eyes in attacking prey. In clear water, a shark can easily pick out a moving object from its background as far as 50 feet (15 meters) away.

—"Sharks," *The World Book Encyclopedia*

The passage above is just one part of one encyclopedia article on sharks. If you read every word on your topic, you would have no time to write your report. Learn to *skim* to find out what is in a selection. *Scan* to look for specific facts.

How to Skim

1. **What is skimming?** *Skimming* is a kind of fast reading. Move your eyes quickly to pick out important information.

2. **Find out what a book is about.** A book with *shark* in its title may or may not have the information you need for your report on sharks. To see what the book contains, look at the table of contents, index, and illustrations.

3. **Read the beginning and the end.** Read the first paragraph or two — just enough to get a general idea. The last paragraph might offer a summary.

4. **Notice the highlights.** To skim a selection, look for titles, headings, highlighted words and phrases, and illustrations. For instance, headings in dark type may help you.

5. **Look at paragraphs.** Read the first and last sentences of paragraphs. Look for key words that tell you the content. For example, words like *food, prey, eat* in a shark book tell you the section has something to do with how sharks feed.

How to Scan

1. **What is scanning?** When you scan, you search for a particular piece of information. For example, you scan the phone book to look for a particular name and number.

2. **Look at highlighted words.** Highlighted words can point your way to the information you need. Look not only at titles and headings but also at other words in **bold** or *italic*.

3. **Look for key words.** What words are key to your topic? Suppose you are writing a report about how sharks see. Zero in on the part of the encyclopedia article headed "Senses." Then look for words like *sight, see, eyes, vision.*

!!! About scan

The word scan *comes from a Latin word meaning "climb."*

Here are four meanings for the word *scan.* (Some of the meanings are opposites!)

scan To examine closely
(*Scan the highway for the yellow truck.*)

scan To look over quickly
(*Just scan the page. There's no time to read it.*)

scan To make a careful search, as with radar
(*We scanned the skies for an approaching plane.*)

scan To analyze the rhythmic pattern of verse
(*I scanned the poem, counting the beats on each line.*)

> ## TIPS on Skimming and Scanning
>
> TO SKIM
> - Skim to look for any important facts.
> - Look at the contents and index of a book.
> - Read the beginning and the end.
> - Notice the highlights —headings, key terms, illustrations.
> - Look for the main idea of each paragraph.
>
> TO SCAN
> - Scan to look for specific facts.
> - Look at highlighted words that are key to your topic.

Writing a Report

Note-taking

SOURCE   *Dingerkus*

SUBJECT   *How sharks find food*

Strong sense of smell
— Can smell drop of blood in 25 gals.
     of water

PAGE   *p. 16*

When you take notes, you collect facts and information to include in a report. Try to use index cards. Then you can arrange and rearrange your notes just by grouping the cards.

How to Take Notes

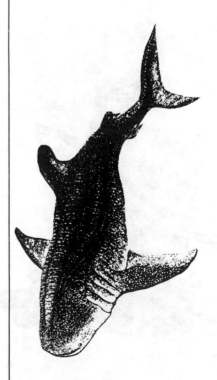

1. **List questions to be answered.** Write down the questions your report should answer. Here, for example, are some of the questions listed by the student who wrote the shark report.

   What have researchers learned about how sharks move?
   What have researchers learned about how sharks find food?
   What old beliefs about sharks now appear to be false?

2. **Make source cards.** On a card, list specific information about each source used. You or your reader may want to consult the source. Save these cards for your list of sources. (See page 214.)

SOURCE CARDS

Book

AUTHOR   *Dingerkus, Guido*

TITLE   *The Shark Watchers' Guide*

PLACE & PUBLISHER   *New York: Franklin Watts*

PUBLICATION DATE   *1985*

Encyclopedia

ARTICLE   *"Shark"*

ENCYCLOPEDIA, DATE   *The World Book Encyclopedia, 1988*

Magazine Article

AUTHOR   *Hennefreund, Beth*

ARTICLE   *"Shark Lady"*

MAGAZINE & DATE   *Ranger Rick March 1989*

PAGES   *49-55*

3. **Put one note on each card.** Put each detail on its own card. Then you can arrange and rearrange notes easily.

4. **Identify the source.** In the upper right-hand corner of each card, write the source of the note. You can use just the author's name or an abbreviation, or you can give each source a number. In the lower right, write the page number.

5. **Identify the topic.** In the upper left-hand corner, write the topic of the note. Usually the topic will be one of the questions with which you started. The topic on the sample card is "How sharks find food" — a short version of "What have researchers learned about how sharks find food?"

6. **Use your own words.** Take notes in your own words. (See "Paraphrasing," page 210.) Then you avoid the risk of *plagiarizing*, or using someone else's words as your own.

7. **Put direct quotations in quotation marks.** If you use someone else's words, put quotation marks around them in your notes. Then you will remember to give the person credit.

8. **Choose what to write.** Do not try to write down everything. Jot down just the important facts that relate directly to your topic. Write only key words, not complete sentences. Use abbreviations wherever you can. Just be sure to write enough so that you will be able to read it back later.

9. **Recognize facts and opinions.** Usually you use facts. If you use an opinion, label it as such. (See page 36.)

TIPS on Taking Notes

- List questions to answer.
- Make a note card for each source of information.
- Write only one note on each card.
- Write the source of each note.
- Label the topic of each note.
- Use your own words.
- Put quotations in quotation marks.
- Note only important information. Write just the key words. Use abbreviations.
- Know the difference between fact and opinion. Label opinions.

!!!
About *note*

Note these notes about *note*. How many meanings does it have?

note Short written record
(*I take notes in class.*)

note Comment on part of a text, usually placed at the foot of the page
(*The note gave the source of the quotation.*)

note Brief, informal letter
(*I got a note from Evan.*)

note Piece of paper money
(*In London I exchanged dollars for pound notes.*)

note Mood, quality
(*A note of sadness crept into his voice.*)

note Importance
(*She is a woman of note.*)

note Observation
(*Take note of this fact.*)

note Call of a bird or animal
(*I heard a trilling note.*)

note Symbol for a musical note
(*That note stands for C.*)

note A musical tone
(*He hit a high note.*)

note Musical instrument key, as on a piano
(*The note for middle C is broken on that piano.*)

Writing a Report

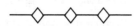

Painful Paraphrases

Paraphrasing is a useful tool, but it isn't meant to improve the original, as you can see from these examples.

DECLARATION OF INDEPENDENCE

We hold these truths to be self-evident, that all men are created equal, that they are endowed by their Creator with certain unalienable Rights, that among these are Life, Liberty and the pursuit of Happiness.

PARAPHRASE

Obviously, we're all born equal. Also, we're all entitled to live, to be free, and to try to be happy.

GETTYSBURG ADDRESS, Abraham Lincoln

Four score and seven years ago our fathers brought forth, upon this continent, a new nation, conceived in Liberty, and dedicated to the proposition that all men are created equal.

PARAPHRASE

A new nation was started here 87 years ago based on everyone being free and equal.

Paraphrasing

☐ **Paraphrasing**   Restating in other words

> The white shark has been seen in all of the world's warmer seas. It is oceanic and travels almost everywhere in the open sea. Besides attacking swimmers off the coast of California, it has attacked people in the United States as far north as Cape Cod. It is a sea monster we encounter just offshore, on our doorstep so to speak.
>
> — *Mystery Monsters of the Deep*, Gardner Soule

Paraphrase: White sharks have been spotted around the world. They live mainly in warm waters but get as far north as Cape Cod (Massachusetts). They have attacked swimmers there and in California and can be a threat close to shore.

The two paragraphs give the same facts, but they use different words. The writer of the second passage has *paraphrased* the first. She has put Soule's information into her own words. When you take notes, paraphrase to avoid plagiarizing (page 209).

How to Paraphrase

1. **Ask yourself, "What is the writer saying?"**   Think about the meaning of the words you read or hear.

2. **Express the same meaning in a different way.**   Change the words but not the meaning.

3. **Be accurate.**   Look for details. For example, white sharks are not found in all oceans, only in warmer ones.

4. **Do not confuse fact and opinion.**   If you are paraphrasing an opinion, say so. (See page 36.)

TIPS on Paraphrasing

- Ask, "What is the writer saying?"
- Express the same meaning in a different way.
- Be accurate. Notice details.
- Distinguish between fact and opinion.

Writing a Report

Outlining

☐ **Outline**   Organized arrangement of main ideas and details

MAIN TOPIC	I. Changes in our beliefs about sharks
SUBTOPICS	A. Not stupid
	B. Not blind
	C. Not generally vicious
	D. Important to ecology of ocean
MAIN TOPIC	II. Other findings
SUBTOPICS	A. Need to keep swimming
	B. Equipped to find food
DETAILS	1. Keen sense of smell
	2. Pick up vibrations

Above is part of an outline for a report on sharks. (See pages 202 – 209.) Use an outline to organize your information.

How to Make an Outline

1. **Sort your note cards into piles.**   Group cards on the same topic and subtopic. Save notes that do not fit any group. They may fit your introduction or conclusion.

2. **Write the topic of each group of cards.**   These topics become the main topics of your outline. Arrange them in a logical order, using Roman numerals. (See pages 202 – 209.)

3. **Write the notes under the appropriate topic.**   The notes on your cards become your subtopics and details. Use capital letters for the subtopics and numbers for the details.

4. **Use standard outline form.**   The outline above is a model.

5. **Have at least two items on each level.**   If you have a I, you need a II. If you have an A, you need a B, and so on.

TIPS on Making an Outline

- Sort note cards into groups by topic and then subtopic.
- Write the topic of each group.
- Below it, add the subtopics and details from your notes.

Roman Numerals

The ancient Roman system for writing numbers lasted until the late 1500s, when the Arabic numerals we use today became common. All Roman numerals are combinations of these seven letters:

I	=	1	C =	100
V	=	5	D =	500
X	=	10	M =	1,000
L	=	50		

Here are some combinations:

$$\begin{aligned} VII &= 7\,(5 + 1 + 1) \\ XV &= 15\,(10 + 5) \\ IV &= 4\,(5 - 1) \\ XIV &= 14\,(10 + 5 - 1) \\ LXXX &= 80\,(50 + 10 + 10 + 10) \\ XC &= 90\,(100 - 10) \end{aligned}$$

Here is the way to write 1 through 10 in Roman numerals.

I	=	1	VI	=	6
II	=	2	VII	=	7
III	=	3	VIII	=	8
IV	=	4	IX	=	9
V	=	5	X	=	10

Your Turn

"Translate" these numerals:

XVI	XXXIV	CLXXXIV
XIX	CXX	CM

900   120   19
184   34   16
Answers

For More Information . . .

See Joseph Gibaldi and Walter S. Achtert, MLA Handbook for Writers of Research Papers *(New York: The Modern Language Association of America, 1988).*

Naming Sources

Scientists have found that sharks are not the stupid animals we once thought they were. Furthermore, not all sharks are vicious. The more we learn about sharks, the more we realize that "Sharks are magnificent animals that deserve respect" (Hennefreund 55).

In a research report, you need to identify the sources from which you obtained your information. When you use a quotation or a technical fact or figure, you identify the source in parentheses after the information, as shown above, or in a footnote at the foot of the page.

. . . we realize that "Sharks are magnificent animals that deserve respect."[6]

[6]Beth Hennefreund, "Shark Lady," *Ranger Rick* March 1989: 55.

How to Give Sources in Parentheses

1. **Give the source right after the information.** Give a source whenever you use someone else's words, facts, or ideas.

2. **Give just enough facts to identify the source.** Usually, the author's last name and the page number are enough. If there is no author, give the title or a shortened version of it. Put the source in parentheses at the end of the sentence. Place it outside any quotation marks. (See the opening paragraph.)

AUTHOR: (Hennefreund 55)   TITLE: ("Sharks")

How to Write Footnotes

1. **Mark the quotation or the fact.** In the text, write a small raised number, or *superscript*, after the item to be noted, like the number *6* above. Notice that the number follows the punctuation. Use as many footnotes as you need in your report, and number them in order.

2. **Skip a space after the last line.**   Leave some space after the last line on the page to separate it from the footnote. Also leave room at the foot of the page for the note.

3. **Follow standard footnote style.**   Notice the punctuation, the superscript, and the paragraph indent in each note.

  a. **Book**   Author's first and last names, *title* (place of publication: publisher, year of publication) page(s).

   [1]Gardner Soule, *Mystery Monsters of the Deep* (New York: Franklin Watts, 1981) 32.

  b. **Magazine article**   Author's first and last names, "title of article," *name of magazine* month and year: page(s).

   [2]Beth Hennefreund, "Shark Lady," *Ranger Rick* March 1989: 55.

  c. **Encyclopedia article**   "Title of article," *name of encyclopedia*, year of edition.

   [3]"Sharks," *The World Book Encyclopedia*, 1988 ed.

  d. **Newspaper article**   Writer's first and last names (if given), "title of article," *name of newspaper* day and month and year, edition (if known): page.

   [4]Geraldo Ruiz, "Lifeguards at Nantasket Beach Issue Shark Warning," *Boston Globe* 20 July 1989, late ed: 25.

  e. **Interview**   Person's name, type of interview, day and month and year.

   [5]Ernest Simon, personal interview, 18 June 1990.

  f. **Repeated reference**   To refer to a work already cited in a footnote, use a short form, plus page numbers if any.

   [6]Soule 44.
   [7]Hennefreund 49.
   [8]"Sharks," *World Book*.

TIPS on Writing Footnotes

• Mark the quotation or fact with a footnote number.
• Number your footnotes in order.
• Leave space for the footnote at the foot of the page.
• Follow standard footnote style.

Writing a Report

For More Information . . .

See Joseph Gibaldi and Walter S. Achtert, MLA Handbook for Writers of Research Papers *(New York: The Modern Language Association of America, 1988).*

!!!
About *bibliography*

The word bibliography *comes from Greek (*biblio-, *"book," + *-graphy, *"write, written").*

Your Turn

You have just learned what biblio- *and* -graph(y) *mean. Take a look at the words below. What might they mean? Take a guess. Then check a dictionary to find out how close you came.*

1. bibliofilm
2. bibliographer
3. bibliomania
4. bibliophile

5. telegraph
6. autograph
7. biography
8. graphology

Now try making up some biblio- *and* -graph(y) *words of your own. For example, what might you call*

— a skywriter?
— a place for washing books?
— a machine for measuring writing?

Answers

(1) type of microfilm used to photograph pages of a book, (2) one who creates bibliographies, (3) exaggerated liking for books (*mania* related to *maniac*), (4) one who loves books (*-phile* = "someone having a love for"), (5) system for sending messages over wires (*tele-* = "distance"), (6) persons signature (*auto-* = "self"), (7) written account of a persons life (*bio-* = "life"), (8) study of handwriting (*-ology* = "study of.")

List of Sources

☐ **Bibliography** List of reference works used for a report

How to Write a Bibliography

1. **Make it the last page.** The list of sources will be the last page of your report. Write *Bibliography* or *Sources* centered at the top of the page. Skip a line between each work.

2. **List all the sources you used.** List works from which you got information even if you did not quote from them directly. Do not, however, list works you did not actually use.

3. **Use alphabetical order.** List the works alphabetically by the authors' last names. Use the first letter of the titles to alphabetize works that have no authors.

4. **Follow standard style.** Here are examples. Notice the punctuation. Also note that the second line is indented.

BOOK	Soule, Gardner. *Mystery Monsters of the Deep.* York: Franklin Watts, 1981.
MAGAZINE ARTICLE	Hennefreund, Beth. "Shark Lady." *Ranger Rick* March 1989: 49–55.
ENCYCLOPEDIA ARTICLE	"Sharks." *The World Book Encyclopedia.* 1988 ed.
NEWSPAPER ARTICLE	Ruiz, Geraldo. "Lifeguards at Nantasket Beach Issue Shark Warning." *Boston Globe* 20 July 1989, late ed: 25.
INTERVIEW	Personal interview. Simon, Ernest. 18 June 1990.

TIPS on Writing a Bibliography

- Make the bibliography your last page.
- List all the sources you used.
  List only the sources you used.
- Use alphabetical order.
- Use standard bibliography style.

Writing a Book Report

☐ **Book report** Composition that tells about a book

Julie of the Wolves
by Jean Craighead George

What would it be like to become part of a pack of wolves? That is what an Eskimo girl named Miyax does in the novel Julie of the Wolves by Jean Craighead George.

Miyax has run away from home to try to join her pen pal in San Francisco, who calls her Julie. On the way, she gets lost in the Alaskan wilderness. She survives by using the traditional Eskimo skills taught her by her father, Kapugen, and by making friends with a pack of wolves led by the great wolf Amaroq. Miyax travels with the wolves, shares their food, and learns their ways. She even learns how to "talk" to them.

In the course of the book, Miyax grows up. Her survival makes her stronger, but some of the things she learns also make her sadder. They made me a little sad too.

The book is both exciting and moving. It gives many fascinating details about wolves and about getting along in the wilderness. You feel that you are in Alaska along with Miyax, trying to survive. Read the book, but only when you have time. You may find it hard to stop reading once you begin. I did.

Notice what this report tells you about *Julie and the Wolves*. It tells you what the book is about, who the main characters are, where the story takes place, and how the writer of the report felt about the book.

Here are the main parts a book report should include:

BOOK TITLE, AUTHOR

INTRODUCTION	– Repeat the title and author. – Tell the type of book and the subject. – Grab the reader's interest.
BODY	– Give a brief summary of the plot. – Tell about characters and setting.
CONCLUSION	– Give an opinion or make a recommendation about the book.

Books for a Report

Here are some well-liked books for different ages. Choose some to read and to use for book reports. (See pages 116, 117, 118, 123; 124 for more lists.)

Across Five Aprils, I. Hunt

Adventures of Sherlock Holmes, A. C. Doyle

And Now Miguel, J. Krumgold

Beowulf, A New Telling, R. Nye

The Cat Ate My Gymsuit, P. Danziger

Charlotte's Web, E. B. White

The Count of Monte Cristo, A. Dumas

Dandelion Wine, R. Bradbury

The Door in the Wall, M. De Angeli

Fahrenheit 451, R. Bradbury

The House of Dies Drear, V. Hamilton

I, Juan de Pareja, E. B. Trevino

In the Year of the Boar and Jackie Robinson, B. Lord

Incredible Journey, S. E. Burnford

Little House on the Prairie, L. I. Wilder

Martin Luther King: The Peaceful Warrior, E. Clayton

Member of the Wedding, C. McCullers

My Side of the Mountain, J. C. George

The Red Badge of Courage, S. Crane

Sixteen: Short Stories by Outstanding Writers for Young Adults, D. R. Gallo, ed.

Summer of My German Soldier, B. Greene

The Wonderful Flight to Mushroom Planet, E. Cameron

- Write a journal entry for one of the characters.

- Write a letter to the author.

- Write a letter to one of the characters.

- Write a letter to a friend, telling about the book.

- Make up an interview with the author or one of the characters.

- Write part of the book as a scene from a play.

- Make a decorated map and use it in a speech about the book.

- Write a news article about an event in the book.

- Give a radio news report about the events in the book.

- Report on the book as one of the characters.

- Make a model of the setting and use it to illustrate a talk about the book.

- Create a comic strip to illustrate the book.

- Create an ad campaign for the book.

How to Write a Book Report

1. **First think about the book.**   Jot down some notes about the book. What was the main idea or theme? How did it affect you? What did you like best? least? For a narrative, make a story chart outlining the story (page 123).

2. **Present the book.**   Use the name and author as your title. Then repeat them in your introduction. Tell what kind of work it is — novel? science fiction? nonfiction? biography? Tell the subject. Make your reader want to know more.

3. **Summarize.**   In the body of the report, summarize the book briefly. For a narrative, describe the plot. Tell only enough to get the reader interested.

4. **Tell about the setting and characters.**   For a narrative, describe the setting and the main characters.

5. **Explain.**   Explain something important about the book, such as why something happened, how the book is put together, or what the author's purpose was. Also mention the *theme* — the general idea of the book, such as survival or growing up.

6. **Support your points with details.**   When you make a statement, back it up with examples or quotations.

7. **Stick to one tense.**   Do not shift tenses needlessly. To tell what a character does, use the present tense only.

   Miyax *travels* with the wolves, *shares* their food, and *learns* their ways.

8. **Give a personal reaction.**   How did you feel?

9. **Make a recommendation.**   Should your reader read the book? Why or why not?

TIPS on Writing a Book Report

- Plan.
- Present the book.
- Give a brief summary.
- For a narrative, tell about plot, setting, characters.

- Explain something important.
- Use examples and details.
- Stick to one tense.
- Give a personal feeling.
- Make a recommendation.

Writing a Summary

☐ **Summary**   A brief statement giving the main points of something

Artifacts are more than just the "things" people make for their use. Artifacts represent the ideas of a culture. (*Culture*, as archaeologists[1] use the word, means any group of people who share a common way of life.) Each culture has its own idea of how something — a spear, a pot, or a basket — should look. For instance, spears made by the Great Lakes Indians are different from those made by Indians from northwest Canada. Each group had its own idea of how a spear should look and passed this design down from generation to generation.

— *Digging the Past,* Bruce Porell

Summary: Every group of people with a common way of life (called a *culture*) has its own idea about what the things it uses (called *artifacts*) should look like. Therefore, objects with the same use look different from one culture to another.

How to Write a Summary

1. **Look for the main ideas.**   Ask yourself, "What is this about?" "What does the writer want to tell me?"

2. **Look for key words.**   Use the key words in your summary. In the passage above, the key words are *culture* and *artifacts*.

3. **Eliminate detail.**   Keep only what is needed to help state the main idea or ideas. Examples are usually not necessary.

4. **Be concise.**   A summary is always shorter than the original. (See "Making Your Writing Concise," pages 158 – 159.)

5. **Keep essentials.**   Do not be so brief that your summary is unclear. If a detail is really needed, use it — briefly.

TIPS for Writing a Summary

- Look for main ideas.
- Look for key words.
- Eliminate detail.
- Be concise.
- Keep essentials.

---

[1]Scientists who study the life and activities of ancient people

???
What Stories Are These?

Can you recognize these familiar stories from their summaries?

While enjoying an outdoor lunch, a girl is driven away by a terrifying spider.

A boy and girl injure themselves falling from a hill they had climbed in search of water.

A shepherdess is informed that her missing flock is sure to return on its own.

Little Miss Muffet; Jack and Jill; Little Bo Peep

Answers

Communicating by Signing

☐ **Signing**   Using a system of hand gestures to communicate, especially with people who cannot hear

When you point to something or raise your hand in class, you are actually "talking" with your hands. It is even possible for you to communicate with hand gestures alone, using different kinds of *sign language.* For example, you can use a *manual alphabet* to spell out words with your fingers, or you can use *American Sign Language (ASL),* a separate language whose "words" are made up of gestures rather than sounds. You can even use both together.

The manual alphabet is shown below, and some words in ASL are shown on the next page.

The Manual Alphabet

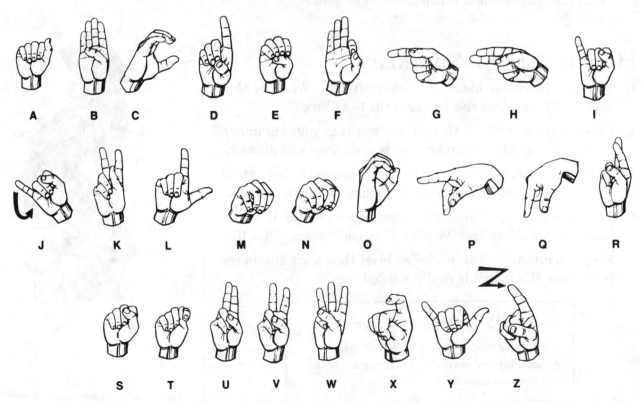

— from *The Perigree Visual Dictionary of Signing,* Rod R. Butterworth

Some Words in American Sign Language

About, Concerning
Move the right index finger in a forward circular direction around the fingers of the left hand.

Cat
Place the index fingers and thumbs of the *F* hands under the nose with the palms facing, then move them out sideways. This sign may also be done with the right hand only.

Center, Central, Middle
Make a clockwise circle with the right curved hand above the left flat hand; then lower the fingertips of the right hand into the left palm.

Hamburger
Cup the right hand on top of the left cupped hand; then reverse.

House, Residence
Form the point of a triangle at head level with both flat hands; then move them apart and straight down simultaneously with the fingers pointing up.

How
Point the fingers of both bent hands down and place the hands back to back. Revolve the hands in and upward together until the palms are flat and facing up.

Negative
Place the right index finger horizontally across the left palm, which is facing out.

— from *The Perigree Visual Dictionary of Signing,* Rod R. Butterworth

Send
Touch the back of the left bent hand with the fingertips of the right bent hand; then swing the right hand forward.

Sentence
Touch the thumb and index fingers of each *F* hand in front of the chest. Pull the hands apart to the sides, either with a straight or wavy motion.

Separate, Apart
Place the knuckles of both hands together and pull the hands apart.

Slow
Draw the right hand slowly upward over the back of the left hand. Begin near the fingertips and move up to the wrist.

Smart, Bright, Brilliant, Clever, Intelligent
Touch the forehead with the right middle finger while keeping the other fingers extended. Direct the middle finger outward and upward. The index finger can also be used.

Your Turn

Use the manual alphabet to sign your name.

See how much you can say. Talk with a friend, using both ASL words and the manual alphabet.

Communicating by Braille

!!!
About Mr. Braille

The Braille system was invented by Louis Braille, a blind French student, at the age of 15. He got the idea from a dot-dash code punched on cardboard and used to send messages to soldiers at night.

Your Turn

Send Braille messages to a friend by punching holes in cardboard or some other kind of stiff paper.

☐ **Braille** Code of raised dots on paper that can be read by touch, used especially by the blind

Braille uses a system based on a six-dot pattern.

With different combinations of these six dots, 63 characters can be formed. Some are shown below.

The Braille Alphabet

A B C D E F G H I J

K L M N O P Q R S T

U V W X Y Z

SOME WORDS

and for of the with

SOME SOUND COMBINATIONS

ch gh sh th wh ed er ou ow

Communicating by Code

Morse, Binary, Semaphore

☐ **Code** Arrangement of words, figures, or signals for sending short and sometimes secret messages

Morse Code

Morse Code is a system of dots, dashes, and spaces once used to send messages by electricity over a wire. The code was developed by Samuel Morse, who invented the telegraph — a device that sent the messages. When a key was pressed on the telegraph, it produced a clicking sound at the other end of the wire. Short clicks were dots, and longer clicks were dashes.

Throughout the later 1800s, the telegraph was the fastest way to send long-distance messages. In fact, in 1866 a telegraph cable was laid across the Atlantic to tie America to Europe.

Sending Morse Code

(1) A dot is short.
(2) A dash is twice as long as a dot.
(3) A space between dots and dashes within a letter is as long as a dot.
(4) A space between words is as long as three dots.

Some Other Useful Codes

BINARY CODE

Binary is the basic code used by today's computers. As in Morse Code, signals are created by on-and-off pulses of electricity. Instead of dots and dashes, binary uses *0* (electricity off) and *1* (electricity on).

Each pulse is called a *bit*, and 8 bits make a *byte*. Given 8 ways to combine the two numerals *0* and *1*, 8 bits can form 256 different patterns! (See also the Glossary on pages 103 – 105.)

BRAILLE

Braille is a system of raised dots that can be read by touch (see page 220).

SEMAPHORE

Semaphore is a way of signaling with flags or targets. It is particularly useful to the navy and to railroad engineers.

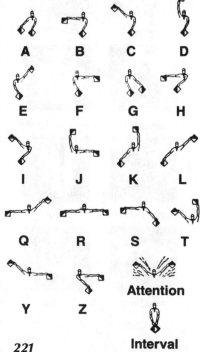

LETTERS

NUMERALS

PUNCTUATION

OTHER SIGNALS

Communicating by Signs

International Airport Signs

Baggage Check-In

Baggage Check-Out

Currency Exchange

Handicapped Access

Men's Lavatory

Women's Lavatory

First Aid

Post Box

Information

Lost and Found

Observation Deck

Restaurant

Telephone

Bus Stop

☐ **Sign** Object used to point out something

Traffic and Road Signs

COLORS OF SIGNS

RED: Stop, yield, do not enter or wrong way.

YELLOW: General warning.

ORANGE: Construction & maintenance warning.

BLACK: Regulatory.

BROWN: Public recreation areas and parks.

BLUE: Motorist services guidance.

GREEN: Distance, direction and information.

WHITE: Regulatory.

ONLY **ONLY**

SLOW MOVING VEHICLE

DO NOT ENTER

STOP

MERGE

YIELD

CATTLE XING

SIGNAL AHEAD

PED XING

DIVIDED HIGHWAY

TWO WAY TRAFFIC

HILL

BIKE XING

DEER XING

SLIPPERY WHEN WET

SCHOOL ZONE

DO NOT PASS

NO PASSING ZONE

NO U TURN

NO RIGHT TURN

NO LEFT TURN

KEEP RIGHT

SERVICE AND GUIDE SIGNS

CAMPING → **CAMPING →**

→ **TRAIL →**

→ **BIKE ROUTE →**

H HOSPITAL →

Communicating by Symbols

☐ **Symbol** Something that stands for something else

Some Weather Symbols

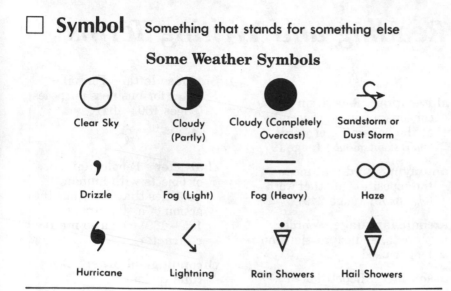

Clear Sky	Cloudy (Partly)	Cloudy (Completely Overcast)	Sandstorm or Dust Storm
Drizzle	Fog (Light)	Fog (Heavy)	Haze
Hurricane	Lightning	Rain Showers	Hail Showers

Some Astronomy Symbols

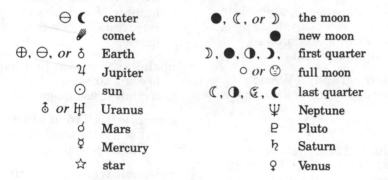

⊖ ☾	center	●, ☾, or ☽	the moon
☄	comet	●	new moon
⊕, ⊖, or ♁	Earth	☽, ●, ◑, ☽,	first quarter
♃	Jupiter	○ or ☺	full moon
☉	sun	☾, ◐, ☾, ☾	last quarter
♁ or ♅	Uranus	♆	Neptune
♂	Mars	♇	Pluto
☿	Mercury	♄	Saturn
☆	star	♀	Venus

Some Music Symbols

𝄞	treble, or G, clef	♮	natural	♪	eighth note	*f*	forte (loud)
𝄢	bass, or F, clef	𝅝	whole note	♬	sixteenth note	*ff*	fortissimo (very loud)
♯	sharp	𝅗𝅥	half note	*p*	piano (soft)	∿	trill
♭	flat	♩	quarter note	*pp*	pianissimo (very soft)		

Some Mathematics Symbols

+	plus; positive
−	minus; negative
×	multiplied by
÷	divided by
=	equal to
±	plus or minus
∓	minus or plus
≠ or ≠	not equal to
≡	identical with
≈	nearly equal to
~	difference
≅	congruent to
>	greater than
≫	much greater than
<	less than
≪	much less than
≧ or ≥	greater than or equal to
≦ or ≤	less than or equal to
≯	not greater than
≮	not less than
:	is to; ratio
∴	therefore
∞	infinity
∠	angle
∟	right angle
⊥	perpendicular
∥	parallel
⊙ or ○	circle
⌒	arc of a circle
○	ellipse
⌀	diameter
△	triangle
□	square

Reading and Writing Terms

A

alliteration Repetition of a consonant sound, especially at the beginning of words (*sweet silent sounds*) (page 197)

antonym Word that means the opposite of another word (*big, small*) (page 249)

archaic language Words, phrases, and expressions no longer used

assonance Repetition of a vowel sound within words (*rosy glow*) (page 197)

audience Person or people to whom a speech, talk, or piece of writing is addressed (pages 119 – 121)

autobiography Person's account of his or her own life

B

ballad Poem that tells a story, usually of a dramatic event; usually includes a **refrain**

bibliography List of books, articles, and other sources of information used in a report; list of books on a subject (page 214)

biography Account of the life of a real person

body Main section of a piece of writing such as a report or a letter

book report Composition that tells about a book (pages 215 – 216)

business letter Formal letter for business purposes (pages 180 – 184)

C

character People, animals, or objects with human qualities that carry out the action of a story (pages 185 – 189) (see also **main character**)

chronological order See **time order**

cinquain Unrhymed poem of five lines with a specific number of syllables on each line, usually 2–4–6–8–2 (page 200)

cliché Expression that has become tired and dull from too much use (page 253)

climax High point of tension in a story; the point at which the conflict peaks (page 186)

coherent writing Writing in which the ideas are clearly connected (pages 156 – 157)

concise writing Writing that is clear and direct, with no unnecessary words (pages 158 – 159)

conclusion Ending of a piece of nonfiction writing (pages 150, 170, 204)

concrete poetry Poetry appealing to the eye rather than the ear, in which the shape of the words on the page helps convey the meaning (page 201)

conflict Problem that sets off the events in a story (pages 185 – 186)

connotation Feelings and ideas associated with a word (page 163)

consonance Repetition of a consonant sound or sounds within words, usually with different vowel sounds (*lovely river*) (page 197)

couplet Pair of rhyming lines (page 200)

creative writing Writing in which writers use their imagination to express themselves and create characters, events, and images, as in stories and poems

D

denotation Exact meaning of a word, as in the dictionary (page 163)

descriptive writing Writing that tells what something is like by appealing to the senses and using vivid language (pages 167 – 168)

dialect The way people in a certain group or area speak

dialogue Actual words said by the characters in a story or play (page 188)

diction Choice of words (pages 162 – 163)

discussion Talking about a subject within a group, often with a particular goal in mind (pages 127 – 129)

E

exaggeration Overstatement of something, often deliberately used for special effect or humor

expository writing Writing that informs or explains (pages 169 – 170)

F

fable Story starring animals that teaches a lesson, or *moral*, often stated at the end

fantasy Fiction involving people or events that could not actually exist or happen

fiction Writing that comes from the author's imagination

figurative language Language that uses vivid images to tell what something is like; figures of speech (pages 192 – 194) (see also **simile, metaphor, personification**)

first person Point of view in a story told by one of the characters, using *I* (page 187)

flashback Interruption of story action to tell something that happened earlier

folktale Traditional story of a certain area or group, usually an oral tale handed down from the past and then written

footnote Piece of information, such as the source of a quotation, placed at the foot of a page (pages 212 – 213)

foreshadowing Hint or clue in a story about what is to come (for example, a weather report predicting a storm as a hint that one of the characters will soon be involved in a storm)

formal language Careful, precise language used for business or formal occasions (page 162)

free verse Verse that does not have a regular rhythm, or meter (page 196)

friendly letter Informal note or letter to friend or relative (pages 174 –179)

H

haiku Japanese verse form; poem of seventeen syllables arranged into three lines that present a single striking image (page 200)

historical fiction Story that comes partly from history and partly from the imagination of the writer

I

image mental picture (page 193)

implied topic sentence The unstated main idea of a paragraph that does not have a **topic sentence** (page 150)

informal language Casual, everyday language (page 162)

interview A question-and-answer conversation that has a purpose (pages 130 – 131)

introduction The opening part of a piece of expository or persuasive writing (page 204)

irony Words that mean the opposite of what is really intended, for example, saying "What a smart thing to do!" to someone who has done something silly or stupid

J

jargon Special or technical language used by people in a special field (page 252)

L

legend Story usually tied to a hero or historical event, sometimes based on truth

limerick Rhymed poem of five lines, usually humorous, in which lines one, two, and five always rhyme (page 27)

literal language Words and phrases that tell about things as they actually are; straightforward, matter-of-fact language (page 192)

lyric poetry Poetry expressing personal feelings and thoughts

M

main character Character who deals with the problem or conflict in a story (page 185)

metaphor Figure of speech based on an implied comparison; says something is something else (pages 168, 193)

meter Regular beat or rhythmic pattern of some poetry (page 196)

mood Atmosphere, feeling, or emotion of a work (page 188)

myth Story giving imaginary explanation of something in nature

N

narrative Story or series of events (pages 164 – 166)

narrative poetry Poetry that tells a story

narrative writing Writing that tells a real or imaginary story or series of events (pages 164 – 166)

narrator Person or character who tells a story (page 187)

nonfiction Writing based on real events, people, things

novel Book-length fictional story

O

onomatopoeia Use of words that sound like what they mean (*quack, plop*) (page 197)

order of importance Arrangement of supporting facts and details according to how important they are; for example, from most to least important or from least to most important (page 152)

outline Organized arrangement of main ideas and details; often used as preparation for writing (page 211)

P

pace Rate at which the action in a story moves; the "rhythm" of a story

parable Story that presents a clear, simple version of a problem in order to teach a lesson or moral

paragraph Group of sentences about one main idea (pages 147 – 150)

paraphrasing Stating something in different words (page 210)

parody Imitation of a particular work or style, designed to be humorous

personal narrative Series of real events told by the person who experienced them (pages 164 – 166)

personification Use of human qualities for nonhuman creatures or objects; a figure of speech (page 194)

persuasive writing Writing that tries to convince someone to believe something or to take an action (pages 171 – 173)

plot Series of connected events in a story, during which a character faces a problem or conflict, the conflict rises to a high point or climax, and the conflict is finally resolved (pages 185 – 189)

poetry Type of writing that uses language to create sounds and images, usually expressing personal feelings (pages 190 – 201)

point of view Position or "eyes" through which a story is told — **first person, third person limited, third person omnipotent** (page 187)

pun Humorous remark based on a word that has more than one meaning or that sounds like another word (page 247)

purpose Reason for speaking or writing; effect a speaker or writer wants to have (pages 119 – 121)

Q

quotation Repetition of someone's exact words; used with quotation marks ("/")

R

rambling sentences Sentences that have too much information and as a result are unclear (page 159)

realistic fiction Fiction based on events that are imaginary but could happen (as opposed to **fantasy**)

redundancy Unnecessary repetition of words or meanings (page 159)

refrain Line or phrase repeated regularly in a poem, usually at the end of each stanza

report Composition, based on research, presenting facts about a topic (pages 202 – 214)

resolution The way the main character finally deals with the conflict or problem in a story (pages 185 – 187, 189)

rhyme Use of words ending with the same vowel and consonant sounds (*beat, feet*) (page 196)

rhyme scheme Pattern of rhyme followed in a particular poem; usually shown by letters of the alphabet, in which each letter stands for a different rhyming sound (*abab*) (page 199)

S

sarcasm Saying one thing but meaning something else, usually to insult or taunt

science fiction Writing that comes from the imagination but uses some aspect of science and usually takes place in another time or another world

sensory words Words that appeal to one or more of the senses — sight, sound, smell, touch/feeling, taste (pages 167 – 168)

setting Time and place of the events of a story (pages 185, 188)

simile Comparison between two unlike things; figure of speech that says something is like something else, using *like* or *as* (pages 168, 193)

sonnet Poem of fourteen lines that follows a certain rhyme scheme

spatial order Arrangement of facts or details in a description according to where the details are located, for example, from left to right or top to bottom (page 152)

stanza Group of lines in a poem that follows a certain rhythmic pattern (page 200)

story (short story) Series of events with a plot, a setting, and characters (pages 185 – 189)

summary Brief statement giving the main points of something (page 217)

symbol Something that stands for something else, such as a flag, which stands for a nation

synonym Word with a meaning similar to another word (*large, big*) (page 249)

T

tall tale Story with exaggerated characters and events, usually told for fun

theme Main or underlying idea or message of a piece of writing; may or may not be stated

thesis statement Sentence that states the main idea of a composition of more than one paragraph, such as a report (pages 172, 204)

third person limited Point of view in a story told by one of the characters using *he* or *she* (page 187)

third person omniscient (all-knowing) Point of view in a story told by an all-knowing impersonal narrator, using *he, she, they* (page 187)

time order Events or steps presented in the order in which they occur (pages 22 – 23, page 152)

tone Attitude of the author conveyed in a piece of writing, such as anger, humor, or **irony**

topic sentence Sentence that tells the main idea of a paragraph (see also **implied topic sentence**) (pages 147 – 150)

transitions Words and phrases that tell how ideas and things are related; for example, *before, above, soon, although, therefore* (pages 154, 157)

U

unified writing Writing in which all sentences and details relate to the topic (page 155)

Part IV –
Using the Tools

Vocabulary

The History of English

Modern languages in the Indo-European family include the following:

Modern Greek

from Latin
  Romanian
  Spanish
  Italian
  Portuguese
  French

from Germanic
  English
  Scandinavian
  Dutch
  Flemish
  German

from Celtic
  Scottish Gaelic
  Irish
  Welsh

Albanian

Armenian

from Balto-Slavic
  Serbo-Croatian
  Czecho-Slovak
  Russian
  Polish
  Bulgarian
  Slovene

from Sanskrit
  Hindi
  Bengali

Persian

A.D. 1000
> on fagne flor feond treddode,
> eode yrre-mod; him of eagum stod
> ligge gelicost leoht unfaeger.
>
> *[on the adorned floor the fiend trod,*
> *he went in an angry way; off his eyes stood*
> *a fire-like, strange light]*
> — from *Beowulf*

Late 1300s
> Whan that Aprill with his shoures soote
> The droghte of March hath perced to the roote,
> And bathed everyveyne in swich licour
> Of which vertu engendred is the flour;
> — from Chaucer, *Canterbury Tales*

1601
> This above all, to thine own self be true,
> And it must follow, as the night the day,
> Thou canst not then be false to any man.
> Farewell. My blessing season this in thee!
> — from Shakespeare, *Hamlet*

1926
> take it from me kiddo
> believe me my country, 'tis of
>
> you, land of the Cluett
> Shirt Boston Garter and Spearmint
> Girl With the Wrigley Eyes
> — from Cummings, *Poem, or*
> *Beauty Hurts Mr. Vinal*

All of the verses above are written in English. Obviously the language has changed, because languages have a history, just as countries do. Nevertheless, you can recognize many of the words Chaucer wrote in the 1300s. With some help, you could even figure out *Beowulf*, written a thousand years ago.

What Do *You* Say?

Do you drink *soda, tonic, pop,* or a *soft drink*? That depends on where you live, because you are likely to speak the way people around you do. The particular form of a language spoken in a particular area by a particular group is called a *dialect*. Here are words that are different in different dialects. Which word in each group do *you* use?

- sub(marine), hoagie, grinder, hero, poor-boy
- bag, sack, poke
- pail, bucket
- flapjack, pancake, hotcake, griddlecake, hoecake
- frying pan, skillet
- belly flop, belly slapper, belly bumper, belly whopper
- white bread, light bread
- peanut, goober
- teeter-totter, seesaw
- hopscotch, potsy
- tadpole, polliwog
- firefly, lightning bug, glowworm
- dragonfly, darning needle, mosquito hawk, spindle
- earthworm, angleworm, fishworm, fishing worm, fish bait, bait worm, mud worm

THE BEGINNING

Linguists (scholars who study language) believe that English and some other languages came from a common ancestor. They call this ancestor *Indo-European*, because it spread from northern India across Europe. Linguists believe there had to have been such a language to explain why some languages are so similar. Look at the similar words for *mother*, for example:

ENGLISH	SPANISH	ITALIAN	FRENCH
mother	madre	madre	mère

ROMANIAN	NORWEGIAN	DUTCH	GERMAN
mama	mor	moeder	Mutter

POLISH	RUSSIAN	IRISH (Gaelic)
matko	matj	mathair

OLD ENGLISH

In A.D. 500, the Celts were living in what is now England. They were conquered by three Germanic tribes — the Saxons, Jutes, and Angles. The Celtic language was replaced by Anglo-Saxon, and the land came to be known as *Angle-land*, then *England*. Anglo-Saxon turned into the earliest stage of English, Old English. Most basic words, such as articles, pronouns, and connecting words, come from Anglo-Saxon.

FROM ANGLO-SAXON	the	you	to	and	do
	a	it	of	that	be
	she	on			go
	I	out			

Like Modern English, Old English adopted words from other languages. There were a few leftovers from the Celtic language and many words from Latin — the language of the Romans, who ruled a large area of the world. Then the Vikings invaded England in the ninth and tenth centuries and added some Old Norse words.

FROM LATIN	school	purple	senate	priest	pork
	candle	column	porch	forest	angel
FROM OLD NORSE	egg	ugly	sky	give	want
	hit	rotten	get	window	skill

The epic poem *Beowulf* (page 231) provides linguists with much interesting information about Old English.

MIDDLE ENGLISH

In 1066 the French-speaking Normans invaded England. French became the official language, but the common people spoke English. Signs of this division can still be seen in the language today. Common everyday words usually come from Anglo-Saxon. "Fancier" words tend to come from Norman French. As a result, English has word pairs like those shown below.

FROM ANGLO-SAXON	FROM NORMAN FRENCH
red	scarlet
cow	beef
king	sovereign

The combination of Norman French and Old English developed into Middle English by the 1200s. See the Chaucer example on page 231, which is written in Middle English.

MODERN ENGLISH

By the time Shakespeare was born in the 1500s, English pronunciation had changed. The final *e* in words like *same* and *side* had become silent. In addition, the vowels that had been pronounced as shown below had taken on the pronunciations they have today.

VOWEL	MIDDLE ENGLISH PRONUNCIATION
same	ah as in father
be	ay as in pay
side	ee as in bee
nose	aw as in law
boot	o as in rose
down	oo as in moon

This change, called the Great Vowel Shift, produced Modern English. The spelling, however, did not change along with the pronunciation. It is still based on the pronunciations of Middle English. That is why the system can seem odd to modern speakers.

English continued to change, as you can see by comparing Shakespeare with Cummings (page 231), and it is still changing today.* A language that is alive and well will always be changing to fit the needs of the people who speak it.

*See "Where New Words Come From," pages 234–236.

!!!
So Many Words!

English has more words than any other language — about 490,000 words, plus about 300,000 technical terms! However, an individual speaker probably uses about 60,000 words at most.

!!!
So Many Speakers!

Of the world's 5,000 or so languages, English is the second most widely spoken (after Mandarin Chinese).

Vocabulary

More Words from Names

leotard tights, usually worn when exercising

—for Jules Léotard, 19th-century French trapeze artist

dungarees jeans

—for Dhungaree, India, where the cloth once came from

cardigan jacket-sweater

—for the Earl of Cardigan, 19th-century Englishman who popularized it

tuxedo semi-formal evening suit

—from Tuxedo Park, New York, where it originated in the 19th century

bloomers loose trousers worn under dresses

—for Amelia Bloomer, 19th-century feminist who introduced them

jersey soft knit fabric

—from island of Jersey, in English Channel, where it was used for sweaters

Ferris wheel amusement park ride

—for G. W. Gale Ferris, its inventor

Where New Words Come From

From Other Languages

Without words from other languages, English would not be the language it is today. Here are just a few examples of words it has borrowed.

AMERICAN INDIAN	Minnesota, Idaho, Chicago, chocolate, skunk, chipmunk, pecan, hickory, moccasin, chocolate
ARABIC	algebra, checkmate, sherbet, zero
CHINESE	chow, silk, typhoon, tea
DUTCH	Brooklyn, sleigh, caboose, boss, Yankee, spook, coleslaw, cookie, waffle, pickle
FRENCH	Vermont, gopher, pumpkin, prairie, rapids, chowder, menu, garage, discotheque
GERMAN	Bismarck, kindergarten, poodle, nickel, noodle, hamburger, frankfurter, pretzel
ITALIAN	opera, stanza, trampoline, pizza, spaghetti, macaroni, pasta, broccoli, soprano, piano
SPANISH	Nevada, San Diego, breeze, barbecue, patio, plaza, cafeteria, tuna, mosquito, tornado, mustang, coyote, canyon, cargo, vanilla, bronco, mesa, rodeo, taco, chili

Words from Names

Items may be named for people or places associated with them.

volt	Unit of electricity Named for Count Alessandro Volta, Italian physicist and pioneer in electricity
saxophone	Musical instrument Named for its inventor, Adolphe Sax
teddy bear	Stuffed toy bear Named for Teddy Roosevelt, U.S. president who spared the life of a bear cub on a hunting trip
cashmere	Soft, luxurious type of wool Comes from Kashmir, India
denim	A strong, coarse fabric often used for jeans From Nîmes in France (*de Nîmes* = "from Nîmes")

Shortened or Clipped Words

Long words in frequent use are often shortened, or "clipped." The clipped form often becomes more common than the original.

ad	advertisement	memo	memorandum
auto	automobile	mod	modern
bike	bicycle	movie	moving picture
bus	omnibus	pants	pantaloons
champ	champion	pep	pepper
exam	examination	phone	telephone
fan	fanatic	plane	airplane
flu	influenza	pop	popular
gas	gasoline	prom	promenade
gym	gymnasium	sub	submarine
lab	laboratory	super	superior
limo	limousine	taxi	taxicab
lunch	luncheon	tie	necktie
math	mathematics	zoo	zoological garden

Word Blends

Sometimes two words are blended so that two meanings are carried by a single word.

bit	binary + digit	o'clock	of (the) + clock
blotch	blot + botch	simulcast	simultaneous + broadcast
brunch	breakfast + lunch		
chortle	chuckle + snort	sitcom	situation + comedy
clash	clap + crash		
clump	chunk + lump	skylab	sky + laboratory
docudrama	documentary + drama	smash	smack + mash
farewell	fare + ye + well	smog	smoke + fog
flare	flame + glare	splatter	splash + spatter
flush	flash + gush	squiggle	squirm + wriggle
hassle	haggle + tussle	telethon	television + marathon
hifi	high + fidelity		
laundromat	laundry + automat	travelogue	travel + monologue
motel	motor + hotel		
motorcade	motor + cavalcade	twirl	twist + whirl

Days of the Week

Sunday	Sun's day
Monday	Moon's day
Tuesday	Tiw's day — Teutonic god of war
Wednesday	Woden's day — Norse god of the hunt
Thursday	Thor's day — Norse god of the sky
Friday	Fria's day — Norse goddess, wife of Thor
Saturday	Saturn's day — Roman god of agriculture

Compound Words

Sometimes whole words are joined to form a compound. The meaning of the compound is not always the same as the meanings of the words that make it up. (See also page 262.)

bareback	gentleman	popcorn	sweetheart
bloodhound	outfield	sandpaper	thumbtack
brainstorm	pancake	spotlight	wristwatch

Words from Sounds

Words can be invented to imitate or "echo" the sounds they name. Here are some *echoic* words. (See also page 167.)

murmur	beep	blip	buzz	clomp	fizz	hiss
honk	moo	plop	quack	slurp	squeal	thump

Acronyms

Rather than using a long title, people often make up a new word out of the first letters or syllables. Some of these *acronyms* are pronounced as words. Others are spelled out.

CD	Compact disk
COD	Cash on delivery
DDT	Dichlorodiphenyltrichloroethane
DJ	Disc jockey
HUD	Housing and Urban Development
JEEP	General purpose (vehicle)
LASER	Light amplification by stimulated emission of radiation
NOW	National Organization for Women
RADAR	Radio detecting and ranging
RSVP	*Répondez, s'il vous plaît* (French: "Reply, please")
SCUBA	Self-contained underwater breathing apparatus
VISTA	Volunteers in Service to America
ZIP	Zone Improvement Plan

New Words for New Things

Here are some other ways in which new words are invented:

1. **Using Latin and Greek roots and stems:** misfire, astronaut
2. **Combining parts of other words:** cheeseburger
3. **Giving old words new meanings:** car (*from* railroad car)

Vocabulary

Understanding Unfamiliar Words

Holding the snickersee firmly, he cut right through the box.

What's a snickersee? Even if you have never seen the word before, you can guess a few things about it from the above sentence. It is something you can hold in your hand and use to cut other things. What is it? It's a large, swordlike knife.

When you come across words you do not know, you can often figure out their meaning from the *context* — the surrounding words.

How to Find Context Clues

1. **Definitions**   Look for an explanation of the word's meaning.

   The *abolitionists* worked for an end to slavery in the
     United States.
   Laws are made by the *legislative* branch of the government,
     that is, by the Senate and the House of Representatives.

2. **Examples**   Look for an example or illustration of the word.

   Draw a *quadrilateral*, such as a rectangle or a square.
     [four-sided figure]
   Among the largest *canines* are Great Danes and Old
     English sheepdogs. [dogs]

3. **Comparisons**   Look for a comparison with a familiar expression.

   Outside the theater, the sidewalk was as *congested* as a
     highway at rush hour. [crowded]

4. **Contrasts**   Look for a contrast with a familiar expression.

   Eva looked *melancholy* until the kitten made her smile.
     [sad]

5. **Synonyms**   Look for a word with the same meaning.

   The sleeping dog was *oblivious* to the noise, unaware
     that a stranger had entered. [unaware]

Roots, Prefixes, and Suffixes

☐ **Root**   The basic part of a word to which other parts may be added

☐ **Prefix**   A word part added before a word to change the meaning

☐ **Suffix**   A word part added after a word to change the meaning

A Word Family

ROOT	_act_
PREFIX + ROOT	en_act_
	re_act_
	inter_act_
	trans_act_
ROOT + SUFFIX	_act_or
	_act_ress
	_act_ion
	_act_ive
PREFIX + ROOT + SUFFIX	inter_act_ion
	hyper_act_ive
	trans_act_ion
	en_act_ment
PREFIX + PREFIX + ROOT + SUFFIX	reen_act_ment
ROOT + SUFFIX + SUFFIX	_act_ivity
	_act_ivate
	_act_ionable

Most words are not just single blocks. Instead, they are made up of several blocks. The blocks can be put together in different ways to build different words, as in the word family above.

The main building blocks of words are _roots, prefixes,_ and _suffixes,_ many of which come from Greek and Latin. Once you can recognize these word parts, you can figure out the meaning of many unfamiliar words. Some common roots, prefixes, and suffixes are listed on the following pages.

SOME GREEK ROOTS

Root	Meaning	Example
aster, astr	star	astronaut
auto	self, alone	automobile
biblio	book	bibliography
bio	life	biography
chron	time	chronology
cosm	universe	cosmonaut
crat, crac	govern	democrat
cycl	circle, ring	bicycle
dem	people	epidemic
gen	birth, race	generation
geo	earth	geography
gram	letter, writing	telegram
graph	write	autograph
hydr	water	hydrant
log	word	apology
logy	study of	biology*
mech	machine	mechanic
meter	measure	thermometer
opt	eye	optical
nym, nom	name, word	synonym
ortho	straight, right	orthodontist
ped	child	pediatrician
path	feeling, suffer	sympathy
phil	love	philosophy
phob	fear	phobia
phon	sound	telephone
photo	light	photograph
pod	foot	podium
poli	city	politics
psych	mind, soul	psychology
scop	see	telescope
soph	wise	sophomore
tele	distant	telephoto
therm	heat	thermometer

*See page 38 for *-ology* words.

What Are You Afraid Of?

With Greek *phobia*, you can give any fear a name.

acrophobia	fear of heights
aerophobla	fear of flying
agoraphobia	fear of open spaces
ailurophobia	fear of cats
amaxophobia	fear of vehicles
arachnophobia	fear of spiders
aquaphobia	fear of water
astraphobia	fear of lightning
brontophobia	fear of thunder
claustrophobia	fear of closed spaces
cynophobia	fear of dogs
gephyrophobia	fear of bridges
herpetophobia	fear of reptiles
murophobia	fear of mice
numerophobia	fear of numbers
nyctophobia	fear of darkness
ornithophobia	fear of birds
pyrophobia	fear of fire
triskaideka- phobia	fear of the number 13
xenophobia	fear of strangers

Your Turn

Add some phobias of your own, using the Greek roots — for example, *philophobia*, "fear of love."

More Word Families

The root *dic(t)* means "say" or "tell." Here are just some of the words formed from it.

diction	contradict
dictionary	verdict
dictate	predict
dictator	prediction
dictation	indict

Below are words with *miss* or *mit*, "send."

missile	transmit
mission	transmittal
missionary	remit
dismiss	remittance
dismissal	remission
remiss	permit
emissary	permission
	admit
	admission
	emit
	emission

SOME LATIN ROOTS

Root	Meaning	Example
act	do	action
alt	high	altitude
ang	bend	angle
aqua	water	aquarium
art	skill	artist
aud	hear	auditorium
brev	short	abbreviation
cam	field	camp
cap	head	captain
capt	take, hold	capture
cede, ceed	go, yield	recede, proceed
ceive, cept	take, get	receive, accept
cogn	know	recognize
corp	body	corpse
cred	believe	incredible
dic, dict	say, tell	dictate
don	give	pardon
fac, fec	make, do	factory, infect
flect, flex	bend	reflect, flexible
fract, frag	break	fracture, fragment
grad	step	graduate
imag	likeness	imagine
ject	throw	reject
junct	join	conjunction
miss, mit	send	dismiss, transmit
nat	born	native
pon, pos	place, put	postpone, deposit
port	carry	portable
scrib, script	write	describe, postscript
sect	cut	section
spec	look, see	inspect
stat	stand	statue
terr	land	territory
vac	empty	evacuate
vid	see	video
viv, vit	live	revive, vitality
volv	roll	revolve

◇——◇——◇

SOME PREFIXES

Prefix	Meaning	Example
a-, ab-	not, away from	abnormal
a-	on	ashore
ad-	to	admit
ante-	before, in front of	antecedent
anti-	against, opposite	antislavery
bene-	good	benefit
bi-	two	bicycle
cent-	one hundred	century
co-, col-, com-, con-, cor-	together, with	coauthor, collect, compile, connect, correspond
de-	away from	defrost
dec-	ten	decimal
dis-	not, away	distrust, dismiss
em-, en-	in, into	embark, enclose
equi-	equal	equality
hemi-	half	hemisphere
il-, im-, in-, ir-	not	illegal, immoral, inactive, irregular
inter-	between, among	international
mal-	bad	malady
micro-	small	microscope
mid-	halfway	midday
mis-	wrong	mistake
non-	not	nonsense
per-	through, throughout	perform
post-	after	postpone
pre-	before	preface
pro-	forward	propel
pro-	in favor of	pro-American
re-	again, back	repeat, repay
semi-	half, partly	semicircle
super-	very large, more than	superhuman
sub-	below, under	subtract
trans-	across	transfer
tri-	three	triangle
un-	not	unhappy
uni-	one	unite

Number Prefixes

Prefix	Meaning	Example
demi-	half	demigod
hemi-	half	hemisphere
semi-	half	semicolon
mon(o)-	one	monorail
uni-	one	unicycle
bi-	two	binary
tri-	three	tricycle
quadr-	four	quadrangle
pent-	five	pentathlon
quint-	five	quintet
hex-	six	hexagon
sex-	six	sextuplets
sept-	seven	September
oct-	eight	octopus
nove-	nine	November
dec-	ten	decade
cent-	hundred	century
milli-	thousand	millimeter
kilo-	thousand	kilogram

Size Prefixes

macro-	large	macrocosm
magni-	great	magnify
mega-	large	megaphone
micro-	small	microscope

SOME SUFFIXES

NOUN SUFFIXES

Suffix	Example

One who does or practices

-ant	assistant
-ar, -er, -or	liar, painter, actor
-arian	librarian
-ee	employee
-ess	actress
-ician	beautician
-ist	scientist

State or quality

-ance, -ence	avoidance, absence
-ation, -tion	starvation, action
-dom	freedom
-hood	falsehood
-ism	heroism
-ity, -ty	equality, honesty
-ment	astonishment
-ness	kindness
-ship	ownership
-th	length

Suffix	Meaning	Example
-archy	form of government	monarchy
-cide	killer, killing	homicide
-ics	science, skill	politics
-itis	inflammation of	tonsillitis

VERB SUFFIXES

Suffix	Meaning	Example
-ate	to make	activate
-en	to make, become	weaken
-fy	to make	simplify
-ish	to take action	punish
-ize	to make, become	dramatize

ADJECTIVE SUFFIXES

	Suffix	Example
Full of		
	-ful	hopeful
	-ose	verbose
	-ous	joyous
Relating to		
	-al, -ial	original, commercial
	-an, -ian	Indian
	-ative, -ive,	talkative, active
	-ic, -ical	comic, economical
	-ish	childish
	-like	lifelike
	-ly	daily
State or quality of		
	-able	comfortable
	-ant	pleasant
	-ate	fortunate
	-ent	excellent
	-ious	anxious
	-y	funny

Suffix	Meaning	Example
-able, -ible	able to be	readable, convertible
-en	made of	wooden
-et, -ette	little	midget, luncheonette
-less	without	worthless
-like	like	lifelike
-most	most	foremost

ADVERB SUFFIXES

Suffix	Meaning	Example
-ily, -ly	manner	happily, slowly
-ward	toward	backward
-wise	manner	clockwise

Switching Roles

Suffixes help languages to be efficient. With the addition of a suffix, a word can move from one job to another. Here are some examples:

ADJECTIVE	happy
ADVERB	happily
NOUN	happiness
VERB	narrate
NOUN	narration
ADJECTIVE	narrative
VERB	avoid
NOUN	avoidance
ADJECTIVE	avoidable
ADJECTIVE	free
ADVERB	freely
NOUN	freedom
ADJECTIVE	wide
ADVERB	widely
VERB	widen
NOUN	width
NOUN	center
ADJECTIVE	central
ADVERB	centrally
VERB	centralize

Vocabulary

Homophones

☐ **Homophones** Words that sound alike but have different meanings and often different spellings

For four days we had been planning a picnic, and we wondered whether the weather would cooperate. What a sight that picnic site was! A horde of ants found our hoard of food. My aunt caught an ant, but then a skunk's scent sent us running. By the side of the road, we sighed and waited. Then a bear, with its bare claws, tried to steal our steel picnic hamper. You have never seen such a scene!

Can you find ten pairs of words that sound alike in the paragraph above? Look for them in the list of homophones below. Also watch out for homophones when you read and when you write. Be sure you can tell the words apart.

Some Homophones

Word	Meaning	Word	Meaning
ad	advertisement	**band**	musical group
add	do addition	**banned**	prohibited
aisle	path	**bare**	unclothed
I'll	I will	**bear**	animal; carry
isle	island		
		base	bottom part
allowed	permitted	**bass**	low tone, voice
aloud	out loud		
		be	exist
ant	insect	**bee**	insect
aunt	female relative		
		beach	shore
ate	did eat	**beech**	tree
eight	number after seven		
		beat	hit
aye	yes	**beet**	vegetable
eye	sight organ		
I	pronoun	**blew**	did blow
		blue	color

Word	Meaning	Word	Meaning
board	lumber, live with	**fair**	honest; carnival
bored	uninterested	**fare**	cost of a ride
boarder	one who boards	**feat**	deed
border	boundary	**feet**	plural of foot
brake	stop	**flea**	insect
break	smash	**flee**	run away
buy	purchase	**flew**	did fly
by	near	**flu**	illness
bye	farewell	**flue**	air shaft
capital	city	**for**	in favor of; purpose
capitol	U.S. Congress building	**fore**	front
		four	number after three
cell	small room (in a prison or religious house); unit of living matter	**foul**	bad
		fowl	bird
		gnu	animal
sell	trade for money	**knew**	did know
		new	not old
cellar	basement	**hair**	growth on head
seller	one who sells	**hare**	rabbit
cent	penny	**hall**	passage
scent	odor	**haul**	carry
sent	did send		
		heal	cure
cheap	inexpensive	**heel**	back of foot
cheep	bird sound	**he'll**	he will
chews	bites	**hear**	listen
choose	select	**here**	this place
coarse	rough	**heard**	listened
course	school subject; path	**herd**	group
creak	noise	**hoarse**	husky voice
creek	stream	**horse**	animal

(Continues)

The Fleeing Flea

A flea and a fly in a flue
Were caught, so what could they do?
Said the fly, "Let us flee."
"Let us fly," said the flea.
So they flew through a flaw in the flue.

A New Gnu

One day I went out to the zoo
For I wanted to see the old gnu,
But the old gnu was dead.
They had a new gnu instead,
And that gnu, well, he knew he was new.

— G. T. Johnson

Word	Meaning	Word	Meaning
its	pronoun	**scene**	setting
it's	it is	**seen**	did see
knot	tangle	**sea**	ocean
not	negative	**see**	look at
know	be acquainted with	**sew**	stitch
no	negative	**so**	in order that
		sow	plant seeds
made	produced	**stair**	step
maid	female servant	**stare**	look hard at
mail	send by post	**steal**	rob
male	masculine	**steel**	metal
main	chief	**tail**	rear appendage
Maine	state	**tale**	story
mane	hair		
meat	food	**their**	pronoun
meet	encounter	**there**	at that place
		they're	they are
oar	of a boat	**theirs**	pronoun
or	conjunction	**there's**	there is
ore	mineral deposit		
one	first number	**to**	toward
won	did win	**too**	also
		two	number after one
pail	bucket	**wait**	remain
pale	light color	**weight**	heaviness
pair	two of	**weak**	not strong
pear	fruit	**week**	seven days
peace	calm	**who's**	who is
piece	part	**whose**	pronoun
read	did read	**wood**	lumber
red	color	**would**	is willing
right	correct	**your**	pronoun
write	pen words	**you're**	you are

Write Right!

Said a boy to his teacher one day:
"Wright has not written *rite* right, I say."
And the teacher replied,
As the blunder she eyed: —
"Right! — Wright, write *rite* right, right away!"

Vocabulary

Homographs

☐ **Homographs** Words with the same spelling but different meanings

The old yak can yak endlessly, telling the story of his two-story bank on the bank of the Rover River. He is an odd kind of animal, kind and gentle. Though he sometimes says mean things, he doesn't mean them. We like him like a grandfather. On his visits, we give him leave to leave early if he looks tired, but he will lean his lean arm on his cane and last to the last minute, yakking away. Does he long for his long-ago life? Maybe.

You may not meet any yakking yaks, but you will certainly encounter homographs. Some homographs are pronounced alike. Others, such as *cóntent-contént*, are pronounced differently.

Some Homographs

Word	Meaning	Word	Meaning
arms	body parts	**bow**	weapon to shoot arrows; kind of knot
arms	weapons		
		bow	bend in respect
bank	place of business		
bank	land next to a river	**bowl**	curved dish
bank	row of items	**bowl**	go bowling
bark	sound a dog makes	**box**	fight with
bark	covering of a tree	**box**	container
bat	flying mammal	**can**	metal container
bat	club to hit ball with	**can**	able to
batter	hit hard	**close**	shut
batter	mixture for a cake	**close**	nearby
batter	ballplayer		
		fair	just
bill	account of money owed	**fair**	beautiful
bill	beak	**fair**	carnival

(Continues)

A pun *is a play on words. It can be based on different meanings of the same word (you* run *one way, but water* runs *another) or on similar sounds of different words (*appeal *sounds like a* peel).

If you like puns, then you are lucky you speak English. With so many homophones and homographs, English is the perfect language for punning.

Punning can be habit-forming, as the following story shows.

A Punny Tale

Once upon a time, there was a jester who drove a king wild with his constant puns. The king declared that he would hang the jester unless the punning stopped. What was the jester's reply? "No noose is good noose." Off he went to the hangman.

Depunitions

illegal — a sick bird

hatchet — what a hen does with an egg

appeal — banana wrapper

alarms — an octopus

knapsack — a sleeping bag

announce — one sixteenth of a pound

debate — what you use to catch de fish

behold — what a bee wrestler uses

lawsuit — judge's clothes

microwave — a little greeting

!!!
A Useful *set*

The English word with the most meanings is set. *It has about 58 uses as a noun, 126 as a verb, and 10 as an adjective.*

Homograph Puns

A doctor fell into a well
And broke his collarbone.
The doctor should attend the sick
And leave the well alone.

Why is a storywriter like a gardener?
— Because they both work on their plots

Overheard in the jungle:
— What will you do if an elephant charges you?
— Pay him!

Overheard in the veterinarian's office:
— What should I do if my dog has ticks?
— Don't wind him.

Overheard on a hike:
— Is it true you jumped off a cliff and didn't get hurt?
— No, that was just a bluff.

Overheard in the emergency room:
— What's the trouble?
— I swallowed a clock yesterday.
— Why didn't you come here sooner?
— I didn't want to alarm anyone.

Word	Meaning
fan	cooling device
fan	admirer
fine	good quality
fine	payment for wrongdoing
fly	insect
fly	move through the air
fresh	not stale
fresh	impudent, rude
kind	considerate
kind	a certain sort
last	final
last	continue
lean	stand slantwise
lean	thin
leave	go away
leave	permission
left	opposite of right
left	did leave
like	similar to
like	have affection for
loaf	mass of bread
loaf	do nothing
long	lengthy
long	wish for
match	stick for lighting fires
match	equal; kind of contest
mean	unkind
mean	intend
pen	writing tool
pen	enclosed yard
pitcher	container
pitcher	ballplayer

Word	Meaning
present	not absent
present	gift
pupil	student
pupil	eye part
rare	uncommon
rare	not cooked much
rest	relax
rest	what remains
ring	sound of bell
ring	circle
row	line
row	use oars in boat
row	noisy quarrel
saw	cutting tool
saw	did see
second	after first
second	$1/60$ of a minute
sock	foot covering
sock	hit hard
squash	vegetable
squash	press flat
story	narrative
story	floor of building
tear	rip
tear	liquid from eye
tire	become weary
tire	wheel covering
top	spinning toy
top	highest part
yak	chatter on and on
yak	ox

Vocabulary

Synonyms and Antonyms

☐ **Synonyms** Words that have similar meanings
☐ **Antonyms** Words that have opposite or nearly opposite meanings

Very few words are exactly the same or even exactly the opposite in meaning. When you speak or write, look for just the right word. Make a list of synonyms or use a thesaurus. (See page 65.) Then think about the precise meaning of each word and also its *connotation* — the feelings associated with it. (See page 163.) Finally, choose the word that best says what you want it to say.

SOME SYNONYMS

arrive, reach, approach, come
hard, difficult, complicated, strenuous
break, crack, shatter, crush, burst, destroy
arrange, group, classify, organize, sort, order, systematize
often, frequently, repeatedly, usually
walk, stroll, pace, step, hike, stride
change, modify, transform, vary, alter, convert
move, budge, shift, stir, maneuver, transport
sound, noise, clamor, clatter, racket
important, vital, crucial, meaningful, significant, major
stop, end, halt, pause, discontinue

SOME ANTONYMS

close–open	together–apart
go–stay	often–rarely
before–after	part–whole
most–least	come–go
smart–ignorant	light–dark
group–individual	work–play
permit–prohibit	nervous–relaxed
same–different	lost–found
follow–precede	clear–unclear
beginning–end	send–receive
even–odd	silence–sound
question–answer	well–badly
friend–enemy	always–never

English or American?

Are American English and British English really the same language? Yes, but . . . there are differences. To understand and speak British, you need to know these synonym pairs.

AMERICAN ENGLISH	BRITISH ENGLISH
apartment	flat
baby carriage	pram
candy	sweet
car bumper	fender
gas	petrol
car hood	bonnet
headlight	lamp
truck	lorry
checkers	draughts
chocolate chips	polka dots
closet	cupboard
corn	maize
cracker	biscuit
diaper	nappy
doctor's office	surgery
drugstore	chemist
elevator	lift
flashlight	torch
French fries	chips
garbage can	dust bin
grab bag	lucky dip
hair spray	lacquer
lemonade	lemon squash
long distance	trunk call
mail	post
movie	cinema, flick
nail polish	nail varnish
zero	nought
tic-tac-toe	noughts and crosses

Ridiculous Relationships

Why is a bad joke like a dull pencil?
— Because they both have no point

Why is money like a secret?
— Because they're both hard to keep

Why is a quarrel like a crossword puzzle?
— Because one word leads to another

Why does a rooster sitting on a fence remind you of a penny?
— Because they both have heads on one side and tails on the other

Analogies

☐ **Analogy**   Comparison between two things that are alike in some way

Writers and speakers use analogies to help them describe things. For example, *The cat's fur was soft as a cloud* is more vivid than *The cat's fur was soft*. To think of and understand analogies, you need to be able to see what certain things have in common, what features they share. This skill is also important when you classify things, or group like things together.

To give practice with analogies, as well as to test the skill, exercises like those below are used. (See also page 81.)

finger : hand :: toe : _____

Read an analogy this way: "Finger IS TO hand AS toe IS TO what?" That is, how is *finger* related to *hand*? A finger is a part of a hand. What is a toe a part of? The answer is a foot.

Here are a few of the relationships covered in analogies.

PART–WHOLE	page : book :: key : typewriter
WORD–SYNONYM	happy : cheerful :: big : large
WORD–ANTONYM	winter : summer :: day : night
GROUP–MEMBER	tree : oak :: planet : Mars
ITEM–USE	needle : sew :: book : read
WORKER–TOOL	singer : voice :: carpenter : hammer
WORKER–PRODUCT	singer : song :: carpenter : shelf

SOME ANALOGIES

1. rich : wealthy :: small : tiny
2. hot : cold :: near : far
3. food : eat :: whistle : blow
4. pen : write :: fork : eat
5. leaf : tree :: doorknob : door
6. pilot : plane :: farmer : tractor
7. color : purple :: shape : square
8. farmer : crop :: artist : painting
9. student : school :: secretary : office
10. velvet : smooth :: sandpaper : rough

Vocabulary

Idioms

☐ **Idiom**   Expression whose meaning is different from the meanings of the individual words

> The idea for a surprise party was planted by Julio, who is always a ball of fire when it comes to pulling a fast one. Earl, of course, would never give the cold shoulder to someone who wanted to throw a party, so he put his two cents in too. Irma did not see eye to eye with them, but she had made up her mind not to be a wet blanket. They promised to button their lips, but in the end Earl let the cat out of the bag.

Every language has its own idioms — expressions that cannot be understood or translated word for word. Julio did not literally dig a hole and plant an idea in it; he just suggested an idea to someone. When not overused, idioms help to give a language a special flavor.

Can you find at least eleven idioms in the paragraph above? Use the following list to help you.

SOME COMMON IDIOMS

at the last minute	crack a joke
at the top of one's lungs	a dead duck
back down	get away with something
back out	give someone the cold shoulder
bail someone out	have a crush on someone
ball of fire	hold one's breath
behind someone's back	let the cat out of the bag
big frog in a small pond	make up one's mind
blow up	plant an idea
break someone's heart	play into someone's hands
bring down the house	pull a fast one
button one's lip	put one's two cents in
call it a day	put one's foot in one's mouth
carry a tune	see eye to eye
catch a bus	throw a party
catch someone red-handed	a wet blanket

Play ball!

Many popular idioms have been born in the baseball park. Here are a few examples.

pinch hit
strike out
play ball with someone
right off the bat
go to bat for someone
take a raincheck
have a strike against one
keep one's eye on the ball
be in there pitching
be off base
come out slugging

Vocabulary

More Jargon

Every field has its own jargon, from ice hockey to chemistry, from pottery-making to banking. If you are interested in a field, you will have to learn its jargon.

The Glossary of Computer Terms (page 103) and the Glosssary of Reading and Writing Terms (page 224) list important terms in those fields. Here is some jargon from other fields.

MUSIC

syncopate	vibrato	refrain
recap	stanza	modulate
theme	interval	beat
flat	pitch	blues

GEOGRAPHY

fiord	ore	belt
altitude	drought	equinox
isthmus	export	nomad
tropic	latitude	grid

ASTRONOMY

black hole	quasar	nova
antimatter	giant	Vulcan
half-life	azimuth	parsec
conjunction	orbit	galaxy

PHOTOGRAPHY

shutter	pose	shadow
exposure	filter	film
shoot	contrast	rewind
negative	focus	develop

Slang, Jargon, Gobbledygook, Clichés

☐ **Slang** Very informal, casual expressions often using common words in new, unusual ways

> Tired of sitting on the shelf, Courtney went to the scrim everyone said was the cat's meow. The dance hall turned out to be a dive, so she scrammed — 23 skiddoo!

In the 1920s, the language in this little story was "the bee's knees" — terrific. Today you can barely understand it. Slang usually fades rather quickly, as the 1960s expressions *groovy* and *far out* did. Sometimes, however, it becomes part of the standard language, like *kidnap* and *highjack*. Occasionally it even stays around for hundreds of years. *Beat it!* and *not so hot* go all the way back to Shakespeare.

Avoid slang in your writing, except in a personal letter or in the dialogue for a short story. Your dictionary will usually tell you whether or not an expression is slang.

☐ **Jargon** Specialized vocabulary of a group or a profession

> The home team's hitters tried everything, but even Romero managed only a ground out, a reach on an error, a fly out, and a strikeout. They came back to life in the sixth, when Greenberg used a one-handed swing to power a home run into the right-field bleachers with one out.

If you are a baseball fan, you can easily follow the events described above. If you do not know the game well, however, the paragraph will sound like a foreign language. Expressions such as *home team, ground out, reach on an error, fly out, strikeout, one-handed swing* are jargon. They are specialized terms used by people familiar with a certain field.

Jargon helps people within a field communicate, but it makes communication more difficult for outsiders. When you write about something you know well but your audience does not, be sure to explain all specialized terms.

☐ Gobbledygook

Wordy language that is difficult to understand because of long words and complicated sentences

Through a multifaceted expansion design, these new computers enable users to maintain their corporate computing environment in situations conducive to both portable and office utilization.

What does the paragraph mean? "The computer has attachments that allow it to be used both in and out of the office." Why didn't the writer just say that? Some people try to sound impressive by using difficult words and complicated sentences. Instead of going directly to the point, they travel around and around it, often leaving the reader behind. Such merry-go-round language is often found in technical articles, legal documents, and political statements.

When you write, avoid gobbledygook. Do not try to dress up your language too much, for you may disguise your message.

☐ Clichés

Expressions that have become dull and worn out from too much use

Down in the dumps? That's the way the cookie crumbles sometimes. If you're at the end of your rope, just remember that every cloud has a silver lining. Don't let the grass grow under your feet! Get busy as a bee and give it your best shot. Soon you'll be fit as a fiddle and having the time of your life. I can feel it in my bones.

Clichés can get a reader down in the dumps. Good writers try to avoid them and use original expressions instead. How can you tell if a phrase is a cliché? Read the first few words and see if the next words spring into your mind.

Here is a sampling of worn-out expressions to avoid.

as thin as a rail	barrel of laughs	cool as a cucumber
all in a day's work	in hot water	time flies
shaking like a leaf	eat like a horse	crack of dawn
a barrel of laughs	scared to death	deep, dark secret
all in the same boat	sink or swim	tried and true
ripe old age	rack your brain	a clinging vine

Spelling

Spelling Plan of Attack

Look at it!
Say it!
Think about it!
Write it!
Check it!

Attack These Words!

Here's a real test. Try your attack plan on these words. (HINT : Your most important step is to sound out the words syllable by syllable.)

supercalifragilisticexpialidocious
"good," according to the Mary Poppins song

antidisestablishmentarianism
support of the church by the state

pneumonoultramicroscopic-silicovolcanoconiosis
lung disease caused by the breathing in of silica dust

floccinaucinihilipilification
evaluating something as worthless

Llanfairpwllgwyngyllgogerych-yrndrobwllllandysiliogogogoch
town in the country of Wales

TIPS

TIPS for Improving Your Spelling

- **Proofread.**   Check everything you write for spelling errors. They can be easy to miss, so look carefully.

- **Keep a list.**   Write down words that give you trouble. Review your list regularly to master the spelling.

- **Use a dictionary.**   Don't guess. If you have any doubts at all about a word, look up the spelling.

- **Pronounce.**   Pronouncing words carefully sometimes helps you spell them. If you pronounce *February* correctly, for example, you are not likely to leave out the first *r*.

- **"See" the letters.**   To review a word, do not just glance at it. Look at the individual letters first and then at the whole word. Close your eyes and picture the word. Write it several times.

- **Think of a memory trick.**   Here are some examples. (See also page 75.)

principal	The principal is my pal.
principle	A principle is a general rule.
committee	2 m's, 2 t's, 2 e's
acquaint	I will seek you (C-Q) to get acquainted.
bargain	You gain from a bargain.

- **Use a plan of attack.**   To learn how to spell a new word, try this strategy.

  1. Look at the word and say it to yourself a few times, syllable by syllable. Look at each syllable as you say it.
  2. Look at each letter and say it.
  3. If the word contains difficult letter combinations, try a memory trick. (See the previous tip.)
  4. Close your eyes and picture the word.
  5. Write the word without looking at it again.
  6. Check to see if you have spelled it correctly. If you have, write it several times more.
  7. If you have spelled the word incorrectly, note your error and start over again.

Spelling

Rules and Guidelines

Plurals

1. **Most nouns**   Simply add *s*.

    book–books   rose–roses   stripe–stripes   dog–dogs

2. **Nouns ending in *s, ch, sh, x, z***   Add *es*.

    bus–buses   wish–wishes   waltz–waltzes
    arch–arches   tax–taxes

3. **Nouns ending in *y***   If a vowel comes before *y*, add *s*.

    day–days   monkey–monkeys   toy–toys   turkey–turkeys

    If a consonant comes before *y*, change the *y* to *i* and add *es*.

    lady–ladies   penny–pennies   trophy–trophies

4. **Nouns ending in *f* or *fe***   In most cases, add *s*.

    belief–beliefs   roof–roofs   safe–safes

    For some nouns, change *f* to *v* and add *es*.

    shelf–shelves   loaf–loaves   knife–knives   leaf–leaves

5. **Nouns ending in *o***   If a vowel comes before *o*, add *s*.

    radio–radios   studio–studios   rodeo–rodeos

    If a consonant comes before *o*, add *es* in most cases. Some words take only *s*, however, so check your dictionary to be sure.

    echo–echoes   photo–photos   tomato–tomatoes

    For musical terms, add only *s*.

    alto–altos   soprano–sopranos   piano–pianos   cello–cellos

America vs. Britain

Don't be surprised if you come across the word *aluminium*, rather than *aluminum*. The British spell the word with two *i*'s. Here are some other examples of American versus British spellings.

American	British
center	centre
check (money)	cheque
color	colour
connection	connexion
curb	kerb
gray	grey
inquire	enquire
jail	gaol
jewelry	jewellery
labor	labour
organization	organisation
pajamas	pyjamas
program	programme
realize	realise
recognize	recognise
theater	theatre

Silent Spoilers

English spelling is famous — or infamous — for its sneaky silent letters. In an earlier stage of the language, these letters were actually pronounced. Today the pronunciation has changed, but the letters remain. Here are the most common examples.

SILENT *b*

debt	climb	dumb	numb
doubt	comb	lamb	thumb
bomb	crumb	limb	womb

SILENT *c*

muscle   indict

SILENT *ch*

yacht

SILENT *g*

gnarled	reign	sign
gnat	campaign	assign
gnaw	foreign	design
gnu	sovereign	resign

SILENT *h*

rhythm	ghost	exhaust
rhyme	ghoul	exhibit
rhinestone	khaki	graham
rhinoceros	shepherd	vehicle
heir	honest	hour
honor	herb	

ALMOST SILENT *h*

whale	whether	whisper
what	which	whistle
wheat	while	white
wheel	whine	why
when	whip	
where	whirl	

6. **Irregular plurals**   Memorize these irregular forms.

tooth–**teeth**	man–**men**	mouse–**mice**
foot–**feet**	woman–**women**	ox–**oxen**
goose–**geese**	child–**children**	

Some nouns are the same in the singular and plural.

sheep	species	Japanese
salmon	series	British
deer	fish	Sioux

7. **Compound nouns**   For most nouns, follow the usual rules.

motorboa**ts**   music box**es**   grandchild**ren**

However, in compounds in which the first word is the only noun or the main noun, make that noun plural.

passer**s**-by *or* passer**s**by   son**s**-in-law   head**s** of state

8. **Letters, symbols, words used as words**   Add an apostrophe and *s* (*'s*).

p's and *q*'s   !'s   four *after*'s on that page

Words with *ie* and *ei*

1. **Remember the rhyme.**

Put *i* before *e*
Except after *c*
Or when sounded like *a*
As in *neighbor* and *weigh*.

bel**ie**ve   rec**ei**ve   r**ei**gn
piece   c**ei**ling   sl**ei**gh

2. **Learn the exceptions.**

ancient   efficient   foreign   either   seize
conscience   species   height   weird

Words with the "seed" sound

1. **Learn the one word that ends with *-sede*.**

   super**sede**

2. **Learn the three words that end with *-ceed*.**

   suc**ceed**   pro**ceed**   ex**ceed**

3. **Use *-cede* for all other words ending in the "seed" sound.**

   pre**cede**   con**cede**   re**cede**   se**cede**

Words with Prefixes and Suffixes

1. **Prefixes**   Do not change the spelling when you add a prefix.

   mis + spell = misspell   re + establish = reestablish
   re + arrange = rearrange   over + rule = overrule
   ir + regular = irregular   il + legal = illegal

2. **Suffixes *-ly* and *-ness***   When you add the suffix *-ly* or *-ness*, do not change the spelling.

   actual + ly = actually   open + ness = openness

3. **Words ending in *e***   When you add a suffix beginning with a vowel, drop the final *e* of the word.

   drive + ing = **driving**   fame + ous = **famous**
   relate + ion = **relation**   note + able = **notable**

   When you add a suffix beginning with a consonant, keep the final *e* of the word.

   hope + ful = **hopeful**   state + ment = **statement**
   like + ness = **likeness**   manage + ment = **management**

   EXCEPTIONS
   true–tru**ly**   argue–arg**um**ent   courage–courage**ous**
   nine–nin**th**   whole–who**lly**   pronounce–pronounce**able**

SILENT *k*

knack	kneel	knit
knapsack	know	knob
knife	knew	knock
knee	knowledge	knot
knuckle	knead	knight

SILENT *l*

could	half	talk	folk
should	calf	walk	yolk
would	salmon	chalk	calm

SILENT *n*

condemn   hymn
column   autumn

SILENT *p*

pneumonia   corps   receipt
psychology   raspberry

SILENT *s*

aisle   isle   island   corps

SILENT *t*

often   glisten
soften   listen
fasten   moisten

castle   hustle
wrestle   bustle
whistle   rustle

SILENT *w*

wrack	wrestle	who
wrap	wriggle	whom
wreath	wring	whose
wreck	wrinkle	whole
wren	write	
wrist	written	
wrong		
wrench		

awry   sword
answer   two

4. **Words ending in *y***   When you add a suffix to most words ending in a vowel and *y*, keep the *y*.

employ + er = employer
play + ing = playing
joy + ful = joyful
convey + ed = conveyed

When you add a suffix to most words ending in a consonant and *y*, change the *y* to *i* before the suffix.

happy + ness = happiness
fifty + th = fiftieth
easy + ly = easily
worry + ed = worried

EXCEPTIONS
When adding the suffix *-ing*: studying
When adding a suffix to some one-syllable words: *shyness*
                                                                                          daily

5. **Words ending in a consonant**   When you add a suffix to a word ending in a consonant, double the final consonant when *both* of the following are true:

a. The word has only one syllable or it is stressed on the final syllable, *and*
b. The word ends in a single vowel plus a single consonant.

ONE SYLLABLE
ENDS IN ONE VOWEL + ONE CONSONANT
bat + ed = batted
sit + ing = sitting
red + est = reddest
run + er = runner

STRESSED ON FINAL SYLLABLE
ENDS IN ONE VOWEL + ONE CONSONANT
prefér + ed = preferred
begín + ing = beginning
admít + ance = admittance
contról + able = controllable

Spelling

Words Often Misspelled

SPELLING DEMONS

about	can't	Friday	muscle	two
accept	careful	friend	neighbor	tying
advise	caught	getting	neither	unknown
again	chief	goes	nickel	until
all right	children	going	ninety	usual
already	choose	grammar	often	wasn't
although	chose	guard	once	wear
always	close	guess	people	weather
answer	color	guide	practice	Wednesday
asked	cough	half	quiet	we'll
aunt	could	handkerchief	quit	we're
author	cousin	hear	quite	weren't
awful	decide	heard	really	we've
babies	didn't	heavy	receive	where
balloon	divide	height	rhythm	whether
been	does	here	right	which
before	don't	hers	Saturday	white
believe	early	hoping	says	whole
blue	easy	hour	straight	witch
bought	enough	house	surely	women
breakfast	every	instead	their	won't
breathe	exact	its	there	would
brother	except	it's	they're	wouldn't
brought	excite	January	though	write
build	favorite	know	thought	writing
business	February	knew	through	written
busy	fierce	listen	tired	wrote
buy	finally	loose	to	your
calendar	forty	lose	too	you're
cannot	fourth	minute	tried	yours

Grammar

— A hair itself is dead, but its root is alive. New cells form at the base of the root and push the old, dead cells up through the skin.

— You can tell whether hair is curly or straight by looking at a cross section of a hair under a microscope. A round shape means straight hair. A longer, flatter shape means curly hair.

— A human hair usually grows about a half inch each month for three or four years. Then the hair falls out, and a new one starts to grow.

— You probably lose from 30 to 60 hairs a day.

— The soft fur on many animals, the thick fleece on sheep, the stiff bristles on hogs, and the sharp quills on porcupines are all various kinds of hair.

— Human hair is made out of the same substance as a cow's horns and a duck's feathers.

— Blond-headed people usually have more hairs on their heads than redheads do.

Parts of Speech

☐ **Part of Speech** The function or job of a word in a sentence

Have you ever seen someone who had a great-looking hair style and thought, "Wow! That's the way I want my hair to look"? Well, you're not alone. Hair styles have been important to people about as long as there have been people. In fact, combs and hairpins have been found from prehistoric times. By 3000 B.C., Egyptians were curling and dyeing their hair. Early Greek men and women carefully gathered their long hair into top knots, although the men later switched to short hair. Extremely fashionable women in ancient Rome dyed their hair and decorated it with gold dust.

PARTS OF SPEECH

NAME	JOB	EXAMPLES
noun	*names* a person, place, thing, or idea	hair, hair style, hairpin, people, times, Egyptians
verb	*expresses* action or being	had, have been, were curling, gathered
pronoun	*replaces* a noun	you, someone, who, their
adjective	*describes* a noun or pronoun	great-looking, alone, ancient, Greek, long
adverb	*describes* a verb, adjective, or adverb	ever, then, carefully extremely
preposition	*relates* a noun or pronoun to another word	to, from, by, into, in, with
conjunction	*joins* words	and, as long as, although
interjection	stands by itself; often *states* strong feeling	Wow! well

Grammar

Parts of Speech: Nouns

So, Bartholomew's Bargain Boutique has a special on yo-yos this week, eh? You can get a hundred yo-yos for only fourteen ninety-five! Hold on. What are you going to do with a hundred yo-yos? Start a yo-yo team? Look. A bargain is only a bargain if you need it.

Never feel forced into buying anything you don't want or can't afford. (Ask yourself, "Do I really need another ___ ?") And don't let a snooty salesperson make you feel "small" if you don't buy the most expensive thingamajig in the store. Remember, a salesperson's job is to help you because you're the customer. You have the right to ask questions, be choosy, and to say no if you decide not to buy.

—*The Official Kids' Survival Kit*, Chaback and Fortunato

About the Noun

1. **What is it?** A noun names a person, place, thing, or idea.

Bartholomew's Bargain Boutique has a *special* on *yo-yos* this *week*.

You can find the following words used as nouns in the selection above.

PEOPLE	PLACES	THINGS	IDEAS
salesperson	Bartholomew's	yo-yos	special
customer	Bargain Boutique	thingamajig	week
team	store		fourteen
salesperson's			ninety-five
			bargain
			job
			right
			questions

2. **Proper or common**

   a. **Proper nouns** name particular persons, places, things, or ideas. They begin with capital letters.

   b. **Common nouns** are general names for persons, places, things, or ideas.

PROPER	COMMON
Bartholomew's Bargain Boutique	store
Boston Bruins	team
Anita	salesperson

!!! About *noun*

Noun comes from a Latin word meaning "name."

Poof! You're a Noun!

Certain endings, or suffixes, can be added to words or roots to turn them into nouns. (See page 242.) Here are some examples.

Added to verb

-age	+ marry	=	marriage
-ance	+ endure	=	endurance
-er	+ use	=	user
-ee	+ employ	=	employee
-ment	+ pay	=	payment
-tion	+ act	=	action

Added to adjective

-ce	+ fragrant	=	fragrance
-cy	+ frequent	=	frequency
-ity	+ secure	=	security
-ness	+ happy	=	happiness

Added to another noun

-cy	+ democrat	=	democracy
-ian	+ library	=	librarian
-ist	+ violin	=	violinist
-ship	+ friend	=	friendship

Your Turn

Be a word maker. Create some words of your own, using the endings listed above.

Noun Jobs

Noun comes from a Latin word meaning "name."

SUBJECT
   Rosa bought a yo-yo.
DIRECT OBJECT
   Rosa bought a *yo-yo.*
INDIRECT OBJECT
   Rosa bought *Jason* a yo-yo.
OBJECT OF PREPOSITION
   Rosa bought a yo-yo for *Jason.*
PREDICATE NOUN
   Rosa is a yo-yo *champion.*
APPOSITIVE
   Everyone cheered the new yo-yo champion, *Rosa.*

Notable Nouns

Even though you know hundreds and hundreds of nouns, there are always more to learn. Try these. (Look up their pronunciations in the dictionary.)

abecedarian   person who teaches or studies the alphabet

crispation   act of crisping or curling

epicure   person with refined taste in food

nonagenarian   person from 90 to 99 years old

physiognomy   facial features

syzygy   term in astronomy

xenophobe   person who mistrusts strangers

zephyr   west wind; gentle breeze

3. **Concrete or abstract**

   a. **Concrete nouns** name objects that can be seen, heard, smelled, touched, or tasted.

   b. **Abstract nouns** name ideas and qualities.

CONCRETE	ABSTRACT
Bartholomew's Bargain Boutique	week
salesperson	question
yo-yo	kindness

4. **Collective**   Collective nouns name groups that act together.

   COLLECTIVE

team	class	club	orchestra	committee	herd	chorus
crowd	group	flock	audience	band	family	fleet

5. **Compound**   Compound nouns have two or more words. They are written as one word, separate words, or words with hyphens.

ONE WORD	SEPARATE WORDS	HYPHENS
salesperson	Bartholomew's	yo-yo
thingamajig	Bargain Boutique	father-in-law
earthworm	station wagon	passer-by

6. **Singular or plural**   Singular nouns name one item. Plural nouns name more than one item. (See pages 255 – 256.)

SINGULAR	PLURAL	SINGULAR	PLURAL
question	questions	yo-yo	yo-yos
chorus	choruses	salesperson	salespeople

7. **Possessive**   Possessive nouns show belonging. (See page 337.)

   POSSESSIVE   *salesperson's* job   *customers'* voices

TIPS on Nouns

- A noun names a person, place, thing, or idea.
- Kinds of nouns: proper—common
                    concrete—abstract
                    collective
- Forms of nouns: singular—plural
                    compound
                    possessive

Grammar

Parts of Speech: Pronouns

Hockey was only one of many sports and games we inherited from the Indians. Hundreds of centuries before Columbus set sail on his historic voyage, Indian athletes were playing their versions of sports we enjoy today: baseball, football, basketball, soccer, wrestling, bowling, and sky-diving — to name just a few.

— *Sports and Games the Indians Gave Us*, Alex Whitney

About the Pronoun

1. **What is it?**   A pronoun is a word used in place of a noun. Hockey is *one* of many sports *we* inherited from the Indians.

   You can find the following pronouns in the selections above.

   one   we   his   their   few

2. **Antecedents**   The *antecedent* of a pronoun is the noun that it stands for. In the sentence below, *his* stands for *Columbus*. Therefore, *Columbus* is the antecedent of *his*.

   Columbus set sail on *his* historic voyage in 1492.

3. **Personal Pronouns**

	Singular	*Plural*
FIRST PERSON	I, me	we, us
SECOND PERSON	you	you
THIRD PERSON	he, him (*masculine*)	they, them
	she, her (*feminine*)	
	it (*neuter*)	

   Use   Personal pronouns are the most common pronouns. They show person, number, and gender.

   a. **Person**

   First person refers to the person speaking.
   Second person refers to the person spoken to.
   Third person refers to the person or thing spoken about

FIRST PERSON	*I* plan to go to the hockey game.
SECOND PERSON	Are *you* going to the game too?
THIRD PERSON	*It* should be an exciting game.

!!!
About *pronoun*

The origin of the word *pronoun* describes it perfectly. The word comes from *pro-* + *nomen* in Latin, which means "in place of the name."

Pronoun Jobs

Since pronouns stand for nouns, they have the same jobs as nouns in a sentence.

SUBJECT
   He admired the writer.
DIRECT OBJECT
   Pedro admired *her.*
INDIRECT OBJECT
   Pedro wrote *her* a letter.
OBJECT OF A PREPOSITION
   Pedro wrote a letter to *her.*
PREDICATE PRONOUN
   Her most devoted fan is *he.*
APPOSITIVE
   She received a letter from a fan, *him.*

From *thou* to *you*

English speakers use *you* no matter whom they talk to — just one person or lots of people, a close friend or a stranger. Other languages handle the second person differently, and English once did too.

Spanish, French, Hebrew, and many other languages have singular and plural forms for *you*. Here are the Spanish forms, for example:

SPANISH   *tú*   "you," singular

ustedes   "you," plural

Some languages also have "familiar" and "polite" forms for *you*.

SPANISH   *tú*   "you," familiar

usted   "you," polite

For example, a Mexican person speaking to an adult he or she did not know well would use the polite form *usted*, not the familiar form *tú*.

English once worked the same way. It had all these forms:

SINGULAR   *thou, thee, thy, thine*

PLURAL   *ye, you, your*

By the eighteenth century, however, all except *you* and *your* had disappeared.

b. Number

Singular pronouns refer to one person or thing.
Plural pronouns refer to more than one.
The pronoun *you* is the same in the singular and plural.

SINGULAR	*She* is sitting in this seat.
	You are sitting in that seat.
PLURAL	*We* are sitting in those seats.
	You are sitting in the two seats next to us.

c. Gender

Third person singular pronouns show gender.
The *masculine* pronouns are *he, him*.
The *feminine* pronouns are *she, her*.
The *neuter* pronoun is *it*.

4. Possessive forms

	Singular	Plural
FIRST PERSON	my, mine	our, ours
SECOND PERSON	your, yours	your, yours
THIRD PERSON	his, her, hers, its	their, theirs

Use   Possessive pronouns are used to replace possessive nouns. They show belonging (See also page 310.)

a. Use *my, our, your, his, her, its, their* before nouns.
b. Use *mine, ours, yours, his, hers, theirs* to stand alone.

BEFORE A NOUN   Indians had *their* version of bowling.
BY ITSELF   The original game of bowling was *theirs*.

5. Reflexive and intensive pronouns

SINGULAR   myself, yourself, herself, itself
PLURAL   ourselves, yourselves, themselves

Use   Reflexive and intensive pronouns have the same form.
Reflexive pronouns refer back to the subject.
Intensive pronouns emphasize a noun or pronoun.
(See also page 315.)

REFLEXIVE   The players enjoyed *themselves*.
INTENSIVE   The players set up the net *themselves*.

6. Demonstrative pronouns

SINGULAR   this   that
PLURAL   these   those

Use   Demonstrative pronouns point out persons or things.* (See also page 315.)

NEARBY   *This* is a bowling ball right here.
DISTANT   *That* is a hockey puck over there.

7. Interrogative pronouns

who   whom   which   what   whose

Use   Interrogative pronouns ask questions.* (See pages 314 – 315.)

Who invented hockey?   *What* was hockey called by the Indians?

8. Indefinite pronouns

Singular			*Plural*	*Singular/Plural*
another	everybody	nothing	both	all
anybody	everyone	one	few	any
anyone	everything	other	many	most
anything	neither	somebody	others	none
each	nobody	someone	several	some
either	no one	something		

Use   Indefinite pronouns refer to persons or things that are not identified. Therefore, they often have no antecedents. (See also page 313.) They can be singular or plural, depending on how many persons or things they refer to.

SINGULAR   *Someone* is here.   PLURAL   *Some* of them are here.

Indian Bowling

Many North American Indian tribes held bowling tournaments. At one Cherokee site in Georgia, diggers uncovered several clay bowling alleys twenty feet long.

Southwestern Indians used wooden bowling balls, which they aimed at corncobs that were standing upright. The Cherokee pitched stone balls at clay objects shaped like the Indian clubs we use today in tenpins and other bowling games.

— Adapted from *Sports and Games the Indians Gave Us*, Alex Whitney

---

TIPS on Pronouns

- A pronoun is a word that replaces a noun.
- Kinds of pronouns: personal pronouns, plus possessive forms
                       reflexive and intensive pronouns
                       demonstrative pronouns
                       interrogative pronouns
                       indefinite pronouns

*Some of these pronouns can be used as adjectives. See page 270.

Verbs are where the action is as far as sentences are concerned. So important are verbs that the word *verb* comes from Latin *verbum*, meaning "word."

Make a Verb

Add certain endings, or one beginning, and you can create verbs. Here are suffixes and a prefix that make verbs out of other words or roots. (See also page 243.)

-ate	oper*ate*
	anim*ate*
-en	sharp*en*
	wid*en*
	loos*en*
-fy	simpli*fy*
	quali*fy*
-ize	recog*nize*
	orga*nize*
	moder*nize*
en-	*en*slave
	*en*liven

Parts of Speech: Verbs

Although athletic shoes can now be found in almost everyone's wardrobe, they have not been around very long. Back in the 1860s, British cricket players were wearing spiked shoes, but these must have been too clumsy for runners. Rubber-soled sneakers, too, had appeared by that time, but the rubber soles did not last long. Distance runners, therefore, used bulky shoes with stiff leather soles — and suffered from sore feet. Although companies made lighter shoes out of canvas and rubber in the 1950s, the modern track shoe did not appear until 1962. In the 1970s, running fever hit, and shoe companies began their own race for new materials and designs. Today there are shoes for every sport. However, most of this fancy footwear just goes for a walk around the block.

About the Verb

1. **What is it?**   A verb states action, being, or a condition. It also tells time.

British cricket players *were wearing* spiked shoes.

You can find these verbs in the selection above:

can be found	must have been	used	did appear	are
have been	had appeared	suffered	hit	goes
were wearing	did last	made	began	

2. **Action verbs**   Action verbs tell what the subject does, has done, or will do. Some tell what the subject has. The verb may show physical action, mental action, or possession.

PHYSICAL ACTION   Anita *walked* two miles this morning.
MENTAL ACTION   She *planned* her route carefully.
POSSESSION   She *has* a new pair of running shoes.

3. **Linking verbs**   A linking verb, or *being* verb, tells what the subject is or feels. It links the subject with another word or group of words.

LINKING VERBS	appear	become	grow	remain
	stay	sound	be	feel
	look	seem	smell	taste

Leather shoes *were* stiff.   The runners' feet *felt* sore.

4. Action or linking?   Some verbs can be used as action or linking verbs. If you can substitute a form of *be* for the verb, it is usually a linking verb. (See also page 319.)

LINKING	ACTION
The shoes *felt* (*were*) comfortable.	She *felt* the blister.
The runner *appeared* (*was*) tired.	Two runners *appeared*.

5. Main verbs and helping verbs   Verbs with more than one word are called *verb phrases*. Verb phrases have a *main verb* and one or more *helping verbs*.

a. Main verbs express action or being.

b. Helping verbs help complete the meaning of the main verb. A main verb may have more than one helping verb. Here are some verb phrases from the opening selection:

Helping Verb(s) + *Main Verb* = *Verb Phrase*
can be | found | can be found
have | been | have been
were | wearing | were wearing
must have | been | must have been
had | appeared | had appeared

Common Helping Verbs

be, been, being   has, have, had
is, am, are, was, were   do, does, did, done

can   shall   will   may   must
could   should   would   might

---

c. Sometimes a helping verb is hidden in a contraction.

He'*ll wear* (= *will wear*) his new running shoes today.
She'*s wearing* (= *is wearing*) her tennis shoes.

d. The words in a verb phrase may be separated by other words or by *n't*. These are not part of the verb phrase.

Athletic shoes *have* now *become* very popular.
They *have*n't *been* around very long, however.

Forms of *be, have, do*

The most common words often have the most irregular forms. This statement certainly holds true for the forms of *be, have,* and *do,* the most frequently used verbs in the language.

be

I	am, was
you	are, were
he, she, it, singular noun	is, was
we, you, they, plural noun	are, were

have

I	have, had
you	have, had
he, she, it, singular noun	has, had
we, you, they, plural noun	have, had

do

I	do, did
you	do, did
he, she, it, singular noun	does, did
we, they, plural noun	do, did

6. Transitive and intransitive verbs

a. A *transitive verb* is an action verb that sends its action to another word. Below, *bought* sends its action to *shoes*.

TRANSITIVE   Ronald *bought* shoes.

b. The word that receives the action is the *direct object* of the verb. The direct object answers the question *what?* or *whom?* after the verb. It is usually a noun or pronoun.

	VERB	DIRECT OBJECT	
Ronald	*bought*	shoes.	(bought what? *shoes*)
Sara	*met*	him.	(met whom? *him*)

c. An *intransitive verb* does not have a direct object.

INTRANSITIVE   Ray *runs* every day. (runs what? no answer)

d. Some verbs can be either transitive or intransitive, depending on how they are used. To decide whether a verb is transitive or intransitive, ask *what?* or *whom?* after the verb. If there is an answer, the verb is transitive.

TRANSITIVE   Ronald *tried* the shoes.
(Tried what? Tried the shoes. *Shoes* is a direct object, and *tried* is transitive.)

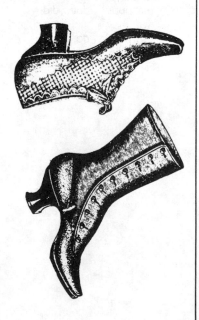

INTRANSITIVE   The runners *tried* harder.
(Tried what? Tried whom? There is no answer here. *Tried* is intransitive.)

TIPS on Verbs

- A verb is a word that states action, being, or a condition. It also tells *when*.
- A verb is used as an action word or a linking word.
- A verb made up of more than one word is a verb phrase.
  A verb phrase has a main verb and one or more helping verbs.
- An action verb may be transitive or intransitive.
  A transitive verb has a direct object.

Grammar

Parts of Speech: Adjectives

As for the space ship, it was truly awe-inspiring. It was long and smooth and cigar-shaped, just as David had planned it, with the big window in front made of fine thick plastiglass which David's mother had given them. On the right side was the door, which could be bolted tight shut when you got inside. At the rear was the sturdy, four-bladed tail, level on the end so that the space ship could be upended to stand firmly. For the ship was separate from the carrier and could quite easily be slipped off when the time came to blast away. Over its entire surface it was covered with cleverly fitted sections of metal sheeting, so that it glistened and gleamed in the morning sun like some marvelous silvery fish. How beautiful it is! . . .

— *The Wonderful Flight to the Mushroom Planet*, Eleanor Cameron

About the Adjective

1. **What is it?**   An adjective *modifies*, or describes, a noun or pronoun. (See also pages 316 – 319.)

It was *long* and *smooth* and *cigar-shaped*, with a *big* window.

You can find these adjectives in the selection above:

the	big	sturdy	entire	marvelous
awe-inspiring	fine	four-bladed	fitted	silvery
long	thick	level	metal	beautiful
smooth	David's	separate	morning	
cigar-shaped	right	its	some	

2. **Recognizing adjectives**   Ask these questions about a noun or pronoun. A word that answers any of them is an adjective.

WHAT KIND?	*big* window	*silvery* fish	*cigar-shaped* ship
	sturdy tail	*morning* sun	*metal* sheeting
WHICH?	*right* side	*the* space ship	*David's* mother
	its surface	*this* morning	*last* week
HOW MUCH	*three* feet	*many* windows	*few* people
OR MANY?	*more* work	*several* days	*less* time

The is a special adjective called a *definite article*. It points out a specific item. *A* is an *indefinite article*. It refers to any one of a group. (*A* becomes *an* before a vowel.)

!!!
About *adjective*

The word *adjective* comes from a Latin word meaning "to add to, to throw to."

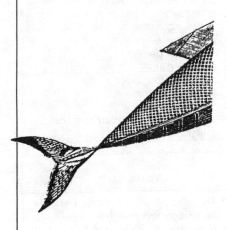

Poof! You're an Adjective!

Many adjectives are created from other words or from roots by adding certain endings. (See also page 243.)

Added to verb

-able	+	move	=	movable
-ive	+	act	=	active

Added to noun

-al	+	nature	=	natural
-ful	+	grace	=	graceful
-ic	+	scene	=	scenic
-ical	+	history	=	historical
-ish	+	child	=	childish
-less	+	harm	=	harmless
-like	+	child	=	childlike
-ous	+	grace	=	gracious

Perfect Matches

Look at these pairs and see why the adjectives are perfect for the nouns.

an offbeat drummer
a classy teacher
a striking batter
a spacey astronaut
a colorful painter
a racey runner
an unsuitable tailor
a spare bowler
an aimless archer
an open-minded brain surgeon
a flighty pilot

Your Turn

Think of an adjective that would make a perfect match with each of these nouns.

pilot   dancer
chef   animal trainer
mechanic   sculptor

3. **Position**

   a. **Before a noun or pronoun**   Most adjectives are placed in front of the words they modify.

   big window   *thick* glass   *entire* surface   *metal* ones

   b. **After a noun or pronoun**   Sometimes, for special effect, adjectives are placed after the words they modify.

   The space ship's tail, *level* and *sturdy*, had four blades.

   c. **After a linking verb**   A *predicate adjective* follows a form of *be* or another linking verb (see page 266).

   The space ship was *separate* from the carrier.

4. **Number**
   More than one adjective can be used to modify a word.

   At the rear was *the sturdy, four-bladed* tail.
   The space ship was *long, smooth,* and *cigar-shaped.*

5. **Proper adjectives**   A *proper adjective* is formed from a proper noun (see page 261). It is capitalized.

   Italy—*Italian*   China—*Chinese*   Britain—*British*

6. **Other words as adjectives**   Some words usually used in other ways can also be adjectives. When they come before nouns and answer one of the questions in item 2, they are used as adjectives.

NOUNS	*morning* sun	*club* meeting	*David's* mother
PRONOUNS	*his* space ship	*some* wood	*what* time
	this morning	*which* door	*many* hours
VERBS	*smiling* boy	*painted* door	*bent* metal

TIPS on Adjectives

- An adjective is a word that modifies a noun or pronoun.
- An adjective answers *what kind? which?* or *how much or many?* about a noun or pronoun.
- It can appear before or after the noun or pronoun. It can also come after a linking verb.
- More than one adjective can be used to modify a word.
- A proper adjective is formed from a proper noun.
- Some nouns, pronouns, and verbs can be used as adjectives.

Parts of Speech: Adverbs

Dicey didn't have much time for thinking about her family. James, she knew, was perfectly happy. He studied at night and went through the heavy wooden doors into the school at a run, every morning. Now and then he would report some amazing fact to Dicey. One time he told her about Alaric's treasure, that disappeared long ago when Rome ruled the world and America wasn't even discovered. Nobody had ever found the treasure because Alaric hid it so well. He diverted a river, then buried the treasure in the river bed, then rerouted the river back to its old path. The treasure was somewhere there, in Italy. Only Alaric knew where.

—*Homecoming*, Cynthia Voigt

About the Adverb

1. **What is it?**   An adverb is a word that modifies, or gives information about, a verb, an adjective, or another adverb.

   James was *perfectly* happy.
   Now and *then* he would report some amazing fact to Dicey.

   You can find these adverbs in the selection above:

n't (not)	then	even	well	there
perfectly	one time	ever	back	where
now	long ago	so	somewhere	

2. **Identifying adverbs**   An adverb usually answers one of the questions below.

HOW?	*quietly* said	hid it *well*
WHEN?	*then* buried it	*now* he knew
WHERE?	buried it *there*	traveled *back*
TO WHAT EXTENT?	*so* well	*extremely* happy

3. **Forming adverbs**   Many adverbs are formed by adding *-ly* to an adjective. There may be a slight change in spelling (see page 257).

perfect + -ly = perfectly	true + -ly = truly
real + -ly = really	happy + -ly = happily

!!!
About *adverb*

Adverb comes from a Latin word meaning "added word."

Some Common Adverbs

HOW?

well	slow	fast
badly	quietly	quickly
carefully	easily	safely

WHEN?

afterward	later	already
always	never	ever
again	today	tomorrow
yesterday	seldom	often
immediately	soon	now
sometimes	then	already
daily	rarely	recently

WHERE?

everywhere	here	there
down	up	away
near	far	nearby
downstairs	upstairs	

TO WHAT EXTENT?

almost	never	fully
completely	not	quite
so	too	very
extremely	really	terribly

Tom Swifties

The name Tom Swifties *comes from a series of books in which a boy named Tom Swift always made statements* crisply, flatly, stonily, *and so on. The adverb related back to a word in his statement in a special way, as you can see from the made-up examples below.*

"I'd like another hot dog," Tom said frankly.

"This lemonade needs some sugar," Tom said sourly.

"The lemonade is too warm," Tom said icily.

"I can't stand seafood," Tom said crabbily.

"I think I'm allergic to clams," Tom said rashly.

"Let's have some French fries," Tom said crisply.

"I think I should stop eating now," Tom said haltingly.

Your Turn

Create some Tom Swifties of your own with these adverbs.

blankly   wildly   sweetly
flatly   squarely sharply

4. **Words they modify** Adverbs modify verbs, adjectives, and other adverbs.

   a. Verbs Most adverbs modify verbs.

   Dicey **waited** *patiently*.
      (adverb *patiently* modifies verb *waited*)
   Now and *then* James **would report** some amazing fact.
      (adverbs *now* and *then* modify verb *would report*)
   Dicey **did***n't* **have** much time.
      (contraction *n't = not*; modifies verb *did have*)

   b. Adjectives and adverbs Adverbs that modify adjectives or adverbs usually answer the question *to what extent?*

   MODIFIES ADJECTIVE James was *perfectly* **happy**.
   MODIFIES ADVERB Alaric hid it *so* **well**.

5. **Intensifiers** Some adverbs that modify adjectives or adverbs are called *intensifiers* because they are used mostly for emphasis. They answer *to what extent?* Here are examples.

   almost   extremely   less   most   rather   so
   too   awfully   least   more   quite   really
   terribly very

6. **Position** Adverbs that modify adjectives or adverbs usually come before the words they modify. Adverbs that modify verbs appear in different places, like the adverb below.

   Happily, James would talk about the treasure.
   James would *happily* talk about the treasure.
   James would talk *happily* about the treasure.
   James would talk about the treasure *happily*.

TIPS on Adverbs

- An adverb is a word that modifies a verb, an adjective, or another adverb.
- An adverb answers *how? when? where?* or *to what extent?*
- Many adverbs are formed by adding *–ly* to an adjective.
- *Intensifiers* are adverbs used to emphasize the meaning of an adjective or adverb.
- Adverbs that modify adjectives or adverbs usually come before the words they modify.
- Adverbs that modify verbs can have different positions.

Grammar

Parts of Speech: Prepositions

You are listening to a mystery on the radio. In the story, a man walks into a house, and you hear the sound of a creaking door. What is actually happening inside the broadcast studio? Instead of a man opening a door, there is someone rubbing the sides of a paper cup together. That's the creaking door!

There are other sound effects that are easy to produce. Pour rice or birdseed over a Ping-Pong ball and listen to the rain falling beside you. Crunch a piece of cellophane between your fingers, and it will sound like an egg frying. Hold an unopened box of corn starch with both hands. Press it with one thumb and then the other. Do you hear footsteps scrunching through the snow? Glue sandpaper onto two wooden blocks. Rub the sandpapered sides together and you will hear a train traveling down a track.

About the Preposition

1. **What is it?**   A preposition shows a relationship between a noun or pronoun and some other word. Look at the sentences below. The prepositions are in italics. The words they relate are in dark type. Notice how different prepositions show different relationships.

   The cup **fell** *off* the **table**.   The cup **fell** *under* the **table.**
   The cup **fell** *near* the **table**.   The cup **fell** *onto* the **table.**

2. **Common prepositions**   Here are words used as prepositions. You can find fourteen of them above.

Some Common Prepositions				
about	at	down	near	to
above	before	during	of	toward
across	behind	except	off	under
after	below	for	on	underneath
against	beneath	from	onto	until
along	beside	in	out	up
among	between	inside	over	upon
around	but (except)	into	since	with
as	by	like	through	without

Old Shoes

In times gone by, you could tell how rich and important people were by the kinds of shoes they wore. Usually, the more ridiculous and uncomfortable the shoes, the wealthier the wearer.

Long, pointed toes were particular favorites. In the 1300s, one fashionable shoe had a toe so long that it had to be held up with a chain so that the wearer could walk.

A wooden shoe called a *chopine* was unusually practical. It had an iron ring on it to help the wearer lift his feet out of the mud.

For over a hundred years starting in 1650, fine gentlemen and soldiers suffered in jack boots — thigh-high boots with a cuffed top. These were so tight and heavy that wearers could not get them on or off without help.

In olden days, it seems, poorer feet were happier feet.

3. **Compound prepositions**   A preposition of two or more words is a *compound preposition*. One appears in the opening selection.

according to	because of	in front of	next to
ahead of	due to	in place of	on account of
along with	in addition to	in spite of	on top of
as if	in back of	instead of	out of

4. **Prepositional phrases**   A preposition is always part of a group of words called a *phrase* (see page 278). A prepositional phrase begins with a preposition. It ends with a noun or pronoun called the *object of the preposition*. The object of a preposition may have one or more modifiers.

				PREPOSITIONAL
PREPOSITION	+ (MODIFIERS +)	OBJECT	=	PHRASE
beside	+	you	=	beside you
in	+ the	story	=	in the story
like	+ a creaking	door	=	like a creaking door

5. **Position of phrases**   A prepositional phrase can appear anywhere in a sentence. A sentence can have many phrases.

On that day, you were listening *to a mystery on the radio*.

6. **Preposition or adverb?**   Some words are used as prepositions and as adverbs. Remember, a preposition is part of a phrase. If it has no object, the word is probably an adverb.

PREPOSITION   The train traveled *down* the track.
ADVERB   Please put the cup *down*.

PREPOSITION   Something happened *inside* the studio.
ADVERB   Let's go *inside* now.

TIPS on Prepositions

- A preposition shows the relationship between a noun or pronoun and another word.
- A preposition is always part of a phrase.
- A prepositional phrase begins with a preposition and ends with a noun or pronoun — the object of the preposition.
- Some words can be used as prepositions and as adverbs.

Grammar

Parts of Speech: Conjunctions

When Harriet Quimby passed her pilot's test in 1911, she became the first woman in the United States with a pilot's license. She also became the first woman to pilot a plane across the English Channel, after she had been flying for only a year. In 1930, Laura Ingalls was the first woman to fly coast to coast, but she had to make nine stops. Two years later, Amelia Earhart not only made the same trip nonstop but also flew solo across the Atlantic. Sadly, Earhart and her plane vanished in 1937 as they tried to fly around the world. Although there were hundreds of female pilots, none were hired as commercial pilots until Emily Howell Warner flew for Frontier Airlines in 1973. Today there are still very few women at the controls of commercial airliners.

About the Conjunction

1. **What is it?**   A conjunction is a word that connects words or groups of words.

Earhart *and* her plane vanished *as* she flew around the world.

Find these conjunctions in the selection above:

when	but		and	although
after	not only ... but also		as	until

2. **Kinds of conjunctions**   There are three kinds of conjunctions: coordinating, correlative, and subordinating.

   a. Coordinating conjunctions   Here is a list:

   and   but   or   nor   for   so   yet

   Use   Coordinating conjunctions connect words that are used the same way.

CONNECTED SUBJECTS	Quimby *and* Ingalls were early pilots.
CONNECTED VERBS	Quimby flew coast to coast *but* made stops.
CONNECTED MODIFIERS	Was Amelia Earhart brave *or* reckless?
CONNECTED SENTENCES	Women have flown planes for decades, *yet* few have become commercial pilots.

!!!
About *conjunction*

The word *conjunction* comes from a Latin word meaning "join together" (*com-*, "together," + *jungere*, "to join").

About *coordinating*

Coordinating comes from a Latin word for "order," plus *co-*, "together." When a coordinating conjunction combines items, it shows that they are "ordered together," or equally important.

About *subordinating*

Subordinating, like *coordinating*, comes from a Latin word for "order." The prefix in this case, however, is *sub-*, "under." When a subordinating conjunction joins items, it puts one "under" the other, or below it in importance.

b. Correlative conjunctions   Here is a list:

| both . . . and | neither . . . nor | whether . . . or |
| either . . . or | not only . . . but also | |

Use   Correlative conjunctions connect words that are used in the same way. The conjunctions work in pairs.

She crossed *not only* the Atlantic *but also* the Pacific.
Neither Quimby *nor* Earhart was a commercial pilot.

c. Subordinating conjunctions   Here are examples:

after	as soon as	in order that	until
although	as though	since	when
as	because	so that	whenever
as if	before	than	where
as long as	if	unless	while

Use   A subordinating conjunction connects a subordinate clause to the rest of the sentence (see page 286). In the sentences below, the subordinate clauses are in dark type. The subordinating conjunctions are in italics.

Earhart vanished *while* **she was flying around the world.**
After **Earhart took off,** she was never seen again.

3. **Conjunction or preposition?**   Some words can be used as subordinating conjunctions and as prepositions. A preposition begins a phrase (page 278). A subordinating conjunction begins a clause (page 284).

PREPOSITION   *After* many years, she became a pilot.
CONJUNCTION   *After* she passed the test, she received a
                license.

!!!
Early Flight Facts

— In 1890 a Frenchman named Clement Ader managed the first engine-powered, piloted takeoff. He lifted his steam-driven craft just a few inches off the ground for a distance of about 150 feet.

— In 1896 a model airplane built by Samuel P. Langley, an American, flew about half a mile. Langley went on to construct a full-size plane powered by a gasoline engine. Twice in 1903 the plane tried to take off from a houseboat, but both times it crashed into the water right after launching.

— In 1903 Orville and Wilbur Wright took their historic flight in a biplane of wood and cloth. The pilot lay on his stomach in the middle of the lower wing. Connected to his waist were wires attached to the wing tips. By moving his hips, he could move the wings to control the flight. The first flight lasted only 12 seconds, covering 120 feet at about 30 miles an hour. Later that day another flight covered 852 feet in 59 seconds.

TIPS on Conjunctions

• A conjunction connects words or groups of words.
• A coordinating conjunction connects words used the same way.
• A correlative conjunction is a pair of words. It is used like a coordinating conjunction.
• A subordinating conjunction begins a subordinate clause.
• Some words are used both as conjunctions and prepositions.

Grammar

Parts of Speech: Interjections

"Hey, there's Janie." Sport pointed up the street . . .
She almost bumped into them.
"Hi."
"Hi."
"Hi."
That over, they all stood there.
"Oh, dear," said Janie, "another year. Another year older
and I'm no closer to my goal."
Sport and Harriet nodded seriously.
— *Harriet the Spy*, Louise Fitzhugh

About the Interjection

1. **What is it?**   An interjection is a word or phrase that is
not connected to the other parts of a sentence. It often
expresses a strong feeling or reaction.

   "*Hey*, there's Janie."
   "*Oh, dear*," said Janie, "another year."

2. **Some interjections**   Here are a few common interjections:

ah	goodness	oh	ouch	shh	uh oh
aha	hey	oh dear	ow	terrific	well
good grief	hooray	okay	phew	ugh	wow

3. **Punctuation**   An interjection is not related to the rest of
the sentence. It is set off by a comma or exclamation point.

   Ugh! I can't stand that song.
   Uh oh, here comes Janie.

!!!
About *interjection*

Interjection comes from a Latin
word meaning "to throw between"
(*inter-*, "between," + *jacere*, "to
throw").

TIPS on Interjections

- An interjection is a word or phrase that is not connected to any
  other part of the sentence.
- An interjection usually expresses a strong feeling.
- An interjection is set off by a comma or exclamation point.

Grammar

Tracking Shadows

Sundials were the earliest timekeepers, and they used shadows to mark the time. One common sundial has a round face that is divided into hours. A thin piece of metal stands up in the center. As the sun moves across the sky, it hits the raised piece at different angles, casting different shadows. On a well-designed sundial, the shadow will hit the number that tells the correct time.

Track the sun yourself. Find a pole or a building in the sun. Early in the morning, put a chalk mark on the ground along the length of the shadow and write the time. Track the shadow every hour or two. Mark the length as well as the position. You may be surprised to see how quickly the shadow changes.

Phrases

☐ **Phrase**   A group of words without a subject and verb, used as a single word

You are bicycling with a friend. Your father asked you to be home by a certain time, but you suddenly realize you forgot your watch. Rather worried, you wonder how to find out what time it is. Just do what people in ancient days did. Look at shadows.

Shadows cast by trees, rocks, or buildings change with the moving sun. Falling one way early in the morning, they shift to the opposite direction later in the afternoon. There are no shadows at all at noon, the middle of the day, for the sun is directly above. Watching shadows can help you guess the time without using a watch. Don't desert your faithful friend the watch, though. You can't carry a shadow around on your wrist.

Kinds of Phrases

1. Prepositional phrase

EXAMPLES	*by a certain time, at noon*
STRUCTURE	Preposition + noun and any modifiers
USE	As adjective: modifies a noun or pronoun
	As adverb: modifies a verb, adjective, or adverb

2. Verbal phrase

a. Participial phrase

EXAMPLES	*Rather worried,* you wonder what time it is.
	Falling one way in the morning, they shift later.
STRUCTURE	*-ed* or *-ing* form + accompanying words
USE	As adjective: modifies a noun or pronoun

b. Gerund phrase

EXAMPLE	*Watching shadows* can help you guess the time.
STRUCTURE	*-ing* form + accompanying words
USE	As noun

c. Infinitive phrase

EXAMPLE	You wonder how *to find out what time it is.*
STRUCTURE	*to* + verb + accompanying words
USE	As noun, adjective, or adverb

3. **Appositive phrase**

> EXAMPLE   Shadows disappear at noon, *the middle of the day.*
> STRUCTURE   noun or pronoun + modifiers
> USE   Identifies or explains another noun or pronoun

Prepositional Phrases

1. **Structure**   A prepositional phrase begins with a preposition and ends with a noun or pronoun. (See pages 273 – 274.)

   a. The noun at the end is the *object of the preposition*.

   > PREPOSITION + NOUN   at *noon*

   b. The object of the preposition may have modifiers.

   > PREPOSITION + MODIFIER(S) + NOUN   by *a certain* time

   c. A preposition may have more than one object.

   > PREPOSITION + NOUNS   by *trees, rocks,* or *buildings*

2. **Use**

   a. **Adjective phrases**   Some prepositional phrases are used as adjectives to modify nouns or pronouns. They tell *what kind, which,* or *how much or many* about the noun.

   > ADJECTIVE   *ancient* people
   > ADJECTIVE PHRASE   people *in ancient days*

   b. **Adverb phrases**   Some prepositional phrases are used as adverbs to modify verbs, adjectives, or adverbs. They tell *how, when, where,* or *to what extent.*

   > ADVERB   Look *there.*
   > ADVERB PHRASE   Look *at shadows.*
   > ADVERB   later *today*
   > ADVERB PHRASE   later *in the afternoon*

3. **In the sentence**

   a. A prepositional phrase can appear in any position.

   > *At noon* there are no shadows.
   > Shadows shift *to the other direction* later in the day.
   > You are supposed to be home *by a certain time.*

   b. A sentence can have more than one prepositional phrase. One prepositional phrase can follow another.

   > *At the end of the day,* the shadow *of the tree* grew long.

Make Your Sentence Grow

Prepositional phrases can help you expand your sentences and make them more interesting. Be careful, though. You have to know when to stop, because you can keep adding them forever!

The man told a joke.

During lunch, the man told a joke.

During lunch, the man told a joke **about a lizard.**

During lunch, the man told a joke about a lizard **with an unusual talent.**

During lunch **at the pizza place,** the man told a joke about a lizard with an unusual talent.

During lunch at the pizza place, the man **behind the counter** told a joke about a lizard with an unusual talent.

During lunch at the pizza place **near the video store,** the man behind the counter told a joke about a lizard with an unusual talent.

During lunch at the pizza place near the video store, the man behind the counter told a joke about a lizard with an unusual talent **for reciting poetry.**

According to Boris, during lunch **on Monday** at the pizza place **with purple tables** near the video store **around the corner,** the man **from Australia** behind the counter told a joke **to my cousin** about a lizard **in India** with an unusual talent for reciting poetry **to herds of cows in the . . .**

About *participle*

Participle and participial have the same origin as participate. They all come from a Latin word meaning "to take part, join with others."

Combining Sentences

Participles come from verbs. Think of them as coming from verbs in sentences of their own.

Shadows change with the sun.

+ The sun is moving.

= Shadows change with the **moving** sun.

When you write, look for sentences you can combine using a participle or participial phrase.

You are worried.

+ You wonder what time it is.

= **Worried**, you wonder what time it is.

Trees cast shadows.

+ The shadows change with the moving sun.

= Shadows **cast by trees** change with the moving sun.

Shadows fall one way in the morning.

+ They shift direction in the afternoon.

= Falling one way in the morning, shadows shift direction in the afternoon.

Verbals: Participles, Participial Phrases

1. **Participles**

   a. A *participle* is a verb form used as an adjective. It tells *what kind, which,* or *how much or many* about a noun.

   b. There are two kinds of participles. *Present participles* end in *-ing*. *Past participles* usually end in *-ed*, but some forms are irregular: *lost, worn, broken* (pages 298 – 300).

   Shadows change with the *moving* **sun**.   (*moving* modifies *sun*)
   Worried, **I** wondered what time it was.   (*worried* modifies *I*)
   The *broken* **watch** was useless.   (*broken* modifies *watch*)

2. **Participle or verb?**   When participles are used as verbs, they have helping verbs with them (page 267). When they are used as participles, they do not have helping verbs.

   VERB   The sun **is** *moving*.   (helping verb *is*)
   PARTICIPLE   Shadows follow the *moving* sun.
           (no helping verb)

3. **Participial phrases**   Participial phrases are made up of participles plus modifiers or other words.

   a. **What do they do?**   Participial phrases are used as adjectives. They modify nouns or pronouns.

   b. **How are they built?**   A participle is a verb form. Any term used with a verb — adverb, prepositional phrase, object — can be used with a participle to build a phrase.

   PARTICIPLE + ADVERB   *Looking carefully,* I found a shadow.
   PARTICIPLE + PHRASE   *Looking at the shadow,* I made a guess.
   PARTICIPLE + OBJECT   *Checking my watch,* I saw I was right.

   c. **Comma or no comma?**   A participial phrase that begins a sentence has a comma. A phrase placed elsewhere has no commas if it is needed to identify a noun or pronoun. A phrase that is not essential — one that can be left out without changing the meaning — is set off with commas.

   BEGINNING   *Walking slowly,* I watched the shadow.
   ESSENTIAL   I saw the shadow *growing longer.*
   NOT ESSENTIAL   The shadow, *growing longer,* told me the time.

Verbals: Gerunds, Gerund Phrases

1. Gerunds   A *gerund* is a verb form in *-ing* used as a noun.

SUBJECT	*Bicycling* is good exercise.
DIRECT OBJECT	I like *bicycling*.
INDIRECT OBJECT	Doctors give *bicycling* a high rating.
OBJECT OF PREPOSITION	You can exercise by *bicycling*.
PREDICATE NOUN	My favorite exercise is *bicycling*.
APPOSITIVE	I found a good exercise, *bicycling*.

2. Gerund or participle or verb?   Gerunds, participles, and verb forms end in *-ing*. To tell them apart, decide how they are used. A gerund is used as a noun. A participle is used as an adjective. A verb is used with the helping verb *be*.

GERUND	*Bicycling* is good exercise. (subject)
PARTICIPLE	*Bicycling*, I lost track of the time. (modifies *I*)
VERB	He *is bicycling* to work today. (used with *is*)

3. Gerund phrases   Gerund phrases are made up of gerunds plus modifiers or other words.

a. What do they do?   Gerund phrases are used as nouns.

GERUND	*Bicycling* is good exercise. (subject)
PHRASE	*Bicycling to work* is good exercise. (subject)

b. How are they built?   Here are some examples.

GERUND PLUS ADJECTIVE	I know the rules of *safe bicycling*.
GERUND PLUS ADVERB	*Bicycling downhill* is fun.
GERUND PLUS PHRASE	*Bicycling to work* is good exercise.
GERUND PLUS OBJECT	Know the time without *using a watch*.

c. Gerunds with possessives   When a noun or pronoun is used before another noun, it is usually a possessive. When a noun or pronoun is used before a gerund, it is also usually a possessive.

POSSESSIVE WITH NOUN	**Carla's** *lateness* surprised us.
POSSESSIVE WITH GERUND	**Carla's** *being late* surprised us.
POSSESSIVE WITH NOUN	**Your** *lateness* surprised us.
POSSESSIVE WITH GERUND	**Your** *being late* surprised us.

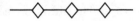

!!!
About *gerunds*

Gerund comes from a Latin word meaning "to carry, to act."

Combining Sentences

Gerunds come from verbs. Therefore, you can think of them as coming from verbs in sentences of their own.

We bicycle.
+ It is our favorite exercise.
= **Bicycling** is our favorite exercise.

When you write, look for sentences you can combine using a gerund or gerund phrase.

Watch shadows.
+ That can help you guess the time.
= **Watching shadows** can help you guess the time.

Do not use a watch.
+ You can guess the time without it.
= You can guess the time without **using a watch.**

The word *infinitive* is related to *infinite*, "numberless, without end."

Combining Sentences

Infinitives come from verbs. You can think of them as coming from sentences of their own.

Guess.
+ It is not difficult.
= **To guess** is not difficult.
or
It is not difficult **to guess.**

When you write, look for sentences you can combine using an infinitive or infinitive phrase.

He cannot read the sundial.
+ He does not know how.
= He does not know how **to read the sundial.**

She decided something.
+ She would leave early.
= She decided **to leave early.**

Leave early.
+ You have no choice.
= You have no choice but **to leave early.**

Verbals: Infinitives, Infinitive Phrases

1. Infinitives   An *infinitive* is a verb form that begins with *to*. An infinitive can be used as a noun, an adjective, or an adverb.

AS A NOUN

SUBJECT	*To guess* is not difficult.
DIRECT OBJECT	Try *to guess.*
OBJECT OF PREPOSITION	You have no choice except *to guess.*
PREDICATE NOUN	The object of the game is *to guess.*

AS AN ADJECTIVE

MODIFIES NOUN	Now is the **time** *to guess.*

AS AN ADVERB

MODIFIES VERB	*To guess,* **look** at the shadows.
MODIFIES ADJECTIVE	Are you **afraid** *to guess?*
MODIFIES ADVERB	Do you know **how** *to guess?*

2. Infinitive or preposition?   An infinitive is made up of *to* plus a verb form. A prepositional phrase is made up of *to* plus a noun or pronoun.

INFINITIVE = *TO* PLUS VERB   *to* move
PREPOSITIONAL PHRASE = *TO* PLUS NOUN   *to* the building

3. Infinitive phrases   Infinitive phrases are made up of infinitives plus modifiers or other words. Here are some examples.

INFINITIVE WITH ADVERB   Carla decided *to leave* **early.**
INFINITIVE WITH PHRASE   She wanted *to leave* **at six o'clock.**
INFINITIVE WITH OBJECT   She tried *to guess* **the time.**

4. Infinitives without *to*   The word *to* is sometimes left out when an infinitive follows such verbs as *let, help, dare, hear, see, watch, feel, make.*

INFINITIVE WITHOUT *TO*   Let me *guess.* *(to guess)*
I helped him *decide.* *(to decide)*
He didn't dare *leave.* *(to leave)*

Appositives, Appositive Phrases

!!!
About *appositive*

Appositive comes from a Latin word meaning "to place near to."

1. **Appositives**   *Appositives* are nouns or pronouns placed next to other nouns or pronouns to identify or explain them.

   My **friend** *Richie* found my watch.
   (*Richie* identifies which *friend*.)

2. **Appositive phrases**   *Apppositive phrases* are made up of appositives plus their modifiers.

   There are no shadows at noon, *the middle of the day.*
   (The prepositional phrase *of the day* modifies *middle*.)

3. **Commas or no commas?**

   a. Do not use commas if the appositive is needed to identify the noun or pronoun.

   ESSENTIAL   My friend *Richie* found my watch.
   (You have other friends. *Richie* identifies which friend.)

   b. Use commas if the appositive is not essential, that is, if it can be left out without changing the meaning.

   NOT ESSENTIAL   Richie, *one of my friends*, found my watch.
   (*Richie* already identifies which friend.)

Combining Sentences

When you write, look for sentences you can combine using an appositive or appositive phrase.

   Don't desert your watch.
   + Your watch is a friend.
   = Don't desert your friend **the watch.**

   There are no shadows at noon.
   + Noon is the middle of the day.
   = There are no shadows at noon, **the middle of the day.**

TIPS on Phrases

- A phrase is a group of words without a subject and verb that is used as a single word.
- Prepositional phrases
    Based on prepositions; used as adjectives and adverbs
- Verbal phrases, based on verb forms:
  Participial phrases
    Based on *-ed* and *-ing* forms; used as adjectives
  Gerund phrases
    Based on *-ing* forms; used as nouns
  Infinitive phrases
    Based on *to* + verb; used as nouns, adjectives, adverbs
- Appositive phrases
    Based on nouns, pronouns; used to identify nouns, pronouns

Clauses

☐ **Clause**   A group of words with a subject and a verb

> The violin is an instrument with two names. The *violin* is played in a concert hall, but the *fiddle* is played in a dance hall. Actually, the fiddle is just a violin that is played in a popular or folk style. Although a fiddle is held differently, it is still the exact same instrument as a violin.

What is the difference between a phrase and a clause? A clause has a subject and a verb. A phrase does not.

PHRASE   The violin is an instrument *with two names.*
CLAUSE   The violin is an instrument *that has two names.*

Independent Clauses

1. **Recognizing independent clauses**   An *independent clause*, or *main clause*, can stand alone as a sentence. In fact, it is called a sentence when it stands by itself.

   INDEPENDENT   *He plays the fiddle.*

   An independent clause can also be part of a sentence.

   INDEPENDENT   *He plays the fiddle* when I sing.

2. **More than one**   A sentence can have more than one independent clause.

   INDEPENDENT   *He plays the fiddle,* and *I play the guitar.*

Subordinate Clauses

1. **Recognizing subordinate clauses**

   a. A *subordinate clause* is also called a *dependent clause*. A subordinate clause cannot stand alone as a sentence. It depends on, or needs, an independent clause.

      SUBORDINATE   when I sing
      INDEPENDENT +   He plays the fiddle
      SUBORDINATE   *when I sing.*

   b. There are three kinds of subordinate clauses: adjective clauses, adverb clauses, and noun clauses.

2. Adjective clauses

a. What they do   An *adjective clause* is used as an adjective. It modifies a noun or pronoun and tells *what kind, which,* or *how much or many.* The adjective and the adjective clause below both modify the noun *fiddle.*

ADJECTIVE	He is playing a *borrowed* **fiddle.**
ADJECTIVE CLAUSE	He is playing a **fiddle** *that he borrowed.*

b. Relative pronouns   The word that connects an adjective clause to the word it modifies is a *relative pronoun.* *

RELATIVE PRONOUN	He is playing a fiddle *that* he borrowed.

Relative Pronouns

who   whom   whose   which   that

Sometimes the pronoun *that* is left out of the clause.

ADJECTIVE CLAUSE	Here is the violin *he wants to borrow.*

The words *when* and *where* are sometimes used as relative pronouns too.

ADJECTIVE CLAUSE	Two o'clock is the time **when** *he practices.*
	That is the place **where** *he practices.*

c. Commas or no commas?   Do not use commas when the clause is needed to identify a noun or pronoun. Use commas when the clause just adds information.

ESSENTIAL	The violin *that she played* belongs to Ben.
NOT ESSENTIAL	The violin, *which is old*, belongs to Ben.

Sometimes the use of commas can change the meaning.

ESSENTIAL	The musicians *who play violin* are good.
	(Only those who play violin are good.)
NOT ESSENTIAL	The musicians, *who play violin*, are good.
	(All play violin and all are good.)

*See pages 314 – 315 for the use of *who, whom, whose.*

A Box with Strings

A violin is a beautifully shaped and polished wooden instrument with strings stretched down its length. The strings make the notes. The lovely container amplifies, or makes louder, the sound of the strings.

Try an experiment. Stretch a string tightly and then pluck it. You will hear a note, but a rather faint one. Now stretch the string across a wooden box and pluck it. The sound will be louder.

You can go one step further and cut an opening in the box, just as a violin has an opening in the wood. Pluck the strings again. Can you hear any difference?

3. Adverb clauses

a. What they do An *adverb clause* is used as an adverb.

ADVERB	I practice *often*.
ADVERB CLAUSE	I practice *whenever I can*.

An adverb clause does all the jobs that an adverb does.

MODIFIES VERB	I **practice** *whenever I can*.
MODIFIES ADJECTIVE	I am **happy** *when I play well*.
MODIFIES ADVERB	I played **better** *than I usually do*.

Like adverbs, adverb clauses tell *how, when, where,* or *to what extent*. They also tell *under what condition* or *why*, or they make comparisons.

WHEN	I practice *whenever I can*.
UNDER WHAT CONDITION	*If she gives a concert*, I will go.
WHY	I will go *because she plays well*.
COMPARISON	She plays better *than I do*.

b. Subordinating conjunctions Adverb clauses are introduced by *subordinating conjunctions* (page 276).

SUBORDINATING CONJUNCTION	I practice **whenever** *I can*.
	Before *I go*, I must practice.

Some Common Subordinating Conjunctions

after	as soon as	so that	until	where
although	because	than	when	while
as	before	unless	whenever	

---

c. Comma or no comma? Use a comma after an adverb clause that introduces a sentence. Also use commas around an adverb clause that interrupts an independent clause.

ADVERB CLAUSE	*After she played*, we all applauded.
	Her playing, *if I may say so,* is wonderful.

d. Incomplete clauses Sometimes the verb and perhaps other words are left out of an adverb clause.

ADVERB CLAUSE	A fiddle is the same *as a violin* (*is*).
	Coretta plays better *than Ben* (*plays*).

Know Your Conjunctions

Each subordinating conjunction joins clauses in its own way. Notice how the meaning of a sentence changes as the conjunction changes. Choose a conjunction that says exactly what you want it to say.

We will leave **after** Sam plays the violin.
We will leave **before** Sam plays the violin.
We will leave **unless** Sam plays the violin.
We will leave **when** Sam plays the violin.
We will leave **while** Sam plays the violin.
We will leave **if** Sam plays the violin.
We will leave **until** Sam plays the violin.

4. Noun clauses

a. What they do   A *noun clause* is used as a noun.

NOUN   The *song* was beautiful.
NOUN CLAUSE   *What she sang* was beautiful.

A noun clause does all the jobs that a noun does in a sentence.

SUBJECT	*What she sang* was beautiful.
DIRECT OBJECT	We liked *what she sang*.
INDIRECT OBJECT	Give *whoever sang* a big hand.
OBJECT OF PREPOSITION	He plays for *whoever will listen*.
PREDICATE NOUN	The fiddle is *what he plays*.

b. Introductory words   Here are some of the words that can introduce noun clauses. (See page 315 for *who–whom*.)

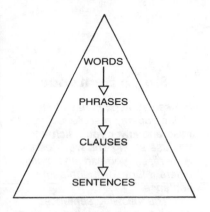

Some Words That Introduce Noun Clauses

how	whatever	which	whom
if	when	whichever	whomever
that	where	who	whose
what	whether	whoever	why

Some of the words above also introduce other kinds of clauses. Identify a clause by what it does, not by the word that introduces it.

NOUN CLAUSE   I wonder **who** *is singing*.
ADJECTIVE CLAUSE   Coretta is the person **who** *is singing*.

TIPS on Clauses

- A clause is a group of words that has a subject and verb.
- An independent clause can stand alone as a sentence.
- A subordinate clause cannot stand alone as a sentence.
  There are three kinds of subordinate clauses:

Clause	Used as	Introduced by
Adjective	adjective	relative pronoun
Adverb	adverb	subordinating conjunction
Noun	noun	one of various words

Grammar

Sing a Sentence

Spoken sentences have tunes. When you say a sentence, you raise and lower your pitch and you use strong and weak beats. As a result, you can sing many different tunes with the same sentence.

The following sentences have the same words but different meanings. The only thing that changes is the way they are said. Say the sentences, emphasizing the words in dark type. Listen to the meaning change.

Rona did not say she hated the violin. (*Someone else said it.*)

Rona did **not** say she hated the violin. (*She didn't say it.*)

Rona did not **say** she hated the violin. (*But the speaker thinks she does.*)

Rona did not say **she** hated the violin. (*Someone else does.*)

Rona did not say she **hated** the violin. (*She said something else about it.*)

Rona did not say she hated the **violin**. (*She hates something else.*)

Sentences: The Four Kinds

"Would you like anything else?" asked the waiter.

The man, a regular customer, replied, "No, that will be all. Give me my check, please." He paid his bill and then walked up a wall, across the ceiling, down another wall, and out the door.

"How odd," said the waiter. "He didn't say goodnight!"

A sentence states a complete thought. Every sentence begins with a capital letter and ends with a punctuation mark.

The Four Kinds of Sentences

1. **Declarative sentences**   A *declarative sentence* makes a statement. It ends with a period.

   DECLARATIVE   That will be all.

2. **Interrogative sentences**   An *interrogative sentence* asks a question. It ends with a question mark.

   INTERROGATIVE   Would you like anything else?

3. **Imperative sentences**   An *imperative sentence* expresses a command or a request. It ends with a period.

   IMPERATIVE   Give me my check, please.

4. **Exclamatory sentences**   An *exclamatory sentence* expresses strong feeling and ends with an exclamation point. You can make any sentence exclamatory.

   EXCLAMATORY   He didn't say goodnight!   That will be all!

TIPS on the Four Kinds of Sentences

- A sentence expresses a complete thought. It begins with a capital letter and ends with a punctuation mark.
- There are four kinds of sentences.

Sentence	What it does	End punctuation
Declarative	makes a statement	period
Interrogative	asks a question	question mark
Imperative	states a command, request	period
Exclamatory	states strong feeling	exclamation point

Sentences: Subjects, Predicates, Complements

☐ **Sentence** Group of words expressing a complete thought

Korea is a land in eastern Asia, on a peninsula that juts out from China. China and Japan are Korea's neighbors, but Korea has always had its own language and customs. In fact, Korea is one of the oldest countries in the world.

Korea's history has not been peaceful. There are now two nations, North Korea and South Korea. The split occurred in 1945 and has caused much conflict. In 1950, a war began. Into the area poured troops from many nations. The United States and other nations helped South Korea. The Soviet Union and China aided North Korea. The war between north and south ended three years later, but the two nations have never signed a peace treaty.

Subjects and Predicates

1. **Two main parts** Every sentence has two main parts.

   a. The *subject* names what the sentence is about.

   b. The *predicate* tells what the subject is, does, has, or feels.

SUBJECT	PREDICATE
A war	began.
Korea's history	has not been peaceful.
The war between north and south	ended three years later.

2. **Complete and simple subjects**

   a. The *complete subject* includes the noun or pronoun that names the subject, plus words that describe it.

   b. The *simple subject* is the key word or words in the complete subject. It is usually a noun or pronoun. (The word *subject* normally refers to the simple subject.)

   c. Sometimes the subject has only one word. Then that word is both the simple subject and the complete subject. Below, the simple subjects are in dark type.

COMPLETE SUBJECT	
It	is divided.
Korea's **history**	has not been peaceful.
The **war** *between north and south*	ended three years later.

!!!
Up-and-Down Sentences

It may seem obvious to you that sentences must be written from left to right across a page. Think about it, though. Is there really a reason that sentences have to be written that way? The answer is no. In fact, in some languages, sentences go in very different directions.

Hebrew writing, for instance, goes from right to left, not left to right. As a result, what is the back of a book in English is the front of a book in Hebrew.

Classical Chinese is written not only from right to left, like Hebrew, but also from top to bottom, in columns. To read a page, then, you start at the top of the rightmost column, read down the column, and then move to the top of the next column on the left.

Read these lines as if they were Hebrew and Chinese:

.SIHT EKIL WERBEH DAER

C	T	T
H	O	H
I		I
N	R	S
E	E	
S	A	I
E	D	S
P	A	H
A		O
P		W
E		
R		

How Natural is Natural Order?

In English, the order *subject-verb* is called the "natural order." What is natural for English in this case is natural for three quarters of the world's languages, including languages as different as French, Hausa, and Vietnamese.

A small percentage of languages, including Welsh, places the verb before the subject.

In a few languages, such as Latin and the Indian languages Quechua and Navajo, words can be arranged in almost any order and still make sense.

3. Complete and simple predicates

a. The *complete predicate* is the verb and the words with it. It includes everything not part of the complete subject.

b. The *simple predicate* is the verb — the key word or words in the predicate. It tells what the subject is, has, does, or feels: *end, begin, occur, help*.

c. A verb that has more than one word is a *verb phrase* (page 267): *has been*. A word or contraction that comes between parts of a verb phrase is not part of the verb phrase.

d. If a verb is the only word in the predicate, it is both the complete predicate and the simple predicate. Below, the simple predicates, or verbs, are in dark type.

COMPLETE PREDICATE

The war between north and south Korea's history **ended** *three years later.*

Korea's history **has** *not* **been** *peaceful.*

A war **began.**

4. Finding the subject

a. Natural order In most sentences, the subject comes before the verb. These sentences are in *natural order*. To find the subject, ask *who?* or *what?* about the verb. (Below, the subject is in italics and the verb is in dark type.)

NATURAL   *Troops* from many nations **poured** into the area. (*Who* poured into the area? *Troops*)

b. Inverted order Sometimes the verb comes before the subject. Such sentences are in *inverted order*. Most questions are in inverted order. So are sentences beginning with *there* and *here*.

INVERTED   Into the area **poured** *troops* from many nations.
Is *Korea* in eastern Asia?
There **are** now two *nations*.

To find the subject, ask *what?* or *who?* about the verb. You can also try putting the sentence in natural order.

There are now two nations. (*what* are? *nations* are)
Is Korea in eastern Asia?   (*Korea* is in eastern Asia.)

c. *you* understood   An imperative sentence states a command or request. Its subject is always *you*. *You* is not stated, but it is understood to be the subject.

IMPERATIVE   Lend me your book about Korea.
(*Lend* = verb; *you* = understood subject)

David, please tell me more about it.
(*tell* = verb; *you* = understood subject)

d. **Other beginnings**   Even a sentence in natural order does not always begin with the subject. To find the subject in any sentence, ask *who?* or *what?* about the verb.

NATURAL   In fact, *Korea* is one of the oldest countries.
(*What* is? *Korea* is.)

5. **Compound subjects and predicates**

a. **Compound subject**   A *compound subject* has two or more simple subjects with the same predicate. A conjunction such as *and, but,* or *or* joins the subjects.

COMPOUND SUBJECT   *China* **and** *Japan* are Korea's neighbors.

b. **Compound predicate**   A *compound predicate* has two or more verbs with the same subject. A conjunction such as *and, but,* or *or* joins the verbs.

COMPOUND PREDICATE   North Korea *is* larger **but** *has* fewer people.

Complements

1. **What are they?**   A *complement* is a word or phrase in the predicate that completes the meaning of the subject or verb.

2. **Verb complements**   A *verb complement* completes the action of a verb. It can be a *direct object* or an *indirect object*.

a. **Direct objects**   A direct object receives the action of the verb. It answers *what?* or *whom?* after the verb and is usually a noun or pronoun. Only action verbs have direct objects (page 268).

DIRECT OBJECT   Several nations **helped** *South Korea*.
(helped *whom?* helped *South Korea*)

Sentence Beginnings

Not every sentence needs to begin with a subject. Here are some other beginnings. Use them to perk up your writing.

PREPOSITIONAL PHRASE
In fact, Korea is one of the oldest countries.
ADVERB
Actually, Korea is one of the oldest countries.
VERBAL
United, Korea was one of the oldest countries.
VERBAL PHRASE
Dating back almost a thousand years, Korea is one of the oldest countries.
APPOSITIVE
An ancient land, Korea is one of the oldest countries.

Subject or Object — Who Saw Whom?

The same word can do different jobs, depending on where it is. Would you rather be the subject or the object below?

Jason saw the lion.
The lion saw Jason.

The Language of Yoda

In the movie Return of the Jedi, *the statements of Yoda sounded odd. Why? They began with complements, not subjects.*

Your father he is.
Sick I've become.
Strong with the Force you are.

Verbs with Indirect Objects

Here are common verbs that take indirect objects.

bring   lend   send   teach
give   make   show   write
hand   offer

Sentence Patterns

Most English sentences are built on one of the patterns below.

S = subject
V = verb
DO = direct object
IO = indirect object
A = adverb
PN = predicate noun
PA = predicate adjective

1. S + V
   People travel.

2. S + V + DO
   Many take airplanes.

3. S + V + IO + DO
   Lisa sent us a card.

4. S + V + A
   The plane flew higher.

5. S + V + DO + A
   Dad drove us there.

6. S + V + PN
   O'Hare is an airport.

7. S + V + PA
   The airport is huge.

Your Turn

Create your own sentences for each of the patterns.

b. **Indirect objects**   An indirect object tells *to what? to whom? for what?* or *for whom?* about a verb. It is usually a noun or pronoun. If the prepositon *to* or *for* is used before the object, it is not called an indirect object.

INDIRECT OBJECT   Several nations **sent** *them* aid.
                   (sent *to whom?* to *them*)
PREPOSITIONAL PHRASE   Several nations **sent** aid *to Korea.*

c. **Position of objects**   An indirect object always comes before a direct object. Above, *aid* is the direct object.

3. **Subject complements**   *Subject complements* complete the action of a subject. They can be *predicate nouns* or *predicate adjectives.*

a. **Predicate nouns**   A predicate noun is a noun or pronoun that comes after a linking verb (page 266) and identifies or explains the subject. Below, the linking verb is *is.*

PREDICATE NOUN   *Korea* **is** a *land.*
                  Korea **is** an ancient *land.*
                  Korea **is** a *land* in Asia.

b. **Predicate adjectives**   A predicate adjective follows a linking verb and describes the subject.

PREDICATE ADJECTIVE   *Korea* **is** ancient.
                       Its *history* **has** not **been** *peaceful.*
NOT PREDICATE ADJECTIVE   Korea is an ancient land.
                           (*Ancient* modifies *land*, not *Korea.*)
                           Its history is not a peaceful one.
                           (*Peaceful* modifies *one*, not *history.*)

TIPS on Subjects, Predicates, and Complements

• Every sentence is divided into a subject and a predicate.
  The subject tells what the sentence is about.
  The predicate tells what the subject is, has, does, or feels.
• A complement is a word or words that complete the meaning of a subject or predicate.
  A verb complement is a direct object or an indirect object.
  A subject complement is a predicate noun or predicate adjective.

Sentences: The Four Structures

If you think that a spider is just another "bug," you are wrong. Spiders are not insects at all. In fact, to a spider, an insect is what a pizza is to you — a good meal. Spiders are famous for their webs, and they spin them to trap the insects that they eat. Spiders are *arachnids*. While insects often have wings, spiders do not. Insects have six legs, but spiders have eight.

The Four Sentence Structures

1. **Simple sentences**   A *simple sentence* has one independent clause only. It may have phrases and compound parts.

   SIMPLE   Spiders and ticks belong to the class *Arachnida*.

2. **Compound sentences**   A *compound sentence* contains two or more independent clauses joined by a conjunction.

   COMPOUND   *Insects have six legs,* **but** *spiders have eight.*

3. **Complex sentences**   A *complex sentence* contains one independent clause and one or more subordinate clauses. Below, the connecting words are in dark type.

   COMPLEX   **While** *insects often have wings,* spiders do not.
   If *you think* **that** *a spider is a bug,* you are wrong.

4. **Compound–complex sentences**   A *compound–complex sentence* contains two or more independent clauses and one or more subordinate clauses.

   COMPOUND–   Spiders are famous for their webs, **and** they
   COMPLEX   spin them to trap the insects **that** they eat.

TIPS on the Four Sentence Structures

- A simple sentence has one independent clause only.
- A compound sentence has two or more independent clauses.
- A complex sentence has one independent clause and one or more subordinate clauses.
- A compound–complex sentence has two or more independent clauses and one or more subordinate clauses.

Compound Predicate or Compound Sentence?

A compound predicate has more than one verb but only one subject.

COMPOUND PREDICATE
I *like* ants but *hate* flies.
COMPOUND SENTENCE
I *like* ants, but I *hate* flies.

I Like *X*, but I Don't Like *Y*

Can you figure out why some things are liked and others are not in these compound sentences?

I like trees, but I don't like flowers.
I like football, but I don't like golf.
I like yellow, but I don't like red.
I like doors, but I don't like windows.
I like spoons, but I don't like forks.

The liked items are spelled with double letters.

Answer

Here's another one for you.

I like lakes, but I don't like the sea.
I like beans, but I don't like peas.
I like ants, but I don't like bees.
I like noses, but I don't like eyes.
I like me, but I don't like you.

The things not liked all sound like letters of the alphabet.

Answer

Diagraming Sentences

When you diagram a sentence, you show how the parts of a sentence are related to one another. Follow the models below to diagram the different sentence parts.

1. **Subject and predicate**   Adam knows.

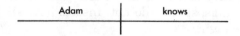

2. **Direct object**   Adam knows something.

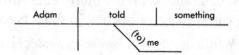

3. **Indirect object**   Adam told me something.

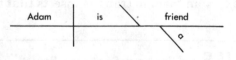

4. **Predicate noun**   Adam is a friend.

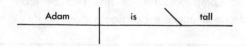

5. **Predicate adjective**   Adam is tall.

6. Adjective, Adverb   Adam really is a good friend.

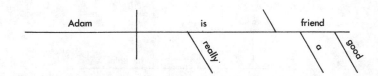

7. Prepositional phrase   Adam went to school.

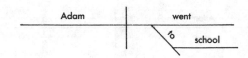

8. Participle, participial phrase   Opening the door, Adam left.

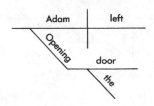

9. Gerund, gerund phrase   Walking fast is healthful.

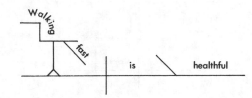

10. Infinitive, infinitive phrase   To walk fast is healthful.

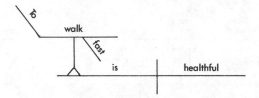

11. Appositive, appositive phrase   Adam, a friend, is visiting.

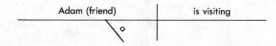

12. Compound subject and predicate   Adam and Sally walked and talked.

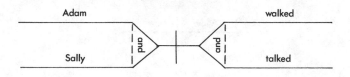

13. Compound sentence   Adam left, but Sally stayed.

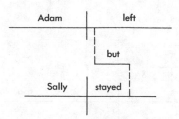

14. Adjective clause   Adam, who left, will return.

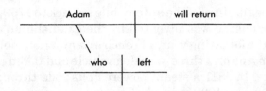

15. Adverb clause   After Adam left, Sally arrived.

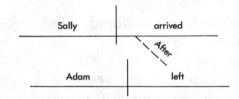

16. Noun clause   I know that Adam left.

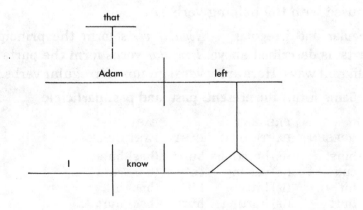

Using Verbs

The beginnings of the automobile go back to 1769, when the steam engine was invented by the Englishman James Watt. By the following year, a French inventor had mounted a steam engine on a three-wheeled vehicle and taken it out for a drive. In 1811 a steam-powered bus rode through London, and by 1829 several of these big, noisy buses were chugging their way down the streets and frightening every horse that came along. The buses frightened the stagecoach companies as well. Because they feared the competition, they fought back. A law was passed saying that a man with a red flag must walk in front of every power-driven vehicle!

Principal Parts

1. Every verb has four basic forms, called *principal parts*. (See also pages 266 – 267.)

PRESENT	PRESENT PARTICIPLE	PAST	PAST PARTICIPLE
walk	(*is*) walk*ing*	walk*ed*	(*has*) walk*ed*

   a. The *present* is the basic form of the verb.

   b. The *present participle* is formed with the verb plus *-ing*. It is used with the helping verb *be*.

   c. The *past* is formed with the verb plus *-ed*.

   d. The *past participle* is formed with the verb plus *-ed*. It is used with the helping verb *have*.

2. **Regular and irregular**   *Regular verbs* form the principal parts as described above. *Irregular* verbs form the parts in different ways. Here are several groups of irregular verbs.

   a. **Same forms for present, past, and past participle**

PRESENT	PRESENT PARTICIPLE	PAST	PAST PARTICIPLE
burst	(is) bursting	burst	(has) burst
cut	(is) cutting	cut	(has) cut
hit	(is) hitting	hit	(has) hit
hurt	(is) hurting	hurt	(has) hurt
let	(is) letting	let	(has) let
put	(is) putting	put	(has) put
set	(is) setting	set	(has) set

Spelling Tips

These tips will help you spell the principal parts of regular verbs correctly.

1. When a one-syllable verb ends in a single consonant, double the final consonant before adding *-ing* or *-ed*.

   hop   ho**pp**ing   ho**pp**ed

2. When a verb ends with *e*, drop the *e* before adding *-ing* or *-ed*.

   close   clos**ing**   clos**ed**

3. When a verb ends in a consonant + *y*, change *y* to *i* before adding *-ed*.

   try   try**ing**   tr**i**ed

b. Same forms for past and past participle

PRESENT	PRESENT PARTICIPLE	PAST	PAST PARTICIPLE
bring	(is) bringing	brought	(has) brought
buy	(is) buying	bought	(has) bought
catch	(is) catching	caught	(has) caught
feel	(is) feeling	felt	(has) felt
fight	(is) fighting	fought	(has) fought
find	(is) finding	found	(has) found
hold	(is) holding	held	(has) held
keep	(is) keeping	kept	(has) kept
lay	(is) laying	laid	(has) laid
leave	(is) leaving	left	(has) left
lend	(is) lending	lent	(has) lent
lose	(is) losing	lost	(has) lost
make	(is) making	made	(has) made
say	(is) saying	said	(has) said
sell	(is) selling	sold	(has) sold
send	(is) sending	sent	(has) sent
sit	(is) sitting	sat	(has) sat
sleep	(is) sleeping	slept	(has) slept
stand	(is) standing	stood	(has) stood
swing	(is) swinging	swung	(has) swung
teach	(is) teaching	taught	(has) taught
tell	(is) telling	told	(has) told
think	(is) thinking	thought	(has) thought
win	(is) winning	won	(has) won

c. Same forms for present and for past participle

PRESENT	PRESENT PARTICIPLE	PAST	PAST PARTICIPLE
become	(is) becoming	became	(has) become
come	(is) coming	came	(has) come
run	(is) running	ran	(has) run

d. Past participle formed from past + -n

PRESENT	PRESENT PARTICIPLE	PAST	PAST PARTICIPLE
break	(is) breaking	broke	(has) broken
choose	(is) choosing	chose	(has) chosen
freeze	(is) freezing	froze	(has) frozen
speak	(is) speaking	spoke	(has) spoken
steal	(is) stealing	stole	(has) stolen

!!!
About *regular*

The origin of *regular* is in a Latin word meaning "rule."

SOME RELATED WORDS

regularity
regulate
regulation
regulator
irregular
irregularity

Are Irregular Verbs Really Irregular?

At one time, what we now call "irregular" verbs were considered as regular as the *-ed* verbs. They simply followed different rules. Those rules date back to an earlier version of the language known as Old English (page 232). Some of the patterns that still exist in the groups of "irregular" verbs on these pages are the leftovers from those Old English rules.

As English developed, verbs either switched over to the *-ed* group or stuck to some of their old patterns. A few, however, could not make up their minds. As a result, there are verbs such as *shine*, which have two forms in the past:

The sun *shone*.
I *shined* my shoes.

e. Past participle formed from present + *-n*

PRESENT	PRESENT PARTICIPLE	PAST	PAST PARTICIPLE
blow	(is) blowing	blew	(has) blown
draw	(is) drawing	drew	(has) drawn
drive	(is) driving	drove	(has) driven
give	(is) giving	gave	(has) given
grow	(is) growing	grew	(has) grown
know	(is) knowing	knew	(has) known
rise	(is) rising	rose	(has) risen
see	(is) seeing	saw	(has) seen
take	(is) taking	took	(has) taken
throw	(is) throwing	threw	(has) thrown

f. Present *i* changes to *a* in past and *u* in past participle

PRESENT	PRESENT PARTICIPLE	PAST	PAST PARTICIPLE
begin	(is) beginning	began	(has) begun
drink	(is) drinking	drank	(has) drunk
ring	(is) ringing	rang	(has) rung
sing	(is) singing	sang	(has) sung
sink	(is) sinking	sank	(has) sunk
swim	(is) swimming	swam	(has) swum

g. Formed in various ways

PRESENT	PRESENT PARTICIPLE	PAST	PAST PARTICIPLE
eat	(is) eating	ate	(has) eaten
fall	(is) falling	fell	(has) fallen
fly	(is) flying	flew	(has) flown
forget	(is) forgetting	forgot	(has) forgotten
go	(is) going	went	(has) gone
lie	(is) lying	lay	(has) lain
ride	(is) riding	rode	(has) ridden
tear	(is) tearing	tore	(has) torn
wear	(is) wearing	wore	(has) worn
write	(is) writing	wrote	(has) written

h. Forms of *be, have, do*

PRESENT	PRESENT PARTICIPLE	PAST	PAST PARTICIPLE
be	(is) being	was, were	(has) been
have	(is) having	had	(has) had
do	(is) doing	did	(has) done

Verb Tenses

1. **What are they?**   Verbs change form to show when something happens. These forms are called *tenses*.

> PAST   Last week I *walked* a mile a day.
> PRESENT   Now I *walk* two miles a day.
> FUTURE   Next week I *will walk* three miles a day.

2. **Simple and perfect tenses**   There are six tenses in English, three simple tenses and and three perfect tenses.

TENSE	EXAMPLE	HOW FORMED
Simple Tenses		
Present	Rita walks they walk	basic form of verb
Past	he walked	verb + *-ed*
Future	he will walk	*will* + verb
Perfect Tenses		
Present perfect	he has walked they have walked	*have* + past participle
Past perfect	he had walked	*had* + past participle
Future perfect	he will have walked	*will have* + past participle

3. **Uses of tenses**

Present	Events in the present; repeated events Rita *walks* every day.
Past	Events completed in the past Rita *walked* yesterday.
Future	Events that will occur in the future Rita *will walk* tomorrow.

Present Perfect	Events that began in the past and may continue;
	Events completed at an indefinite time in the past
	    Rita *has walked* every day this week.
	    Rita *has left* already.

Past Perfect	Past event that came before another past event Rita *had walked* a mile when we met her.
Future Perfect	Event that will occur before another event Rita *will have walked* two miles by noon.

Tense comes from the Latin *tempus*, meaning "time." (The word *tense* meaning "nervous" is a different word with a different origin.)

Croakers

Practice the past tense by trying to think of more punning verbs such as these:

"I'm dying," he croaked.

"I simply must have a raspberry ripple cone!" I screamed.

"Company's coming," she guessed.

"Was that the doorbell?" she chimed.

"Perhaps we'll strike oil," he gushed.

"Smile for the camera," she snapped.

The word *conjugation* comes from the Latin "to yoke or join together" (*com* "with," + *jugare* "yoke").

4. **Verb conjugation**   A *conjugation* shows all the forms of a verb. Here is the conjugation of the verb *walk*. Notice that some forms change in the third person singular:

a. *-s* is added to the verb in the third person singular: *she walks, he walks, it walks.*

b. *Has* is used to form the third person singular present perfect: *she has walked, he has walked, it has walked.*

Conjugation of *walk*

	SINGULAR FORMS	PLURAL FORMS
Present		
1st person	I walk	we walk
2nd person	you walk	you walk
3rd person	he, she, it walks	they walk
Past		
1st person	I walked	we walked
2nd person	you walked	you walked
3rd person	he, she, it walked	they walked
Future		
1st person	I will walk	we will walk
2nd person	you will walk	you will walk
3rd person	he, she, it, will walk	they will walk
Present Perfect		
1st person	I have walked	we have walked
2nd person	you have walked	you have walked
3rd person	he, she, it has walked	they have walked
Past Perfect		
1st person	I had walked	we had walked
2nd person	you had walked	you had walked
3rd person	he, she, it had walked	they had walked
Future Perfect		
1st person	I will have walked	we will have walked
2nd person	you will have walked	you will have walked
3rd person	he, she, it will have walked	they will have walked

---

5. Progressive forms   The progressive form is used for a continuing event. It is made up of *be* plus the present participle (*-ing* form). Each tense has a progressive form. The verb *be* changes form to show the tense.

	Progressive Forms
Present	Rita *is walking* now.
Past	Rita *was walking* when we met her.
Future	Rita *will be walking* all afternoon.
Present Prefect	Rita *has been walking* for an hour.
Past Perfect	Rita *had been walking* for an hour when the rain began.
Future Perfect	Rita *will have been walking* for an hour by the time we start.

6. Avoiding shifts in tense

a. Use verbs in the same tense to talk about events occurring at the same time.

INCORRECT   The bus *chugged* along and *frightens* the horses.
CORRECT   The bus *chugged* along and *frightened* the horses.

b. Use verbs in different tenses only to show that one event occurs before another.

CORRECT   If the bus *is* noisy, it *will frighten* the horses.
CORRECT   The bus *had left* by the time we *arrived*.

Active and Passive Voices

1. Active voice   When the subject of a sentence performs the action, the verb is in the *active* voice.

ACTIVE   Watt *invented* the steam engine.
(*Watt* is the subject. It performs the action.)

2. Passive voice   When the subject of a sentence receives the action, the verb is in the *passive* voice.

PASSIVE   The steam engine *was invented* by Watt.
(*Steam engine* is the subject. It receives the action. *Watt* still performs the action.)

Mixed-up Tenses

Tenses are not always what they seem. For example, you often use the present progressive to talk about future time.

I'm starting school tomorrow.

Newspaper headlines often abandon standard tenses, but you probably have no trouble understanding headlines like this one:

Governor Dies

The governor has been dead long enough for the newspaper to find out about it and print the story, yet the headline is in the present tense.
    Now think about this one:

TV Star to Quit

It is not the future tense that tells you the star's plans are still in the future. Instead, it is an infinitive: to quit.

3. **Forming the passive**   A verb in the passive is made up of the helping verb _be_ plus the past participle (page 298). The helping verb shows the tense: _was invented._

4. **Active to passive**   Compare the active and passive below. Notice that the subject and object change places, though not exactly. In the passive, _by_ shows who performed the action.

   ACTIVE   The _inventor_ tested the _car._
   PASSIVE   The _car_ was tested by the _inventor._

5. **Transitive verbs only**   Only transitive verbs have objects. Therefore, only transitive verbs can be passive.

6. **Performer left out**   In the passive, the performer is not always mentioned.

   ACTIVE   The inventor _tested_ the car.
   PASSIVE   The car _was tested_ by the inventor.
   PASSIVE   The car _was tested._

7. **Using the passive**   Use the passive when the person or thing that receives the action is more important than the person or thing that performs it. Use the passive when the performer is not known or not important. Otherwise use the active.

   PASSIVE   The car _was tested_ by the inventor.
   (_car_ is more important than _inventor_)
   The car _was tested._
   (performer unknown or unimportant)

TIPS on Using Verbs

- A verb has four basic forms: the present, present participle, past, and past participle.
- Regular verbs form the present participle with _-ing_ and the past and past participle with _-ed._
  Irregular verbs form the principal parts in other ways.
- Tenses are the verb forms that show time.
  There are six tenses: present, past, future, present perfect, past perfect, and future perfect.
  Each tense has a progressive form for continuing action.
- Verbs can be in the active voice or in the passive voice.

Usage

Making Subjects and Verbs Agree

Different countries of the world celebrate different milestones in people's lives. In Egypt, one of the most important celebrations is the party given for a week-old infant. News of the birth spreads, and into the baby's house stream friends and relatives. Everyone is handed a bag of fruits and sweets.

To the Chinese, the first-year birthday is a milestone. Eggs are dyed red and served at a feast. Another food served is noodles. Both are seen as symbols of long life. For many Chinese, there are no more birthday parties until the age of sixty-one!

Japan honors each seven-year-old girl, five-year-old boy, and three-year-old child on November 15, "Three-Five-Seven" Day. He or she visits a shrine and receives special gifts.

Fifteen years is an important stretch of time for Mexican girls, for they are considered grown up when they reach that age. A feast and a dance band help mark the occasion.

How to Make Subjects and Verbs Agree

1. **Agree on what?** The *number* of a word tells whether there is one or more than one. A *singular* word refers to one thing, and a *plural* word refers to more than one. A noun can be singular or plural (page 262), and so can a verb (page 302). This fact is connected with an important rule of English.

   SUBJECT-VERB AGREEMENT:
   A verb must agree with its subject in number.

   If a subject is singular, then its verb must be singular. If a subject is plural, then its verb must be plural.

2. **Singular and plural forms**

   a. **Nouns** Plural nouns usually end in *s* (page 255).
   b. **Verbs** The only verb forms that change to show number are third person singular forms. They usually add *s* to agree with a singular noun (page 302).

   | SINGULAR | one boy **celebrates** |
   | PLURAL | two boys **celebrate** |

!!!
About *agree*

Agree comes from a Latin word meaning "to be pleasing to" (*ad-*, "to," plus *gratus*, "pleasing, beloved").

SOME RELATED WORDS
agreeable
agreement

grace
grateful
gratitude
gratify

congratulate

c. Personal pronouns Some personal pronouns take singular verbs, and others take plural verbs, as shown below.

Agreement with Personal Pronouns

he, she, it	singular verb
we, they	plural verb
you	plural verb
I	singular form of *be*; otherwise, plural verb

SINGULAR VERB   *he* **celebrates**   *I* **am** celebrating
PLURAL VERB   *they* **celebrate**   *you* **celebrate**

3. Verb phrases In a verb phrase, the first helping verb agrees with the subject. (See the margin and page 267 for singular and plural forms of the helping verbs *be, have, do*.)

SINGULAR   One boy **is** *singing.*
PLURAL   Two boys **are** *singing.*

4. Interrupted subjects Words that separate the subject from the verb do not usually affect agreement.

a. A noun in a prepositional phrase is never the subject of a verb.

PLURAL   Different *countries* of the world **celebrate** different milestones.
(verb agrees with *countries*; phrase *of the world* does not affect agreement)

b. Phrases beginning with expressions such as *with, including, as well as, in addition to* do not affect agreement.

SINGULAR   *China*, as well as other Far Eastern countries, **considers** the one-year birthday a special time.
(verb agrees with *China*; phrase that begins *as well as* does not affect agreement)

5. Linking verbs A linking verb agrees with its subject, not with a noun that follows the verb.

SINGULAR   Another special *food* **is** noodles.
(*Noodles* does not affect agreement.)

Forms of *be*

SINGULAR

am
is
was
has
been

PLURAL

are
were
have
been

6. **Inverted sentences**   The verb always agrees with its subject, even when the subject follows the verb (page 290). Do not be fooled by the object of a preposition. It is never a subject.

> PLURAL   Into the house **stream** *friends and relatives.*
> (*House* is the object of the preposition *into,*
> not the subject of the sentence.)
> PLURAL   There **are** no more birthday *parties* for a long time.
> (*There* is not a noun. It is never the subject.)
> SINGULAR   **Do** the *guests* at the party know one another?

7. **Compound subjects**

   a. **With *and***   A compound subject whose parts are joined by *and* is always plural.

   > PLURAL   A feast *and* a dance band **help** mark the
   > occasion.

   b. **With *or***   When the parts of the subject are joined by *or* or *nor*, the verb agrees with the part nearer to it.

   > SINGULAR   He *or* she **dresses** up for the occasion.
   > SINGULAR   The girls *or* their brother **is** having a party.
   > PLURAL   Daniel *or* his sisters **are** having a party.

   c. **After *each***   When *many a, every,* or *each* comes before a compound subject, the subject is considered singular.

   > SINGULAR   *Each* seven-year-old girl and five-year-old boy
   > **is** honored on September 15 in Japan.

   d. **Bread and butter**   Some very common compounds are thought of as units. They are considered singular.

   > SINGULAR   *Bread and butter* **is** served at every meal.
   > *Rock and roll* **was** the band's specialty.

8. **Special nouns**

   a. **Collective nouns**   A *collective* noun names a group: *team, class, crowd, committee* (page 262). When the noun refers to the group as a unit, it is singular. When the noun refers to the individual members, it is plural.

   > SINGULAR   The *family* **is** arriving this afternoon.
   > PLURAL   The *family* **are** arriving at different times.

b. Singular nouns ending in *s*   Some words that end in *s* are singular in meaning: *scissors, eyeglasses, news, measles, physics*. They take singular verbs.

SINGULAR   The *news* **spreads** quickly.

c. Titles   A single title is always considered singular.

SINGULAR   *Gullivers' Travels* **was** written by Jonathan Swift.

d. Amounts and time   An expression of amount, time, or measurement is singular when considered as a unit.

SINGULAR   *Fifteen years* **is** a long stretch of time.
PLURAL   *Fifteen years* **have** passed.

9. Pronouns with *doesn't, don't*   Use *doesn't* with the pronouns *she, he, it*. Use *don't* with all other pronouns.

SINGULAR   *She* **doesn't** know about the party yet.
PLURAL   **Don't** *they* know about it either?

10. Indefinite pronouns   Some indefinite pronouns are always singular, some are always plural, and some can be either singular or plural. (See the margin for a list of pronouns.)

SINGULAR   *Everyone* at the party **is** handed a bag of sweets.
PLURAL   *Both* **are** seen as symbols of life.

Some indefinite pronouns can be either singular or plural (see margin). They are singular when they refer to one thing. They are plural when they refer to more than one thing.

SINGULAR   *Some* of the bread **has** been eaten.
        (*Bread* refers to one thing.)
PLURAL   *Some* of the guests **have** arrived.
        (*Guests* refers to several things.)

Indefinite Pronouns

SINGULAR

another	everybody	nothing
anybody	everyone	one
anyone	everything	other
anything	neither	somebody
each	nobody	someone
either	no one	something

PLURAL

both	others
few	several
many	

SINGULAR OR PLURAL

all	none
any	some
most	

TIPS on Making Subjects and Verbs Agree

• A verb must agree with its subject in number.
  A singular subject takes a singular verb.
  A plural subject takes a plural verb.

Usage

Using Pronouns

Nancy and I walked home, Beauty and the Blimp, Wonderwoman and the Blob Who Ate Brooklyn. Nancy was really excited about Smedley. She kept saying how much fun it would be, how she liked to get to know people, and how she thought it would be good for me. I asked her why.

"Oh, Marcy. You know. You're so hung up about your weight . . . you and your family don't talk to each other . . . and you're so afraid of things . . . and you shouldn't be."

I just clumped along, biting my nails and thinking about what she had said.

— *The Cat Ate My Gymsuit*, Paula Danziger

Cases of Personal Pronouns

1. **The three cases**   Just as verbs change form to show tense, pronouns may change form to show *case*. The case of a pronoun depends on its job in the sentence.

   a. **The nominative case** is used for subjects: *I*. Pronouns in the nominative case are *subject pronouns*.

   b. **The objective case** is used for objects: *me*. Pronouns in the objective case are *object pronouns*.

   c. **The possessive case** is used to show possession: *my*. Pronouns in the objective case are *possessive pronouns*.

	Singular	*Plural*
NOMINATIVE CASE = SUBJECT PRONOUNS		
1st Person	I	we
2nd Person	you	you
3rd Person	he, she, it	they
OBJECTIVE CASE = OBJECT PRONOUNS		
1st Person	me	us
2nd Person	you	you
3rd Person	him, her, it	them
POSSESSIVE CASE = POSSESSIVE PRONOUNS		
1st Person	my, mine	our, ours
2nd Person	your, yours	your, yours
3rd Person	his, her, hers, its	their, theirs

!!!
15 Cases!

English has only three cases, but Finnish has fifteen! In addition to having cases that show subject, object, and possession, Finnish has cases that show the relationships expressed by *in, out of, into, on, from, to, as, part of, change to, without, by,* and *with.*

Actually, things are not as complicated as they seem. All those cases are really like prepositions. The forms are just attached to the ends of words instead of being separate words as they are in English.

2. Using subject pronouns

a. As subjects   Use a subject pronoun when the pronoun is the subject of a verb.

b. As predicate pronouns   Use a subject pronoun when the pronoun is a predicate pronoun. A *predicate pronoun* is used like a predicate noun (page 292). It follows a linking verb and identifies or renames the subject.

SUBJECT   *I* just clumped along.
PREDICATE PRONOUN   That **must be** *he*.
The winner **was** *she*.

In conversation, you might hear or use *That must be him* instead of *he*, or *It's me* instead of *I*. In formal speaking and writing, however, use the nominative form.

3. Using object pronouns

a. As direct objects   Use an object pronoun when the pronoun is the direct object of a verb. A direct object answers *what?* or *whom?* after a verb (page 291): *saw me.*

b. As indirect objects   Use an object pronoun when the pronoun is the indirect object of a verb. An indirect object answers *to or for what?* or *to or for whom?* after a verb (page 292): *wrote me a letter.*

c. As objects of prepositions   Use an object pronoun when the pronoun is the object of a preposition. The object of a preposition follows a preposition (page 279): *to her.*

DIRECT OBJECT   Nancy liked *me.*
INDIRECT OBJECT   I asked *her* a question.
OBJECT OF PREPOSITION   It would be good for *me.*

4. Using possessive pronouns

a. Before nouns   Use a possessive pronoun before a noun to show possession: *our club*

b. By themselves   Use a possessive pronoun by itself to show possession: *ours.* Possessive pronouns used alone have special forms (see page 309).

POSSESSIVE BEFORE NOUN   The cat ate *my* **gymsuit** again.
POSSESSIVE USED ALONE   That gymsuit is *mine.*

c. Pronoun or contraction? Possessive nouns have apostrophes, but possessive pronouns do not. Never use an apostrophe with a possessive pronoun.

POSSESSIVE NOUN   Is that gymsuit *Marcy's?*
POSSESSIVE PRONOUN   Is that gymsuit *hers?*

Use apostrophes only in *contractions*. In a contraction, the apostrophe stands for a missing letter or letters.

POSSESSIVE PRONOUN   You and *your* family should talk.
CONTRACTION   *You're* so afraid of things.
              (= You are)

PRONOUN	its	your	their
CONTRACTION	it's	you're	they're
	(it is)	(you are)	(they are)

5. ***we* and *us* with nouns**   If *we* or *us* is used with a noun, use the form you would use if the noun were not there.

SUBJECT   **We students** planned the trip.
OBJECT   The trip was planned by **us students.**

6. **In compounds**   To decide on the right pronoun in a compound, separate the parts of the compound.

SUBJECT   Nancy and (*I? me?*) walked home.
           Nancy walked home. *I* (not *me*) walked home.
           Nancy and *I* walked home.

OBJECT   She invited Nancy and (*I? me?*).
           She invited Nancy. She invited *me* (not *I*).
           She invited Nancy and *me*.

OBJECT   That is a secret between Nancy and (*I? me?*).
           That is a secret between *me* (not *I*).
           That is a secret between Nancy and *me*.

When you use *I* or *me* in a compound, you should not only use the right case, but you should also put yourself last.

POOR   Me and him had a talk after school.
CORRECTED   *He and I* had a talk after school.
POOR   He spoke to me and Nancy.
CORRECTED   He spoke to *Nancy and me*.

7. In clauses

a. Look in the clause.
A clause is a group of words with a subject and a verb (pages 284 – 287). When a pronoun occurs in a clause, its form depends on how it is used *within its own clause.*

SUBJECT OF CLAUSE Nancy arrived **after** *I* **did.**
OBJECT OF PREPOSITION Nancy arrived **after** *me.*

b. After *than* and *as*
In clauses beginning with *than* or *as*, words are sometimes left out (page 286). Choose the pronoun you would use if all the words were there.

SUBJECT OF CLAUSE Nancy arrived later **than** *I* (did).
OBJECT IN CLAUSE She likes Joel as much **as** (she likes) *him.*

Agreement with Antecedents

1. Antecedent The *antecedent* of a pronoun is the noun that the pronoun stands for.

ANTECEDENT AND PRONOUN Has **Marcy** lost *her* gymsuit?
(= Has Marcy lost Marcy's gymsuit?)

2. Agreement A pronoun must agree with its antecedent in three ways: *person* (first, second, or third), *number* (singular or plural), and *gender* (masculine, feminine, or neuter). Only third person pronouns show gender.

Third Person Pronouns

MASCULINE he, him, his
FEMININE she, her, hers
NEUTER it, its

The **cat** just ate *its* supper. (3rd person, singular, neuter)
Nancy just ate *her* supper. (3rd person, singular, feminine)
Joel just ate *his* supper. (3rd person, singular, masculine)
They just ate *their* supper. (3rd person, plural)

!!!
About *antecedent*

You might be able to guess the origin of *antecedent.* It comes from a Latin word based on *ante-* "before" + *cedere* "to go," meaning "to go before."

!!!
About *gender*

The origin of the word *gender* is the Latin word *genus,* meaning "kind, sort, race."

Masculine and Feminine vs. Male and Female

Masculine, feminine, and *neuter* are grammatical terms. Often, they have little to do with "male-ness" and "femaleness." The English pronouns *he* and *she* do correspond to "male" and "female," but they are the exceptions rather than the rule.

Many languages have masculine, feminine, and neuter nouns. In German, for example, *fork* is feminine, *spoon* is masculine, and *knife* is neuter. Obviously, the gender of these words has nothing to do with their "maleness" or "femaleness."

3. Compound antecedents

a. If a pronoun refers to two or more singular antecedents joined by *and*, use a plural pronoun.

PLURAL **Nancy *and* Marcy** are on *their* way home.

b. If a pronoun refers to two or more singular antecedents joined by *or, nor, either–or,* or *neither–nor,* use a singular pronoun.

SINGULAR ***Either* Nancy *or* Marcy** left *her* gymsuit here.

4. Indefinite pronouns as antecedents

a. Agreement   When the antecedent is an indefinite pronoun (page 265), the personal pronoun agrees with it.

SINGULAR **Each** of the girls has *her* gymsuit.
PLURAL **Both** have *their* gymsuits.

b. *his or her*   The phrase *his or her* may be used when the indefinite pronoun can refer to a male or a female. When possible, substitute a plural pronoun and use *their*.

SINGULAR **Everyone** has *his or her* sneakers.
PLURAL **All** have *their* sneakers.

c. Singular or plural?   Some indefinite pronouns can be either singular or plural. Use the meaning to decide. If a prepositional phrase follows the pronoun, look at the object of the preposition. As a general rule, if it is singular, the pronoun should be singular. If it is plural, the pronoun should be plural.

SINGULAR **Most** of the *floor* has lost *its* shine by now.
          (*floor* is singular; pronoun has a singular meaning)
PLURAL **Most** of the *schools* have had *their* floors waxed.
          (*schools* is plural; pronoun has a plural meaning)

d. With prepositional phrases   Do not be confused by a phrase that comes after an indefinite pronoun.

SINGULAR Did **one** of the girls forget *her* gymsuit?
          (*Her* agrees with *one,* not *girls.*)

5. Clear antecedents Be sure that every pronoun has a clear antecedent. Rewrite any sentence that is not clear.

UNCLEAR I saw a cat's tail, and then *it* ran away.
(What ran away, the cat or its tail?)
CLEAR I saw a tail, and then the cat ran away.

UNCLEAR Marcy called Nancy whenever *she* had a problem.
(Who had a problem, Marcy or Nancy?)
CLEAR Whenever Marcy had a problem, *she* called Nancy.

UNCLEAR *It* says that gym classes are important.
CLEAR The article says that gym classes are important.

UNCLEAR *They* say that gym classes are important.
CLEAR *Some experts* say that gym classes are important.

UNCLEAR Gym class gives *you* a chance to exercise.
CLEAR Gym class gives *students* a chance to exercise.

Other Kinds of Pronouns

1. *who, whom, whose*

a. As interrogative pronouns *Whom* and *whose* are just case forms of the interrogative pronoun *who* (page 309). Use *who* as a subject pronoun, *whom* as an object pronoun, and *whose* as a possessive pronoun.

SUBJECT *Who* has lost her gymsuit?
OBJECT *Whom* did you meet?
To *whom* does this gymsuit belong?
POSSESSIVE *Whose* gymsuit is this?

b. In adjective clauses *Who, whom,* and *whose* are also used as relative pronouns, in the front of adjective clauses (page 285). The form depends on how the pronoun is used *within its own clause.* (*Whoever* is used like *who,* and *whomever* is used like *whom.*)

SUBJECT OF CLAUSE I feel like the Blob **Who Ate Brooklyn.**
(*who* ate Brooklyn)
OBJECT IN CLAUSE He is the one **whom I met.**
(I met *whom.*)
POSSESSIVE He is the one **whose sister I met.**
(I met *his* sister.)

c. In noun clauses *Who, whom,* and *whose* can introduce noun clauses (page 287). Which form is used depends on what the pronoun does within the noun clause. (*Whoever* is used like *who,* and *whomever* is used like *whom.*)

SUBJECT OF CLAUSE I wonder **who she is.**
(She is *who.*)
SUBJECT OF CLAUSE Give the gymsuit to **whoever calls.**
(*Whoever* is the subject of *calls,* not the object of *to.*)
OBJECT IN CLAUSE I don't know **whom he called.**
(He called *whom.*)

d. *whose* or *who's?* Do not confuse the pronoun *whose* with the contraction *who's.*

CONTRACTION *Who's* going to gym now? (= Who is)

2. ***-self, -selves***

a. A pronoun in *-self* (page 264) always has an antecedent. The pronoun agrees with the antecedent in all ways.

I found the gymsuit *myself.* (NOT Myself found the gymsuit.)

b. Use *himself, themselves.* Avoid *hisself* and *theirselves.*

Marcy and Nancy found it *themselves.* (NOT theirselves)

3. ***this, that, these, those***

a. The demonstrative pronouns (page 265) agree with their antecedents in number. *This* and *that* are singular. *These* and *those* are plural.

b. Do not use *here* or *there* right after the pronoun.

SINGULAR *These* are my cats right here.
(NOT These here are . . .)
PLURAL *That* is his cat over there.
(NOT That there is . . .)

TIPS on Using Pronouns

- Personal pronouns have three case forms: subject, object, and possessive.
- Personal pronouns agree with their antecedents in person, number, and gender.
- Most other pronouns agree with their antecedents in number.

Using Adjectives and Adverbs

One of the most famous routines in the early days of movies was pie-throwing. Audiences seemed to think that a pie thrown in someone's face was one of the funniest things in the world.

Who started this messy practice? Supposedly, during a lunch break, silent movie star and comedienne Mabel Normand grabbed a cream pie and threw it, for reasons that are not known. A movie camera was going at the time, and someone captured the whole scene on film. To the director, the scene was really funny. Audiences agreed, and pie-throwing quickly turned into a big hit. A busy baker soon became busier than ever, baking thousands of pies for the movie studio. Gooey custard pies worked best.

Keystone Studio, the studio where Mabel Normand worked, was probably better known than any other studio of the time. Its comedies did well with audiences, especially those starring the Keystone Cops, the zaniest comics of all. In fact, the studio was even more famous for its cops than for its pie-throwing.

Comparing with Adjectives and Adverbs

1. **The three degrees of comparison**   Adjectives and adverbs describe, or modify, other words (pages 269 – 272). They are also used to compare things. There are three degrees of comparison, and the forms for each are different.

   a. **Positive**   The *positive* form is the basic form. It is used to describe, not to make comparisons: *funny*.

   b. **Comparative**   The *comparative* form is used to compare two things: *funnier*.

   c. **Superlative**   The *superlative* form is used to compare three or more things: *funniest*.

   ADJECTIVE
   POSITIVE   The comedian was *funny*.
   COMPARATIVE   He was *funnier* than Mabel.
   SUPERLATIVE   Charlie was the *funniest* of the three.
   ADVERB
   POSITIVE   That comedian really runs *fast*.
   COMPARATIVE   He runs *faster* than any of the others.
   SUPERLATIVE   Of all the comedians, he runs the *fastest*.

!!!
About *compare*

Compare comes from a Latin word meaning "to pair, match" (from *com-* "mutually," and *par*, "equal").

SOME RELATED WORDS

comparable
comparative
comparison

2. **Regular forms**   Most adjectives and adverbs form the comparative and superlative degrees in regular ways.

a. **One-syllable words**   Modifiers of one syllable add *-er* in the comparative and *-est* in the superlative.

	Positive	Comparative	Superlative
ADJECTIVE	light	light**er**	light**est**
ADVERB	fast	fast**er**	fast**est**

b. **Two-syllable words**   Some two-syllable words add *-er* in the comparative and *-est* in the superlative. Others use *more* to form the comparative and *most* to form the superlative. To check the form, use the dictionary.

	Positive	Comparative	Superlative
ADJECTIVE	funny	funn**ier**	funn**iest**
	famous	**more** famous	**most** famous
ADVERB	early	earl**ier**	earl**iest**
	quickly	**more** quickly	**most** quickly

c. **Three-syllable words**   Modifiers of three or more syllables always use *more* to form the comparative and *most* to form the superlative.

	Positive	Comparative	Superlative
ADJECTIVE	difficult	**more** difficult	**most** difficult
ADVERB	easily	**more** easily	**most** easily

d. *less* **and** *least*   Comparisons can also be made to show less rather than more. *Less* always forms the comparative. *Least* always forms the superlative.

She was *less funny* than I.   He was the *least funny* of all.

3. **Irregular forms**   Learn these irregular forms.

Positive	Comparative	Superlative
bad, badly	worse	worst
good, well	better	best
little	less	least
much, many	more	most
far	farther	farthest

Hollywood!

In the early 1900s, Mack Sennett was fascinated by movies. He decided that this exciting new industry could use an exciting new location, one that was better suited to outdoor filming than the New York City area was. So off he went across the country to sunny California. He settled in a small, sleepy suburb of Los Angeles. There, in 1912, Sennett founded his Keystone Studios, and Hollywood came to life.

Sennett's specialty was comedy. He started with simple chase scenes and added slapstick and surprises. For example, if an actor shut the door of a house, the whole house collapsed. He also used techniques such as slowing the camera down to speed up the action.

These were the early days of movies. If anything at all was happening in the neighborhood, out Sennett went with his camera to film it and make it part of a movie, often grabbing passers-by as extra actors. Moviemaking was still a long way from being the huge and complicated industry it is today.

4. Avoid double comparisons   To make a comparison, use either an ending or the word *more* or *most*. Do not use both.

DOUBLE   She was the most cheerfulest person on the set.
CORRECT   She was the *most cheerful* person on the set.
DOUBLE   Did she throw the pie more better that time?
CORRECT   Did she throw the pie *better* that time?

5. Avoid double negatives   Here are common negatives.

Negatives					
neither	not	nobody	nowhere	none	hardly
no	-n't	no one	nothing	never	scarcely

a. Do not use two negatives to express one negative idea.

DOUBLE   Nobody didn't throw any pies in that movie.
CORRECT   *Nobody* threw *any* pies in that movie.

b. One way to correct a double negative is to use a positive word instead of a negative one. (See the margin.)

DOUBLE   She didn't throw no pies in that movie.
CORRECT   She did*n't* throw *any* pies in that movie.

6. Avoid unclear comparisons

a. Use *other* or *else* when comparing members within a group.

UNCLEAR   Keystone was better known than any studio.
    (seems to say that Keystone was not itself a studio)
CLEAR   Keystone was better known than any *other* studio.

UNCLEAR   Mabel threw more pies than anyone.
    (seems to say that Mabel is not anyone)
CLEAR   Mabel threw more pies than anyone *else*.

b. Be sure that you compare like things.

UNCLEAR   Mario liked the movie better than Mom.
    (seem to compare *movie* with *Mom*)
CLEAR   Mario liked the movie better than Mom *did*.

UNCLEAR   Mario's joke was funnier than Mark.
    (seems to compare *joke* with *Mark*)
CLEAR   Mario's joke was funnier than *Mark's*.

Think Positively

Here are some negative-positive word pairs. Switch to the positive word to correct a double negative.

NEGATIVE	POSITIVE
neither	either
never	ever
no	any
no one	anyone
nobody	anybody
none	any
nothing	anything
nowhere	anywhere

Adjective or Adverb?

1. **Which modifier is it?** Ask these questions to decide.

   a. **What does it modify?** An adjective modifies a noun or pronoun. An adverb modifies a verb, adjective, or adverb.

   b. **What does it tell?** Adjectives tell *what kind, which, how much/many.* Adverbs tell *how, when, where, to what extent.*

2. **With linking verbs** After a linking verb, use an adjective to modify the subject (pages 266, 270).

   ADJECTIVE The pie smells *sweet.* (*Sweet* modifies *pie.*)

3. **Troublesome pairs** Know which is which in these pairs.

ADJECTIVE	ADVERB
He was *good* in the role.	He played it *well.*
He felt *bad* yesterday.	He played it *badly.*
The scene looked *real.*	It was *really* funny.

   Well can be an adjective when it refers to health: *felt well.*

Placing Modifiers

1. ***only, almost*** Place adverbs such as *only, almost, even, just, nearly* as close to the modified word as you can.

   He *only* acted in movies. (He didn't direct or produce.)
   He acted *only* in movies. (He didn't act in plays or TV.)

2. **Avoid misplaced modifiers** Place a modifying word, phrase, or clause as close as you can to the word it modifies.

   MISPLACED Alex served a pie to a man with lots of custard.
   CORRECT Alex served a **pie** *with lots of custard* to a man.

3. **Avoid dangling modifiers** Be sure that a modifying word, phrase, or clause has a word to modify.

   DANGLING Expecting a hit, the movie was finished.
   CORRECT *Expecting a hit,* the **director** finished the movie.

TIPS on Using Adjectives and Adverbs

- Use the correct comparative or superlative form to compare.
- Know the difference between adjectives and adverbs.
- Place modifiers as close to the modified words as possible.

Watch Those Modifiers

You can get some surprising results if you are not careful about where you place modifiers.

Yesterday a burglar was seized by police carrying silverware.

Last night, a man saved a kitten going to a rock concert.

Making a funny noise, the mechanic finally fixed the car.

Please look over the insurance policy sent to you in the mail with your family.

Last night Jason Jones died in the old farmhouse in which he was born at the age of 92.

Two sisters were reunited after twenty years in the ticket line of a movie.

Soaring thousands of feet, we watched the plane take off.

The jury decided to find the defendant guilty of driving without a license to please everyone.

Writing Sound Sentences

The thirteen original American colonies were prosperous, with rich farmland available. Artisans in New England crafted fine objects for trade. Farmers in the South filled ships with cotton, rice, and tobacco. Cities flourished, including New York and Charleston. To ease travel, colonists built roads, opened inns, and wrote guidebooks. Mail routes and stagecoach lines were set up, though a trip between Boston and New York could take as long as five days. Many colonists could read, and more and more newspapers appeared. Although they did not yet realize it, the colonies were readying themselves for revolution.

Avoiding Fragments and Run-ons

1. **Avoid sentence fragments.** A *sentence fragment* is a group of words that does not express a complete thought. It usually leaves the question *who?* or *what?* unanswered.

   FRAGMENT   Were crafting fine objects. (Who were?)
   SENTENCE   *Artisans* were crafting fine objects.

   a. **Kinds of fragments** A *phrase fragment* lacks a subject and a verb (page 278). A *subordinate clause fragment* needs another clause to complete its meaning (page 284).

   PHRASE FRAGMENT   With rich farmland.
   SENTENCE   With rich farmland, they grew prosperous.

   PHRASE FRAGMENT   Preparing for revolution.
   SENTENCE   They were preparing for revolution.

   CLAUSE FRAGMENT   Although they did not realize it.
   SENTENCE   Although they did not realize it, they were preparing for revolution.

   b. **Correcting fragments.** Correct a fragment in one of two ways: (1) attach it to the sentence before or after it, or (2) add words to make it a complete thought.

   FRAGMENT   They built roads. *To make travel easier.*
   SENTENCE   *To make travel easier,* they built roads.
   SENTENCE   They built roads. They tried *to make travel easier.*

2. **Avoiding run-on sentences**   A run-on sentence results when two or more sentences are written as one. Such a sentence confuses the reader because ideas are run together.

a. **Kinds of run-on sentences**   There are two kinds of run-on sentences: (1) sentences joined without punctuation, and (2) sentences joined with a comma.

NO PUNCTUATION   Roads were built travel increased.
COMMA FAULT   Roads were built, travel increased.

b. **Correcting run-on sentences**   To correct a run-on sentence, you can rewrite it as (1) separate sentences, (2) a compound sentence, or (3) a complex sentence.

TWO SENTENCES   Roads were built. Travel increased.
COMPOUND SENTENCE   Roads were built, and travel increased.
COMPLEX SENTENCE   When roads were built, travel increased.
Roads were built as travel increased.

Using Parallel Structures

Parallel structures are structures of the same kind. Be sure to use parallel structures for expressions that are used the same way, especially with (1) coordinating conjunctions (page 275), (2) comparisons, and (3) correlative conjunctions (page 276).

NOT PARALLEL   They started to build roads, open inns, and began writing guidebooks.
PARALLEL   They started to build roads, open inns, and write guidebooks.

NOT PARALLEL   They cared more about wealth than being free.
PARALLEL   They cared more about wealth than about freedom.

NOT PARALLEL   Most were either artisans or farmed the land.
PARALLEL   Most were either artisans or farmers.

TIPS on Writing Sound Sentences

- Avoid sentence fragments.
- Avoid run-on sentences.
- Use parallel structures.

A Sentence Game

Play "Sentences" by yourself or with one or more partners. Choose a word of at least five letters. Then take turns making up sentences that consist of words beginning with the letters of the word you chose. If you use a sentence fragment, you're out. Suppose you began with the word *begin*. Here are some sentences you might make up:

Beautiful **e**meralds **g**low **i**n **N**ovember.
Boys **e**at **g**reen **i**ce **n**eatly.
By **e**vening, **g**entlemen **i**magine **n**othing.

!!!
About *parallel*

The word *parallel* comes from a Greek word meaning "beside one another" (*para-* "beside" + *allelon* "of one another"). Parallel lines in geometry are lines that remain an equal distance apart at every point, meaning that they go in exactly the same direction. Things that are parallel, then, are alike.

Glossary of Word Usage

The listings below show *standard* usage, the usage most widely accepted by English speakers. In general, follow standard usage in formal situations and when you write.

a, an   Use *a* before words beginning with consonant sounds. Use *an* before words beginning with vowel sounds.

> Is there *a* meeting tonight?   It is *an* early meeting.

accept, except   *Accept* is a verb meaning "to receive." *Except* is usually a preposition meaning "but, other than." It is sometimes used as a verb meaning "to leave out."

> He *accepted* the invitation to the party.
> Everyone *except* Todd was going.
> If you *except* Todd, people will miss him.

advice, advise   *Advice* is a noun. *Advise* is a verb.

> What *advice* did the doctor give you?
> She *advised* me to get more exercise.

affect, effect   *Affect* is a verb meaning "to influence." *Effect* is usually a noun meaning "result." *Effect* is sometimes used as a verb meaning "to accomplish or produce."

> The last test *affected* my grade in French.
> What *effect* did it have on your French grade?
> Studying *effected* an improvement in my grades.

all ready, already   *All ready* means "completely ready." *Already* means "by or before the time" or "even now."

> I am *all ready* to leave.
> The bus had *already* left when I arrived.
> Are you ready *already?*

all right   Spell *all right* as two words, not one.

> Are you *all right* now?

all together, altogether *All together* means "everyone together." *Altogether* means "wholly, thoroughly."

> The family is *all together* now.
> He talks *altogether* too fast.

a lot Write *a lot* as two words, not one. Use it only in informal writing.

> There is *a lot* of spaghetti left in the pot.

among, between Use *among* when referring to three or more things. Use *between* when referring to two things.

> *Among* the three of us, we can think of some solution.
> *Between* the two of us, we had only a dollar.

amount, number Use *amount* to refer to items that cannot be counted. Use *number* to refer to things that can be counted.

> There has been only a small *amount* of rain.
> There have been a *number* of rainy days this week.

anywhere, everywhere, somewhere, nowhere Do not add *s* to any of these words.

> I could not find them *anywhere*. (NOT anywheres)

at Do not use *at* after *where*.

> Where is Maria? (NOT Where is Maria at?)

bad, badly *Bad* is used as an adjective and *badly* as an adverb.

> She felt *bad*. (linking verb + adjective)
> She played *badly*. (action verb + adverb)

beside, besides The preposition *beside* means "next to." The preposition *besides* means "in addition to."

> Ricardo sat *beside* me during the play.
> *Besides* Ricardo, Lynn and Juliet were there.

borrow, lend   To *borrow* is to "receive something *from* someone." To *lend* is to "give something *to* someone temporarily."

May I *borrow* your pen?   *Lend* me your pen.

bring, take   Use *bring* to show motion toward the speaker. Use *take* to show motion away from the speaker.

Please *bring* it with you when you come.
You can *take* it with you when you go.

farther, further   *Farther* means "more distant." *Further* means "additional."

I cannot go any *farther* today.   Do you have *further* plans?

fewer, less   *Fewer* is used with a plural word, that is, with items that can be counted. *Less* is used with a singular word, that is, with something that cannot be counted.

There are *fewer* calories in milk than in cream.
There is *less* fat in milk than in cream.

from, off   Do not use *off* where the preposition *from* is needed.

I borrowed a warm sweater *from* my aunt. (NOT off my aunt)

good, well   *Good* is an adjective. It may follow a linking verb. *Well* can be used as an adjective only when it refers to health. Otherwise, it is an adverb.

You don't look *good* today.   Don't you feel *well?*
You did very *well* on the history test.

its, it's   *Its* is a possessive pronoun. *It's* is a contraction of *it is.*

The umbrella has lost *its* handle.   *It's* raining now.

lay, lie   *Lay* means "to put or set down." It is usually followed by a direct object. *Lie* means "to rest or recline." It is never followed by a direct object.

Lay your head on the pillow.   *Lie* here and rest.

learn, teach *Learn* means "to get knowledge *from.*" *Teach* means "to instruct or give knowledge *to.*"

I *learned* a new dance today.   *Teach* me that new dance.

leave, let *Leave* means "to depart, go away from." *Let* means "to allow, permit."

Before I *leave, let* me help you.

like, as *Like* is usually used as a preposition. *As* is usually used as a subordinating conjunction.

My brother looks *like* me.   We can go just *as* we are.

passed, past *Passed* is the past form of the verb *pass.* As an adjective, *past* means "gone by" or "of a former time." As a preposition, *past* means "beyond."

We have *passed* Jessica several times in the *past* few days as we walked *past* the video store.

raise, rise *Raise* means "to lift up." It is usually followed by a direct object. *Rise* means "to move upward." It is never followed by a direct object.

Raise the window shade so that you can watch the sun *rise.*

real, really *Real* is an adjective meaning "true, actual." *Really* is an adverb meaning "very" or "actually."

That is a *real* orchestra playing.   It sounds *really* good.

set, sit *Set* means "to put or place." It is usually followed by a direct object. *Sit* means "to rest in a seated position." It is never followed by a direct object.

After you have *set* the table, please *sit* down.

than, then *Than* is a subordinating conjunction that introduces the second part of a comparison. *Then* is an adverb meaning "next" or "at that time."

Cheryl is taller *than* he is now.   She was shorter *then.*

that, which, who   All three words can be used as relative pronouns. *That* can refer to people, animals, or things. *Which* refers to animals or things. *Who* refers to people.

> The dog *that* followed us home is brown and white.
> The dog, *which* followed us home, is brown and white.
> The person *who* called is the owner.

their, there, they're   *Their* is a possessive pronoun. *There* can be an adverb or can begin an inverted sentence. *They're* is a contraction of *they are*.

> *Their* reports were interesting.
> *There* are several pages lying *there*.
> *They're* discussing the reports now.

theirs, there's   *Theirs* is a possessive pronoun. *There's* is a contraction of *there is*.

> This book is ours, and that book is *theirs*.
> *There's* only one book left.

to, too, two   *To* is a preposition. *Too* is an adverb. *Two* is a number.

> We are all going *to* the football field.
> Are you going there *too*, or is it *too* late?
> *Two* other people are going with us.

who, whom   *Who* is used as a subject or a predicate noun. *Whom* is used as a direct object, indirect object, or object of a preposition.

> *Who* will be at the party?   *Whom* did you invite?

whose, who's   *Whose* is a pronoun. *Who's* is a contraction of *who is*.

> *Whose* is that scarf?   *Who's* wearing that red scarf?

your, you're   *Your* is a possessive pronoun. *You're* is a contraction of *you are*.

> *You're* taking *your* dog with you, aren't you?

The basketball game of November 22, 1950, would have to be included in any list of "The Dullest Games in History." As dull as it was, though, the game changed basketball forever.

In the early 1950s, the Minneapolis Lakers ruled professional basketball. When the star center George Mikan was playing, the only way to stop the team was to stall. That was the strategy of the Fort Wayne Pistons in Minneapolis on November 22, 1950. The Pistons froze the ball, passing it around, dribbling — anything to keep it out of the Lakers' hands. The game dribbled on, boring everyone and ending in a Pistons win, 19–18. It set records for the fewest shots at the basket and the fewest points scored.

People were furious. One fan complained, "If this happens again, I'm giving up basketball!" Maurice Podoloff, president of the National Basketball Association, replied, "It'll never happen again." It didn't. The 24-second rule was soon adopted, requiring a team to shoot within 24 seconds or give up the ball.

Capitalizing First Words and *I*

1. The first word in a sentence

The team froze the ball.

2. The first word of a line of poetry

Water, water, everywhere,
Nor any drop to drink.
— Samuel Taylor Coleridge

3. The first word of a direct quotation

He declared, "It'll never happen again."

If a quotation continues, do not capitalize the first letter of the second part unless it begins a new sentence.

"It won't happen again," he said, "for a good reason."
"It won't happen again," he said. "There's a good reason."

4. The pronoun *I*

"If this happens again, I'm giving up basketball!"

!!!
About the Letter *I*

– The first person pronoun

– The seventh most used letter in English

– The symbol for *iodine*

– Roman numeral for *one*

Proper Nouns

1. **Names of specific people and animals**

   George Mikan   P. T. Barnum   Carmen   Muffin the cat

2. **Names of specific groups and businesses**

ORGANIZATIONS	National Basketball Association, Pistons, Democratic Party, Drama Club
BUSINESSES	General Motors, Kodak
INSTITUTIONS	Yale University, Mesa High School, Museum of Modern Art, Jericho General Hospital
GOVERNMENT BODIES	U.S. Congress, State Department

   BUT Do not capitalize words such as *club, team, high school, museum* unless they are part of a proper noun.

   Our high school has a baseball team and a marching band.

3. **Names of specific places**

COUNTRIES	Costa Rica, Pakistan, Canada
STATES, PROVINCES	New York State, Alberta
CITIES, TOWNS	Vancouver, San Diego
COUNTIES, TOWNSHIPS	Dade County, Lincoln Township
SECTIONS OF COUNTRY	the South, the Northeast, West Coast
CONTINENTS	South America, Asia
ISLANDS, BEACHES	Sea Island, Singing Beach
BODIES OF WATER	Indian Ocean, Charles River, Lake Huron
MOUNTAINS	Rocky Mountains, Mount McKinley
PARKS, FORESTS	Grand Canyon, Zion National Park
STREETS, ROADS	Middle Road, Fifth Street, Route 1
BUILDINGS, MONUMENTS	Empire State Building, Grant's Tomb

   BUT Do not capitalize words such as *state, mountain, park, island, street* unless they are part of a proper noun.

   The city of Seattle is in the state of Washington.

   BUT Do not capitalize *east, west, north, south* unless they refer to specific regions.

   Drive south to Georgia and you're in the South.

4. **Names of specific ships, trains, planes, spacecraft, and planets and other heavenly bodies**

SHIPS, TRAINS   *Mayflower, Sunset Limited*
PLANES, SPACECRAFT   *Spirit of St. Louis, Apollo 12*
HEAVENLY BODIES   Mars, Earth, North Star, Milky Way

BUT   Do not capitalize *earth* when used with *the*.

From the space capsule, they photographed the earth.

5. **Names of specific brands, awards, and courses**

BRANDS   Dove, Coca-Cola, Reebok, Jordache, Chevrolet, Apple
AWARDS   Nobel Prize, Oscar, Heisman Trophy
COURSES   History II, Latin, English

BUT   Do not capitalize the product after a brand name.

Put the Dove soap next to the Pert shampoo on the shelf.

BUT   Do not capitalize the name of an unnumbered course unless it is the name of a language.

Today I have to study math, history, and Spanish.

6. **Names of historical events and periods, and documents**

EVENTS   World War II, Boston Tea Party, Middle Ages
DOCUMENTS   Bill of Rights, Declaration of Independence

7. **Names of special events, days, months, and holidays**

SPECIAL EVENTS   World Series, Junior Prom, Easter Parade
DAYS, MONTHS   Wednesday, January
HOLIDAYS   Thanksgiving Day, Fourth of July

BUT   Do not capitalize the names of the seasons of the year.

Labor Day means the end of the summer.

8. **Names of nationalities, languages, and religious terms**

NATIONALITIES   a Korean, a Colombian, a Spaniard
LANGUAGES   Russian, Swahili, Vietnamese, Italian
RELIGIOUS TERMS   a Baptist, Buddhism, the Bible, the Koran

In Other Languages

When you learn another language, you may have to learn the rules of capitalization all over again, for different languages capitalize differently. Here are just a few examples:

– English capitalizes *I* but not *you*, while German capitalizes *you* (*Sie*) but not *I* (*ich*).

– English capitalizes the days of the week and the months, but Spanish, for example, does not.

– English capitalizes the names of languages, but Spanish, French, Portuguese, and other languages do not.

– In case you're beginning to think that English uses more capital letters than any other language, you should know that German begins every single noun with a capital letter.

Do you feel strongly about an issue? Write to your senator, representative, mayor, or other public official and let him or her know. Here are some of the titles you might want to use in a letter. The first shows how to address the letter. The second shows how to write the greeting of the letter.

CHIEF JUSTICE

The Chief Justice
Dear Mr./Madam Justice

U.S. SENATOR

The Honorable John/Jane Jones
Dear Senator Jones

U.S. REPRESENTATIVE

The Honorable John/Jane Jones
Dear Mr./Mrs./Ms. Jones

U.S. AMBASSADOR

The Honorable John/Jane Jones
Dear Mr./Madam Ambassador

FOREIGN AMBASSADOR

His/Her Excellency John/Jane Jones
Excellency
or Dear Mr./Madam Ambassador

GOVERNOR

The Honorable John/Jane Jones
Dear Governor Jones

MAYOR

The Honorable John/Jane Jones
or His/Her Honor the Mayor
Dear Mayor Jones

Proper Adjectives

Adjectives formed from proper nouns

Alaska–**Alaskan** oil Italy–**Italian** restaurant
Queen Victoria–**Victorian** times Maine–**Maine** lobster

Titles

1. **Titles used with names of people**

   Governor Ruiz **Dr.** Mayo **Officer** Quigley **Bishop** Tutu

   BUT Do not capitalize titles when used alone, except for high government officials: *President, Queen of England.*

   The governor met the **President** in the White House.

2. **Titles used in direct address**

   I'm pleased to meet you, **Senator.** Yes, **Captain,** I will.

3. **Titles showing family relationships** Capitalize family titles before a name and in direct address.

   I just spoke to **Uncle** Sid. When are we leaving, **Dad?**

   BUT Do not capitalize family relationships after a possessive unless the title is considered part of a name.

   We met Maria's dad and mom but not her **Aunt** Carmen.

4. **Written works, movies and plays, musical works, works of art**

WRITTEN WORKS	*Seventeen* magazine, *The Red Badge of Courage,* "The Gift of the Magi," the *Boston Globe*
MOVIES, PLAYS	*The Wizard of Oz, West Side Story*
MUSICAL WORKS	"The Star-Spangled Banner," the opera *Carmen*
WORKS OF ART	the painting *The Last Supper*

   BUT Do not capitalize prepositions, conjunctions, articles unless they begin the title: "The Gift of the Magi." Capitalize *the* or *a* at the beginning only if it is officially part of the title: the *Reader's Digest.*

Central America is perfectly named, for it connects South America to North America. On this bridge of land are seven countries: Belize, Guatemala, Honduras, El Salvador, Nicaragua, Costa Rica, and Panama. They lie between the Pacific Ocean on one side and the Caribbean Sea (a part of the Atlantic Ocean) on the other. The 51-mile-long Panama Canal, opened in 1914, joins the two seas.

Who are the people of Central America? They are the descendants of native Indians, African slaves, and Spanish colonists, as well as others. Athough many groups have made their home in this rich, beautiful land, only the Indians, of course, were the original inhabitants.

Using End Marks

1. **Sentences**

   a. A *period* ends a statement and an imperative sentence.

   STATEMENT   Central America is perfectly named.
   IMPERATIVE   Tell me more about it.

   b. A *question mark* ends a question.

   QUESTION   Who are the people of Central America?

   c. An *exclamation point* ends an exclamation and some interjections (page 277).

   EXCLAMATION   What a great trip that was!
   INTERJECTION   Wow! That was quite a trip.

2. **Most abbreviations end with a *period*.**

   BUT   Abbreviations for certain names formed from initials, names of states, and metric measurements use no periods.

   NASA   (National Aeronautics and Space Administration)
   TX   (Texas)   km   (kilometers)   cm   (centimeters)

Looking at It Another Way

In Spanish, question marks and exclamation points are placed not only at the ends of sentences but also at the beginnings — upside down.

¿Qué tal?
   "How are things?"
¡Qué lástima!
   "What a shame!"

Some Abbreviations

A.D.	*anno domini*, Latin: "in the year of our Lord"
A.M.	*ante meridiem*, Latin: "before noon"
B.C.	before Christ
e.g.	*exempli gratia*, Latin: "for example"
et. al.	*et alii*, Latin: "and others"
etc.	*et cetera*, Latin: "and others"
ft	foot
ibid.	*ibidem*, Latin: "in the same place"
i.e.	*id est*, Latin: "that is"
in.	inch
lb	pound
M.D.	doctor of medicine
P.M.	*post meridiem*, Latin: "after noon"
P.S.	postscript
qt	quart
sq.	square
viz.	*videlicet*, Latin: "namely"
yd.	yard

etc.

Using Commas

The comma is the most frequently used punctuation mark. It is usually used to show a reader which words should be grouped together and which should be separated.

1. **Use commas to separate items in a series.** A series is made up of three or more items of the same kind. A series may contain words, phrases, or clauses.

   WORDS   Nicaragua, Costa Rica, and Panama are three Central American countries.

   PHRASES   They swam in the ocean, hiked up a mountain, and visited some ancient ruins.

   CLAUSES   The guidebook explained what to see, when to go, and how to get there.

   BUT   Do not use commas if _and, but_, or _or_ connect the items.

   We swam _and_ hiked _and_ then rested.

   BUT   Do not use a comma to separate pairs of words that are thought of as a unit.

   We ate _bread and butter_, fish, and a salad.

   BUT   Some writers do not use a comma before the conjunction. To avoid confusion, however, the comma should be there.

   CONFUSING   They ate fish, salad, corn and bran muffins. (Did they eat corn muffins or plain corn?)

2. **Use commas between two or more adjectives before a noun.**

   Many have made their home in this rich, beautiful land.

   BUT   Do not use a comma if one adjective can be thought of as part of the noun. Also do not use a comma if one of the words modifies another. Try this test. Say _and_ between the adjectives. Use a comma if _and_ sounds natural.

   COMMA   It was a hot, sunny day.   (hot **and** sunny? yes)

   NO COMMA   It was a hot summer day.   (hot **and** summer? no)

   NO COMMA   There was a bright blue sky.   (bright **and** blue? no)

3. **Use a comma before the joining word in a compound sentence** (page 293).

Central America is perfectly named, *for* it connects South America to North America.

BUT You do not need a comma if the clauses are very short.

She swam but Roberto rested.

BUT Do not use a comma when a joining word like *and* joins verbs rather than clauses.

Central America *lies* between two oceans **and** *connects* two continents.

4. **Use a comma after a word, phrase, or clause that introduces a sentence.**

WORD *Actually,* there were natives, slaves, and colonists.
      Oh, the scenery is beautiful.
PHRASE *Because of the location,* people came there.
        Searching for gold, Spanish explorers arrived.
CLAUSE *Before the Spanish came,* the Indians flourished.

BUT You can omit the comma if the opening phrase is short. Do use a comma if there is more than one phrase.

By noon they had arrived at the canal.
By noon on Monday, they had arrived at the canal.

BUT Do not use a comma if a phrase is followed by a verb.

Down the mountain *scrambled* the hikers.

5. **Use commas to set off one or more words that interrupt a sentence.**   These "interrupters" are only loosely connected to the rest of the sentence. They can appear in the middle, at the end, or at the beginning of a sentence (see margin).

Only the Indians, *of course,* were the original inhabitants.
Later came the colonists and slaves, *as well as others.*
After all, Belize once belonged to Britain.

Watch That Comma!

Look carefully at these sentence pairs. Watch the meaning change as the comma moves around.

I hear some singing boys.
I hear some singing, boys.

She is pretty smart, but shy.
She is pretty, smart, but shy.

I can tell Shirley that you don't agree.
I can tell, Shirley, that you don't agree.

Some Common Interrupters

after all	I suppose
by the way	I hope
for example	I guess
however	I know
therefore	nevertheless
of course	in general
furthermore	at any rate
to tell the truth	in my opinion
in fact	moreover

6. Use commas to set off a noun of direct address. The name or title of someone to whom you speak directly is a *noun of direct address*. Use commas around such nouns.

Eva, let's take the other trail.
When you climb, *boys*, keep your partner in sight.
I am glad you are with us, *Mom*.

7. Use commas to set off most appositives. An *appositive* is a noun, plus any modifiers, that identifies or explains another noun or pronoun. Most appositives are set off with commas. (See page 283.)

The Panama Canal, *an artificial waterway*, opened in 1914.

BUT Do not use commas if the appositive is needed to identify the noun. Usually such appositives are single words.

My friend *Jorge* was born in Guatemala. (tells *which* friend)

8. Use commas to set off phrases and clauses that are not essential to the meaning. (See pages 280 and 285.) Is the phrase or clause needed to identify something? If not — if it just adds some information — then set it off with commas.

The Panama Canal, *opened in 1914*, joins the two seas.
(not needed to tell *which* canal; just adds information)

9. Commas in dates, places, addresses, and letters

DATES On Monday, June 4, 1990, he left Costa Rica.
PLACES Miami, Florida   Managua, Nicaragua
ADDRESSES He lives at 4 Gates Road, Provo, Utah 84601.
LETTERS Dear Juan,   Yours truly,

BUT Do not use a comma between a month and year: *May 1980*.
There is no comma before a ZIP code.

10. Commas with quotations Use commas to set off the speaker tag from a quotation (page 338). Put a comma inside the quotation marks when it occurs at the end of a quotation.

BEFORE She said, "That's Costa Rica."
AFTER "That's Costa Rica," she said.
MIDDLE "That's Costa Rica," she said, "next to Panama."

Using Semicolons and Colons

1. **Using semicolons**   Think of a *semicolon* as a combined comma and period. It marks a break that is stronger than a comma but weaker than a period.

   a. Use a semicolon to join the parts of a compound sentence when a joining word such as *and* is not used.

   The Pacific Ocean is on one side of Central America; the Caribbean Sea is on the other.

   b. Use semicolons between parts of a series with commas.

   The capital cities I visited were Guatemala City, Guatemala; Tegucigalpa, Honduras; and San Salvador, El Salvador.

   c. Use a semicolon between independent clauses joined by a word such as *therefore, for example*. (See the margin.)

   Some capitals are named for the country; *for example*, the capital of Panama is Panama City.

2. **Using colons**   Colons usually point out what comes next.

   a. Use a colon before a list of items, especially after expressions such as *the following, these*.

   Central America includes these countries: Belize, Guatemala, Honduras, El Salvador, Nicaragua, Costa Rica, and Panama.

   BUT   Do not use a colon after a verb or a preposition.

   The people in the group *are* Linda, Manuel, Oscar, and Rosa.

   b. Use a colon to introduce a long statement or quotation.

   As the governor said:

   c. Use a colon in these special situations:

BETWEEN HOURS AND MINUTES	3:24 P.M.
	6:18 A.M.
IN SALUTATIONS IN BUSINESS LETTERS	Dear Sir or Madam:

Some Connector Words

Here are some of the words that can be used with a semicolon to join the parts of a compound sentence. (Most of them can also be used as "interrupters" in sentences — page 333.)

therefore
furthermore
for example
for instance
however
moreover
nevertheless
otherwise

Using Dashes and Parentheses

1. **Use a dash to set off words that interrupt the main idea.** Dashes show a more sudden break in thought than commas do.

    The campers gathered around the fire — the air had grown cold suddenly — and made plans for the next day.

2. **Use parentheses to set off added information that may be interesting but is not closely connected to the main idea.**

    The Caribbean (actually part of the Atlantic Ocean) is known for its beautiful blue-green color.

Using Hyphens

1. **Use a hyphen in numbers from 21 to 99 and in fractions used as adjectives.**

    NUMBERS   twenty-nine eighty-six forty-seven
    FRACTIONS a two-thirds share (BUT two thirds of the voters)

2. **Use a hyphen in certain compound nouns.**

    COMPOUND NOUNS   mother-in-law great-grandfather

3. **Use a hyphen between words in a compound adjective used before a noun.**

    COMPOUND ADJECTIVES well-planned report
                         light-colored dress

    BUT   Do not use hyphens in compound adjectives after nouns. Do not use hyphens with adverbs ending in *-ly*.

    It was well planned.   It was a beautifully written report.

4. **Use a hyphen with *ex-*, *self-*, *all-*, with *-elect*, and with prefixes before proper nouns and adjectives.**

    ex-senator self-control all-star mayor-elect pro-British

5. **Use a hyphen to break a word at the end of a line.**   Divide words only between syllables: *enor-mous* (NOT *eno-rmous*).

Using Apostrophes

1. **Use an apostrophe to form possessive nouns.**

   a. Add apostrophe + *s* to a singular noun.
   b. Add only an apostrophe to a plural noun ending in *s*.
   Add apostrophe + *s* to a plural noun not ending in *s*.

   SINGULAR   hiker's shoe   boss's desk   sister-in-law's note
     PLURAL   hikers' shoes   bosses' desks   men's clothes

   c. To show that more than one person owns something, add apostrophe + *s* to the last noun only.
   d. To show that each person owns something separately, add apostrophe + *s* to each noun.

   OWN TOGETHER   Sara and Jessie's dog
   OWN SEPARATELY   Sara's and Jessie's dogs

2. **Use an apostrophe + *s* to form the possessive of an indefinite pronoun** (page 265).

   INDEFINITE PRONOUNS   somebody's   everyone's

   BUT   Never use an apostrophe with a personal pronoun.

   PERSONAL PRONOUNS   hers   its   yours   theirs

3. **Use an apostrophe + *s* to form the plural of a letter, a number, or a word used as a word.**

   LETTERS   four *X*'s   *p*'s and *q*'s   *ABC*'s
   NUMBERS   five *6*'s   eight 10's
   WORDS AS WORDS   four *yes*'s and eight *no*'s

   BUT   Years usually have no apostrophe: *1990s*.

4. **Use an apostrophe to show missing letters in a contraction.**

   CONTRACTIONS   it's   = it is   who's = who is
     they're = they are   can't = cannot
     you're = you are   we'll = we will

!!!
About *apostrophe*

The word *apostrophe*, which often replaces letters that have been "turned away," or left out, comes from a Greek word meaning "to turn away."

A Look Backward

Considering the age of the world, our system of punctuation is practically brand new. It has been in use, in one form or another, for only about 400 years.

What did people do before then? In ancient times, words were usually just run together, although paragraphs did exist.

Different marks turned up here and there. In some ancient texts, for example, a raised period meant a full stop, while a lower period meant a comma. The comma that we use today made an appearance sometime in the 800s. It was not until the 1500s, however, that Italian printers decided to try to make punctuation marks standard.

Using Quotation Marks

1. **Use quotation marks to show someone's exact words.** A direct quotation tells someone's exact words. Quotation marks show where those words begin and end. (For capitalization with quotations, see page 327.)

    DIRECT QUOTATION "I'm from Honduras," Alberto said.

    BUT An *indirect quotation* does not give the speaker's exact words. Do not put it in quotation marks.

    INDIRECT QUOTATION Alberto said that he was from Honduras.

    a. **Speaker tags** A speaker tag — words that identify the speaker — may come before, after, or in the middle of a quotation. Place the tag outside the quotation marks.

    SPEAKER TAG *He continued,* "I was born in Tegucigalpa."
    "I was born there," *he told us,* "in 1975."
    "We moved here when I was five," *he stated.*

    b. **Commas with quotation marks** The speaker tag is usually set off from the quotation with one or more commas. A comma goes inside the quotation marks.

    "That's the capital of Honduras," he explained.

    c. **Periods with quotation marks** When a quotation ends a sentence, put the period inside the quotation marks.

    Alberto stated, "Nicaragua is below Honduras."

    More than one sentence can appear inside quotation marks.

    He said, "There are many volcanoes. They're beautiful."

    d. **Exclamation points and question marks with quotation marks** Put exclamation points and question marks inside the quotation marks only if they are part of the quotation. If they are not, put them outside.

    She exclaimed, "What a great speech Roberto gave!"
    Did she say, "My cousin's name is Quintero"?

!!!
About *quotation*

Quotation goes all the way back to Latin *quot*, meaning "how many." From *quot* came Middle English *coten*, "to mark with numbers." Thus, *quotation* is not related to words having to do with "say" or "speak," but rather to words having to do with counting, such as *quota* and *quotient*.

2. **Use quotation marks with dialogue.** When you write dialogue, begin a new paragraph for each new speaker.

> "Do you really want to see the volcano?" he asked, hoping Adam would say yes.
> "Of course!" exclaimed Adam eagerly. "When can we go?" Adam looked as if he were ready to start immediately.
> "Well, how about first thing in the morning?"

3. **Use quotation marks with titles of short works.** Use quotation marks with the kinds of titles shown below.

SHORT STORIES	"The Gold Bug" by Edgar Allan Poe
ARTICLES, ESSAYS	the *Time* article "Three Young Governors"
CHAPTERS	Chapter 7, "The First Microscope"
POEMS	"Mending Wall" by Robert Frost
SONGS	"Tomorrow" from the show *Annie*
TV EPISODES	"Rudy Huxtable Gets Lost"

Underlining

1. **Underlining and italics** Italics is a special kind of slanty print that is used in printed material to mark certain expressions. Unless you have a word processor, you cannot use italics when you write. Use underlining instead.

2. **Underline letters and numbers. Also underline foreign words and words used as words.**

LETTERS, NUMBERS	I thought those <u>7</u>'s were <u>T</u>'s.
WORDS	<u>Kindergarten</u> comes from German <u>Kinder</u>.

3. **Underline titles of long works, works of art, and vehicles.**

BOOKS	<u>All Creatures Great and Small</u>
NEWSPAPERS	the <u>Washington Post</u>
PERIODICALS	<u>Life</u> magazine
MOVIES, PLAYS	<u>The Wizard of Oz</u>, <u>A Raisin in the Sun</u>
LONG POEMS	<u>Paradise Lost</u> by Milton
RADIO, TV SERIES	<u>Live from Lincoln Center</u>, <u>The Cosby Show</u>
MUSICAL WORKS	<u>The Pirates of Penzance</u>
WORKS OF ART	Mary Cassatt's <u>The Bath</u> (painting)
VEHICLES	<u>Mayflower</u> (ship), <u>Challenger</u> (spacecraft)

Awful Authors

Write your own book titles, capitalizing and underlining them correctly, of course. Then match them with an appropriate author, like each of the titles below.

Crime Does Not Pay by Robin Banks

King Kong by Hugh Jape

At the Stroke of Midnight by Justin Time

The Open Window by Eileen Doubt

The Dog's Dinner by Nora Bone

A Visit to the Dentist by Phil A. Kavity

Using Standard Manuscript Form_____

Before you write the final draft of a composition, check with your teacher for specific instructions. Here is the most common form for the final copy of a piece of writing.

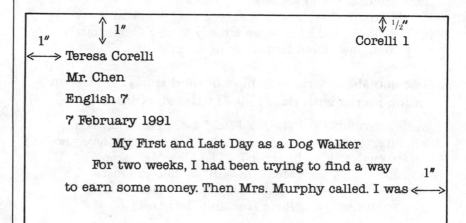

1. **Paper**   Use standard-size 8½″ by 11″ white paper. Use just one side of the paper.

2. **Writing**   If you are writing by hand, use black or blue ink. Write as neatly as you can. If you are typing or using a word processor, use a dark ribbon.

3. **Margins**   Leave a 1″ or 1½″ margin at the left of the page and a 1″ margin at the right, at the bottom, and at the top, except for page numbers. Make the left margin even, starting the first letter of every line at the same place (except for paragraph indents — see item 8). Make the right margin as even as you can, without using too many hyphenated words. However, if you are using a word processor, do not *justify* the margins, that is, do not set the right-hand margin to come out even automatically.

4. **Spacing**   Double-space everything you write. That is, write on every other line rather than on every line. If you are using a word processor, set the spacing for double-spacing before you begin. Double-space all parts of your composition, including the heading, title, quotations, and notes.

5. Top margin and heading   At the left margin, on separate lines, write or type your name, your teacher's name, the name of the course, and the date. Double-space the heading.

6. Title   Write the title on the middle of the line below the heading. Follow the rules for capitalizing titles (page 330). Do not use all capital letters, underlines, or quotation marks (unless you need them for other reasons — pages 338 – 339). Begin your composition on the line below the title.

TITLES   My First and Last Job as a Dog Walker
The Mother in <u>The Cat Ate My Gymsuit</u>

7. Page numbers   Write the page numbers in the upper right-hand corner of each page, a half inch from the top. Write just the number, without *p.* or *page*. It is a good idea also to write your last name in front of the page number in case the pages get separated. If you are using a word processor, begin the file by setting up a running head that automatically writes your name and the page number on each page. Place the running head against the right margin and leave a double space before the first line of text.

8. Paragraph indent   Start each new paragraph five spaces from the left margin.

9. Long quotations   Start long quotations ten spaces from the left margin.

10. Writing numbers

    a. Spell out numbers that you can write in two words or less. Use numerals for other numbers (but see *b* and *c*).

    b. Spell out a number at the beginning of a sentence.

    c. If you have to use numerals for one number, then use numerals for all related numbers.

    d. You can combine numerals and words for large numbers.

Forty-one students were present, and *four* were absent.
Of the *122* items, only *12* had to be returned and *4* discarded.
There are about *11 million* people in the state.

11. Make a copy.   If possible, keep a copy of your final draft.

Index

C

call numbers, 56 – 58, 59
capitalization
   brand names, 329
   checklist, 145
   of first words and I, 327
   in foreign languages, 329
   in letter parts, 181
   outline, 211
   proper adjective, 330
   proper noun, 328 – 329
   in titles, 119, 208, 215, 330, 340,
      341
   of words after possessives, 330
captions, 69, 91, 70
card catalog, 55 – 58
case, 309
categorizing. *See* classifying
category chart, 20
cause and effect
   chain, 16
   defined, 15
   order, 153, 154
   strategies for determining, 15 – 16
-*cede*, 257
-*ceed*, 257
character (story)
   defined, 224
   development, 124, 186, 187
   profile, 188
charting. *See also* graphic aids, plan
   as analysis tool, 25.
   to organize topic, 136
Chaucerian English, 231, 233
Chinese, 233, 289
choosing a topic, 169
   for an argument, 171
   for a report, 202 – 203
   for a personal narrative, 165
   for a poem, 191
chronological order. *See* time order
cinquain, 200, 224
circle (pie) graph, 97
classification systems, library, 57, 58
classifieds, 68
classifying, 19 – 21
clause
   adjective, 285
   adverb, 286
   clear antecedents for, 314
   comma after, 333
   fragments, 320
   incomplete, 286
   independent, 284
   noun, 287

objects, 315
   pronouns in, 312
   subjects in, 314 – 315
   subordinate, 284 – 287
   vs. phrase, 284
cliché, 194, 224, 253
climax, 186, 187, 189, 224
clipped (shortened) words, 22, 235
closings, letter, 174, 175, 180, 181
cluster diagrams, 5, 114, 134
codes, 221
coherent writing, 156, 224
collective nouns, 262, 307 – 308
colon, 181, 335
color and brightness words, 167
combining sentences. *See* sentence
   combining
comma
   and appositives 283, 334
   and clauses, 280, 283, 334
   before joining words, 333
   between modifiers, 332
   in dates and places, 334
   in letter parts, 175, 181, 334
   in series, 332
   with interjection, 277
   with interrupter, 333
   with nonessential clause and
      phrase, 334
   with noun of direct address, 334
   with participial phrase, 280
   with phrases, 281, 285, 286
   with quotations, 338
   vs. dash, 336
   vs. semicolon, 335
comma fault, 321
common nouns, 261
comparative adjectives and adverbs,
   316 – 317
comparing and contrasting, 13, 95, 97,
   101, 154
comparisons. *See also* metaphor, simile
   as context clues, 237
   parallelism in, 321
   unclear, 318
compass rose, 99
complaint letter, 184
complements, 291
complete predicate, 289
complete subject, 289, 296
complex sentence, 293
compound adjectives, 336
compound antecedents, 313
compound nouns, 256, 262, 336
compound predicate, 291, 293, 296

compound sentence, 293, 296, 333, 335
compound subject, 291, 296, 307
compound words, 236, 262
compound-complex sentence, 293
computerized catalogs, 55, 59
concise writing, 158 – 159, 224
concluding sentences, 150
conclusion (ending)
   book report, 215
   expository writing, 170
   paragraph, 150
   personal narrative, 166
   report, 204
   speech, 126
   story, 124, 189
conclusions
   drawing, 33 – 35
   limiting, 39
concrete nouns, 262
concrete poetry, 201, 224
condition, verb of. *See* linking verb
conflict (story), 185, 186, 187, 189, 225
conjugation, 302
conjunction
   jobs, 275, 276
   kinds of, 275 – 276
   in titles, 330
   vs. preposition, 276
connectors. *See* coherent writing,
   conjunctions, transition words
connotation, 44, 163, 225, 249
consonance, 197, 225
consonance pairs, 197
consonant + *y*, 298
context clue types, 237
contractions, 162, 267, 311, 315
contrast, as context clue, 237. *See also*
   comparing and contrasting
coordinating conjunctions, 275, 321
copyright page, 66, 67
correlative conjunctions, 276, 321
couplet, 200, 225
course names, capitalizing, 329
creative writing, 3 – 6, 8, 10, 14, 225.
   See also ideas
criteria, establishing, 47
critical thinking and evaluating,
   46 – 47
cubing, 136

D

dash, 336
dates
   in books, 56, 66

comma in, 334
copyright, 66, 67
ending in -s, 337
on source cards, 208
punctuating, 334, 337
days, months, and holidays, 109, 235,
329
etymologies, 64
declarative sentence, 288
deductive reasoning, 38, 40 – 41
definite article, 269
definition, as context clue, 237. *See also*
dictionary, thesaurus
definition label, in dictionary entry, 63
definitions, humorous, 247
degrees of comparison, 316
delivering a speech, 126
demonstrative pronouns, 265, 315
denotation, 163, 225
dependent clause, 276, 284, 293
description, as supporting detail, 148,
153
of story characters, 188, 189
descriptive writing, 167 – 169, 189,
192 – 194, 196 – 197, 225
detail chart, 168
details
in book report, 216
in outline, 211
in summary, 217
organizing, 170
supporting, 147 – 149, 152 – 153
Dewey, Melvil, 59
Dewey Decimal cards, 58
Dewey Decimal System, 57, 58
diagrams. *See also* graphic aids, plan
cause-and-effect chain, 23
category chart, 20
charts and tables, 25, 88, 89
cluster, 30
diagram map, 100
graphs, 92 – 94
idea (spider) map, 30
labeled sketch, 26
time line, 20
dialect, 225, 232
dialogue
defined, 225
punctuating, 338, 339
writing, 188
diction, 64, 162 – 163, 173, 181, 225
dictionary
contents, 63
entries, labeled, 64, 65
guide words, 63

order, 63
pronunciation key, 64
as spelling aid, 254
types of, 30, 62,
direct address, noun 334
direct cause, 16
direct object, 262, 263, 268, 281, 291,
294, 310 – 312
direct quotations, 209, 327
directions on compass, 328
directions, giving. *See* instructions
discussion
defined, 225
guidelines, 127 – 129
leader's role, 129
member's role, 128
steps, 128
three purposes of, 128
do- forms, 267
doesn't/don't agreement, 308
double bar graph, 94 –95
double comparisons, 318
double negatives, 318
drawing, to explore topic, 136
drawing conclusions, 35, 89, 92, 93, 95,
96. *See also* critical thinking and
evaluating

E

each, with compound subject, 307
echoic words, 236
editorial page, 68
ei/ie rule, 256
either-or argument, 44
elements of story, 185
empty expressions, avoiding, 204
empty words and phrases, avoiding, 158
Enc., 182
encyclopedias, 30, 61, 205, 208, 213, 214
endings. *See* conclusion
end marks, 288, 331
English, history of, 231 – 233
entry, dictionary, 63 – 64
entry, thesaurus, 65
envelope addresses, 174, 180
essay question tests, 82
essential clauses, 285
etymologies. *See also* word families
capitalization and punctuation
words, 70, 332, 335, 336, 337, 338
grammar/revision words, 210, 275,
278, 280, 283, 284, 291, 301, 302,
304, 312

parts of speech names, 261, 266, 269,
271, 273, 275, 277, 282, 312
persons, places, and things, 22, 43,
60, 88, 134, 176, 179, 206,
214, 220, 234 – 235
etymology
in dictionary entry, 63
patterns, 22
word sources, 176, 179, 234 – 235, 238
euphemisms, 163
events
capitalizing names of, 329
order of, 149, 150
as supporting details, 148, 153
evidence gathering, 172
exaggeration, 225
examples
as context clues, 237
as supporting details, 148, 150
in expository writing, 170
in instructions, 133
exclamation point, 277, 331, 338
exclamatory sentence, 288
explanations, 169
exploring a topic, 135 – 137
expository writing, 169 – 170, 225

F

fable, 225
fact
defined, 36
as supporting detail, 148, 150, 153
vs. conclusion, 35
vs. generalization, 32
vs. opinion, 36, 172, 209, 210
fact gathering, 38, 39, 169
familiar *you,* 264
fantasy, 225
far-to-near order, 154
faulty cause and effect, 45
faulty reasoning, 42 – 45
feminine, 312
fiction
call numbers, 57, 58
defined, 225
kinds of, 113, 185
figurative language, 168, 192 – 194, 225
figures of speech, 193
fill-in tests, 80
film review, 46
final consonant, doubling, 258, 298
final draft, 340 – 341
final *e,* 298

imperative sentence, 288
implied topic sentence, 150, 226
importance order, 149, 152, 154
indefinite article, 269
indefinite pronouns, 265, 308, 337
indenting, 147, 339, 341
independent clauses, 293, 333, 335
indexes
    book, 66
    newspaper, 69, 70
    specialized, 61
indirect object, 262, 281, 292, 294, 310
indirect quotations, 338
Indo-European language groups, 232
inductive reasoning, 37, 38 – 40
inferences, making, 33 – 34, 35
infinitive
    jobs, 281
    diagraming, 296
    phrases, 278
    vs. preposition, 282
informal closing, 175
informal (friendly) letters, 174 – 179
informal language (diction), 64, 162,
    226
informal note, 176
information gathering, 203
inside-to-outside order, 154
instructions, 132 – 133, 170
intensifiers, 272
intensive pronouns, 264
international airport signs, 222
interrogative pronouns, 265, 314
interrogative sentence, 288
interrupted subjects, 306
interrupters, 290, 313, 335, 336
interview
    in bibliography, 214
    defined, 226
    footnoting an, 213
    guidelines, 130 – 131
intransitive verbs, 268
introduction,
    book, 66, 67
    book report, 215
    defined, 226
introductory words and comma, 333
inventors and inventions, 3, 4, 5, 6, 28,
    50, 51, 151, 234, 235, 328
inverted order, 290, 333
inverted sentences and agreement, 307
invitation, 179
irony, 226
irregular comparatives and
    superlatives, 317

irregular nouns, 256
irregular verbs, 298 – 300
ISBN number, 66
"It doesn't follow" argument, 44
italics, 206, 339
item-use analogies, 250

J

jacket, book, 66
jargon, 68, 226, 252. *See also* Glossary
    of Computer Terms
joining words, comma before, 332, 333
journal keeping, 135
jumpline, 69, 70

K

key (legend), 99, 100, 101
key words, 156, 206, 209, 217

L

labeled sketch, 26
labels in graphic aids, 91 – 97, 100
Latin influence on English, 22, 232,
    331. *See also* prefixes, word families
lead headline, 69, 70
lead story, 69, 70
least, less, 317
legend, 226
legend (key), 99, 100, 101
letters. *See* business letters, friendly
    letters
levels of speech, 162 – 163, 225, 226
library
    card, 54
    catalogs, 55 – 59
    classification systems, 57, 58
    how to use, 29, 53 – 54
    reference section, 30
    rules, 54, 60
    sections, 53, 58
Library of Congress cards, 56, 58
Library of Congress system, 57 – 58
library resources
    computerized catalog, 59
    dictionaries, 62 – 64
    librarian, 54, 59, 60, 61
    reference materials, 60 – 61
    special equipment, 54, 60
    special events, 53
    thesauruses, 65
limerick pattern, 27, 226

limericks, 25, 195, 200, 245, 246, 259
limiting conclusions, 39
limiting topic, 203
line graph, 96
linking-verb/subject agreement, 306
linking verbs, 266, 267
listing
    as analysis tool, 24, 51
    to find ideas, 6
    to improve spelling, 254
listening guidelines, 122
lists. *See also* etymologies, word families
    abbreviations, 331
    astronomy symbols, 223
    common interrupters, 333
    conjunctions, 275, 276, 286
    connectors, 335
    genres, 113, 185
    homographs, 247 – 248
    homophones, 244 – 246, 247
    indefinite pronouns, 308
    interjections, 277
    irregular comparatives and
        superlatives, 317
    kinds of supporting details, 148
    mathematics symbols, 223
    music symbols, 223
    negatives, 318
    prefixes, 241
    prepositions, 273, 274
    proofreading symbols, 143, 144
    questions advertisers ask, 120
    revising goals, 140
    sensory words, 167, 168
    silent-letter words, 256 – 257
    spelling demons, 259
    suffixes, 243, 266, 269
    transition words, 154, 157, 166
    troublesome adjective-adverb
        pairs, 319
    U.S. and Canadian holidays, 109
    weather symbols, 223
literal vs. figurative language, 192, 193,
    194, 225, 226
loaded language, 173
loaded words, 44
logic, 37 – 41. *See also* coherent writing,
    unified writing
logic games and puzzles, 39, 40, 41, 48,
    49
logical order, 157
long quotations, 341
"loose ends," tying up, 124
-ly, 243
lyric poetry, 226

M

magazine article
  in bibliography, 214
  footnoting, 213
  source card, 208
Magazine Index, 61
main character, 185, 187, 226
main clause, 282
main idea
  in conclusions, 170
  developing, 148 – 150
  in summary, 217
  in unified writing, 153
  ways to find, 205 – 206
main topic of outline, 211
main verbs, 267
manual alphabet, 218
manuals, 61
manuscript form, 212 – 213, 340 – 341
maps
  diagram map, 100
  idea (spider) map, 30
  road and street, 99
  time zone, 102
  weather, 101
masculine, 312
matching tests, 80
mathematics symbols, 223
measurement abbreviations, 331
memorization strategies, 20, 21
memorizing hints
  i before *e*, 256
  spelling, 254
  3-minute list + classifying, 21, 75
metaphor, 168, 194, 226
meter (poetry), 196, 227
metric measurements, 331
metric system, 106
microfilm and microfiche, 60
Middle English, 233
mind-opening techniques, 135
misplaced modifiers, 319
mnemonics, 75
Modern English, 231 – 235
modified (semi-block) style, 180, 181
modifiers. *See* adjectives, adverbs,
  demonstrative pronouns, clauses,
  participles, phrases, possessive
  pronouns
modifiers, dangling and misplaced, 319
mood, 227
Morse Code, 221
movement words, 167
"movie" technique, 124

multiple-choice tests, 79
multiple meanings, 63, 209, 248
myth, 227

N

name-calling, 43
names
  capitalizing, 328
  as word sources, 176 – 179, 234, 235,
    328
naming sources, 212 – 213
narrative planning chart, 165
narrative poetry, 227
narrative writing, 123, 165 – 166,
  185 – 190, 227. *See also* book report
narrator, in story, 188, 227
narrowing a topic, 203
nationalities, languages, and religious
  terms, capitalizing names of, 329
natural order, 290
near-to-far order, 154
negative-positive word pairs, 318
negatives, double, 318
neuter, 312
Newbery medalists, 116, 117, 118
newspaper article, in bibliography, 214
newspaper
  front page, 69
  jargon, 68
  sections, 68
nominative case, 309
nonessential clauses, 285
nonfiction, 113, 227
nonfiction call numbers, 57, 58
Norman French influence on English,
  232, 233
note cards, 126, 207, 208, 211
note-taking, 8, 10, 30, 116, 131, 133, 203
noun
  as adjective, 270
  clauses, 297, 315
  compound, 256
  endings, 255
  forms, 262
  gerund as, 281
  infinitive as, 281
  jobs, 262
  kinds of, 261 – 262
  of direct address, 334
  prefixes, 241
  plural, 262, 255 – 256
  in prepositional phrase, 279
  singular, 262
  suffixes, 269

noun clause, diagraming, 297
number. *See also* pronoun-antecedent
  agreement
  of collective nouns, 307
  of indefinite pronouns, 308, 313
  prefixes showing, 241
  of pronouns, 264
  of titles, 308
numerals
  hyphenated, 336
  in outlines, 137
  Morse Code, 221
  plurals of, 337
  Roman, 108, 137, 211
  spelled vs. numeral, 341
  superscript, 212
novel, 227

O

obituary page, 68
object of preposition, 262, 263, 281, 307,
  310
object pronouns, 309, 310
objective case, 309
observing tips, 9 – 10
Old English, 232, 233, 300
Old Norse influence on English, 232,
  233
omitted letters. *See* apostrophe, contractions
omitted words
  after *than* and *as*, 312
  in contractions, 267
  in infinitives, 282
  in passive sentences, 403
omniscient ("all-knowing") point of
  view, 187, 229
only, 319
onomatopoeia, 197, 227
onomatopoeic words, 167
op-ed page, 68
opinion vs. fact, 36
optical illusions, 9
-*or* and subject-verb agreement, 307
order
  cause-and-effect, 153, 154
  inverted, 290
  of details, 149
  of footnotes, 212
  natural, 290
  spatial, 149, 152, 154
  step-by-step, 170
  subject-verb, 290
  time, 149, 152, 154, 170

syllogism, 40, 41
syllogism circles, 41
symbol
   defined, 229
   lists (astronomy, math, music, weather), 223
   plural of, 256
sympathy note, 178
synonym
   defined, 229
   in dictionary entry, 63, 64
   lists, 121, 249
   as revision tool, 141
   tests, 86
   in thesaurus entry, 65
synonym use,
   in analogies, 250
   as context clue, 237
synthesizing, 50 – 51

T

table logic, 40
table of contents, 66, 67
tall tale, 229
taste words, 168
"telescoping" to observe, 10
temperature systems, 107
tense
   in book report, 216
   avoiding shifts in, 303
   chart, 301
   etymology, 301
tests
   analogy, 81
   essay question, 82
   fill-in, 80
   matching, 80
   multiple-choice, 79
   true-false, 79
test-taking
   classroom tests, 78
   key words in directions, 82
   standardized tests, 83 – 87
   tips, 77
testimonial (propaganda tool), 43
than and *as* clauses, 321
thank you note, 177
that, 285, 315
the, 269, 330
theme, 229. *See also* main idea
thesaurus, 65
thesis statement, 172, 204, 229
thinking skills, 17, 18
third person pronouns, 263, 264

third-person limited point of view, 187, 229
third-person omniscient point of view, 187, 229
this/that, these/those, 315
thou/you, 264
time
   abbreviations, 331
   colon in, 335
   expressions, and number, 308
time line, 23
time order, 149, 152, 154, 166, 170, 188, 229
time zone map, U.S., 102
timing a discussion, 129
title card, 56 – 58
title page, 66, 67
titles
   as research aid, 206
   as story starters, 188
   book report, 215
   commas with, 334
   in note cards, 207, 208
   in quotation marks, 341
   movie and play, 330
   number of, 308
   of art works, 330
   of written works, 330
   underlined, 339, 341
titles (names)
   of family relationships, 330
   of government and public officials, 330
   for royalty, 119
   underlined, 339, 341
   used alone, 330
to, left out of infinitives, 282
toe-to-head order (spatial), 149
Tom Swifties, 272
tone, 175, 181, 229. *See also* diction
top-to-bottom order, 154
topic
   choosing a, 125, 169, 202 – 204
   in outline, 211
   limiting a, 203
   on source card, 209
   sticking to, 155
topic sentence, 147 – 149, 155, 170, 229
topic sentence, implied, 150
touch/feeling words, 168
traffic and road signs, 222
transfer technique, 43
transition words, 154, 157, 166, 229
transitive verbs, 268, 304
tree diagram, 20, 26

troublesome word pairs, 322 – 326
true-false tests, 79
types of writing
   description, 167 – 169
   exposition, 169 – 170
   narration, 164 – 166
   persuasion, 171 – 173

U

unabridged dictionary, 62
unclear antecedents, revising, 314
unclear comparisons, 318
underlining, 339, 341
underlying cause, 16
U.S. customary system, 107
unified writing, 155, 229
usage
checklist, 145
   label in dictionary entry, 64
   label in thesaurus entry, 65
usage errors. *See also* Glossary of Grammar, Mechanics, and Usage
   double negatives, 318
   -self words, 315
   this here, that there, 315
   in object pronouns, 311
   troublesome adjective-adverb pairs, 319
   unclear antecedents, 314
   unclear comparisons, 318

V

validity, testing for, 41
varied sentences, achieving, 160 – 161, 291
vehicle names, 329
verb
   agreement with subject, 305 – 308
   complements, 291
   conjugation, 302
   irregular forms, 298 – 300
   phrases, 267, 268, 290
   prefix *en-*, 266
   principal parts, 298 – 300
   progressive forms, 303
   regular forms, 298, 300
   suffixes, 266
   tenses, 301
   vs. gerund, 281
   vs. participle, 286

Acknowledgments

(continued)

Great and Small by James Herriot, Copyright © 1972 by James Herriott, St. Martin's Press, Inc., New York. *Page 9: Born Free: A Lioness of Two Worlds* by Joy Adamson. Pantheon Books, a division of Random House, Inc. Copyright © 1960 by Joy Adamson. Forward copyright © 1987 by George B. Schallter. *Page 9:* Reprinted by permission of Sterling Publishing Co., Inc., 387 Park Ave. South, New York, NY 10016, from *The World's Best Optical Illusion* by Charles H. Paraquin, © 1977 by Sterling Publishing Co., Inc. *Page 24: What's What*, edited by Reginald Bragonier, Jr. and David Fisher. Published by Ballantine Books, a division of Random House, Inc. Entire contents copyright © 1981 by Reginald Bragonier Jr. and David Fisher. Reprinted by permission. *Pages 25, 26:* From *Laughable Limericks*, compiled by Sara and John E. Brewton. Published by Thomas Y. Crowell, 1965. *Page 26: What's What*, edited by Reginald Bragonier, Jr. and David Fisher. Published by Ballantine Books, a division of Random House, Inc. Entire contents © copyright 1981 by Reginald Bragonier Jr. and David Fisher. Reprinted by permission. *Page 31: Never Cry Wolf* by Farley Mowat. Published by Little, Brown and Company. Copyright © 1963, 1973 by Farley Mowat. *Page 33:* from "They Go In When Planes Go Down" by Richard Saltus, November 24, 1989. Reprinted courtesy of The Boston Globe. *Page 42:* From "It's Natural! It's Organic! Or Is It?" from *Consumer Reports* magazine. Copyright 1980 by Consumers Union of United States. *Page 46:* Review of *Young Guns II*, "Emilio Estevez in Reprise of Billy the Kid Role" by Janet Maslin, August 1, 1990. Copyright © 1990 by The New York Times Company. Reprinted by permission. *Page 47:* From *Rotten Reviews*, edited by Bill Henderson. Published by Pushcart Press. Copyright © Pushcart Press, 1986. *Page 50:* Adapted from *Be an Inventor* by Barbara Taylor. Harcourt Brace Jovanovich, Publishers. Copyright © 1987 by Field Publications. *Page 60:* Entry adapted from *Readers' Guide to Periodical Literature*, copyright © 1984, 1985 by The H.W. Wilson Company. *Pages 63, 64:* Entries adapted from *The American Heritage Student's Dictionary*, Copyright © 1986 by Houghton Mifflin Company. Adapted and reprinted by permission from *The American Heritage Student's Dictionary*. *Page 65:* Entry adapted from *The Clear and Simple Thesaurus Dictionary* by Harriet Wittels and Joan Greisman, published by Grosset & Dunlap, Inc. Copyright © 1971 by Grosset & Dunlap, Inc. *Page 67:* Reproduced from *Wolf Pack* by Sylvia Johnson and Alice Aamodt. Published by Lerner Publications Company. Copyright © 1985 by Lerner Publications Company. *Page 69:* Copyright 1990, *The State Journal-Register*, Springfield, Illinois. Reprinted with permission. *Pages 78, 79:* Questions taken from *Can You Pass These Tests?* edited by Allen D. Bragdon. Copyright © 1987 by Allen Bragdon Publishers, Inc. Reprinted by permission of Harper-Collins Publishers. *Page 90:* Amtrak, National Passenger Railroad Corporation, Washington D.C. *Page 91: What's What*, edited by Reginald Bragonier, Jr. and David Fisher. Published by Ballantine Books, a division of Random House, Inc. Entire contents copyright © 1981 by Reginald Bragonier Jr. and David Fisher. Reprinted by permission. *Page 93:* Graph: "Emptier Nets in the World Cup," (Accompanying "Soccer Federation's Goals Are Just That," by Paul Gardner), February 1, 1990. Copyright © 1990 by The New York Times Company. Reprinted by permission. *Page 94:* Graph: "Starters and Finishers," (Starting and Finishing Runners, New York Marathon, 1970–1989), 1989. Copyright © 1989 by The New York Times Company. Reprinted by permission. *Page 97: Statistical Abstract of the United States*, Public Information Office, Bureau of the Census, Department of Commerce, Washington, D.C. *Pages 98, 99:* Map and Legend, The H.M. Gousha Company, California. *Page 100:* From *Plane Talk*, a publication of the Massport Public Affairs Department, Boston, Massachusetts. *Page 101:* Map: "Today's High Temperatures and Precipitation," April 21, 1990. Copyright © 1990 by the New York Times Company. Reprinted by permission. *Pages 113, 115: Keepers and Creatures at the National Zoo* by Peggy Thomson. Published by Thomas Y. Crowell. Copyright © 1988 by Peggy Thomson. *Page 117: Charlotte's Web* by E.B. White, Published by E.P. Dutton. Copyright © 1959, 1988 by Jean Craighead George. *Page 123: The Singing Ringing Tree* by Selina Hastings, published by Henry Holt & Company, Text copyright © 1988 by Selina Hastings. *Page 125:* Speech excerpt from *Speak For Yourself — With Confidence* by Elayne Snyder with Jane Field. A Signet book, published by New American Library. Copyright © 1983 by Elayne Snyder. *Page 130:* From "Interview With a Young Diplomat" by Gail Greco, from *Cobblestone* magazine, February 1985. Published by Cobblestone Publishing, Inc. *Page 130: How to Talk with Practically Anybody About Practically Anything* by Barbara Walters, Doubleday, a division of Bantam,

Doubleday, Dell Publishing Group, Inc., 1970. *Page 132:* Adapted from *Funny Side Up!* by Mike Thaler. Published by Scholastic, Inc. Copyright © 1985 by Mike Thaler. *Page 147: Care of Uncommon Pets* by William J. Weber, D.V.M, published by Holt, Rinehart and Winston. Copyright © 1979 by William J. Weber, D.V.M. *Page 154:* Adapted with permission of Atheneum Publishers, an imprint of Macmillan Publishing Company, from *The Teenager's Survival Guide to Moving* by Patricia C. Nida and Wendy M. Heller. Copyright © 1985 by Patricia C. Nida and Wendy M. Heller. *Page 155: Amazing Creatures of the Sea*, published by National Wildlife Federation. Copyright © 1987 National Wildlife Federation. *Page 156:* From *National Geographic World*, November 1989. Published by The National Geographic Society, Washington, D.C. *Page 160: My Side of the Mountain* by Jean Craighead George, published by E. P. Dutton, a division of NAL Penguin Inc. Copyright © 1959, 1988 by Jean Craighead George. *Page 164: Desert Exile* by Yoshiko Uchida, published by University of Washington Press, Copyright © 1982 by Yoshiko Uchida. *Page 165: I Dream a World: Portraits of Black Women Who Changed America*, photographs and interviews by Brian Lander, edited by Barbara Summers. Published by Stewart, Tabori & Chang, Inc. Copyright © 1989 by Brian Lanker. *Page 167: Dandelion Wine* by Ray Bradbury. Doubleday & Company, Inc., publisher. Copyright © 1957 by Ray Bradbury. *Page 169:* Reprinted with permission of Bradbury Press, an Affiliate of Macmillan, Inc. from *Dinosaurs Walked Here: And Other Stories Fossils Tell* by Patricia Lauber. Copyright © 1987 by Patricia Lauber. *Page 171:* "Keep Greenhouse at Bay" from *Greenpeace* magazine, Washington, D.C., July/August 1989. *Pages 180–184: Free Stuff for Kids*, published by Meadowbrook, Inc. Copyright © 1990 by Meadowbrook Creations. *Page 185:* From "Theft" by Elizabeth Webster, in *Merlyn's Pen* magazine, October 1989. Copyright © 1989 by Merlyn's Pen, Inc. *Page 190:* "Heat Wave" by Cheri Johnson, "Heat Wave" by Jeremy Bell from *Cricket* magazine, December 1987. Reprinted by permission of *Cricket* Magazine, Vol. 15, No. 4. © 1987 by Carus Corporation. *Page 192:* "Ill tell you how the Sun rose" by Emily Dickinson. Reprinted by permission of the publishers and the trustees of Amherst College from *The Poems of Emily Dickinson*, Thomas H. Johnson, ed., Cambridge, Mass: The Belknap Press of Harvard University Press, Copyright 1951, © 1955, 1979, 1983 by the President and Fellows of Harvard College. *Page 192:* "the drum" from *Spin a Soft Black Song* by Nikki Giovanni. Copyright © 1971, 1985 by Nikki Giovanni. Reprinted by permission of Farrar, Straus and Giroux, Inc. *Page 195:* "Whispers" from *A Song I Sang to You* by Myra Cohn Livingston, Harcourt Brace Jovanovich, 1984. *Page 195:* "A Lazy Thought" from *Jamboree: Rhymes for All Times* by Eve Merriam. Dell paperback, 1984. Copyright © 1962, 1964, 1966, 1973, 1984 by Eve Merriam. *Page 198:* "About the Teeth of Sharks" from *You Read to Me, I'll Read to You* by John Ciardi. Published by J.B. Lippincott Co. © 1962 by Curtis Publishing. *Page 198:* "Love Song for a Jellyfish" from *Earthworks* by Sandra Hochman, Viking Penguin Inc., 1970. *Page 199:* "Neither Out Far Nor In Deep" from *The Poetry of Robert Frost*, edited by Edward Connery Lathem. Copyright 1939, © 1967, 1969 by Holt, Rinehart & Winston, Inc. *Page 199:* "The Termite" from *Verses From 1919 On* by Ogden Nash, Copyright © 1942 by Ogden Nash. Published by Little, Brown and Company. First appeared in *The Saturday Evening Post. Page 199:* "The Sloth," from *The Collected Poems of Theodore Roethke* by Theodore Roethke, Doubleday & Company, Inc. Copyright © 1966 Beatrice Roethke as Administratix of the Estate of Theodore Roethke. *Page 201:* "Trees" by Denise F. from *The English Journal*, April 1973. Copyright 1973 by the National Council of Teachers of English. Reprinted with permission. *Page 202:* "The Shark," from *Custard and Company: Poems by Ogden Nash* by Ogden Nash, Little, Brown and Company, 1980. *Page 202:* From the Preface by Eugenie Clark to *The Shark Watchers' Guide* by Guido Dingerkus. Published by Julian Messner, a Division of Simon & Schuster, Inc. Text Copyright © 1985 by Guido Dingerkus. *Page 205:* "Sharks" from *The World Book Encyclopedia* published by Field Enterprises Educational Corporation. *Page 210: Mystery Monsters of the Deep* by Gardner Soule. Published by Franklin Watts. Copyright © 1981 by Gardner Soule. *Page 212:* "Shark Lady" by Beth Hennefreund in *Ranger Rick* magazine, March 1989, published by the

Porell. Addison-Wesley Publishing Company, Inc. Copyright © 1979 by Bruce Porell. *Pages 218, 219:* From *The Perigree Visual Dictionary of Signing* by Rod R. Butterworth. A GD/Perigree Book published by The Putnam Publishing Group. Copyright © 1983 by Rod R. Butterworth and Mickey Flodin. *Page 231:* "Poem, or Beauty Hurts Mr. Vinal" from *IS 5, poems by E. E. Cummings.* Liveright Publishing Corporation. *Page 236:* Information from *They Have a Word for It* by Howard Rheingold. Published by Jeremy P. Tarcher, Inc. Distributed by St. Martin's Press. Copyright © 1988 by Howard Rheingold. *Page 261: The Official Kids' Survival Kit* by Elaine Chaback and Pat Fortunato. Published by Little, Brown and Company. Copyright © 1981 by Elaine Chaback and Pat Fortunato. *Pages 263, 265: Adapted from Sports and Games the Indians Gave Us* by Alex Whitney. Published by David McKay Company, Inc. Text Copyright © 1977 by Alex Whitney. *Page 269: The Wonderful Flight to the Mushroom Planet* by Eleanor Cameron. An Atlantic Monthly Press Book. Published by Little, Brown and Company. Copyright 1954, by Eleanor Cameron. *Page 271: Homecoming* by Cynthia Voigt. A Fawcett Juniper Book published by Ballantine Books by arrangement with Atheneum Publishers, a division of The Scribner Book Companies, Inc. Copyright © 1981 by Cynthia Voigt. *Page 277: Harriet the Spy* by Louise Fitzhugh. Published by Dell Publishing Co., Inc., by arrangement with Harper & Row, Publishers, Inc. Copyright © 1964 by Louise Fitzhugh. *Page 309: The Cat Ate My Gymsuit* by Paula Danziger. Published by Dell Publishing Co., Inc., by arrangement with Delacorte Press. Copyright © 1974 by Paula Danziger.